The Trauma Spectrum

A Norton Professional Book

THE TRAUMA SPECTRUM

Hidden Wounds and Human Resiliency

Robert Scaer

W. W. Norton & Company
New York • London

For information about permission to reproduce
selections from this book, write to
Permissions, W. W. Norton & Company, Inc.,
500 Fifth Avenue, New York, NY 10110

Manufacturing by Quebecor World Fairfield Graphics
Composition by Paradigm Graphics
Production manager: Leeann Graham

Library of Congress Cataloging-in-Publication Data

Scaer, Robert C.
 The trauma spectrum : hidden wounds and human resiliency / Robert Scaer.
  p. cm.
 Includes bibliographical references and index.
 ISBN 0-393-70466-1.
 1. Psychic trauma. 2. Post-traumatic stress disorder. I. Title.

RC552. T7S33 2005
616.85'21—dc22   2005047298

W. W. Norton & Company, Inc., 500 Fifth Avenue, New York, N. Y. 10110
www.wwnorton.com

W. W. Norton & Company Ltd., Castle House, 75/76 Wells St., London W1T 3QT

0 9 8 7 6 5 4 3

This book is dedicated to the loving memory of my late mother, Ada Gressens Scaer, whose painful journey through life I have finally come to understand and cherish through my studies of life trauma and its consequences.

Contents

Foreword by Peter Levine ix

Preface: An Autobiographical Study of Trauma and Meaning xiii

Acknowledgments xvii

Introduction: Trauma and Meaning 1

Part I. Brain Mechanisms and Trauma

1. The Brain/Mind/Body Continuum 13
2. How the Brain Helps Us to Survive 28
3. Trauma As Imprisonment of the Mind 58
4. Genes, Experience, and Behavior 77

Part II. The Trauma Spectrum

5. Preverbal Trauma 99
6. The Spectrum of Societal Trauma: From Neglect to Violence 126
7. The Trauma of Illness and Its Treatment 151

Part III. Trauma in Health and Disease

8. Somatic Dissociation: Conversion Hysteria, Stigmata, and Reflex Sympathetic Dystrophy 177
9. Diseases of Stress and Trauma 205

Conclusion: Healing Trauma and the Power of the Human Spirit 252

Epilogue: Understanding Your Life 285

References 291

Index 299

FOREWORD

Robert Scaer, M.D., in a four decade career in neurology and rehabilitation medicine, has devoted himself to the alleviation of pain and suffering. In his previous book, *The Body Bears the Burden*, Dr. Scaer illuminated the wide ranging and often hidden, though pervasive, effects of trauma upon our bodies. In addition, he described the broad and unexpected spectrum of the often "ordinary" causes of trauma.

At the onset of his "second" career in traumatology, Dr. Scaer began to observe how the debilitating symptoms of his chronic pain patients seemed to have occurred after seemingly minor motor vehicle accidents. Many of these same patients had histories fraught with childhood trauma. Dr. Scaer's observations concerning the cause of chronic pain challenged many of the existing medical theories and treatment practices in pain rehabilitation. As Dr. Scaer pursued his observations and their clinical implications, he was able to help his patients understand that their symptoms were not "only in their heads," and that the body had its own very real reasons for these chronic pain experiences. With great wisdom and compassion, he helped them, not only to decipher these hidden messages, but also to find effective treatment. An avid skier, Bob was now traversing new slopes. He dedicated the next years to reviewing his clinical observations and to an extensive study of trauma literature, with the development of fresh and practical insights culminating in *The Trauma Spectrum*.

A major accomplishment of this exciting and revealing new book is its broad exploration of the pervasive effect that trauma has on all facets of one's daily life and inner experience. Dr. Scaer starts where the core diagnosis that is used to describe the psychological effects of traumatic stress leaves off. He argues convincingly that "the cumulative experiences of life's 'little traumas' shape virtually every single aspect of our existence." This accumulation of negative life experiences moulds one's "personality, choices of mate, profession, clothes, appetite, pet peeves, social behaviors, posture, and, most specifically, our state of physical and mental health and disease."

This bold premise is both an extension of, and radical theoretical departure from, the classical definition of *posttraumatic stress disorder*—"PTSD"—as a sharply defined group of symptoms. Dr. Scaer offers us a new understanding of the undercurrents that unconsciously dominate many of our feelings and life preferences. This book describes how the sum and trajectory of our traumas, including the "little, long forgotten" ones, are at the root of how we make order and meaning.

An implicit assumption made in conventional psychological understanding and treatment is that people are able to talk about their traumas. Because traumas frequently stem from preverbal events, methods that rely on "the talking cure" are often of limited value. Dr. Scaer describes further that all trauma is fundamentally non-verbal. That is to say, we store the effects of trauma in our brains and, therefore, our bodies, often in the form of chronic pain and dysfunction such as migraines, asthma, fibromyalgia, and severe PMS. Many people suffering from these disorders go from doctor to doctor, and from alternative healer to alternative healer, often with little lasting relief.

Dr. Scaer helps both physicians and their patients to identify and sort through the many and varied forms that trauma-related symptoms can take. In addition, he brings our attention to the innate capacity of the human organism to restore itself in the aftermath of terror and helplessness. *The Trauma Spectrum* presents a very positive vision by demonstrating that people have a profound ability to heal from trauma given guidance and appropriate therapeutic techniques. It also offers a description and comparison of various promising newer therapies that make use of our capacity for self-regulation and resilience to promote healing. In doing this, the book presents powerful tools that can help people overcome the debilitating symptoms of trauma and restore wholeness.

Another exciting feature of this book is its debunking of the extreme positions of "nature vs. nurture." The thrilling search for the complete human genome has led many behavioral scientists to attribute the majority of human behavior and illness to our genetic heritage. On the other hand, behavioral scientists, beginning with Freud, have attributed human behavior to the sum of life experiences, imprinted as patterns on the brain. Employing an exten-

Foreword

sive overview of current literature, Dr. Scaer attempts to bridge this divisive polarity. By establishing how negative life experience plays a role in the expression of our genetic make-up, he demonstrates that we are neither the victims of our genes nor our past. This book, well written and accessible for lay and professional audiences, substantiates our magnificent capacity for emotional and physical health and resiliency.

—Peter A. Levine, Ph.D.
Author of *Waking the Tiger* and *Healing Trauma*

An Autobiographical Study of Trauma and Meaning

The memories are there, but they are indistinct and largely unformed: Wisps of images, often perceived as cartoons, with me as an observer, not a participant. Memories of pain without the physical sensation but with a familiar chest-clenching feeling of apprehension. Impressions of deep emotional upset, but with the emotions as names, definitions, not as body/mind experiences. Gaps where there should be a flow, a continuum—a childhood full of holes and a vague impression that there should be more to it. But at the same time, startling images, sensations, intense experiences that are so vivid that shapes, colors, sounds, and context never vary every time they emerge.

I am told that my mother had ether when I was born, and that forceps were used. She had suffered a postpartum depression and psychosis after the birth of my sister 8 years before and was told by her doctor never to have another child or she might end up in a mental institution. Several years ago I found what may have been the cause of her mental illness: Her father, a minister, was reputed to have "done bad things to her" as a child. One didn't talk about such things in those days.

My mother became pregnant again a few years after my sister was born and had an illegal abortion, a shocking decision for the wife of a minister and college professor in the first half of the 20th century. Finally my father's gamete once again fought its way through a contraceptive used once too often, and my parents decided that another abortion was clearly not possible. I was on my way, although the product of a mistake.

Pictures of me as a child show a strange configuration of my skull, remarkably flat in back. I suspect that I spent a lot of time flat on my back in a crib.

I was told that I was a voracious thumb sucker—so bad that my parents fashioned tiny wire cages to fit over my thumbs to keep them out of my mouth. But I was a beautiful little "towhead," the youngest of a dozen much older cousins, and I was praised and adored by my whole family.

When I was 4, my life changed forever. I was playing with my best neighborhood friend, and we were arguing over the ownership of a straightened wire clothes hanger that I found in the street. My friend threw the hanger at me, piercing the pupil of my left eye. I recall my mother standing in the front door of the house, screaming herself when she came to answer my screams. That image is a metaphor for her emotional state thereafter, throughout my childhood until her death when I was 42.

My parents took me to the hospital, where I had my first of many experiences with ether anesthesia. I recall every minute detail of being taken from my parents, strapped securely to a table in a room filled with masked giants and muffled voices. A mask was clamped without warning over my nose and mouth, and I was told to "blow the bad smell away." My head filled with a loud roar and hallucinations of a line of black elves, all identical as if they were cutout paper dolls, marching slowly from right to left and singing, "O sesame, O sesame. . . . " The smell was overwhelming, and then there was nothing. When I awoke, both eyes were bandaged. The left one hurt fearsomely and I was in a room alone, blind and confused. There I remained, blindfolded, for 4 weeks, my parents visiting me during visiting hours in the evening, my only toy a windup miniature organ that I played incessantly.

Upon my discharge from the hospital, I was given sulfa, the only antibiotic available in those days, but after several weeks my wounded eye became infected. I was readmitted to the hospital and reexperienced the whole scenario of the operating room, complete with the smells and the marching trolls, as my eye was surgically removed. Over the next 4 years I was twice again treated to the ether/surgical experience with the removal of my tonsils and appendix.

I was a little boy with a host of "nervous tics." When anxious, I would squint my left eye repetitively. I was chided by my parents to stop this nervous habit. I had a host of strange respiratory tics, repeatedly clearing my throat and making a clicking sound in my larynx that I still can't figure out how I do.

At age 12, while running to get back in line after recess in seventh grade, I ran into a boy on my left (my inattentive side), fell, and fractured my left wrist—a Colles fracture with the distal parts of the radius and ulna broken off and jammed under the proximal ends. I again was taken to the doctor, who, without any anesthesia, grabbed my left hand and arm and pulled and twisted the bones to set the arm. It was the most painful event of my life. Ever dutiful, I sobbed, "Thanks, doc." Not surprisingly, X rays 2 weeks later showed that the bones had been improperly set, and I was again taken to the operating room to have the wrist set under ether anesthesia. This time they weren't going to have it so easy. I had to be forcibly restrained and tied down as I screamed, "No ether, no ether!" I was exhorted by the masked nurses to act like a "big boy" before I blessedly left the arena of terror.

Would it surprise anyone that I decided to become a doctor? Traumatic reenactment exerts a powerful force on one's life choices. In early college I began to spend my summers as a hospital orderly, eventually moving up to an operating room technician. By my last 2 years in college, I was advanced to the position of scrub nurse, assembling the surgical tools, needles, and sutures and passing instruments to the surgeons. In the process I was able to exorcise the demons of hospital smells, especially the smell of ether.

But there were other demons to battle. My mother's mental illness, diagnosed as depression and anxiety, provided the pervasive background to events in our family. She functioned fairly well during the day, but at night her private memories and terrors emerged, dampened but also distorted by sedatives and alcohol. I would pray that she wouldn't scream and cry, a chorus of misery accompanied by the exhortations of my father. My own sleep was disturbed. I was terrified of the creatures under my bed, and I often experienced micropsia, a dissociative visual distortion that objects in my darkened room were shrunken and tiny. I would also pray that I wouldn't die while asleep, and I was terrified of the mindless state of nothingness that I perceived sleep to be, a state that, I realized in retrospect, mimicked the immediate experience of "going under" with surgical anesthesia.

I had no concept that these feeling states, emotions, tics, and behaviors were in any way unusual or abnormal. For all intents, I was a happy, well-adjusted child, teenager, student, and, ultimately, adult. My tics irritated my wife, but they had subsided a great deal as I matured. I eventually successfully helped raise four children with my wife, and I pursued a rewarding medical career. My marriage, however, gradually unraveled after many years, leading to a divorce when I was 62. It was around this time that I became fascinated by the field of traumatic stress, and I realized that, in my marriage, I had begun to "leave the scene" and clearly dissociate during episodes of stress. I also realized that I had done this unconsciously many times in my life, always at times of conflict and emotion. This unconscious tendency had created a huge void in my marital relationship that neither my wife nor I could fill. Always the "good guy," I had actually contributed to an environment that could not be healed in the presence of my emotional abandonment.

As I immersed myself in trauma theory, I underwent dozens of sessions of Somatic Experiencing with Peter Levine and many other therapists who became my colleagues. Amazingly, virtually all of my somatic tics disappeared—they were no longer necessary to "protect" me. I became aware that my entire field of perception on my left side was dissociated and without any sense of safe boundaries. Neck and back pain, always on the left, were clearly remnants of the original contraction of my whole body at the time of my eye injury. My rounded shoulders and forward head weren't due to too many hours hunched over books—they were shaped by all of the threatening medical experiences that I had experienced throughout a painful and helpless childhood.

I was able to recognize that in my own relationships with other people, I had previously tended to set up defensive barriers that inhibited intimacy. I became able to experience and express anger, usually appropriately, whereas earlier my anger had represented potential personal annihilation. I realized that in many ways I was a bit strange, but I was comfortable with my new self-perception. In essence, having found the *meaning* for who I was, and why I was that way, I could live with the image of myself—an image that in previous years had not actually been different but rather altogether *absent*! The many tics, behaviors, and unexplained pains ceased to be threatening because their *meaning* was instantly obvious to me whenever they resurfaced. They were no longer symptoms; instead, they were barometers of my own state of stress, and emotional wellbeing, and they served as tools that helped me to reassess my life and recognize factors that I could change to resolve stress.

Just as Pavlov's dogs were reconditioned to salivate to a bell 10 years after this conditioned response had been extinguished, so too the conditioned tics, postures, sensations, and somatic messages of trauma do not disappear completely with therapy. They still emerge, often in fragments, under stress. But in the presence of the cognitive awareness of their *meaning*, they no longer provoke fear and contribute to the trauma. Healing from trauma may entail not only extinguishing the cues and memories that perpetuate the process, but also providing a meaning for the messages provided by the body. Healing, in fact, may represent the return of consciousness and of the wisdom of the self.

Acknowledgments

First and foremost, I am indebted to all of the patients that I have had the good fortune to meet and to come to know. I include in this large and varied group of courageous people, not only those whom I treated after I had my late career "epiphany," when I came to realize the role of traumatic stress in their illness. The thousands of patients that I treated with all of the biases of my allopathic medical training also provided me with a wealth of experience and knowledge that prepared me for the massive paradigm shift that occurred for me in 1996.

After that time, I learned most of what I know from the stories of my trauma victims and what these stories actually meant. The trust that these patients gave to me has been an incredible gift, because in trauma, trust always carries a risk. The trauma victim is often more generous than the caregiver.

I particularly would like to acknowledge my patient, Caroline Douglas, who generously shared with me the beautiful and uncannily insightful works of ceramic sculpture that she created during her recovery from a terrible trauma, both as a creative expression, and as a means of healing. Samples of her work are presented throughout this book as metaphors for the process of healing in trauma.

I greatly appreciate the comments and suggestions of colleagues who have taken their valuable time to review the original manuscript, including Belleruth Naparstek, Charles Whitfield, Bob Tinker, Alan Schore, and Peter Levine. Their input has been extremely helpful in making important editorial changes. I am indebted to my editor at Norton, Deborah Malmud, who has provided a constant source of support and wisdom as I have traveled the challenging path of editing, dealing with my at-times nitpicking concerns. My copy editor, Casey Ruble, deserves the most credit for making this book comprehensible. She taught me the art of semantic parsimony, a skill usually lacking in medical writers. She also provided me with the task of cutting, rewriting, dividing, combining, moving, and deleting what seemed like endless phrases, paragraphs, and portions of chapters. She did so with discipline and humor, making the editing process actually enjoyable. Michael McGandy and Andrea Costella, my managing editors through the final stages of preparation of the book, were models of efficiency in handling the myriad of details in its final organization.

Finally, I have benefited greatly from my intense interaction with my large cohort of colleagues in the field of trauma therapy, a diverse group that includes psychotherapists, psychologists, psychiatrists, physical, occupational, speech and recreational therapists. Among many others, I would particularly like to acknowledge the contributions of Marcus Kurek, Rita Bowman, Joe Kurtz, Mel Grusing, Veronique Mead, Helene Mentzel, Konstanze Hacker, Dianne La Tourette, Ana do Valle, Marianna Amicarella, Cass Reich, Rachel Katz, Dianne Heller, Bob Whitehouse, and Carol Schneider. Their suggestions, observations, intuitions, and critiques have influenced and enhanced many of the concepts that are included in this book.

The Trauma Spectrum

INTRODUCTION
Trauma and Meaning

This book arose out of a need to redefine what our culture and medical and mental health professions consider life trauma. Over the past 150 years, the evolution of what defines a traumatic event and its medical consequences has been tortuous. Perhaps this is related to the early introduction of the Cartesian concept of mind/body dualism into the developing science of medicine, which asserted a purely physical concept of human disease and precluded the idea that a *sentinel* experience could produce a predictable cascade of emotional behavior and physical symptoms in an otherwise healthy individual. According to this logic, the symptoms produced by a stressful event must be *psychological* and therefore relegated to a separate—and less important—class of ailments. Thus, the early victims of conversion hysteria in 19th-century Paris and the soldiers suffering from "shellshock" in Word War I were often accused of malingering (faking their symptoms), perhaps for the purpose of the secondary gain achieved by their disability.

The emergence of consistent sets of symptoms after cataclysmic events such as war forced society to once again consider these unfortunate victims and attempt to develop methods of treatment. Unfortunately, time and the aging of the traumatized population usually resulted in their abandonment and a loss of interest in pursuing the study of life trauma. It wasn't until the latter part of the 20th century that the most important research into the field of trauma was produced, perhaps as a result of the terrible ambiguity and societal distress produced by the Vietnam war, which may have rattled our cultural cage enough to force the current keen awareness of the consequences of trauma.

However, despite our growing understanding of trauma, behavioral science has, until recently, continued to define a traumatic event in terms of the horrific extremes of human experience. In this book, I attempt to redefine trauma as a continuum of variably negative life events occurring over the lifespan, including events that may be accepted as "normal" in the context of our daily experience because they are endorsed and perpetuated by our own cultural institutions. More importantly, I suggest that the traumatic nature of those experiences is also determined by the *meaning* the victim attributes to them. That meaning is based on the cumulative burden of a myriad of prior negative life events, especially those experienced in the vulnerable period of early childhood.

Because trauma victims are conditioned to their early experiences, the emotions and physical symptoms they experience during and after a trauma that occurs during adulthood may be based more on the childhood trauma than on the current event. The rape victim who is surreptitiously fondled on a bus may have an "exaggerated" physical and emotional response to the event due to its meaning based on her past experience. The victim may be baffled by the symptoms that arise from an apparently innocuous event, when, in fact, that event has resurrected old emotions and physical sensations related to a trauma that has been locked in unconscious memory. These new "insignificant" experiences may then become an independent source of anxiety and threat. Understanding the *meaning* of these often complex and obscure associations may represent the critical missing link between states of health and disease, emotional calm and distress, empowerment and helplessness.

The other major goal of this book is to explore the pervasive effect that life trauma has on all facets of our existence. The core diagnosis used to describe the psychological effects of traumatic stress is *posttraumatic stress disorder* (PTSD), a sharply defined group of symptoms in the fourth edition of the *Diagnostic and Statistical Manual of Mental Disorders* (DSM-IV). The growing community of behavioral scientists specializing in the study of trauma has recognized that the DSM-IV definition is now antiquated and does not address the broad spectrum of symptoms that trauma victims may experience, especially over the course of many years. Attempts to rewrite the definition of PTSD are currently in progress but probably will continue to ignore the pervasive influence of life trauma. In this book I argue that the cumulative experiences of life's "little traumas" actually shape virtually every aspect of our existence—our personality, choice of mates, profession, clothes, appetite, pet peeves, social behaviors, posture, and, most specifically, our state of physical and mental health and disease.

As I already have implied, the mantle of culture may expose most of the population to events that are actually traumatizing but condoned by cultural institutions. For example, increased violent behavior in males is correlated with exposure to violence in our entertainment industry, a trend that is increasing despite these societal concerns. Separation of the newborn infant from the mother at birth has been shown to cause long-term and even permanent effects on the infant in animal studies, but this practice continues to be common and accepted in hospital births. Accepting these cultural rituals as universal and trivializing their traumatic nature obscures that intrinsic traumatic nature. Furthermore, in the context of acculturation of societies, the installation of such rituals (which may be important to the culture for political and economic reasons) may lay the seeds for societal degeneration and destruction. This societal damage is based on the effects that insidious and recurrent trauma may have on the structure and function of the brain, the stability of the mind, and the health of the body. Trauma as a ubiquitous societal experience therefore far exceeds the definition of a psychiatric disease.

Discovering Trauma

I spent most of my 34-year career in the field of neurology as the medical director of a freestanding rehabilitation center. As such, I primarily treated patients who had suffered medical illnesses or injuries that resulted in varying degrees of disability requiring the services of a team of rehabilitation specialists. Motor vehicle accidents (MVAs) were perhaps the most frequent cause of injury, pain, and disability in these patients; I probably treated 5,000 to 10,000 MVA victims over the course of my career. Our team also treated patients suffering from chronic pain originating from a variety of causes.

The severity of the pain and disability experienced by both these patient groups frequently exceeded the severity of the physical injury. Physical examinations and imaging studies often did not explain the patients' symptoms. Their pain was also often resistant to physical and behavioral therapies of many kinds, as well as to medications. Striking symptoms of emotional distress were also commonly evident. Because my rehabilitation center generally treated the severe end of the pain and disability spectrum, those characteristics of our patient population were not terribly surprising. Nevertheless, many of these patients arrived at my office with negative labels from their treating physicians. They were often described as suffering primarily from psychological problems or from a psychosomatic condition, or they were branded as a "chronic pain patient," a diagnosis that implies symptom magnification or secondary gain.

Admittedly, many of these patients seemed to be demanding, fearful, insecure, and at times suspicious of their caregivers. Many also suffered from a variety of other medical conditions or symptoms, especially bowel problems, chronic fatigue, and sleep disturbance. And yet the paramount goal of virtually all of these patients was to return to basic functions of daily life, including work, recreation, and a satisfying social life. My staff and I seldom doubted that the pain, distress, and disability experienced by these patients were anything but real.

Many of my MVA victims carried the diagnosis of whiplash, and these patients in particular seemed to suffer from a wide variety of problems involving many systems of the body. These symptoms were neurological, emotional, and physical, including dizziness, blurred vision, headache, neck and back pain, depression, irritability, and cognitive problems. In fact, these symptoms are so common among MVA patients that doctors began to attribute them to a closed head, or brain, injury, postulating that rapid changes in velocity in an MVA could damage the brain and cause a cluster of symptoms termed *postconcussion syndrome*. This diagnosis included primarily the neurological, cognitive, and emotional disorders accompanying whiplash.

Thus, I supervised the rehabilitation of hundreds of patients suffering from what I presumed to be closed head injuries, postconcussion syndrome, and injuries to the ligaments of the spine. Many patients gradually recovered with long and at times exhaustive courses of physical therapy, occupational therapy, cognitive therapy, counseling, biofeedback, and physical conditioning programs. Many eventually emerged from "the fog," as they often called it; attaining a level of functioning close to their preaccident state of well-being often took 2 to 3 years. Some patients, however, never completely recovered. Others essentially remained completely physically and emotionally disabled.

In 1995, I experienced an epiphany of sorts when I came across the writings of Peter Levine, a psychologist who developed a rather unique method of therapy for victims of traumatic events. His method of treatment was based on the theory that PTSD is caused by a truncated or uncompleted freeze response by the victim of a severe threat to life. The freeze response is well known in animals—we all are familiar with the phrase "playing 'possum," which comes from the animal's instinct to feign death when threatened by a predator. Levine's technique, called somatic experiencing (SE), was a somatic behavioral therapy based primarily on responses of the body rather than on "talk." I referred several patients to Levine, realizing that they suffered from, among other problems, symptoms consistent with the diagnosis of PTSD. To my amazement, the first two of these patients treated reported improvement not only in their symptoms of PTSD but also in their chronic spinal pain, cognitive problems, and postconcussion symptoms. My second patient commented after her second session, "I don't know what that guy does, but my brain injury is better."

I soon realized that I had stumbled onto something new—a concept of brain function and disease that didn't make sense in the paradigm that covered most of my medical education. It became quite clear to me after introducing dozens of my patients with brain injury, spinal injury, and PTSD to SE that the entire whiplash syndrome was primarily a conditioned behavioral response to a traumatic event. The emotional and physical experiences of the accident were stored in unconscious procedural memory as part of the freeze. Thereafter, for variable but usually prolonged periods of time, they were replicated as physical symptoms triggered by a variety of conditioned cues related to the traumatic event. I also discovered that the greatest predictor of delayed recovery in MVA whiplash was the cumulative burden of prior life trauma, especially trauma that had occurred during childhood.

In order to find a scientific rationale for these rather radical conclusions, I immersed myself in the psychophysiological scientific literature in the field of PTSD. Thanks to the information provided by scientists before me, I found many of the answers to the mind/body puzzle of how a diverse physical syndrome of such remarkable specificity as whiplash could be caused solely by an *experience* rather than by any proven physical injury. The result of my research was a series of articles and a book in which I tried to provide a neurophysiological rationale for the experiential basis for whiplash. I also expanded this thesis to address a host of related chronic diseases that I felt were ultimately caused by the neurological, endocrinological, and autonomic cascade produced by the exposure to an episode of traumatic stress experienced in a state of helplessness.

The Risks of Controversy

This book, then, is an attempt to expand the conceptual horizons of trauma, to remove it from the restraints of medical definitions designed to break it up into manageable pieces for the purpose of scientific investigation and statistical study. Viewed from this perspective, societal and personal trauma assume a different meaning for each individual while at the same time being part of the universal human experience. Such a viewpoint also allows us to recognize that the effect of the experience of trauma over the lifespan lays the seeds for most chronic, poorly understood disease processes that defy explanation by our current concepts of health and disease. These chronic diseases make up the majority of symptoms for which patients present to doctors' offices.

The book is often purely speculative, although these speculations are based on the fairly solid foundation of the rapidly expanding study of the neurophysiology of traumatic stress. It also may be controversial, because it attacks many of the firmly held beliefs of established medical science. It may anger certain professionals because it challenges perceptions that have been basic to our medical training. Hopefully it will, in a sense, liberate victims of life trauma by validating many of the emotional and physical experiences that they know to be true but that have been rejected by family, societal peers, and medical caregivers.

Any exploration of the bad ways that people treat each other raises issues that some members of a culture do not want to hear. The primary areas of predictable conflict in human relations are probably those relating to race, gender, wealth (or lack of it), religion, and nationality. Although I hope to make the case for a broad range of relatively ignored sources of traumatic stress in our culture, the characteristics of race, gender, wealth, religion, and nationality continue to represent the overwhelmingly dominant sources of conflict, persecution, and trauma in our species. In his book *The Territorial Imperative*, Robert Ardrey (1966) presented a compelling case for the role of this basic animal instinct, manifested throughout many species, in causing much of human conflict and warfare. Territory, of course, is more than the boundaries of a physical realm. It also represents the boundaries of influence, control, and management of a population by institutions, including religions, corporations, armed forces, and governments. Certainly more wars have been fought, more atrocities committed, more pogroms advanced, and more people slaughtered in the names of religions and nations than for any other cause. Poverty, enslavement, and racial, religious, and gender persecution and discrimination have been used throughout recorded history as methods of controlling the behavior of the populace. They constitute yet another means of maintaining cultural control through inflicting traumatic stress.

Many of these issues, especially those related to religion, race, and gender, are closely linked to societal taboos, however, and addressing them in the interests of science and societal reform often elicits the rage and recriminations of cultural leaders. These sensitive issues related to societal trauma have been met with periodic repression, denial, and amnesia by society. I am well aware of the danger inherent in implicating well-established institutions within our culture as sources of significant trauma. Fortunately social gadflies no longer are subjected to the ingestion of hemlock. Nevertheless, as Sigmund Freud discovered after his career was almost destroyed by the publication of the pinnacle work of his career, "The Aetiology of Hysteria" (which suggested that sexual violence against children was perpetrated even by the wealthy classes of society), implicating important cultural figures or institutions as perpetrators of societal trauma can be disastrous to one's reputation and career (Freud, 1962). At this point, in the twilight of my career, I am blessed with the opportunity to take such a risk with relative professional impunity.

A Brief Outline of This Book

Part I of this book, Brain Mechanisms and Trauma, provides a scientific pedestal for the rest of the book. Chapter 1 discusses concepts proffered by the emerging field of mind/body medicine and discusses the effects of emotions and life experiences on the body as factors in health and disease. It emphasizes the role of brain mechanisms and body sensations in producing the perceptions that are usually seen as products of the mind, and it places the brain, mind, and body on a continuum, with each continuously and reciprocally affecting and changing the others.

Chapter 2 provides a scientific basis for the brain physiology that governs and regulates how we respond to a life-threatening event. It describes how this response may be altered and corrupted by the interruption of the basic response to threat: the fight/flight/freeze sequence of behavior. It details the all-important role of memory mechanisms in this process and describes the basic roles of conscious and unconscious memory. Pavlovian classical conditioning is discussed to illustrate the primary mechanism that humans and other species use to learn behavior necessary for survival. Finally, the chapter analyzes how conditioning underlies both the process of traumatization as well as effective treatment models for PTSD.

Chapter 3 explores the complex spectrum of symptoms and experiences (far exceeding the symptoms presented in the DSM-IV) that constitute the life of the victim of unresolved trauma and that are part of the widespread change in the physiology and structure of the trauma victim's brain.

Chapter 4 addresses the relationship among genes, experience, and behavior. Experience may "switch on" and alter genes, affecting how they are expressed. This process raises issues regarding the relative roles of genes and experience in such supposedly genetically-based conditions as mental illness and personality traits. Trauma victims inevitably seem to be compelled to pursue behaviors that replicate past traumas, and the often-bizarre behaviors of repetition and recapitulation of past trauma are explored in depth.

Part II, The Trauma Spectrum, addresses the sometimes subtle but also broad spectrum of life events that must be considered when one evaluates patients who present with emotional and physical symptoms of trauma. Chapter 5 is devoted to preverbal trauma, including trauma to the unborn fetus and especially to the infant. Medical interventions are a major source of trauma in this age group, and intrauterine trauma, the neonatal intensive care unit, and the American system of childbirth are specifically addressed. Animal models of maternal/infant bonding illustrate the crucial importance of this bonding process in optimal brain development as a requisite for life-long resilience to trauma.

Chapter 6 delves into cultural anthropology and forms of trauma from neglect to violence. It identifies sources of unappreciated, often institutionally sanctioned traumatic stress. The topics in this chapter are wide-ranging but relate to the basic theme of the ubiquitous presence of traumatic experience within a variety of cultures.

Our Western allopathic system of the delivery of medical care as a massive, relatively unappreciated source of societal trauma is presented in Chapter 7. The training of the American physician, the use and abuse of technology, and the loss of the healing quality of the doctor-patient relationship are discussed in this context. The chapter offers observations on what may be required to change this dysfunctional system.

Part III, Trauma in Health and Disease, addresses the somatic manifestations of trauma: the changes in appearance, posture, and health that occur in the traumatized individual. These physical syndromes may be explained by the specific experience associated with the traumatic event and the changes in systems of the body that present as symptoms and disease processes. Chapter 8 focuses on the unusual syndrome of conversion hysteria (an arcane diagnosis originating in 19th-century psychiatry and largely abandoned in the DSM-IV), stigmata, and reflex sympathetic dystrophy. I suggest in this chapter that hysteria is a prototype for the somatic manifestations of life trauma. I define somatic dissociation and explore the physiological rationale for this definition in detail.

Chapter 9 is devoted to a lengthy discussion of the types and classes of physical diseases and syndromes that I believe are directly attributable to changes in critical systems of the traumatized body. These systems primarily include the autonomic nervous system, the endocrine system, and the immune system. All of these diseases tend to be characterized by disruption of autonomic regulation and are resistant to laboratory diagnosis because of their cyclical nature. Consequently, many fall into the category of psychosomatic disorders. Although the material in this chapter is purely theoretical, a plausible scientific rationale is provided for this speculation.

The book's conclusion, Healing Trauma and the Power of the Human Spirit, outlines concepts of treatment, resilience, and the transformation of the trauma victim. Rather than discussing the myriad therapeutic techniques for treating PTSD, I explore a basic physiological rationale—based on the theories of traumatic stress presented in this book—for trauma treatment in general. Although I have incorporated many existing studies and opinions regarding the neurophysiology of trauma in the process of developing these theories, I have departed from them in many ways. I obviously emphasize the role of somatic processes in the extinction of the conditioned reflexes of trauma. The chapter also critiques the expanding use of psychotropic medications in PTSD.

The epilogue reemphasizes the ubiquitous nature of life trauma and the pervasive effect it has in shaping every aspect of our lives. It concludes by exploring the concept of transformation in the context of the acquisition of wisdom, both with regard to ourselves and with regard to others.

PART I
Brain Mechanisms and Trauma

To state the obvious, the existence of a species or individual is dependent upon its survival—its ability to avert or live through a life-threatening event and to remember what it learned from that event so that it can avoid similar situations in the future. In accordance with principles of Darwinian selection, species that continue to exist have evolved physiologically to promote such survival. Behavioral studies of animals, such as those conducted on dogs by Ivan Pavlov in the 1800s, have demonstrated how the mechanisms of the brain function to deal with the potential trauma of life-threatening events and how those traumatic events in turn shape the brain. These animal studies have been critical in contributing to our understanding of the human brain, which for ethical reasons is more difficult to study in terms of its response to trauma.

Also hindering the study of the human brain in response to trauma is medical science's devotion to the use of the Cartesian model of mind/body separation. I present a different theoretical concept: that the brain, mind, and body exist on a continuum, wherein sensory input from the body shapes and changes the structure and function of the brain, which concurrently shapes and alters the body in all of its parts, particularly those that provided this sensory input to the brain. This concept implies that the brain and body are intimately interrelated rather than two distinct parts of the greater whole. These two parts of the continuum form a dynamically changing servo system, constantly and reciprocally adapting based on the influence of the other. In my model, the mind is basically a receptacle for perceptual experience, including body sensations or feelings, and the positive or negative emotions that are related to that information. The mind is based on brain activity and is the conscious manifestation of what we sense and feel based on the dynamic interaction of the brain/body. As such, it is a vital part of this continuum.

11

The Trauma Spectrum

It goes without saying that a life-threatening experience may also be a traumatic experience if it occurs in a state of helplessness. The field of psychology accepts the premise that such trauma affects the mind. Through imaging studies, we now know that trauma affects the structure and physiology of the brain as well. If we accept the idea that the mind, brain, and body exist on a continuum, then we must also consider the ways in which trauma affects the brain/body. Ideally, the brain/mind/body uses what it learns from a traumatic event to develop resiliency and fortify the individual against future similar occurrences. However, depending on the individual's prior experience and the nature and outcome of the event, the trauma may actually lead to dysfunctional physiological changes in both the brain and body. The dynamic interaction of the brain/body in turn sends cues to the mind, affecting what it senses, feels, and perceives. If the brain/body has been overly conditioned and sensitized to react to life threats, the mind will perceive threat in situations where none may exist. This hypersensitivity to threat amounts to what I call the "imprisonment of the mind"—a state in which the mind is primed to perceive threat, is continually assaulted by and frozen in the past, and cannot conceive of a self that is free of physical and emotional pain.

The nature versus nurture, genes versus experience dilemma is especially important in the field of development of the brain and behavior. Many mental illnesses and behavioral and personality traits are considered to be primarily genetic in nature. In fact, genes are routinely activated or "switched on" by experience, often only during a window of opportunity in early infancy. The long-term effects of early life experience on behavior throughout the lifespan must be considered when diagnosing and treating behavioral disorders, especially when considering the perplexing tendency for victims of trauma to repeat behavior closely associated with prior life trauma.

Viewing trauma-related disorders as simply products of the mind confines our understanding of them and severely limits our ability to treat them. The chapters in this part of the book make a scientifically based case for a broader conceptualization of such disorders that is based on the inclusion of the brain/body in the response to trauma. Considering the brain and body in conjunction with the mind paves the way for a more holistic—and successful—treatment of trauma-related disorders.

CHAPTER 1

The Brain/Mind/Body Continuum

Concepts of "mind/body medicine" have emerged in recent years and reflect an attempt to address the needs of the patient as a "whole person," incorporating both emotional and physical needs. Also called "holistic medicine," this approach acknowledges that the emotional state of patients may affect their physical state of health and disease. Holistic medicine, however, remains a small, radical offshoot of current medical philosophy. Through the work of Hans Selye (1956) and others, we know that severe life stress can contribute to a variety of diseases, but disorders of emotional states and diseases of the body are still widely considered to be separate—and unequal—entities. Medical science has claimed that psychological symptoms and physical symptoms are intrinsically unrelated—that the mind and the body are separate and discrete.

However, throughout history, many physicians, philosophers, and other theorists have viewed the concepts of emotions, the mind, and the soul as closely intertwined. Theodore M. Brown (1989) reviewed the thoughts of some of the original thinkers and philosophers in concepts of the mind, soul, and body. He noted that Hippocrates connected emotional agitation to diseases of the body: "If the soul is burned up it consumes the body" (p. 323). Brown also reviewed Thomas Wright's early-17th-century assertions that "passions, or movements of the *soul* [italics added] . . . alter the body humors" and that "perturbations and affections of the *mind* [italics added] create changes in the body" (p. 323).

Descartes, the 17th-century philosopher credited with subsequent concepts of mind-body dualism, also appeared to intermingle the ideas of the soul and the mind. He referred to the soul as "rational," equating its properties and functions to an entity that we currently refer to as the mind. In addition, he connected the soul with the body through the intermediary of the pineal gland, a small gland in the very center of the brain whose function was unknown at the time. Descartes felt that the body was associated with "animal spirits," that the soul was associated with the "will," and that the two forces interacted at the pineal gland, forcing it from side to side based on the strength of each opposing force at any given time. He also felt that all affective/emotional states, or "passions," are primarily somatic in nature. These passions remained in the body and could affect it but become emotions only when the soul perceived them (Brown, 1989, p. 327). One could argue that the "animal spirits" that Descartes referred to in fact are the instinctual genetic legacy, the inherited unconscious knowledge whose primary function is to ensure our day-to-day survival and whose behavioral expressions may reflect the actions of nonhuman species that we perceive as primitive, violent, or uncivilized.

In this book I present the mind and body as being measurable physical entities intrinsically linked to the brain and each other, with each part of this triad influencing and changing the others as part of a dynamic and continuous process. The brain operates based on continuous sensory input provided by the body, and on a vast accumulated storage of conscious and unconscious memories based on prior experiences. The body not only provides sensory input to the brain but also responds to and is changed by the resulting dictates of the brain. The mind, a more ephemeral concept, may be a perceptual state that is determined by the status of the brain and the sensory information it is receiving at a given moment. Operating on the brain's vast storehouse of old memories, the mind may then direct the behavior of the body and affect the content of ongoing memory storage. It may even generate novel behavior, based on old memories and current experience.

It goes without saying that my proposal of a brain/mind/body continuum is presumptuous. It presumes that we know far more than we actually do regarding the internal workings of the brain, as well as about what we might call the intangible world. Our concept of reality is tightly bound by the amount of meager information that our sensory organs are able to provide us at any given time. Other species possess organs of sensory perception that we totally lack. Sharks are able to sense magnetic fields through sensory organs along their body. At tremendous speed of flight, bats use emitted vocal sounds to detect insects in the air through a type of sonar sense. Pigeons and other birds have a remarkable sense of direction, possibly based on pineal function, that allows them to travel thousands of miles in unerring flight to a distant island. Most mammals possess an astoundingly sensitive and accurate olfactory (smell) sense that serves as a critical tool for survival. Clearly our perception of reality differs dramatically from these species.

In some humans, senses have been trained to enhance perception of what can be called "subtle energies." Practitioners of some the body-centered therapies, including massage, physical therapy, and acupuncture, report the ability to sense disturbances in organ function that even the trained physician may be unable to perceive. Based on the consistency of such perceptions by skilled practitioners of these arts, I have no reason to doubt their abilities or the accuracy of their perceptions. By the same token, the tracking abilities of various indigenous human tribes are notorious, and they represent fine-tuning of otherwise latent sensory and perceptual skills. But even such subtle differences in perception can expand to alter one's views of reality drastically. Reality indeed is in the eye (or nose, skin, ear) of the beholder. The function of the mind and its perception of the world, even the function of the brain, can be changed by the quality of the body's sensory input based on the sensory tools at its disposal. The entire function of the brain/mind/body continuum will therefore be altered by the nature and quality of the sensory information that the body provides.

Our perceptions of reality (the mind), the primary source of information regarding that reality (the body), and the "computer" that collates all of this information (the brain) may be shaped not only by our ability to access the full spectrum of sensory information in the environment, but also by its meaning based on our storehouse of primarily unconscious memory. It is said that the Native Americans who first viewed Columbus's ships on the ocean horizon could not see the boats themselves because they had no prior reference to such an image. If a natural event, such as an eclipse of the sun, is beyond our ability to explain or comprehend, it may assume mystical or religious connotations or catastrophic implications. Similarly, reported "near death" experiences, which often involve an out-of-body experience with movement toward a bright or white light, tend to reinforce our often religiously based belief in the hereafter following death, as well as our belief in the immortality of the soul. Psychiatrists and mental health practitioners view these experiences as dissociative episodes in the face of life-threatening circumstances, an example of the phenomenon of depersonalization. So is the near-death experience the beginning of a metaphysical state produced by the shedding of our corporeal being and the accessing of our intrinsic immortal spirit? Or are those pesky neurotransmitters that help with the transfer of brain messages simply fooling us once again? It seems that the brain/mind/body continuum may also be altered as a whole by the content of our legacy of stored memories (the brain).

Finally, the functions of the body are clearly shaped and altered by functions of the mind and brain. Perhaps the simplest example of this is the basic acquisition of skills. The mind may govern the repetition of a stereotyped motor task (a golf swing, a sequence of chords on the piano). The brain is sequentially altered by its storage of unconscious memory related to that skill. And the body is changed by increased strength in the muscles involved in the task and by the increasingly accurate sensory information provided with its performance. Each limb of the brain/mind/body continuum therefore operates as part of a servo system, with all parts changing constantly with input from the others.

Now that I have linked the three parts of our system in a constant interactive dance, I would like to look at each of the three limbs in more detail. This does not diminish the continuity of the system that we are discussing. Although all parts are constantly changing, each of the three has a unique contribution to make in the process. Although reciprocity and continuity provide adaptability within such a system, specialization of role and function within the brain/mind/body continuum is necessary in order for the system to provide a wide range of options and responses.

The Brain

For the purposes of this book, I will define the brain as: *a plastic, fluid, and ever-changing electrical/chemical/structural system that generates new synapses and neurons and discards old ones in response to sensory input from changes in the environment.* We know from emerging data obtained through new brain-imaging techniques that the brain, throughout our waking and sleeping states, undergoes continuous fluctuation in the flow of arterial blood and the utilization of glucose and oxygen within widely varying regions. Areas of the brain that serve vision receive increased blood flow when the person gazes at, for example, a painting, a movie, or the face of a loved one. They may also "light up" on a scan if the person imagines a picture of, for instance, the battle scene where he was wounded in combat. If a person reads aloud, the area in the left hemisphere of the brain that serves speech and verbal comprehension burns more glucose, uses more oxygen, and becomes especially prominent in the scan. The areas of the brain that control our response to threat or danger receive more blood flow if the person tells a story or reads a script describing an assault, car accident, or rape.

The prominence of these changes in brain blood flow and energy use varies from person to person based on the individual's specific pattern of life experience. These life experiences are represented by complex, often unconscious memories for the sensory perceptions that accompanied the experiences, and therefore they are reflected in the unique patterns of dominance in regional energy use in the brain. Life experience, based on specific sensory experiences, therefore changes the brain permanently in the way that it specifically reacts to subsequent similar experiences. These brain-imaging studies provide compelling evidence for the examples of unconscious patterns of learned behavior: Function in specific regions of the brain is patterned by the somatic experiences related to that region.

Similarly, there is now evidence that the physical structure of the brain also changes based on life experience. New connections are formed between neurons, and, at least in the hippocampus (which serves conscious memory), new neurons may be formed and existing neurons may be discarded based on the nature of life experience. Not only may patterns of energy use be altered in specific brain regions, but areas of the brain also may shrink or expand and become more or less functional based on experience.

It is well known that unconscious learned behavior in all species is primarily directed toward survival-based activities. This behavior is established primarily through the repeated chance association of successful forms of complex behavior with escape from a life-threatening situation or with access to a life-sustaining reward. The behavioral patterns emerging from this learned association have been called *conditioning*.

In his studies of conditioned responses in animals, Ivan Pavlov routinely used threatening (electric shock) or life-affirming (food reward) stimuli to produce consistent conditioned behavior (Kaplan, 1966). These conditioned responses, which are based on cumulative life experiences, are the basic means by which species accumulate knowledge to enhance survival. Because this knowledge must be available at all times and at a moment's notice—and must be independent from the complexity of conscious problem solving—it is basically unconscious knowledge. Such unconscious knowledge constitutes the primary source of learning and behavior, not only in animals but also in human beings.

Other sources of unconscious knowledge also exist. Underneath the layering of these learned behaviors, of course, lies a rich template of genetic instinctual responses that literally provide animals with a running start in the survival race. This genetic template is hardwired and is the product of our genetic legacy. There is also evidence, however, that life experience and exposure to environmental influences may alter the degree to which the expression of those genes occurs. Several factors therefore may affect how successful our genetic inheritance is in facilitating our survival through instinctual behaviors. For example, the changing nature of environmental threats may render our inherited survival skills less effective, leading to our early demise. The introduction of alien species into isolated environments clearly illustrates this, as was the case with the island bird population on Guam, which was decimated after the introduction of the alien brown snake because these birds had evolved their survival-based behaviors in the absence of this particular threat.

Genetic instinctual patterns of behavior and learned conditioned behavior therefore are part of well-established brain pathways and are the primary source of the means for survival in probably all species. Nevertheless, they are subject to many challenges. Under certain circumstances, if the intense arousal that was associated with a traumatic event is conditioned to the cues derived from sensory messages from the body at that moment, arousal may be triggered with these cues even though the traumatic event was resolved. The altered brain will now interpret these cues to mean that the past traumatic event is still present. For example, a woman who managed to successfully thwart an assault from a man wearing a green sweatshirt may thereafter find that she experiences anxiety whenever she sees a green sweatshirt, and her brain will interpret this cue (man wearing green sweatshirt) as a threat. This aberrant form of classical conditioning may then contribute to the symptoms of PTSD: arousal triggered by memory-based sensory cues related to the old trauma. Under these circumstances, conditioned responses may be counterproductive in the process of survival-based acquisition of unconscious knowledge.

Many researchers now believe that threatening life experiences in early childhood may especially alter genetic expressions of what we consider to be personality or character. Such experiences may override genetic influences and create dysfunctional personality traits that may threaten long-term survival. Harlow's (1958) studies with monkeys raised in the absence of a nurturing maternal figure dramatically illustrate how such early alteration of survival instincts may lead to lifelong dysfunctional behavior that is harmful to survival.

The brain, then, might be considered to have a variety of roles in the brain/mind/body continuum. They all involve concepts of director, organizer, and regulator—perhaps the CEO of this organization. But this concept belies the fact that the brain itself—its neurochemical state, its structure, even its genetic template—is subject to change based on sensory input from the body, and perhaps the perceptual dictates of the mind. Although the brain's reciprocal responses to sensory experience are central to its role, they may be corrupted by traumatic experiences, which drastically alters its ability to be an effective participant in the goal of survival.

The Mind

As primates evolved, the frontal third of the cerebral cortex dramatically expanded. These greatly enlarged frontal lobes have been credited, or blamed, for the development of what we now consider to be the human mind. These areas of the brain have been associated with uniquely human states of perception and conception. Associated with this perception has been a significant degree of hubris that allows us to refer to other species as subhuman. These unique characteristics involve such concepts as logic, insight, problem solving, abstracting, creating, innovating, and judging, among others. Perhaps most notably, these functions permit the human species to derive information from experience, and from this information to derive novel concepts previously absent from thought, behavior, or expression. They also include the development of language, including verbal, symbolic, and ultimately written language. (Certainly many nonhuman species possess vocal and behavioral communication, and many students of animal behavior would contend that this in fact represents language as well.) In humans, frontal lobe functions also involve concepts of intangible parts of the self, including the soul, the spirit, and the mind. These human functions are also associated with the need to conceive of a state of existence other than that of our earthly life.

Well-documented behavior in other animal species certainly suggests an awareness of death as a specific process or state. An example is the behavior of elephants in choosing remote places to die, often with the attendance of specific members of the elephant herd. Although again it may be presumptuous to conclude that the comprehension of death as a state distinct from life is uniquely human, we, as a species, have learned to attach mystical and intangible characteristics to death that are intricately involved in the development of the concepts of religion and the immortal soul. The soul in the religious sense encompasses both a "self" that is separate from the body and a spiritual entity that is not only separate from the body but also continues to exist in the absence of the body.

My model of the brain/mind/body continuum obviously avoids concepts of the soul and spirit. At the same time, it acknowledges the entirely possible existence of entities and forces that are as yet beyond our poor capabilities to perceive or understand except by what we currently term faith. Although it is by no means definitive, I put forth the following definition of the mind for the purpose of building a meaningful structure on which to develop the model of trauma suggested in this book: *a perceptual experience, generated by a complex set of synapses, neurons, and neurochemical states and determined by genes, instinct, and experience, that is capable of developing and directing novel behavior.*

Basically, the complex cognitive processes of the mind are unnecessary for survival and may even be a hindrance. The last thing a person should do when suddenly presented with a life threat demanding immediate fight or flight motor activity is reflect on the various possible modes of behavior in order to pick the most logical choice. In this circumstance, the frontal lobes are deactivated so that the automatic and instinctual functions of the survival brain can take control of the situation and initiate the motor behavior necessary to avoid the threat. One doesn't need logic or language to fight or flee.

However, after successful resolution of the life threat, the mind reflects, problem solves, and incorporates conscious information from the experience, both to avoid future exposure to a threat and to develop additional means of assuring safety. In addition to unconsciously incorporating survival-enhancing motor skills, the mind develops future self-protective and avoidant behaviors that also promote survival. This process of conscious skill acquisition, based on mind/body interaction, constitutes a continuum of mind and body.

The Body

In this context, when I refer to the body, I basically mean the whole of our corporal being other than the brain. This can be broken down into dozens of subsets, organ systems, physical entities, and processes, such as the skin, the muscles, the bony skeleton, the glands, the digestive system, the vascular system, and so forth. More generally, but also more appropriately, we can break it down into the musculoskeletal and the visceral systems.

The Brain/Mind/Body Continuum

The musculoskeletal system includes the muscles and bony skeleton, the tendons that attach muscles to bones, and the ligaments that connect bones across the joints. The functional activity of the musculoskeletal system is governed by the *voluntary* or *somatic* nervous system, as it incorporates at least in part consciously directed behavior. Using this system, we can physically and intentionally change the world around us and therefore actively control our own physical environment. We can also initiate and complete survival-based motor behavior.

Messages from the somatic body, via the skin, tendons, ligaments, and muscles, affect the brain's perception of the environment and govern the behavior that the brain then calls forth in the area of the body that has sent this information to the brain. For example, if your foot twists while walking on uneven ground, messages sent from the tendons and ligaments of your ankle joint to the brain's balance centers will initiate messages to specific muscles in your leg to support the ankle. The skin contains sensory receptors for pressure, pain, and temperature that provide specific areas of the brain with information about the state of the environment. The tendons that attach muscles to bones and the muscles themselves contain complex sensory receptors that detect changes in movement, tension, position, and stretch. They provide messages to the brain that allow it to regulate complex patterns of body movement and balance through integration of movement within specific muscle groups. If those messages contain information vital to survival, a permanent change will take place in brain centers that are critical to survival in order to incorporate a skillful response of the musculoskeletal system to that particular threatening experience. For instance, in martial arts and military training for combat, the acquisition of complex motor skills is enhanced by the perceived threat underlying the training. As part of this process, the muscle groups that participated in the motor act of survival develop unique qualities and abilities to respond to future similar threatening experiences. These unique qualities and abilities are based on the unconscious memory of these movements in the survival brain. Like skilled movements learned by an athlete or dancer, the skilled movements learned in a survival experience remain stored forever.

Patterns of body movement that are acquired in an effort to gain a skill, as in athletics, also produce permanent changes in brain function and structure, although they are likely to decay in the absence of practice, as anyone who has tried to pick up and play an instrument abandoned earlier in life can attest to. The skill, however, is never totally lost, as the brain and body have been changed by the experience. The brain and body *as a unit* develop new qualities and characteristics based on their continuing alteration by the influence of ongoing experience. This process is repeated hundreds of times a day in the lifespan of a person or animal, and behaviors are enhanced or inhibited by this constant feedback servo system of information and response determined by unconscious brain mechanisms. The function and processes of the somatic nervous system thus set up a continuum between the brain and the musculoskeletal system of the body.

The visceral system (the term *viscera* refers to organs of the chest and abdomen) involves all of the unconscious regulatory processes of our body and the organs that they regulate. Examples of functions of the visceral system are the regulation of circulation of blood, respiratory, digestive, and excretory functions, glandular secretions of the skin, respiratory tract, and gut, body temperature control, endocrine hormone secretions, and cellular function of the immune systems. This system involves the *involuntary* or *autonomic* nervous system and is generally thought to be unconscious and beyond our control. It operates and controls all the processes that determine the energy-using or energy-storing status of the animal. The autonomic nervous system operates on a continuous basis based on messages from the environment, from the brain, and from the body itself. The unconscious nature of the autonomic nervous system is necessary because it would basically take all of our time, effort, and goal-directed behavior to manage these continuous and self-regulating processes if this system were not autonomic and automatic. Both the somatic and autonomic nervous systems contain *afferent* (incoming) nerves that carry messages to the brain from the musculoskeletal and visceral organs, and *efferent* (outgoing) nerves that cause changes in these organ systems. The special senses of smell, vision, hearing, balance, and taste also add afferent sensory input. Information from these special senses may affect all aspects of the body, the somatic and autonomic nervous system, and the brain, and they play a definitive role in the survival game. They probably affect brain function more specifically than other senses, and they are addressed a great deal more throughout this book.

Much of our somatic behavior also occurs without our intention. Many musculoskeletal reflexes are quite automatic and are governed unconsciously by neuronal pathways in our spinal cord and brainstem that are genetically present in all species. For example, the stretch reflex, elicited by tapping most muscle tendons (e.g., the knee jerk) or simply stretching any muscle, is a primitive, so-called spinal reflex that is designed to allow us to move quickly away from a threatening sensory stimulus and literally to maintain an upright posture. Simply stretching a muscle activates sensory messages that lead to an involuntary contraction of that muscle. Many brainstem reflexes that influence posture are instinctual and hardwired in the brain before birth, are common to all species, and provide the unconscious, built-in movement patterns on which learned motor skills are later built. The voluntary motor system is therefore also governed by instinctual and unconscious patterns of so-called postural reflexes. In addition, certain basic motor skills that we learn throughout our life also are permanently wired in the brainstem and other lower brain centers that control movement patterns. We never forget certain basic learned skills, such as walking or throwing an object.

Traumatic life experiences often contribute to learned habits of movement and posture that reflect the self-protective movement patterns associated with those threats. Many of these trauma-based learned movement patterns affect the way that we move, sit, and stand. They may lead to patterns of movement and posture that are abnormal, and they may inhibit our normal coordination and our learning of other desirable motor skills. For example, a patient of mine who was a teacher attempted to break up a fight between two students. One of them struck her, and she fell back against the blackboard, bracing her left leg to keep herself from falling. She recalled feeling rage and wanting to strike the boy, but she knew that he belonged to a particularly vicious street gang and that she and her family might face retribution. As a result, she contained herself and sent both combatants to the principal's office. Thereafter, however, she developed spasm and pain in her back and left leg, as well as a pronounced limp. Progressive pain and loss of motion in her right neck and shoulder developed, eventually resulting in a frozen, immobile shoulder. No physical causes for her pain and immobility could be found. What had happened, of course, was that the self-protective movement patterns of the aborted assault had been stored in survival memory.

These learned dysfunctional patterns persist because they are, in a metaphorical sense, necessary for defense against future life threats similar to those that elicited the defense in the first place. The interaction of the brain and the body region represented by these postures and patterns of movement constitutes part of a sensory information/motor activation continuum. Linking the brain and the body into a continuous whole, these learned habits are associated with newly established brain pathways and may or may not serve a useful function.

Our autonomic nervous system, supposedly unconscious and outside of our voluntary control, may be affected by many aspects of our experience and even by our habits and our learned patterns of behavior. The autonomic nervous system actually organizes the response of our organ systems to arousal and emotion on an unconscious basis. It is the system most sensitive to low-grade stress, which, if prolonged, may cause harm to the organ systems controlled by it. The emerging science of biofeedback is based on the obvious connection of stress with a wide variety of abnormal symptoms and conditions. Examples include migraine, tension headaches, hypertension, and other so-called psychosomatic ailments. Early biofeedback practitioners found that an individual can consciously learn to alter the unconscious response of the somatic nervous system to stress (e.g., painful muscle spasm). They also found that they could alter the stress response of the autonomic nervous system (migraine, rapid heartbeat, cold hands, acid secretion in the stomach). They accomplished this by feeding information back to a person through a conscious signal, such as a sound, light, or color. Each signal represented a measure of various states of the autonomic nervous system, such as electrical measurement of muscle contraction, skin temperature, or heart rate. By comparing the signal to the desired goal (relaxing the muscle, warming the hand), the person could learn to exert voluntary control over unconscious somatic and autonomic functions of the nervous system.

The visceral system of the body is even more intimately involved in continual reciprocal feedback with the brain than is the somatic system. Everyone is quite familiar with the concept of "gut feelings." Viscerally based emotions are often felt to be uniquely accurate, perhaps because they are unconscious and bypass the often-misleading filter of learned bias. The abdominal viscera indeed have unique neuronal connections with parts of the limbic system (the part of the brain that governs and regulates emotions and memory, among other things). People are generally aware that emotions are also often manifested by conscious visceral discomfort, such as pressure in the chest, a hollow feeling in the pit of the stomach, palpitations of the heart, and tightness in the throat. Such sensations not only warn the person that he or she may be in danger but also may enhance the autonomic nervous system response that is causing the physical experience itself. Damasio (1999) asserted that what we term a *feeling* is in fact our conscious interpretation of such visceral sensations. Our assessment of our well-being at any given time may be based on this shifting subtle awareness of messages from the gut.

If traumatic memories are implanted in the brain, internal cues, such as dreams, may trigger the autonomic response to threat without any feedback from the external environment and may cause shifts in our feeling state based on the visceral response to the autonomic shift. Thus the brain and the visceral body again clearly constitute a continuum.

There is also a constant interplay between the activity in the frontal lobes (the parts of the brain that most closely determine functions of the mind) and messages to and from both the somatic and visceral peripheral nervous systems. These messages from within the body and from the external environment are interpreted consciously, which ultimately leads to appropriate changes in behavior. For example, if we eat contaminated food at a restaurant, the resulting nausea and vomiting may prompt us to avoid that restaurant in the future. If the food that caused the sickness had a unique flavor, smell, or texture, we may find ourselves nauseated at the thought of eating such a dish again. Our unconscious brain has been conditioned to experience negative aversion to the food, and our conscious brain has developed a plan of action to avoid the threat implied by our negative experience. Further, the brain region that processed the message (nausea) and the body part (stomach) that produced the response (vomiting) both now have a new and fairly permanent connection with the mind that is specifically based on that negative life experience.

Perhaps the best-known example of Pavlovian conditioning is the elicitation of salivation in a dog by pairing the act of feeding with the ringing of a bell. After relatively few trials, the dog salivated when a bell was rung. As with most of Pavlov's studies, the conditioned response involved a survival-based behavior, the need for food. Pavlov extinguished this conditioned response by eliminating the conditioning stimulus (the food) while continuing to ring the bell for a sufficient number of trials. It is of considerable interest that years later, the same dogs were once again able to be conditioned to salivate at the ringing of a bell, but with far fewer trials than they had first required. Both the brain and the visceral body are therefore changed by this process of learning.

Thus far I have suggested that a change primarily in behavioral aspects of the body occur via the process of brain/mind/body interaction. Certainly learning a motor skill results in hypertrophy of the muscles that have gained this skill through increased use. Athletes develop increased capacity for dissipation of body heat through improved patterns of perspiring and dilatation of skin blood vessels. These changes, however, are adaptive to demand and quickly disappear in the absence of demand. The concept that certain brain states and mechanisms can actually induce regional bodily changes that are abnormal enough to constitute a disease is much more controversial. If this is true, however, we have powerful evidence for the presence of actual structural change at each end of the brain/body continuum.

The Brain/Mind/Body Continuum

If you really think about it, nature, evolution, or Darwinian natural selection wouldn't have it any other way. If a species is to survive, each member must be a unitary whole, with all parts intimately connected and interactive with all other parts of the whole, however separate and distinct they may seem to be. Nevertheless, we humans, as a species, have been driven, perhaps by our desire to understand the unexplainable and perhaps unknowable, to find a separate logical compartment in which to place such ethereal and evanescent concepts as the spirit and the mind. We attribute creativity, novelty, insight, and other "executive functions" of the frontal lobes to the mind rather than to a unique evolutionary neuronal development that has allowed us to perform certain mental gymnastics that we are convinced are lacking in other animal species. We find a separate conceptual niche for emotions, attributing them to a unique process of the mind that we define as psychological, and we deny the fact that emotions actually primarily dwell in physical sensations of the body rather than in cognitive perceptions. We then develop a body of theoretical science, or in some instances, a religion, on which to base our certainties about the unexplainable.

In medical science we compartmentalize, partly in the interests of conceptual economy, partly in order to fit a body of information (as opposed to knowledge) into arbitrary subunits that we can then submit to "scientific investigation." Medical science in particular abhors a continuum for this very reason, and thus it may blind us to the fact that all of nature is in fact a continuum. Each process in nature, at every level of existence, within the systems of the body, between individuals, at the level of the pack, herd, tribe, society, or culture, is eventually affected by and affects every other process throughout nature. The analogy of the flap of a butterfly wing in Brazil affecting wind patterns in Mongolia is trite, but it contains a measure of truth. Using the term psychological as opposed to physical to explain a physical symptom or somatic feeling state defies the obvious—that all perceptions, thoughts, symptoms, or experiences have a physiological basis within the brain/mind/body continuum.

CHAPTER 2

How the Brain Helps Us to Survive

The world that all creatures inhabit on this beautiful planet of ours is completely impartial when it comes to their survival. It may not be all kill-or-be-killed, eat-or-be-eaten, tooth-and-claw nastiness, but the term "survival of the fittest" certainly applies to all animal endeavors, including those of the human species. Natural selection has its place in every facet of our day-to-day existence.

Because our brains drive our every action (shaped of course by processes of the mind and body), they must possess centers, pathways, and chemicals that govern what we might term "survival behavior." This capacity to respond to a life threat is instinctual, inherited, and common to all species with varying levels of complexity. It must be adaptable to a vast—in fact, infinite—array of life experiences and be able to change based on those experiences. And, of course, it must be instantaneous and unconscious. The prey animal has one chance to learn all about the behavioral complexities of each of its potential predators. With few exceptions, the prey/predator relationship is also a continuum, with most predators having the potential to be the prey of another animal higher on the survival pecking order. So all animals must have the capacity to learn from life-threatening experiences.

All animals learn to survive through the functions of the areas of the brain that process information through a complex behavioral process that has been termed the *fight/flight/freeze response*. The brain pathways and behaviors in this response are common to all animals, from reptiles to primates. But these instincts only form a template on which exposure to a series of life threats builds specific survival skills. Whether one fights or flees when exposed to a specific threat must be learned very quickly through such experiences. This process of learning by definition involves mechanisms of *memory*, the stored acquisition of bits of information that we can dredge up when needed. In this case, however, that information must be *unconscious* in order to be of use in the survival game. It must be capable of triggering a predictable behavioral response learned through trial and error without thinking or planning. The process by which we learn these survival skills is called *classical conditioning*. By pairing a previously neutral, or meaningless, environmental stimulus (such as a bell) with an unconscious body message that is intrinsically linked to survival (hunger/food) one may produce a survival behavior in a dog (salivation). The dog *learned* to equate a bell tone with food. The brain pathways used in this process also include those that the dog uses to *learn* about threats in the environment that needed to be avoided. The process involves intrinsic or unconscious memory, part of which is procedural memory (the part that we use to learn skills). Survival depends on classical conditioning through procedural memory.

Sometimes the fight and flight options are no longer available, particularly in animals that are weak or slow. Under these circumstances, a third survival option is available: the freeze response. One very slow mammal, the opossum, has given its name to the immobility or freeze response—"playing 'possum." In this unique response, the animal remains immobile, unresponsive to pain or external stimuli, and has been accused of "feigning death" as a means of duping the predator. This freeze response, common to all species, indeed may allow the animal to survive, but in mammals it sometimes comes at a terrible cost. Animals who survive the freeze response experience an unconscious "discharge" of all of the energy and stored memories of the threat and failed escape through stereotyped body movements as the animal "awakens." If they don't experience this discharge, a host of adverse behavioral and health problems may follow, problems that indeed are the core topic of this book. Classical conditioning in this context can fool the brain and lead to a host of inappropriate and ineffective survival behaviors. When this happens, we say that trauma has occurred.

We can study these unique problems faced by the absence of the freeze discharge in animals quite easily and gain useful information that we can then apply to our human species. However, the study of the laboratory of life in the human species also provides amazing insights into this unique physiological event. Understanding the freeze discharge and the implications of its absence requires that one suspend the mind/body, psychological/physical dichotomy. Only by studying behavior solely as a neurophysiological event can we fully understand trauma.

Pavlovian Conditioning and Survival

Russian physiologist Ivan Petrovich Pavlov (1849–1936) has probably done more to dispel the validity of Cartesian dualism than any other scientist or philosopher. A passionate and innovative investigator, he derived his data and theories through the laborious effort of measuring the physiological responses of dogs to a variety of induced environmental stimuli. In the process, he developed and established the concept of classical conditioning. He was initially interested primarily in the digestive reflexes, especially salivation and secretion of digestive juices of the stomach. The responses of his dogs to a variety of sources of stimulation, however, led him to some unusual findings. He repeatedly exposed his dogs to a wide variety of external sensory stimuli, such as noises, electrical shocks, and visual images, that activated parts of the cerebral cortex. Pavlov found that these stimuli, if presented along with instinctual stimuli such as food or pain, would stimulate and enhance secretions of the digestive glands, whose neural control came solely from the "hindbrain," or unconscious brainstem. Once established, these reflex responses and their paired association often persisted for prolonged periods of time.

Classical Conditioning

Classical conditioning involves presentation of a neutral or *conditioned stimulus*, such as a bell or tone, simultaneously with a primary eliciting, or *unconditioned stimulus*, such as food or pain. The unconditioned stimulus involves some form of sensory information that has implications for survival. By its very nature, it elicits a specific unconscious and involuntary physical response, such as salivation or increased stomach secretions. If the conditioned and unconditioned stimuli are presented simultaneously a sufficient number of times, the conditioned stimulus will soon produce the unconscious behavior by itself. In other words, the body's unconscious response becomes associated with and conditioned to occur with this previously neutral stimulus. The dog will now salivate when hearing a bell. Almost any sensory perception—related to smell, sight, taste, hearing, touch, pain, temperature, visual size, shape, texture, and so on—can be used as the conditioned stimulus.

Such conditioned responses shape our perceptions, preferences, and behavior on a constant basis. For example, if we develop food poisoning after a meal of fish, we may experience a prolonged, and even permanent, aversion to smelling, tasting, and certainly eating fish. Future exposure to fish is likely to produce the physical sensations (nausea), motor responses (gagging), and emotional responses (disgust) we experienced during the food poisoning event. All of these are conditioned responses. If we become stuck in an elevator for a prolonged time, we may develop not only an aversion to elevators but also to any enclosed space—the well-known condition of claustrophobia. Conditioned physical responses to closed spaces may include rapid heartbeat, nausea, weakness, and tremulousness. All threatening experiences, even those that are successfully resolved, will prompt unconscious conditioned responses related to cues from that experience. Therefore, if a person experiences a car accident in which he is broadsided by a red car, future glimpses of the color red may affect his driving and his body's autonomic responses. The linking of driving with the image of a red car may elicit the conditioned response of rapid heartbeat and the physical sensations of anxiety (stomach tightness, palpitations), both of which are unconscious responses of the autonomic nervous system to the cue. In some cases, the individual is consciously aware of a cue, but generally such cues are perceived unconsciously, leading to seemingly bizarre responses to stimuli that appear innocuous.

Persistence of the conditioned response to the conditioned stimulus and is often dependent on *reinforcement*. Repeated pairing of the conditioned and unconditioned stimuli is often necessary to maintain the connection of the conditioned stimulus with the response. Multiple car accidents, even those that are minor, will reinforce symptoms of anxiety related to driving. *Extinction*, or disappearance of the conditioned response (salivation), may occur if the conditioned stimulus (bell) is presented enough times without reinforcement (food). For example, a person who experiences anxiety about horseback-riding related to a recent fall from a horse may find that her anxiety gradually diminishes as she rides many times over a long period without falling—hence the familiar "if you fall, get right back on the horse" maxim. This example, however, belies the incredible complexity of the process of conditioning and extinction. Both animals and humans can be conditioned to extreme subtleties of differentiation of the conditioned stimulus, such as a minute change in frequency of a metronome's ticking or the slight change of a circle into an ellipse.

This complexity is due to two other processes: *irradiation* and *concentration*. When an animal is conditioned to respond to a certain stimulus, the conditioned response will also be prompted by a fairly large spectrum of stimuli in the general range of the initial stimulus. For example, the dog conditioned to salivate in response to a musical note will also salivate upon hearing a variety of musical sounds. This process is termed *irradiation*. Furthermore, the conditioned response may irradiate not only to variations in the stimulus, but also to unrelated sound stimuli. Indeed, if the conditioning environment contains stimuli not involving sound, these other stimuli might later elicit the conditioned response. For example, the noises, smells, visual images, and even reflexive movement patterns of the body that occur during a car accident may be incorporated in memory as conditioned stimuli and may later evoke physical symptoms of anxiety.

Concentration of excitation occurs when a consistent stimulus is presented for an ongoing duration: The conditioned response will progressively be elicited only by that specific stimulus. This is obviously the opposite of irradiation. In other words, if food is paired with a tone of a specific frequency for a long period of time, the dog will be more likely to salivate only upon hearing that specific tonal frequency. The capacity to precisely identify the exact stimulus capable of producing the conditioned response through concentration is logically necessary for efficiency and precision of learning and information processing. By the same token, early spread of the stimulus through irradiation would facilitate the best opportunity for the animal to learn from the experience. Thus, both irradiation and concentration are important for the survival of the animal.

Conditioning and Survival

Pavlov noted that "the conditioned reflex does not disappear without a trace" (Cuny, 1965, p. 69). Reinstatement of the conditioned response will occur with only a few pairings of the original stimuli, even after many intervening years. This persistence of conditioning in the case of a learned, unconscious skill whose main purpose is enhancement of survival is not surprising. The gazelle's learned conditioned response (flight) from the conditioned stimulus (spotted cat) allows only one trial for successful conditioned/learned association with the unconditioned stimulus (threat). The conditioned response of flight of the gazelle must be permanent across the lifespan for survival, even with years of lack of reinforcement with exposure to the leopard.

Pavlov clearly believed that the phenomenon of classical conditioning was rooted in the necessity for experience-based, rapid, and unconscious learning to take place continuously if the animal is to survive. He acknowledged the existence of *instincts*, which he considered to be "the essential basis of the animal's external activity" (Cuny, 1965, p. 80). On the other hand, he considered instincts, these "special unconditioned reflexes," to be "inadequate to preserve the individual and the race" (Cuny, p. 80). In other words, without continuous unconscious learning through the process of conditioning, the animal will die. Pavlov was able to elicit behavioral changes in his dogs by specifically using instinctual survival-based visceral activity as a means of measuring the conditioned response.

Experimental Neurosis
Pavlov discovered that the dogs that served as subjects for his experiments fell into variations of two consistent behavioral types: *weak*, or cowardly, and *strong*, or courageous. Of the strong group, he noted subgroups of *equilibrated* (behaviorally stable) and *unequilibrated* (behaviorally unstable) animals. These variations of apparently instinctual behavior were defined by the aggressiveness or passivity with which the dogs responded to the rigors of the experiments and by how long it took for aggressive dogs to adapt. Weak animals tended to be passive and submissive. Although easy to handle, they sometimes tolerated the rigors of the experiments poorly. Strong dogs were assertive and, when equilibrated (behaviorally stable), were the best subjects for training. In addition, they specifically handled the techniques used to induce experimental neurosis most successfully.

Psychological concepts of the development of neurosis in humans have often been related to the *approach/avoidance conflict*. The approach/avoidance conflict occurs when an event or aspect of one's life contains implications of being both essential/desirable and negative/threatening. As such, it elicits emotions such as frustration, fear, and anxiety. For example, leaving an undesirable job might involve loss of accrued benefits. A sense of enforced immobility, or helplessness, is also implied by this state. Neurosis seems to be limited to more advanced cultures, especially human civilizations, and is seldom seen in animals in the wild. One might speculate that the opportunity for approach/avoidance conflict increases incrementally in proportion to the complexity of a culture.

Pavlov devised ways to instill neurosis in his dogs through a number of techniques that replicated this painful state. In his first series of experiments studying neurosis, he subjected dogs to intense and painful electrical stimuli to the skin. These stimuli elicited either flight or ferocity depending on the dog's weak or strong behavioral type. If the shock was presented simultaneously with food, however, both types of animals salivated and had a diminished behavioral response to the shock. Eventually they salivated with the shock alone, as long as reinforcement of the shock with food was periodically provided. The animal had developed a visceral conditioned response to pain. This process represented an aberration of survival-based behavior that obviously involved the inhibition of pain while sustaining a connection to it. In other words, the reward not only overrode the response to pain, a clear threat, but also became linked to it. This phenomenon has implications for what we term masochistic behavior, as well as possibly for the phenomenon of traumatic reenactment, as is discussed later.

In addition, if a series of shocks was applied at a subtly increasing distance from the initial conditioned place on the skin, at some point an abrupt change in behavior occurred in the dogs. They would suddenly stop salivating to the shock, would exhibit strong defensive reactions, and would no longer salivate with subsequent shocks. Thereafter they also became extremely sensitive and defensive to stimulation with even a weak, nonpainful shock. In other words, the demand for increasingly subtle distinctions between conditioned stimuli eventually created an approach/avoidance conflict—and neurotic behavior. When it comes to survival, we need black-and-white definitions for learning.

In another, more subtle experiment, animals were conditioned to salivate to the visual shape of a circle. Presentation of the shape of an ellipse, however, did not produce salivation. When the shape of the circle was gradually altered toward that of an ellipse, the dogs continued to salivate, an example of irradiation. However, when the image approached the halfway point between the circle and the ellipse, the dogs manifested behavior similar to that of the dogs exposed to the regional spreading shock administration: They stopped salivating and exhibited defensive behavior. Ambivalence creates anxiety in the process of learning, even unconsciously.

Neurosis in both experiments was induced by creation of a state of ambivalence. In the case of the shock stimulus, ambivalence involved the linking of a life threat (pain) with a reward (food). This situation may be expected to create a state of *tension*, a classical approach/avoidance conflict that was sustainable as long as it was contained within the rigid conditioned association of pain (avoidance) in one point of the skin and rewarded with food (approach). Experimental irradiation of the pain stimulus to adjacent body regions literally enlarged and enhanced the perceived intensity of the threat, ultimately breaking down the conditioned response. Interestingly, this process also permanently changed the animal's subsequent behavior and, by definition, its brain. The animal developed a permanent, exaggerated defensive response to a minimal conditioned stimulus, a state that might be termed *phobia*. Even though this was an unconscious process, in a sense the animal was traumatized by the experience of being unable to control the orderly sequence of learning a survival skill. The ambivalence associated with the approach/avoidance conflict created a state of helplessness.

In the circle/ellipse experiment, *inhibition* of perception was required in order for the dogs to differentiate the ellipse from the circle. As the circle gradually approached the ellipse in shape, the dog eventually reached a threshold where differentiation was impossible. At that point the dog stopped salivating, became agitated, and lost all of his conditioning to the link between the circle and salivation. Again, one might conclude that presentation of progressively more ambiguous conditioned stimuli posed a threat significant enough to induce neurosis. As I noted earlier, the dogs responded more or less adaptively to these conflicted experiences based on their type, with the stronger and more equilibrated dogs being very little affected. This finding might suggest the presence of hereditary factors, analogous to personality types, that might affect the vulnerability of the dogs to the development of neurosis. As is discussed later, such "innate" characteristics also may be rooted in the exposure of the animal/human to experiences in infancy that might affect, or even determine, the animal's vulnerability to develop neurosis, even in the laboratory environment of Ivan Pavlov.

In both cases, the dogs were exposed to increasingly ambiguous situations, linked to both punishment and reward, and neurotic behavior appeared when the meaning of the conditioned stimulus blurred. As Pavlov said, "the collision between the two contrary processes, one of excitation and the other of inhibition, which were difficult to accommodate simultaneously, or too unusual in duration or intensity, or both, causes a breakdown of equilibrium" (Cuny, 1965, pp. 108–109). This breakdown of equilibrium is manifested in the defensive reactions that he noted in those dogs subjected to threatening and ambiguous conditioned stimuli. These exaggerated reactions replicate in large part the experience and behavior of human victims of unresolved traumatic stress.

35

Hypnosis and Immobility

Pavlov also made important observations on the behavior of dogs that he termed *animal hypnosis*, a response of self-immobilization in a state when the dog could not escape a threat through fight or flight. We now call this behavior the *freeze response*. Despite his general areas of significant disagreement with Pavlov, Freud also equated hypnosis to "a sort of paralysis of the will, and the power of movement; a paralysis produced by the influence of an omnipotent person on a defenseless, impotent subject" (Cluny, 1965, p. 105). This behavior is reminiscent of the hypnosis produced in animals by fear. Pavlov apparently thought that animal hypnosis was also a survival skill, "a self-protecting reflex of an inhibitory nature" (Cluny, 1965, p. 105). He documented a number of interesting features of animal hypnotism, including persistence of the reflex response of salivation when food was offered, reflex following eye movements, and persistence of reflex motor postures imitating the last position of the limbs before hypnosis ensued (*cataplexy*).

Pavlov also noted that hypnosis could be induced by the prolonged presentation of monotonous stimuli to his dogs, much like the current techniques for inducing hypnosis in humans in a therapeutic setting. The similarity of this process of induced immobilization to the onset of sleep in his dogs led him to conclude that "the so-called inhibition is nothing more than sleep, but partial and localized" (Cluny, 1965, p. 106).

Pavlov observed that some dogs were more susceptible to hypnosis than others, and that several slipped into the hypnotic state every time they were placed in the usual experimental conditions. Throughout his work, he took every measure to ensure that the surgeries performed were relatively painless, and that the dogs were well treated. He did not address issues of trauma, either in human behavior or in the effect of the confinement and forced immobilization on his dogs' behavior. I believe that it is clear, however, that references to the varied behavior of his animals to hypnosis probably reflected not only the instinctual behavioral types described by him but also the varied responses of his animals to a basically traumatic experience.

As noted, Pavlov was clearly describing the freeze response in his animals, and he equated it with various states of sleep. It is of great interest that Freud equated the state of hypnosis in humans to the state of fear-induced immobility seen in animals, thereby implying that induced human immobility constituted the freeze response. Many clinicians and researchers now feel that hypnosis is an induced state of dissociation (a major topic of consideration of this book), a concept that would strongly support my contention that the freeze response is indeed a state of dissociation, not only in animals but also in humans.

Pavlov's Legacy

Pavlov's theories have withstood the test of time, although they have never been subjected to rigorous statistical analysis or validation through the current medical scientific benchmark of randomized controlled trials. His experiments were often elegantly simple, and he was subjected to bitter criticism by many of his scientific peers for the dramatic conclusions that he was able to derive from them. These discoveries led him inexorably to the study of the brain and behavior, initially of dogs, but eventually of the human species. The last years of his career were spent in intense study of patients suffering from hysteria, neurosis, and schizophrenia in the clinics and hospitals of Russia. He produced a vast body of literature based on his lectures and writings and was awarded the Nobel Prize in 1904 (Cuny, 1965).

Although the concept of learning by association had been accepted in the scientific community for centuries, Pavlov, through his research, provided a simple and logical scientific explanation for why this phenomenon occurs in all species. He generalized his concepts of conditioning to the extent that he maintained that all thought, emotions, motor behavior, and processes of the viscera were based on conditioned responses of infinite variety and interaction, determined by life experiences after the moment of birth. He considered the mind to be a vast array of learned perceptions and reflex responses, acquired through a lifetime of conditioned experiences and responses.

He also addressed the concept of creative thought. Human beings have the capacity to focus their internal concentration on thoughts, feelings, and memories and to create new thoughts and concepts from them. In the process of developing concepts and ideas that are totally novel, are we indeed using unique functions of the brain that are separate from the process of conditioning? Pavlov would maintain that we are not, that such creative thinking is based on the complex matrix of preexisting patterns of memory developed through the process of experiencing a myriad of life events. He would even question the validity of "wants or desires" independent of the conditioned response that leads to seeking behavior. He conceived of the cerebral cortex as a "grandiose mosaic" of neuronal interactions, layered on the matrix of inherited instinct, that allowed for the complexities of human perception, creative thought, and behavior (Cuny, 1965, p. 60).

Memory Mechanisms and Survival

We tend to think of memory in terms of what we are able to dredge up from our storehouse of life stories and experiences, with all of the sounds and images associated with them. Or we equate memory with names, phone numbers, and other facts of our daily life that at times elude us to our great consternation. This type of memory of course is only a tiny fraction of the information and learning stored in the areas of the brain that serve the process of memory. Most of our stored memories are unconscious

As presented above, the lessons of life that are necessary for survival are primarily acquired through trial-and-error conditioned associations. Although an unconscious process, conditioning represents a type of learning, and learning requires memory. The type of memory used in conditioning is procedural, or skill-based memory, a concept that will be revisited many times in the book.

Explicit/Declarative Memory

Most of us relate the concept of memory to things that we *remember* (events, facts, words, faces, information, etc.). We specifically equate memory with *learning*, a process that we are exposed to from our very first—well, memory! We learn letters, numbers, words, sentences, and names. We remember specific objects and images, but usually in the context of the names that we assign to them. The type of memory that we use in this specific process of conscious learning is called *explicit* or *declarative* memory. We use this type of memory in reading and trying to incorporate or retain information in our bank of conscious knowledge. Declarative memory may be *episodic* (the type that we use in the course of personal experience to guide our immediate activities and behavior) or *semantic* (the type that we use intentionally for the purpose of learning or gathering information). Different types of declarative memory are assigned to the specific sensory system (visual, auditory, verbal, etc.) that perceived the information to be remembered. Access and retention of conscious, declarative memory is in part a learned skill based to a degree on native intelligence, and it is exquisitely sensitive to decay with distraction, emotional distress, impaired attention, or, for that matter, the passage of time. When paired with an intense emotional event, it may assume features of unconscious memory, including long-term accuracy and resistance to decay. We constantly access and discard information based on the incidental cues that we perceive and process from moment to moment in our activities of daily living. When a memory is incidental and unimportant, we rapidly filter it out, with immediate decay and disappearance.

Declarative memory is notoriously unstable, is subject to prior preference or bias, and may change significantly with the passage of time. It is often distorted by subsequent life experiences and memories. Simple parlor games reflect its innate inaccuracy—if a group of 10 people is sequentially and privately told a specific story by the person next to them and then pass it on one at a time to the next person, the content of the final story often has little bearing on the original story. Descriptions by witnesses of ordinary events or of faces at the scene of an accident often vary markedly. Nevertheless, the performance of most occupations and the pursuit of most human relationships are based on the retention and application of declarative memory. It is predictably enhanced by repetition and training, but even solidly imprinted declarative memories, if unused, will decay and disappear. Doctors probably remember less than 20% of all of the vast volume of facts that they had to learn (temporarily!) in medical school.

The area of the brain that processes declarative memory is called the *hippocampus*. This small brain center in the temporal lobes, represented on both sides of the brain, processes incoming information from the sense organs of the body. It begins the process of bringing that information to consciousness and aids the frontal lobes and other parts of the cerebral cortex in developing memory for the event based on the sensory information provided. At birth, the axons (nerve fibers) that serve the hippocampus are not myelinated (covered with the fatty sheath that allows conduction of electricity) and only gradually undergo myelination during the first few years of life. This probably accounts for our lack of consistent conscious memory for most of those early years of life. The unusual occurrence of damage to the hippocampus on both sides leads to a rather bizarre syndrome in which the victim processes information, responds briefly and appropriately, but within seconds loses memory for the event. Such patients live in the immediate present, cannot use incidental episodic memory to guide their behavior, and are quite disabled, asking the same questions over and over in an attempt to orient themselves. Loss of declarative memory is often the first sign of Alzheimer's disease and other diseases associated with diffuse degeneration of the brain. A concussion from a blow to the head or a profoundly traumatizing emotional event may also be associated with declarative amnesia, the former due to physical/chemical injury and the latter due to dissociation.

Implicit/Nondeclarative/Procedural Memory

Survival skills acquired by life experience through the process of conditioning are dependent on specific memory mechanisms and structures in the brain. Given that virtually all species contain this capacity to some degree, much of this learned behavior must be processed and stored in our most primitive, or reptilian brain: the midbrain, cerebellum, and brainstem. Because these brain centers frequently operate separately from higher centers that control conscious thought and emotions, information stored in these parts of the brain is intrinsically unconscious in nature. Generally we refer to behavior generated by the reptilian brain as being *reflexive* in nature, occurring automatically without regard to planning or intent and without being based on specific input from the thinking brain. This certainly makes sense from the standpoint of initiating behavior intrinsic to survival. The amount of time between experiencing a threatening message and exercising the life-saving motor reaction depends on the number and complexity of the brain circuits the message needs to travel in order to produce the necessary defensive behavior. The defensive motor response must be automatic, preprogrammed, specific, and immediate. Although certain inborn instincts may contribute to this behavior, existence and its dangers are much too complex for instinct alone to be sufficient. Only through repeated and varied exposures to different forms of threat can the human/animal develop the conditioned responses necessary for survival in their particular world. And only by bypassing the conscious brain and its complex circuits can this system work effectively. These features require a type of learning (memory) that fulfills these very specific needs.

The type of memory that serves conditioned responses is called *implicit*, or nondeclarative, memory. By definition, it is unconscious and is acquired constantly through our daily existence without intent or effort. Memory that is associated with intense emotional states is relatively permanent and the brain pathways that mediate it are partly unconscious. This feature of emotional enhancement of memory storage is common to animals other than humans as well. Emotional memory is readily retrievable into conscious memory and remains remarkably accurate over time. Emotional associations that contribute to this type of implicit memory include both intensely negative and positive events. Positive memories of weddings, winning games, receiving awards, and the successes of our children are quite intense and permanent. In the United States, our most recent and vivid negative implicit (and of course explicit) memory obviously is that associated with our experience of the events of the 9/11 terrorist attack on the World Trade Center in New York City. There is considerable debate over how the repetitive televised replay of those horrific events affected the national psyche. Even a simple mention of the attacks will cause most people who spent the day glued to their television sets to immediately reexperience the images and sounds of that event. Reading a passage like this may even provoke the same body sensations that were produced by the stimuli of watching the broadcast. Memory linked with emotional associations in these respects also involves the process of classical conditioning and is relatively accurate and permanent. Because emotional tone is associated with the relative state of affairs regarding survival, it is not surprising that this type of memory is also relatively permanently hardwired in the brain.

As noted earlier, when implicit memory pertains to memory for motor skills and to conditioned sensorimotor responses, it is called *procedural memory*. Procedural memory is the process of acquiring sensorimotor skills, and it employs the centers of the brain that we use to gain those skills. These skills may be athletic, musical, related to the use of tools or machinery (such as driving)—all of the activities that we pursue on a daily basis without having to think very much. If these activities were not automatic and relatively unconscious, we would be cognitively overwhelmed by them and unable to replicate them.

Procedural memory, in general, is also hardwired in the brain. It is consistent, accurate, and relatively resistant to decay through lack of use or exposure. We never really "forget" how to ride a bicycle, ski, skate, dance, or run and jump. Although the skill may deteriorate with neglect and the passage of time, the relearning curve is faster than the initial process. Procedural learning of a skill may be enhanced by the emotional tone of the environment during the training process. Reward systems promote acquisition of the learned motor behavior and enhance its retention. As in Pavlov's induction of experimental neurosis, punishment may also enhance learning, although it presents the predictable risk of inducing a breakdown in behavior and performance. The pressures on our increasingly juvenile competitors in such sports as figure skating and gymnastics, and the rate of emotional collapse, anorexia, and injury in these sports, may well be an example of this phenomenon, as they replicate the dangerous approach/avoidance conflict.

When procedural motor learning takes place in a situation of threat to life, that pattern of unconscious memory is rendered more permanent and resistant to decay. The unconscious sensations that the body experiences during a life-threatening event are therefore permanently retained in procedural memory. The pattern of movements of muscles and tendons used in the act of defense during the threat also become a permanent procedural memory. The sensory experience and motor response then become parts of a survival skill that will be used in the face of future similar threats. The acquisition of this skill, of course, occurs through the process of conditioning. The learned, conditioned motor skills related to a succession of life threats indeed are the primary means of survival of the animal in the wild. These "street smarts" in animals begin to be acquired at the moment of birth; if they are successful, they continue to grow and develop throughout the lifespan until the sensorimotor application of these accumulated skills begins to decay with aging, leading to eventual death.

Along life's paths, however, one faces experiences that may turn procedural memory from a source for learning survival skills to a source of confusion of the past and the present. Such experiences may constitute an aberration of conditioning as a means of survival and a source of dysfunctional emotions and negative physical experiences. In unresolved traumatic stress, procedural memory turns inward, responding to internal cues of a threat that no longer exists, evoking inappropriate somatic and autonomic experiences and responses that pertain to cues unwittingly emerging from past memory rather than from present external experiences.

The varied symptoms of trauma, of which a small number are included under the diagnosis of PTSD, fall under the definition of conditioned responses. These symptoms are incredibly varied. They include abnormal memories (flashback images, intrusive conscious memories, recurring physical sensations, nightmares), abnormal arousal (panic, anxiety, startle), and numbing (confusion, isolation, avoidance, dissociation). The broad spectrum of expression of these symptoms reflects a basically cyclical, bipolar dysfunction involving the brain and most of the regulatory systems of the body—autonomic, endocrine, and immune. They are based on a disruption of the usually modulated regulation of brain centers that govern arousal, emotional tone, memory, and perception. The core of this problem is the fact that procedural and declarative memories for the traumatic event, and the conditioned sensory perceptions and reflex motor responses associated with those memories, continue to replicate the failed efforts at successful fight or flight responses.

Survival Behaviors: The Fight/Flight/Freeze Response

The basic survival behavioral sequence termed the fight/flight/freeze response is familiar enough to be in general usage outside of the scientific community. In fact, it is a complex series of body states that involve the brain and the body in a finely tuned balance between both systems. Altering this primitive and instinctual balance may lead to a wide variety of emotional and physical disorders.

Fight and Flight

Most animal species, including humans, have also developed a series of instinctual behaviors that are automatically triggered by any experience that contains a threat to survival. This response may be set off by a threat to the individual animal but can also be triggered by a threat to a member of the family, pack, societal grouping, or larger related community. The response to threat also varies a great deal depending upon many innate factors, such as the size of the animal, its weapons of self-defense or aggression, its relative placement on the predator/prey ladder, and its gender. The basic choices available in the face of threat include fighting or fleeing, and these behaviors are generally determined by the specific threat the animal faces. Of course, most animals may be defined as either predators or prey by nature and design, but depending on the state of the animal and the nature of the threat, any animal may become a prey. For example, a polar bear, an otherwise primary predator, may become the prey of a helicopter pursuing it for the purpose of tagging.

Humans are unique among animals in that they lack intrinsic weapons of defense and would be expected to assume the role of prey when threatened. However, from the time of the early hunter-gatherers in prehistoric times, the human species has usually behaved like a predator. They have achieved this primarily through the development of tools designed both for defense and predation. Using a variety of spears, arrows, and knives, and progressing to the more sophisticated weaponry of today, humans have reigned as the supreme predator. Except for the occasional feline attack in the wild, humans have only other humans to fear in the pecking order of predators. This fact alone may explain why man is the primary source of traumatic stress for his own kind.

The capacity to initiate the fight/flight response is determined by the *sympathetic nervous system*. Fighting and fleeing demand immediate and intense activation of the cardiovascular and motor systems of the body. The heart must supply increased blood to the brain and muscles, and blood vessels in these organs must dilate to provide it. Glucose must be mobilized from the liver to provide energy for brain and muscles. These needs are provided by the release of epinephrine (adrenaline) from the adrenal medulla, a part of the peripheral sympathetic nervous system. The animal is fine-tuned for the vigorous physical activity required to fight or flee.

The Freeze Response

When fight and flight are unsuccessful or not possible, a third instinctual and quite unconscious option will be exercised. The animal collapses and becomes immobile. Both Freud and Pavlov commented on this *immobility response* as a self-protective behavior in certain animals and likened it to the states of sleep and hypnotism. In fact, immobility behavior is present in most species, including reptiles, and has also been called the *freeze response*. This state of the brain and body has been referred to as suspended animation, as feigning death for the purpose of survival, and as "playing 'possum."

The freeze response can be useful in several ways. First, many predators attack simply because of an instinctual response to movement cues in the prey. The freeze response may inhibit the predator's instinct to attack, causing it to lose interest in the immobile prey. Second, in some situations, the predator is hunting for food for its offspring. In these cases the predator, believing the prey is injured or dead, will leave the area to gather its brood, giving the prey the opportunity to arouse and escape. Third, the analgesia associated with the freeze response, induced by release of large amounts of brain endorphins, allows injured prey to refrain from nursing its wounds, a behavior that might precipitate another attack.

If the freeze response is successful in preventing the animal from being killed, the animal will gradually emerge from immobility. If the animal has pursued an unsuccessful attempt at flight before the freeze response occurred, it will exhibit a remarkable and relatively stereotyped pattern of movement that often resembles a grand mal seizure. There are many variations in this response, from relatively slight twitching movements to violent shaking. Slow-motion video recordings of animals experiencing recovery from a freeze often reveal running movements although the animal is lying on the ground. It is almost as if the movements are a continuation of the last movements of attempted

How the Brain Helps Us to Survive

escape. There are a number of names for this process, but the most accurate might be a *freeze discharge*. The severity and length of the freeze discharge sometimes reflects the severity of the attack and the intensity of the escape attempts.

Observation and physiological studies of the freeze response in the mammal reveal that the animal is remarkably analgesic to painful stimuli and, although quite immobile, not unconscious. At times it may be frozen in unusual postures that reflect its position at the moment of freeze. Pavlov noted that one could induce "immobility" in a dog by turning it onto its back and restraining it, which caused the dog to remain "stuck" in the posture in which it was placed.

Because the freeze response follows a life threat, one would expect that blood pressure and pulse would be elevated as a result of release of large amounts of adrenaline associated with heightened arousal. Indeed, the blood pressure and pulse are elevated, and blood vessels constrict in the skin as evidence for high levels of adrenaline. However, this is only part of the autonomic response. More prominently, the pulse also periodically falls to extremely low levels, the blood pressure drops, and blood vessels dilate, indicative of activity of the parasympathetic, or vegetative, nervous system. The animal in freeze is in a precarious state of abnormally dysregulated and fluctuating autonomic nervous system activity.

One seldom sees the dramatic immobility of the freeze response in humans. Video recordings of spectators watching the collapse of the World Trade Center on 9/11, however, reveal numerous graphic illustrations of the freeze. Many spectators stood transfixed with their hands over their mouth, others sat on the curb with their head in hands, others stood motionless with their jaw dropped and eyes staring widely. All were in a state of shock, stunning, and trance, numbed to emotion and cognitively fogged. When questioned, some described a dramatic slowing of the passage of time, others a sense of unreality to the point of looking down on the scene as a third person. The perceptual experience at that moment is called *dissociation*. It is physiologically the same as the freeze.

Freezing and the Vagal System: In Search of Energy Efficiency
Survival behavior differs between mammals and reptiles, primarily because mammals have evolved a system of utilizing energy that allows for great speed and mobility. This may be a result of their progression from an aquatic to a land-based existence. Compared to reptiles, which maintain a relatively cooler body core and blood temperature, mammals have a much higher body

temperature and an ability to produce dramatic increases in circulation of blood throughout the body. This means they must be able to suddenly increase the utilization of oxygen in the face of immediate demands for energy, a skill that gives them the advantage of mobility and speed in the survival race. It also enables them to travel for relatively long distances in search of food to meet the higher number of nutritional calories that these characteristics demand.

Reptiles, on the other hand, are hampered by slow circulation and a low potential for increasing oxygen utilization. As a result, they exhibit slow speed and limited endurance. On the other hand, these characteristics make reptiles more energy-efficient, allowing them to survive for long periods of time without any food and even, in some physical states, without any oxygen. These features obviously also have survival advantages.

The physical activities of the mammal that require the highest energy use are fleeing a predator, pursuing prey, and mating. The prey animal faces the potential need for flight from a predator many times in the course of a day. Initiating flight in response to every threatening noise, image, or scent would be impractical—the animal would expend more energy fleeing than it would gain through feeding. Thus, mammals developed an adaptive "early-warning system" for executing survival behavior short of the flight response. Faced with a potential threat while feeding, the prey animal becomes almost entirely motionless, with the exception of slight side-to-side movement of the head to allow it to scan the environment for visual or olfactory (smell) cues. This behavior is called the *orienting response*. If no danger is detected, the animal will resume its activity without wasting energy on a false alarm. For example, a rabbit may "freeze" momentarily upon hearing a dog in the distance and then resume its activity once the threat has passed. (Some investigators call this brief period of immobility a "freeze" response, but I reserve this term for the more dramatic behavior of immobility I discussed earlier.) However, if danger is clearly imminent, the prey animal will initiate a flight response. Prey animals with weapons, such as horns, may initiate group defense or fight behavior. In humans, this orienting response is harder to identify. An example might be the sudden crouching and immobility with head turning by the soldier in combat at the sound of gunfire.

Steven Porges (1995) presented a compelling theory addressing the relative roles of the vagus nerve in energy conservation and survival. His theory suggests, among other things, that the true freeze response is dangerous to mammals. The vagus nerve regulates all of the visceral organs and selectively slows the heart, dilates the blood vessels, and lowers the blood pressure. The *dorsal vagal complex*, a cluster of connected neurons in the brainstem medulla, slows down the energy-expending processes in reptiles, allowing them to hibernate. It also governs the dive reflex in reptiles, where they remain submerged for long periods of time to pursue prey or escape predators. Excessive influence of the dorsal vagal complex in mammals may be hazardous to life, causing cardiovascular events that may precipitate sudden death (Porges, 1995). When wild rats in a laboratory are immobilized by being held tightly in a gloved hand, almost all of the rats will freeze, and a significant number will die during the freeze. Autopsies reveal that the rat's heart is dilated, relaxed, and engorged with blood, a state of fatal activation of the dorsal vagal complex. In mammals facing a life threat while helpless, the freeze response therefore may not only be lifesaving but also life-endangering.

The attention and orienting reflex discussed above is also mediated by the dorsal vagal complex, but it is modulated by another center in the vagus nerve, the *ventral vagal complex*, a group of neurons unique to mammals. The ventral vagal complex puts a damper on the dorsal vagal system, protecting the mammal from the dangers of dorsal vagal effects while at the same time conserving vital energy stores (Porges, 1995). However, if the threat is severe and the freeze profound, the influence of the ventral vagal complex in protecting the mammal may be insufficient.

A number of studies on sudden, unexplained death clearly reflect the dangers of excessive activation of the freeze response and the dorsal vagal complex in humans. George Engel (1971) studied 170 cases of sudden death in patients. Life events preceding these deaths included great personal loss—grief and mourning of the death of a loved one, loss of jobs or self-esteem, and ambivalent, conflicted situations that created helplessness with no hope of resolution of the problem. Many cases presented an insoluble approach/avoidance conflict. Helplessness and hopelessness were the key elements in all cases. Most victims died of heart failure, similar to the wild rats that died during enforced immobility. Saul (1966) describes a case that exemplifies the combination of helplessness and hopelessness that may be associated with a profound approach/avoidance conflict:

A 45-year-old man found himself in a totally unbearable situation and felt forced to move to another town. But just as he was ready to make the move, difficulties developed in the other town that made the move impossible. In an anguished quandary, he, nonetheless, boarded the train for the new locale. Halfway to his destination, he got out to pace the platform at a station stop. When the conductor called, "All aboard," he felt he could neither go on nor return home; he dropped dead on the spot. He was traveling with a friend, a professional person, with whom he shared his awful dilemma. Necropsy showed myocardial infarction (Saul, 1966, p. 89).

Walter Cannon made similar observations in indigenous tribal members in Africa cursed by a medicine man or shunned by the tribe for some misdeed. In situations creating helplessness and hopelessness through social taboos, the shunned tribal member would retreat to his hut, compose himself, and die in a state popularly termed "voodoo death." Similarly, a curse may be placed on a member of the tribe by the medicine man for some societal misdeed. A magical animal bone is pointed at the victim while the curse is invoked. Voodoo death may occur in these victims who have been "boned" (Cannon, 1957). These fatal reactions are probably mediated by the dorsal vagal complex of the brainstem medulla as part of a profound freeze response. Prolonged, severe slowing of the heart and of circulation carries the risk of death in the mammal. In addition, chronic exposure to the influences of the freeze response in humans may lay the seeds for a wide variety of chronic disease states, many of them without any other explainable cause.

The Critical Importance of the Freeze Discharge

Psychologist Peter Levine (1997) derived a unique hypothesis from his extensive studies regarding the role of freezing and discharge in animals and its relationship to the effects of traumatic stress in humans. He noted that animals in captivity seem to have lost much of their instinctual ability to experience a healthy freeze/discharge sequence in the face of threat, and suffer from symptoms of depression and a shortened lifespan. Similarly, Levine found that his PTSD patients experienced a dramatic clearing of many of their symptoms when they were allowed to complete the motor discharge of the freeze through unique behavioral therapeutic techniques. In the absence of this freeze discharge, the "energy" of the intense arousal associated with the threat and attempted escape remains bound in the body and brain, leading to a host of abnormal symptoms that we attribute to PTSD. Levine also noted that repeated freeze events without discharge seemed to be cumulative, adding to a progressive worsening of posttraumatic symptoms and to the development of progressive helplessness in the face of threat.

The key to this dilemma of inhibited discharge seems to lie in the attainment of empowerment, freedom, and ultimately completion. The healthy animal freezes only when it enters a state of helplessness. This may occur because it has been run to the ground, because it is trapped and cannot initiate a flight response, because it is physically incapable of defense through fighting, or because it has been injured and rendered incapable of further attempts at saving itself. Pavlov demonstrated what he called a *freedom instinct* in his dogs, which if sufficiently thwarted, led to experimental neurosis (Cuny, 1965). Entrapment or caging of a wild animal seems to inhibit the process of freeze and discharge and may account for the abnormal behavior in zoo animals, including self-harm, social withdrawal, and early death. Other animals denied freedom of movement and the exercise of basic instinctual behavior exhibit similar behavioral abnormalities, health problems, and early death. This includes animals in laboratories, circus animals, and domestic animals. And lest we ignore the obvious, it also includes the acculturated human.

Brain Pathways for Adaptation and Survival

Survival behavior of a threatened animal basically begins with receiving messages from the environment that the animal has been conditioned to respond to as being dangerous. The head and neck contain the primary means of accessing these threat-based stimuli through the primary senses of smell, sight, and hearing, as well as the proprioceptive senses of the muscles of the neck that process messages of movement of the head. Messages from these sources of information in the head have a special priority for early processing in centers of the brain that are designed to promote survival. They also are closely connected with the parts of the brain that regulate emotional tone and memory. As noted earlier, procedural memory is the primary source of storage of survival-based information. Emotions, including fear, rage, joy, and sadness, also reflect positive and negative life experiences and are closely tied into the repertoire of acquired survival skills.

The muscles of the head and neck also are closely linked to reflexes associated with survival. In the human embryo, during the first weeks and months of development, the head and neck go through a stage where gills appear on each side of the neck, much like those of fish and amphibians. As the embryo develops, the gills disappear, and the muscles that move the gills gradually transform into many of the muscles of the face, jaw, mouth, and neck. These are the only voluntary muscles that are supplied specifically by the autonomic nervous system, which otherwise innervates the involuntary muscles of the viscera: the heart, lungs, and digestive muscles. Like the gill muscles from which they developed, these muscles are intimately related to instinctual as well as voluntary behaviors that are linked to survival.

In the human species, the muscles of the face have become closely associated with subtle human forms of communication, including communication of love, joy, fear, rage, threat, and terror. Infinitely subtle shades of these emotions are also possible through variations in facial expression, and they constitute a poorly recognized but important source of communication between humans that is critical for eventual survival. Such nuances of facial expression also undoubtedly play a role in survival with other mammals as well.

The muscles of the jaw perhaps have the most obvious survival implications. They participate in predation (killing the prey by throttling with clenched jaws) and in defense (through biting). They also participate in alimentation (eating), an obvious survival-based behavior. A "clenched jaw" is widely recognized as a sign of rage or frustration. The syndrome of bruxing (involuntarily clenching or grinding the teeth, especially at night) is also a reflex related to inordinate stress in one's life. Like the facial muscles, the muscles of the jaw are closely linked to emotions, especially those associated with the response to threat.

The sternomastoid muscles at the side of the neck that turn the head from sided to side, as well as forward and backward, are also derived from the gill muscles. Their primary and intrinsic function is probably also based on the orienting reflex discussed earlier as the instinctual initial motor response of the body to impending threat. These movements position the head, with its primary senses of smell, vision, and hearing for optimal access to threat-based messages.

The head and neck movements associated with the orienting response and the fight or flight behavior that may follow it are clearly innate. Once these reflex responses are initiated, however, the subsequent survival behavior is patterned by the ongoing experience of the attempt to survive, which is based on the sensory input from many systems, and the motor behavior in response to that input. The brain centers that guide this complex sensorimotor response are primarily those that deal with arousal, memory, emotions, and organization of behavior.

The Neurophysiology of Threat

In the interests of clarity, I would like to present a relatively simplistic model for the structures and pathways in the brain that bring the brain "on line" in response to a threatening experience. Basically, the frontal and central areas of the right cerebral hemisphere are the regions of the brain that attend to the arousal response to threatening information. The parts of the brain that then must organize behavior in order to survive the threat are recruited based on the information processed in this area of the right side of the brain. In general, the parts of the brain that function in an executive fashion (thinking, planning, communicating, using any type of rational thought) are not really necessary for this type of emergency behavior. As a result, most of the frontal and central areas of the left cerebral hemisphere (which organize speech, use of symbols, and higher thought processes) are not called into play immediately. One does not need words when faced with imminent death.

Usually the first information that warns us of impending threat is accessed by the primary senses of smell, vision, and hearing. Messages coming primarily from these basic senses are routed to a tiny cluster of cells in the brainstem called the *locus ceruleus*, or blue center (Figure 2.1). This brain nucleus

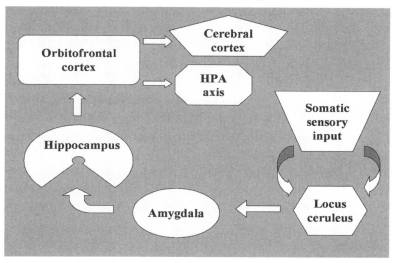

Figure 2.1: Brain pathways for trauma. Sensory input from the primary senses and from the body are sent to the *locus ceruleus*, where they are evaluated for threat-based content. Messages then are sent to the *amygdala*, which assesses their emotional content and sends this information to the *hippocampus*. The hippocampus assigns a cognitive meaning to the information and sends messages to the *orbitofrontal cortex* (OFC). The OFC then activates the *hypothalamic/pituitary/adrenal* (HPA) axis to organize the autonomic and endocrine responses, and to the *cerebral cortex* to organize complex survival behavior.

is composed of blue-staining cells that send messages to many brain centers, employing primarily the neurotransmitter *norepinephrine*, a chemical that excites or stimulates reaction in these centers. Most importantly, messages from the locus cereleus are sent to the *amygdala* (the "olive"), which is the center for memory for emotionally laden information. The amygdala sends messages to the *hippocampus* (the "sea horse"), the nerve center for declarative memory, in addition to other regions of the brain. Any part of the brain receiving information that has been processed by the amygdala is likely to respond to the emotional content of the experience, which of course is higher if the experience is threatening. The hippocampus forms a conscious structure for this threat-based message that includes its emotional importance, and then sends it on to the *orbitofrontal cortex*, the master regulator of survival behavior, both conscious and unconscious.

The orbitofrontal cortex then sends information to many parts of the brain that may then organize and initiate the necessary behavior patterns to help the animal survive. It also activates the body's endocrine response through the *hypothalamic/pituitary/adrenal* (HPA) axis. The *hypothalamus* is a center deep in the middle and base of the brain. In addition to regulating many other complex functions, such as sleep and appetite, it also regulates the autonomic nervous system. In the case of a threat, the sympathetic nervous system (the energy-burning survival part) is activated. The *pituitary gland*, the master endocrine gland, is also activated and initiates the body's endocrine response. The pituitary gland, through the hormone *adrenocorticotropic hormone* (ACTH), stimulates the adrenal glands to release *cortisol*, which puts a brake on norepinephrine, modulating the brain's further arousal response. In the event that the animal survives the immediate threat, cortisol also prepares the animal to manage ongoing stress through changes in its circulation, metabolism, and immune responses. This complex interaction of nerve centers, glands, and chemicals is typical of the multiply interactive feedback systems by which the body is designed to regulate itself and to promote stability of the entire organism, a state of autonomic balance called homeostasis.

Stress, Trauma, and Homeostasis

Homeostasis was described by Walter Cannon (as quoted in Selye, 1956, p. 23) as "the coordinated physiological processes which maintain most of the steady states in the organism." All of the systems of the body work to maintain this steady state. They do so by reacting to any stimulus, internal or external, and by integrating the information from that stimulus into all of the adaptive systems of the body. These systems include the brain, endocrine, and immune systems, which then generate a response that most effectively maintains the steady state of homeostasis.

In order to maintain a state of resiliency in this process, all of these response systems must be flexible and, like much of nature, operate on the principle of a sine wave. When you drop a pebble into the smooth surface of a lake, you produce a circular pattern consisting of rhythmic elevation and depression of the rings of water, the elevated portion of which we call the wave. These waves spread away from the impact point, lessening in amplitude based on the distance from the impact. This is an appropriate analogy for the method with which the systems of the body respond to stimuli. Any message or input to the body elicits such a wavelike response in all systems; the response gradually diminishes until a new, altered but steady state has been achieved. This pattern may also be viewed as rhythmic cycling, a phenomenon that typifies most of nature, including the seasons, the monthly cycles of the moon, day-night cycles, the menstrual cycle, the sleep-wake cycle, and so on. Maintenance of the body's systems in such a smoothly regulated cycle of function allows it to respond to constant input from the environment in an adaptive fashion that prevents excessive responses that would disrupt homeostasis.

Under certain life circumstances, however, stimuli from the environment demand more drastic responses of the body and may disrupt homeostasis. In these life-threatening cases, adaptive responses are called upon to allow the body to adjust to the immediate needs for survival at the expense of homeostasis. Hans Selye spent his career studying the body's response to such stressful experiences. He demonstrated that the prolonged need to adapt to ongoing stress resulted in many of the chronic diseases of civilization, including hypertension, heart disease, kidney disease, and alterations of the intestinal and immune systems (Selye, 1956). Although Selye's stressed animals automatically adapted to ongoing threat, selected parts of their body deteriorated in the face of persisting high levels of the stress hormone cortisol, a process that he termed the *general adaptation syndrome* (GAS).

The pathways in the nervous and endocrine systems that are implicated in trauma, as opposed to stress, are similar to those that Selye (1956) studied in his experiments with stress in animals. Indeed, many victims of life trauma exhibit chronic diseases similar to those produced as part of the GAS. In traumatic stress a series of experiences—or, for that matter, a single traumatic event—can lead to an alteration of the cycle of homeostasis and produce a process that is self-perpetuating even in the absence of ongoing external stressors or threats. The animal or human has "learned" a response or behavior that persists even though it alters and prevents the resumption of healthy homeostasis. Thus, one might logically conclude that the stimuli perpetuating the disruption of homeostasis in trauma are generated internally.

Animal Models of Trauma:
Learned Helplessness Versus Learned Resiliency

In a simple study done by H. J. Ginsberg (1974, referenced in Seligman, 1975), newborn chicks were studied for their survival instincts. The freeze response was induced in the chicks by holding them until they became immobile. The first group of chicks was allowed to recover from the freeze response and to go through the process of discharge without interference. A second group of chicks was also immobilized in the same manner, but the experimenter disrupted the freeze discharge by prodding the chicks on their breasts until they aroused. A third group was not subjected to immobilization. Resiliency was measured by the length of time it took each group of chicks to drown when place in a vat of water. (The time it takes for an animal to drown in such a controlled and obviously fatal environment is a widely used test for stress resiliency in animals.)

The group of chicks who had experienced the freeze response but had spontaneously and naturally emerged from it swam the longest (Figure 2.2). The third group, which had never experienced the freeze, swam the next longest. This appears to testify to the value of "completing the escape" from a life-threatening event through freezing and spontaneous recovery. The group of chicks that had frozen but were not allowed to complete the freeze discharge put up little struggle and quickly drowned. They apparently lacked the instinctual resiliency to face another life threat.

This simple experiment exemplifies concepts of vulnerability and resiliency in the face of a life threat. Animals raised in a closed environment, protected from danger and never exposed to the freeze response, such as a pet or domestic livestock, may not display behavior typical of having been trau-

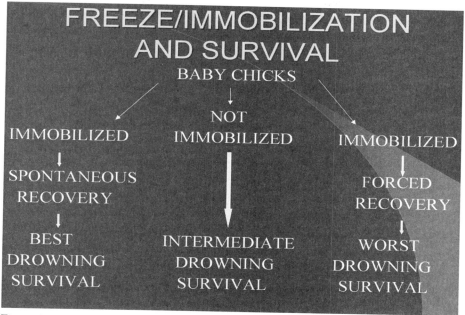

Figure 2.2. Resiliency and the freeze discharge. Producing a freeze response in chicks and allowing them to proceed through the discharge enhances their survival abilities in the face of future threat. Preventing the freeze discharge, however, renders them vulnerable and helpless in the face of future threats (Ginsberg, 1974).

matized. Nevertheless, if exposed to a life threat in a natural environment, they probably would lack many of the survival skills of an animal raised in the wild. Having experienced many instances of threat, even sufficient to cause the freeze response, animals raised in the wild have developed resilience to further traumatic stress. Finally, animals that have experienced threat in a state of helplessness, as in a zoo, and have never "escaped" will be completely vulnerable and helpless in any state of future threat and, in fact, will be vulnerable to dying from the experience. This phenomenon almost certainly accounts for the astoundingly high rate of fatality (approaching 50%) in animals captured in the wild and transported to zoos. Confinement in a cage and ongoing helplessness prevent any freeze discharge and perpetuate the trauma.

However, the animal in the wild that has experienced the freeze response, discharged it, and survived has retained the memories of the threat and of survival: Procedural memories for the experience now contain memories of escape. These memories represent learned behaviors that contribute to increased resilience for later threatening experiences. In a sense, it has added to its basic instinctual storehouse of survival skills.

Many scientific investigators who have studied the state of helplessness in animals have used the technique of "inescapable shock." One means of applying this technique is to place an animal, usually a cat or a dog, in a box separated into two halves by a barrier. On the floor of one side of the box is an electrical grid; on other side the floor is wooden and therefore benign. The animal is placed on the side with the grid and is subjected to a shock. This naturally causes marked agitation and attempts to escape from the shock, but the animal is prevented from doing so by the barrier. With successive shocks, the animal makes fewer and fewer escape attempts and eventually lies down, passively accepting the shocks in a state of immobility. Having frozen in the face of an inescapable threat, the animal is traumatized and unable to complete the freeze discharge. Repeatedly threatened in a state of helplessness, the animal develops *learned helplessness*, a state that is now felt to be analogous to traumatization in humans and a state that is basically derived from a conditioned response.

Remarkably, if the barrier preventing the traumatized animal from escaping is removed, the animal will remain immobile, passively accepting the shock and making no attempt to move to the safe side of the box. Learned helplessness—or, for that matter, being traumatized—inhibits subsequent survival instincts and behavior. The logical conclusion would be that the unresolved freeze response creates learned helplessness, and that learned helplessness must be significantly mediated by the parasympathetic/vagal nervous system, as is the freeze response. Indeed, many investigators, including Seligman (1975), have documented that blocking the parasympathetic nervous system with the drug *atropine* blocks the development of learned helplessness in animals. Learned helplessness therefore appears to represent the learned persistence of the parasympathetic-dominant freeze response in the face of any threat.

The model of learned helplessness helps to differentiate the concept of life stress from that of trauma. It takes a permanent conditioned response in the animal to establish the ongoing self-perpetuating state that characterizes the external behavior and internal state of disrupted homeostasis caused by trauma. The establishment of this conditioned response is specifically dependant on the experience of a life-threatening event in a state of helplessness, a situation guaranteed to induce the freeze response. The experiences associated with the threat are consolidated in procedural memory and learning because the animal is unable to discharge or complete the process of recovery from the freeze response. Furthermore, the future tendency to freeze is perpetuated by repetitive internal stimuli derived from the storage in procedural memory of all of the sensorimotor experiences of the traumatic experience.

CHAPTER 3

Trauma As Imprisonment of the Mind

In Chapter 1, I defined the mind as "a perceptual experience, generated by a complex set of synapses, neurons, and neurochemical states, determined by genes, instinct, and experience, that is capable of developing and directing novel behavior." In the brain of the trauma victim, the synapses, neurons, and neurochemicals have been substantially and indefinitely altered by the effects of a unique life experience. Not surprisingly, the perceptual experience that constitutes the mind has been equally altered. This alteration more than anything else is a corruption of procedural memory, that part of our intrinsic memory that is most involved in acquisition of survival skills. We depend on learned cues in our environment to distinguish positive versus negative survival-based information. If we have not learned to distinguish between these types of cues, we lose our edge in the survival game. In trauma, cues to an event that is over and done with are stored in procedural memory as if the event had never been completed.

Trauma thus represents a time-based corruption of learning. The brain in trauma has lost its ability to distinguish past from present, and as a result it cannot adapt to the future. This confusion of time further immobilizes the trauma victim, who still remains immobilized by a thwarted freeze discharge. Procedural memory is bombarded by environmental and internal cues that represent old, unresolved threat. Declarative memory is assaulted by intrusive thoughts, memories, and dreams that repetitively warn the person of potential danger. Furthermore, the constant activation of brain circuitry related to threat alters and suppresses structure and function in the verbal and thinking brain. Trauma indeed is a state of imprisonment.

Cues and Traumatic Memory

One of the most important functions of procedural memory as a tool for survival is its unconscious detailed storage of the cues associated with life-threatening experiences. Thus, a gazelle that has experienced an attack by a cheetah has the cat-with-spots visual cue deeply embedded in its implicit memory, and that cue serves the gazelle's survival by initiating a flight response when needed. As noted earlier, cues that are related to a severe threat (like the cat-with-spots) are conditioned to the appropriate response much more quickly and easily than more subtle survival-based cue associations, such as salivating and bell ringing.

This basic survival memory, however, may be corrupted by the experience of traumatization, which is characterized by the process of learned helplessness that occurs when completion of the act of escape from the threat has not been accomplished. Procedural memories in this state are linked with explicit and implicit emotional memories of the event but are inappropriately integrated into one's bank of old survival skills. Although the threat of the event is past, stored procedural memory for the event continues to operate as if the threat were still imminent. The intrusive thoughts, flashbacks, and nightmares associated with this unique process suggest that the past danger remains present and imminent in memory and awareness. Because these memories have been acquired in a state of helplessness, the victim is again unable to overcome the danger that they represent and resumes a response of helplessness by freezing/dissociating, ensuring their persisting and inevitable reoccurrence. In this state, the victim cannot differentiate between imminent threat and memory of old threat. The victim is thus repetitively assaulted by the past and destined to repeat it.

When a traumatic event laden with many intense cues occurs, such as an automobile accident, most of these cues are immediately stored for future reference in procedural memory. If the trauma was associated with helplessness, subsequent exposure to these environmental cues will elicit fear, along with the autonomic and sensorimotor responses that we have learned to associate with fear. Thus, a person's first car ride after an MVA may provoke spasm and pain in the neck muscles that were reflexively braced for self-protection in the accident. Dizziness reflects the intense vestibular stimulation experienced in the impact. Palpitations are related to the sympathetic arousal associated with fear. Weakness and nausea are associated with the parasympathetic component of the freeze response. In other words, faced with cue-related reminders of the recent severe life threat, the brain will resurrect sensory experiences that have been stored in procedural memory for the purpose of self-defense.

With time, the body will increasingly respond to more general situations associated with stress and arousal. The brain will differentiate less and less between specific cues related to the MVA and general stressful experiences. The patient's symptoms related to subsequent stressful or threatening life experiences will replicate the symptoms experienced in the car accident. Trauma victims will develop specific body symptoms that they associate with stress, such as tightness on one side of the neck, which they may call their "stress" point. They usually do not realize that their "stress point" is actually a dysfunctional survival-based procedural memory related to their old MVA.

This leads to the development of stereotyped learned defensive motor behaviors, as well as replication of the sensory experiences under situations of threat, a process that I believe explains a number of syndromes, including whiplash. I have concluded that whiplash syndrome is based on procedural memory for the somatic sensations, perceptions, and motor behavior that occurred during an MVA. These symptoms and behaviors emerge with exposure to cues to that event (even if perceived unconsciously) and eventually with exposure to any ambient stress. This abnormal memory retention of vivid, accurate, and reproducible somatic experiences in trauma only occurs when the victim has frozen and been unable to discharge the freeze response. In other words, in whiplash syndrome "the gain in pain comes mainly from the brain," not from damaged ligaments, brain cells, or other tissues of the body. This process unfortunately leads to the eventual acquisition of a host of vague somatic symptoms that physicians are usually unable to explain.

Because emotional symptoms are frequency related to whiplash and the degree of the patient's distress is often disproportionate to the physical injury, many physicians who have studied the syndrome have maintained that it is primarily psychosomatic in nature. Admittedly, the postures and sensory experiences that result from dissociation and procedural memory don't make sense from the standpoint of actual damage to structures of the body or the central nervous systems. They do, however, make eminent sense as residual sensory experiences (warnings) and motor responses (defensive postures) that reflect patterns of behavior that are unconsciously and mistakenly perceived as being necessary for ongoing survival defense. The persistence of these old experiences and defensive motor behaviors is clearly dependent on the unconscious perception that the threat still exists, an inevitable part of traumatization.

Another graphic example of this process is phantom limb pain, which occasionally occurs in victims of limb amputation. Often it occurs when the limb was traumatically injured or when severe intractable pain in the limb preceded the amputation. This type of pain clearly represents procedural memory for a threat-based message that was never successfully resolved. In fact, many types of chronic intractable pain not associated with a specific cause on diagnostic tests are probably due to trauma-based procedural memory.

In the absence of further similar traumatic life experiences, the passage of time may erode these learned sensory and motor responses through the process of extinction of conditioning. On the other hand, through irradiation of conditioning, fear may gradually be produced by cues related to but not identical to the original cue, leading to a worsening of symptoms. Persistence of a low-grade threat, such as ambient life stress, may indefinitely perpetuate and sustain cues from an old trauma and the body's response to them. Such conditioned associations that thereafter govern our behavior are far more common than we think.

For example, a colleague of mine who had experienced a tonsillectomy under ether anesthesia as a young child was unable to sustain a full yawn for 7–8 years after the surgery. Initiating a yawn caused him to choke, ending the reflex inhalation that accompanies yawning. When ether anesthesia was a common practice, physicians usually urged the patient to "blow away the smell," thus producing hyperventilation and more rapid induction of anesthesia. This hyperventilation was usually associated with intensification of the smell and hallucinations associated with ether. The experience produced intense sympathetic arousal and fear, traumatizing the patient. Trouble swallowing, stutter and abnormal speech patterns, and compulsive habit spasms (tics) of the throat all represent possible involuntary somatic expressions of the trauma produced by ether anesthesia or, for that matter, any trauma associated with perceived asphyxiation. Enhanced sensitivity to smells, especially those associated with organic chemical compounds such as alcohol, might be another somatic response to this experience.

Similarly, a young patient of mine who recovered completely after 18 months of treatment for neck pain after a rear-end MVA experienced a recurrence of identical pain when she entered high school over 3 years later. The stress of going from a small one-room class to the complex social environment of secondary school, along with her own high academic expectations of herself, resulted in the emergence of old, supposedly extinguished patterns of pain and muscle spasm. This case is clearly an example of irradiation of a latent conditioned response to an entirely new but also stressful event.

Another patient of mine returned to see me after I had referred her to a therapist. The patient noted that the therapist was very pleasant and supportive but said that she found something about the therapist unsettling. With a little exploration, we discovered that the therapist favored scarlet nail polish, as had the patient's abusive grandmother. Conditioned associations such as these may be extremely subtle and revealed only after a thorough exploration of the *meaning* of the patient's response has been conducted.

Such deeply rooted conditioned associations have a great deal to do with how we view the world—through the clear lens of safety or through the murky glass of danger. From preferences to phobias, our life choices are often influenced by procedural memories for old, unremembered, and supposedly trivial life trauma. The myriad environmental cues stored in our unconscious memory shape our personalities, preferences, and social behaviors. They are deeply learned habits, both good and bad, and changing them is difficult at best. On the negative side, they limit the breadth of our behavioral options and may not only be self-perpetuating but also lead to more symptoms. In such cases, the body sensations representing old traumatic procedural memory may themselves serve as a message of threat, eliciting low-grade arousal as part of fight/flight preparation. Images, explicit memories, and other internal cues to the original trauma may also trigger the cycle of neuronal connections that initiate the brain's neurophysiological cycle of arousal (see Figure 2.1). The quantum shift in endocrine and immune responses resulting from these "trivial" events may sow the seeds of many common somatic diseases and emotional disorders throughout the lifespan.

Internal Cues and Kindling

When internal cues of the trauma become part of the source for arousal related to a specific traumatic event, a process called *neurosensitization* or *kindling* takes place. Taken from the word for wood that burns easily, the term *kindling* refers to a process of neurosensitization within neuronal pathways that leads to spontaneous activity that is independent of external sensory stimulation.

Trauma As Imprisonment of the Mind

In 1969, Goddard and colleagues (1969) discovered a unique model of self-driven neuronal circuits in rats. By electrically stimulating various regions of the brain in newborn rats at a critical frequency, Goddard was eventually able to produce seizures. If he stimulated these brain regions enough times, the seizures became permanent and self-perpetuating: The rats had developed permanent changes in the functions of selected neurons. These changes apparently caused persisting spontaneous electrical transmission between the neurons that were in the area of the originally stimulated brain centers. In other words, these brain centers were being activated simply through stimulation of the sensitized neurons by other similar neurons. The amygdala, the center within the limbic system for assessment and mobilization of emotions, was the easiest brain region in which to induce this kindling. Many researchers in the field of trauma believe that PTSD represents an example of this type of neurosensitization. In PTSD, the conscious and procedural memories of the traumatic event serve as the spontaneous internal cues that cause the emergence of symptoms even in the absence of external environmental cues.

The process of kindling may explain why both internal and external cues trigger arousal in traumatized patients. It may also explain the close link between trauma-related emotions and sensations and the perpetuation and replication of these symptoms. The elicitation, or "recovery," of a suppressed traumatic memory during a massage or other type of therapeutic bodywork occurs when a deep-seated somatic cue is involuntarily accessed. It is not due to "body memory" but rather to the resurrection of kindled procedural memory of somatosensory features of the traumatic experience.

Kindling may also explain the tendency for painful body symptoms and associated emotions to actually worsen with the passage of time, almost as if they had a life of their own. In cases of trauma and learned helplessness, the brain and body are literally on automatic pilot, following pathways of old survival cues that warn of long-past threats. First acquired to warn the unwitting victim of the original trauma, these cues now trigger useless reflexive self-protective motor responses, pain, or other intense sensory experiences and emotional states disproportionate to the current experience. And each time these old cues elicit arousal, they "up the ante," increasing the self-protective response to the perceived threat and rendering the victim increasingly sensitive to them. Eventually the trauma victim may respond to almost any ambient excessive environmental stimulus, such as smells, loud noises, or flashes of light. This phenomenon of progressive cue-based sensitization through kindling explains the fact that PTSD often worsens with time, and develops an increasing assemblage of somatic symptoms. It also explains the progressive sensitivity to even minor stressors that is so apparent in victims of multiple, sequential life trauma. This exquisite sensitivity to the environment often results in the medical profession's labeling of victims of this type of cumulative and complex trauma as "hypochondriacs."

As mentioned earlier, when searching a patient's history for the cause of his or her distress, one must always attend to the *meaning* of the ambient cues of the traumatic experience. A patient of mine with a history of childhood trauma, as well as several significant MVAs, moved to a new city to escape an abusive personal relationship. The day after she arrived, she went grocery shopping. As she pulled her car into a spot in the parking lot, the person parked next to her opened her door and forcefully bumped the patient's passenger-side door. The patient jumped and then "went numb" for a time. She thereafter developed severe stiff neck, vertigo, headache, hypervigilance, and cognitive impairment—essentially the symptoms of whiplash. Fleeing to a strange town to escape ongoing abuse by her partner, and with a history of substantial prior life trauma, the patient was set up for being traumatized again by what was truly a trivial event. The key was not only the already-kindled state of her brain's alarm system, but also the trivial but meaningful cue of the sound of steel on steel that was embedded in her procedural memory due to prior MVAs.

Assaulted by the Past

Researchers and theoreticians often refer to victims of PTSD as living in the past, destined to experience trauma-related memories and physical sensations that constantly intrude on their daily lives. This intrusion may take the form of persistent thoughts, which are often stereotyped, repetitive, and usually of a negative nature, even if they don't directly relate to the traumatic event. Intrusive thoughts are the hallmark of many syndromes of emotional distress. Patients suffering from depression often find that negative thought intrusions are one of their most unpleasant and debilitating symptoms. These thoughts usually arise whenever the mind is left even slightly unoccupied, and the victims find themselves ruminating unwittingly over worries, just as a cow endlessly chews its cud.

Intrusive thoughts predictably interrupt the normal stream of thought and can produce significant periods of time when the brain can't properly process information through working memory. They compete with a person's attempts to concentrate on the routine activities of daily living and therefore interfere with basic attention span. As a result, they are implicated in the common impairment of memory seen in depression, PTSD, and panic or anxiety disorders. A person plagued by intrusive thoughts may find that they frequently go to a different room in the house to find something and then can't remember what they were looking for. When I interview patients with this common complaint, I usually find that, when they explore an episode of forgetfulness, they realize that they have experienced several unrelated thoughts that have intruded on their awareness while they were looking for something. These intrusive thoughts erased the memory for their original intent.

Clearly this type of event is common enough in everyday experience that it cannot be called a hallmark of emotional distress by itself. At times it may be attributable simply to an excessive volume of demands for one's attention, although this scenario in itself implies a degree of inordinate life stress. In the individual with significant past life trauma or current life conflict, however, it probably represents a continuing attempt to deal with the threat or stress of daily life by resurrecting old, emotionally related implicit memories for the purpose of dealing with a current stressful situation. People with this distressing symptom often say, "I can't keep my mind quiet!" or "My mind keeps running all the time!" Not surprisingly, tests of cognitive function in such people often reveal objective and measurable impairment of memory that may actually interfere with the performance of daily life activities.

As part of the symptom complex of PTSD, intrusive thoughts usually have an identifiable connection to the events of the trauma itself and often are a form of reexperiencing or reliving the trauma. Such thoughts frequently are more than semantic, word-based recall and may be closely linked to other sensory events of the trauma, such as images, sounds, or smells. They also may be linked to the alterations of the autonomic nervous system function that accompanied the trauma, and therefore may be associated with palpitations, chest tightness, dizziness, or nausea. Intrusive thoughts or memories of this nature may be so specific and intense that they accurately replicate all of the emotional and physical experiences of the trauma and may once again be associated with terror. Such events may be experienced as panic attacks or flashbacks, and they are often emotionally wrenching. Across this broad spectrum of somatic and cognitive reexperiencing, intrusive thoughts are indeed examples of perversion of the normal functions of memory.

Memory and Dreams

In the daily cycle of life, the sleep period is often most vulnerable to such intrusive thoughts. Dreams have been studied and discussed for many millennia. Some primitive societies believed dreams were emanations from supernatural beings and predicted future events. Aristotle believed that they were embedded in the psychic activity of the dreamer and therefore were based on processes of the mind. Sigmund Freud (1938) also placed great importance on dream content, maintaining that they had specific meaning with regard to the dreamer's prior life experiences, especially those of a conflicted nature. Freud felt that the meaning of dream content could be allegorical and wrote at length on the meaning of dreams.

In victims of trauma, early terrifying nightmares often replicate the visual, sensorimotor, emotional, and autonomic experiences of the traumatic event with exactitude and vivid clarity. The victim of a recent MVA might be awakened from a dream with vivid images and actual sensory experiences of the impending crash—the loud noise, the smell of burning rubber, the sensations of body movement, and the racing heartbeat associated with the event. Distorted images of the environment in which the trauma occurred may be experienced, often intermingled with equally distorted images of other old traumatic events. Soldiers suffering PTSD may experience similar graphic nightmares of images and sounds of battle. Such vivid nightmares may persist for long periods of time after the event, often with remarkably accurate sensorimotor representation.

Gradually, however, the very specific nature of the nightmare related to the recent traumatic experience will begin to fade, and content from new life events may be inserted into the nightmares. These new and more complex dream structures still tend to reflect the fact that the new dream material also is derived from experiences of conflict and threat that may be useful for future reference in the accumulation of survival-based "knowledge." In addition, old traumas, such as medical experiences, threats in childhood, or social traumas, are often randomly integrated with the new but fading traumatic dream material. These seemingly random and bizarre combinations of images account for people's viewing dream content as symbolic or allegorical rather than as an actual reexperiencing of a memory. It is clear, however, that one function of dreaming seems to be the integration of the threat-based content of one's daily life experience into survival-based procedural memory. By integrating this new learning material with old memories of trauma, the dreamer enhances his repertoire of survival-based skills stored in procedural memory for future use in the face of new threats.

On the other hand, the persistence of vivid nightmares from a specific trauma suggests that the trauma was not resolved and that the victim may have frozen or dissociated at the moment of the experience. Such persistence of a nightmare is usually accompanied by other symptoms of PTSD, including phobias related to events and objects associated with the trauma, waking intrusive thoughts and images of the traumatic event, periodic anxiety states, and exaggerated startle.

It is quite clear that dreams are an essential part of the life experience, and that artificial interference with the dream process will produce significant problems. An experimental model of dream deprivation involves observing the EEG pattern of a patient and awakening him whenever he enters REM (rapid eye movement) sleep, the period when dreams occur, roughly on the average of six times a night. If this interruption is done often enough, the dream-deprived victim eventually will begin to hallucinate—or dream—while clinically awake. When he is once again allowed to sleep without REM sleep being interrupted, the victim will experience numerous and at times continuous REM cycles until the "dream debt" has been paid, so to speak. Dreaming is an instinctual process clearly necessary for survival.

Frozen in the Past

One of the most unusual conceptual processes that accompanies learned, trauma-induced helplessness is the perception that the victim is stranded in time, like the Paleolithic fly suspended in amber. This state of suspension may be related to the victim's ongoing perception that the threat is still quite real, imminent, and dangerous. Being flooded with images, sensations, memories, and dreams related to the trauma certainly suggests the persistence of the immediacy of the threat itself. In the absence of the capacity to flee, defend, or initiate any reasonable behavior that would reestablish the aborted and frozen life path, trauma victims are no longer able to learn even rudimentary new adaptive behaviors. Their repertoire of survival skills remains confined to those skills that were acquired up to the time of the trauma, and they lack the resilience to learn new strategies, even through their instinctual and automatic accommodative reflexes. Basically, the late effects of trauma seem to lead to a state of increasing lack of resiliency in dealing with subsequent life trauma. Once they have frozen/dissociated in the face of threat and helplessness without experiencing the freeze discharge/completion, they will continue to dissociate in response to further threat and remain unable to assimilate adaptive survival skills in procedural memory.

Most of the skills that the trauma victim continues to apply to subsequent life threats or stress are directly related to the actual physical responses elicited by the old trauma. Until the trauma victim physically completes the successful resolution of the traumatic experience, he continues to demonstrate behavior that is stereotyped, repetitive, and counterproductive to ongoing daily life experiences. He responds to new events, relations, and challenges as if he were responding to the old threat. This behavioral response may involve old conditioned behaviors that are irrelevant to the new experience. The victim of a rape may scream and experience a full-blown panic attack when bumped in the back on a crowded bus. The child who has undergone ether anesthesia may panic and experience terror when a sibling holds his hand over the child's mouth to keep her quiet during a game of hide-and-seek. The victim of an MVA may jam his right foot into the floorboard of the car and experience panic if he is a passenger and the driver comes too close to the car in front. The victim's survival brain repeatedly goes back to old traumatic defensive patterns of motor behavior from a threat that was never resolved, behaviors that now are useless for protection from the current threat.

For example, a patient of mine who suffered soft-tissue injuries in an MVA was left with a persistent area of pain underneath her left shoulder blade. Upon examining her, I noted a slightly reddened area of skin in the region of her symptom. Lightly touching the area to detect underlying muscle spasm, I was surprised when she jumped and cried out. When I apologized for causing her discomfort, she reassured me that I had not hurt her. What had caused her to cry out was the sudden image of being hit with a switch in that specific region by the nuns who ran the residential elementary school that she attended as a child. It was the habit of the nuns to make nightly rounds for students who had misbehaved and to hit them with a switch while they took their baths. The deeply embedded procedural memory for this painful and repeated traumatic event was resurrected by the pain and trauma of the car accident, which not surprisingly involved her car being hit from behind, just as she was as a child. The persistent pain reflected the pain from the physical abuse that she had experienced as a child, and the spasm and bracing of the underlying muscles reflected the old defensive motor behavior to that abuse, now ineffectively applied to the new traumatic experience of the car accident.

The behavior of the trauma victim may appear strange even to the victim, and it is often the source of considerable emotional distress and embarrassment. As noted in the previous example, symptoms are often related to the meaning of long-past experiences, not to any current identifiable source. To others, the trauma victim may appear labile, overreactive at times, and inappropriate in social behavior. Because victims' conditioned responses to environmental cues have irradiated to a host of stimuli that only slightly reflect the original traumatic cues, victims may experience painful arousal manifested as anxiety or panic in apparently benign situations. There is nothing "inappropriate" or "psychological" about these responses, for they are precipitated by new pathways in brain centers that remain devoted to the endless task of escaping from the old, unresolved threat.

When these old defensive behaviors prove useless or counterproductive in response to new threats, the trauma victim may become perplexed and blame external factors for their failure. This blame often spreads to people who form part of the victim's social support system, further isolating the victim from the social support that is so critical to his stability and ultimate recovery. This process of social isolation further serves to enforce old patterns of defensive behavior and to perpetuate the victim's state of being persistently embedded in the past.

Social isolation often occurs in the later stages of a person's response to severe trauma. Part of this response, of course, is due to the inevitable exposure to ambient environmental stimuli that are associated with social intercourse. Stimuli that might be perceived as pleasurable and exciting, such as laughter, music, and conversation, may well be perceived as irritating, threatening, and exhausting to the victim of trauma. Many of my patients specifically use the term *overwhelmed* to describe their experience when exposed to public gatherings, viewing television programs or movies, or shopping in large stores. These feelings are associated with more specific symptoms of constriction and dulling of cognition and thinking, a feeling of confusion and fogginess, low-grade fear, and profound physical exhaustion. The symptoms suggest that such people enter into a state of freeze/dissociation with exposure to very nonspecific but nevertheless threatening stimuli.

Unfortunately, this process of social isolation deprives the victim of trauma from a basic necessity in the process of recovery. Social support systems have been found to be one of the most important factors in helping the trauma victim to heal. Judith Herman (1997) emphasized the crucial role of the healing relationship with the therapist, with groups of similar trauma survivors, and with family systems.

Adults who have experienced significant traumatic abuse as children often reflect to a disturbing degree many of the maturational features that were normal at the age that the trauma occurred. This is primarily true of adults who experienced interpersonal childhood trauma at a very early age. Not only may they respond excessively to minor life threats or stresses, but also they seem not to have acquired new adaptive social skills beyond the age that the trauma occurred. Their adaptive social behaviors at times appear to be childish, lacking the ability to adapt to changing social demands. They also seem to lack the capacity to change this behavior through teaching or encouragement, although with appropriate cognitive and somatic psychotherapy, they may become more appropriately adaptive to life's stresses as the trauma becomes a story from their past as opposed to an ongoing threat.

This state of suspension in time is predictably associated with a rather dramatic distortion of time perception. Because past experience remains of prime importance for survival, they remain frozen in that past event. Because many of the ambient cues of their daily existence turn them back to the old traumatic event and the behaviors that it demanded, they have only a dim sense of a future different from their immediate experience. Indeed, one of the symptoms of PTSD is a sense of a "foreshortened future" (American Psychiatric Association, 1994). It is almost as if victims cannot perceive of a future when they will not be continuously preoccupied by a battle with their past demons. Because they operate on the premise that a life threat is always lurking or present, many trauma victims strongly feel that they will die while they are still young. Not surprisingly, the rate of suicide is significant in this group of patients.

The Shattering of the Self

Another major area of perceptual impairment in trauma victims lies in their sense of self. The past continues to assault them—during the day in unstable cycles of physical, autonomic, and emotional symptoms, and at night in nightmares, pain, and intrusive fear-based thoughts. With the passage of time, their self-perception becomes focused on physical and emotional pain and the inability to control even the most simple of basic body functions. Many say that their life ended at the moment of the traumatic event and that since then they are a different, unrecognizable person. They no longer have a sense of who they are in the context of their past memories. Trauma indeed is a disorder of the perception of time, of the body, and of the self.

Antonio Damasio (1994) presented a theoretical model in which he postulated that the self was formed on the basis of conscious declarative memory for accumulated past experiences, or one's "autobiography," associated with the "primordial representation of an individual's body." I would define this somatic "primordial representation" as the accumulation of procedural memories for the host of sensorimotor messages and experiences over one's lifetime, ranked in order of influence and importance by their relative importance to the person's survival. Damasio also emphasized the fact that this somatic self-image changes constantly with the passage of time, so that the perception of one's self is ever-evolving and based on the somatic experiences of the moment. The "self," then, is shaped by these conscious memories of one's past, which also is dependent upon the body perceptions of the moment and which is changing constantly as one moves through a fleeting present into an immediate future.

Changing the Brain

Obviously, experiential trauma is not good for the brain. At this point it should be clear that I equate all emotional experiences and, for that matter, all psychiatric diagnoses and psychological symptoms with measurable changes in brain function and processes. Mental illness is a functional neurological problem. Abnormalities in emotional function are sometimes unique enough for the psychiatric profession to break them down into a rigorously defined group of diagnoses. If indeed we can split abnormal behavior into different mental disorders based on unique symptoms, one might conclude that each disorder would therefore show unique changes in the architecture, chemical composition, or dynamic function of the brain, as well as specifically produce changes in different brain regions.

The Role of Imaging Studies

The most effective means of studying measurable changes in brain structure and function today is by imaging, or developing pictures of the brain. The three most useful imaging techniques include positron emission tomography (PET), single photon emission computed tomography (SPECT), and functional magnetic resonance imaging (fMRI). Computerized tomography (CT) is an older and less specific technique that has been used less frequently recently, especially with the rapid improvements in fMRI technology. The concept of tomography, implicit in all of these techniques, is based on the differences in density and chemical composition of adjacent but different regions and organs of the body. By rotating the device that one uses as a measuring tool around the body part to be examined, a computer algorithm is able to reconstruct the raw image of the object being studied into a two-dimensional image (more recent advances allow a three-dimensional view). The head, as a sphere, is uniquely adaptable to this technique.

CT scans use X-rays as the means of measuring the relative density of various regions of the brain. MRI scans use a magnetic field combined with radio frequency waves to produce a more detailed image of the brain. With functional MRI, you can also measure the volume of selective areas of the brain, as well as dynamic functions, such as circulation in different regions. PET and SPECT scans use injectible radioactive isotopes to map blood flow or metabolism in different areas of the brain. The volume of blood flow and the intensity of metabolism in a brain region are related to the degree of activity in that region at the moment of measurement. These techniques therefore allow the examiner to identify specific brain areas that control specific tasks and functions, and they can therefore localize the parts of the brain that regulate such functions as speech, vision, problem solving, and emotions.

Weight and Bigler (1998) have reviewed the scientific literature regarding the use of brain imaging to further define specific psychiatric diagnoses. The diagnoses that were reviewed included anxiety disorder, PTSD, obsessive-compulsive disorder, attention deficit hyperactivity disorder, mood disorders, and schizophrenia. Despite isolated exciting findings that might distinguish these disorders based on regional brain function or dysfunction, there were many inconsistencies of findings within the same diagnoses. Sadly, as of 1998, the authors could only conclude that patients with the same diagnoses often showed conflicting imaging findings and that further studies were needed. The problem with this approach may be that categorizing a patient population based only on observations of behavior lacks sufficient specificity to be applied to an unbiased test such as imaging.

The psychiatrist usually does not have an X-ray or blood test to validate his clinical diagnosis, which is based on a comparison of a cluster of symptoms to the criteria of the DSM-IV. In addition, many forms of mental illness are characterized by wide variations in symptoms and behavior. Structural diseases, such as strokes, produce a fixed anatomical and functional change in the brain that one can measure objectively. Trauma, on the other hand, produces many clinical changes in behavior that at times are almost diametrically opposite to each other. Interpreting the meaning of changes in imaging in such cases must be based on the specific metabolic state that exists in the brain at the time of the imaging. This dilemma has long been a burden of the behavioral sciences.

Nevertheless, imaging techniques are improving rapidly, and despite the barriers noted previously, there is much to be learned from their use with regard to mental illness. These techniques may be especially applicable in the field of trauma because of the unique cluster of emotional, autonomic, and sensorimotor symptoms associated with trauma. Douglas Bremner (2002) provided a comprehensive review of the latest findings in brain imaging in trauma-related disorders in his book *Does Stress Damage the Brain?* He also made a plea for the application of the diagnostic term *trauma-related disorders* to the complex spectrum of symptoms seen in trauma victims, rather than solely to the standard diagnosis of PTSD. This plea is based on trauma researchers' placing increasing importance on the fact that the spectrum of symptoms and conditions related to trauma far exceeds the prescribed definitions of PTSD.

As previously noted, when we perform any type of task, physical or mental, the region of the brain that serves that particular function shows increased neuronal activity. This process results in an increase in utilization of glucose and oxygen within those brain regions. Increased blood flow allows for the provision of the glucose and oxygen required to meet the increased demands. When one talks, the speech area of the brain receives more blood; when one reads, the area for verbal comprehension lights up on the blood flow scan. We know that the right cerebral hemisphere is primarily responsible for processing the information related to a threat, and that the regions involved include the thalamus, amygdala, hippocampus, and orbitofrontal cortex, a part of the medial prefrontal cortex (see Figure 2.2). While a trauma victim is reading a script describing the event of the trauma, imaging studies of the brain show increased blood flow to the right cerebral hemisphere. During this high state of arousal, the area for speech and verbal expression receives less blood (Rauch et al., 1996). Once again, one doesn't need speech to fight or flee.

In a state of sustained arousal, however, blood flow scans in victims of old abuse show reduction of blood flow in the right hippocampus and the medial prefrontal cortex. These scans also show decreased blood flow in the anterior cingulate gyrus, a region that plays a role in maternal infant bonding and social behavior and an area that also may inhibit the amygdala. The medial prefrontal cortex also plays a role in modulating the arousal response by inhibiting the amygdala and therefore inhibiting the process of fear conditioning (see Figure 2.1). Bremner noted that inhibition of function of the medial prefrontal cortex and hippocampus at the time of a traumatic event could result in distortion and fragmentation of memory for the event itself and even complete amnesia.

Trauma Damages the Brain

For over a decade, researchers have found that the same conditions of stress that produced Selye's GAS, with its specific somatic disease processes, also caused damage to the hippocampus (which participates in processing declarative memory). Most of the somatic diseases produced by stress in Selye's studies with animals were found to be due to sustained levels of the hormone cortisol (Selye, 1956). Researchers exposed the brains of animals to high levels of cortisol and found that prolonged exposure produced damage to the hippocampus. Not only was the volume of the hippocampus decreased, but both the number of neurons and their synaptic connections also were decreased. Imaging studies in the brains of victims of various types of trauma, especially trauma experienced in childhood, have also consistently shown decreased hippocampal volume, presumably due to prolonged cortisol exposure as part of PTSD. Bremner deduced that loss of hippocampal volume in these individuals caused deficits in memory, and he therefore studied memory function by testing veterans with combat-related PTSD and victims of childhood physical or sexual abuse. Not surprisingly, both groups of trauma victims showed deficits in a variety of types of memory function, including declarative memory, short term memory, immediate and delayed recall, and percent retention of memory (Bremner, 2002).

Interestingly, not all people subjected to a traumatic event develop these memory deficits. Only those who go on to develop the PTSD/dissociation spectrum of symptoms appear to suffer hippocampal damage, with its associated memory deficits. As I have implied, I consider dissociation to be part of the freeze response, perhaps the subjective perceptual experience that accompanies the physiology of freezing. These perceptions generally involve a fragmentation of the perception of reality. Examples include the out-of-body experience, a slowing of time, a sense of intense familiarity or strangeness, and even amnesia for the event. Studies show that individuals who experience dissociation at the time of the trauma later have a much higher incidence of clinical PTSD. This finding would certainly be in keeping with the concept of an unresolved freeze response with associated fear conditioning being the basic substrate for traumatization. Traumatization, in turn, may result in sustained exposure to abnormal levels of cortisol, resulting in real physical damage to the brain in the form of loss of neurons and synapses in the hippocampus.

The experiencing of a traumatic event alone, however, is not sufficient to produce the anatomical and physiological changes in the brain just described. Damage to the hippocampus requires prolonged exposure to elevated levels of cortisol, and this only occurs if the trauma is ongoing or there is a continual reexposure to threat. This situation, of course, may occur in an abusive household, where the child victim is repeatedly threatened in a helpless state. It may also be replicated by any sudden threat to life in a state of helplessness, where the freeze/dissociation response will predictably occur and where lack of completion through freeze discharge perpetuates the events of the trauma in procedural memory. This process, with incorporation of cues in procedural memory, contributes to the development of kindling in selected brain regions.

Once the cycle of kindling is established, the patient will automatically cycle in and out of states of abnormal arousal, inevitably activating the HPA axis, with production of high levels of cortisol and resulting hippocampal damage. It must be noted that there is controversy regarding how, and even whether, cortisol is the primary agent in this process, and also how hippocampal atrophy can be explained by it. Nevertheless, the existing information presents a compelling case for the fact that traumatization leads to neuropathological changes in brain structure and neurophysiological changes in brain function. Bremner (2002) actually cautions clinicians about encouraging their trauma victims to use retraining and schooling to recover from their memory deficits. He warns that problems with new learning and memory will hinder their performance in a school setting that demands the functions of memory that they lack. This caution is tempered by the fact that the severity of memory problems often correlates with the levels of traumatic exposure that they have experienced.

The good news, however, is that the hippocampus is one of the most plastic and adaptable of brain regions. It is the one area where replication of new neurons has been demonstrated in humans. Many studies show that, even in old age, intensive verbal and memory training can improve cognitive function. Remarkably, temporary functional improvement in these areas with this type of therapy has been shown in Alzheimer's disease patients. You can teach an old dog new tricks. The concept of brain plasticity has ramifications not only for the progressive deterioration of function in complex trauma, but also for rehabilitation, recovery, and ultimately transformation. The therapeutic success stories among my patients contain many cases of victims of trauma with substantial cognitive deficits related to their PTSD who have improved significantly in functional cognitive performance with appropriate therapy.

CHAPTER 4

Genes, Experience, and Behavior

During the search for the complete human genome, many behavioral scientists attributed the majority of human behavior to our genetic heritage. In some ways, this was a comforting thought. It relieved us of considerable anxiety and guilt over aspects of our own and our offspring's negative behavior. We could always blame our parents, or their parents for that matter, for transferring the nasty little genes that made us act badly at times. Along with our wispy hair, big noses, and flat chests, we could attribute our moodiness, irritability, or laziness to a familial gift that governed our emotions and appearance. The propensity to blame our ill fortune on the devious activities of others or on events beyond our control is one of the less functional evolutionary attributes that the human species seems to have developed along with the neocortex.

As with everything in life, it's not that simple. We are not slaves to the dictates of our genetic heritage. It seems that genes, like all systems of the body, are flexible and changeable based on the influence of life experiences. Although they're not very flexible when it comes to hair and eye color, in many body systems, including the brain, they actually form a template—a temporarily fixed structure—on which layers of life experience establish the conditions for how our life evolves. Negative life experiences, especially in early childhood, may mold our brains and influence the expression of genetic traits, including those for personality and certain types of mental illness. They may also plant the seeds for a variety of illnesses to which we may be susceptible. I suppose we can now blame—or credit—our parents for the way they raised us as well as for the genes they gave us.

In fact, we can probably blame our early life experiences rather than our genes for much of our behavior and many of our choices that make up the fabric of our lives. One of our most odd and inexplicable behaviors is the tendency to make the same bad choices over and over, including in friendships, choice of mates, and job decisions. We often seem to need to recapitulate such choices and experiences until we finally get it right. When we are conditioned in childhood to respond to a negative experience through the only adaptive behavior available to us, we tend to respond repeatedly in the same way to future experiences that are similar. This process of repetition is so automatic and unconscious that it seems almost instinctual and genetic. And it often leads us to be attracted to mates and other people who possess the negative traits of our childhood caregivers. As I will explain, however, this very trait represents an unconscious, conditioned survival-based response common to us all.

Genes and Mental Illness

Other behavioral scientists in the past, particularly Freud, could be classified as empiricists or nurturists: They attributed all of human behavior to the sum of life experiences, which inexorably imprinted patterns of behavior on the brain. It was easy to blame the parents, especially the mother, for the quirks and oddities of human behavior. As a young medical student studying psychiatry, I was struck by the absolute certainty with which my professors of psychiatry blamed schizophrenia on mothers who manifested particularly ambivalent nurturing styles, referring to them as "schizophrenogenic mothers." The concept that a certain maternal nurturing style could predispose offspring to a very stereotyped psychosis in young adulthood is today viewed as ridiculous. The genetic propensity for the development of schizophrenia of course is now well documented, although, as I hope to establish, negative life experience also plays a role in the expression of that gene.

Nevertheless, scientific studies addressing the intergenerational transmission of psychiatric disorders are numerous and contradictory. For one thing, diagnoses applied to behavioral and mental disorders are based on certain common features of behavior, not on standard reproducible laboratory testing. The precise diagnosis of psychiatric disorders therefore frequently suffers from vagueness of definition. The various editions of the DSM reflect this dilemma in their constantly shifting criteria and categories for the subsets of mental illness. PTSD is actually one of the more specific psychiatric diagnoses based on criteria, and in general has lent itself fairly well to epidemiological study. Specific criteria that define the nature of things, however artificial, are a source of comfort to scientists and allow them to apply statistics to what otherwise might seem an amorphous mass of epidemiological points of data. This use of the scientific method as a means of acquiring knowledge has long been a problem for not only behavioral science, but also for medical science in general, as I have implied and will explore further.

The Holocaust has provided a unique laboratory for the study of PTSD, allowing many researchers to study the effects of a horrific societal trauma across several generations. Rachel Yehuda and colleagues (1998) published a number of studies linking PTSD in Holocaust survivors and their offspring. Not surprisingly, they documented that symptoms of PTSD in offspring seem to be related to the incidence and severity of symptoms in the parent/survivor, especially if the parent/survivor suffered from full-blown PTSD. There certainly could be a genetic trait that predisposes a person to susceptibility to traumatization, and those people therefore would be more likely to develop PTSD. Because not all Holocaust survivors developed PTSD, the fact that those who did tended to bear children who later also developed PTSD could suggest a genetic vulnerability in the offspring. This study, however, suggests that the type of *symptoms* experienced by the survivor/parent—not the simple diagnosis of PTSD—seemed to be the primary predictor of PTSD in their offspring. In other words, the specific behavioral dysfunction of the parent/survivor (to which their offspring were exposed) seemed to be the critical factor. This finding suggests that transmission of symptoms of PTSD across generations might more likely be due to the adverse experience of the child rather than to genetic heritage.

This concept would be in keeping with the influence of maternal behavior and bonding on the ability of the developing infant to achieve optimal states of self-regulation in the face of arousal in later life. The maternal trauma victim, experiencing varying states of arousal and dissociation, may well have lost the instinctual ability to achieve the facial attunement and bonding that is necessary for modulating her infant's subsequent state of arousal. Victims of trauma suffer from disordered mood regulation as well as dissociation. The resulting disruption of the basic stability of family life may lead to low-grade fear and vigilance in children who never know when the next emotional shoe will drop. This type of latent, almost invisible social trauma may contribute to states of vulnerability to subsequent life trauma as the child matures and may explain what appear to be exaggerated emotional responses to negative events later in life. Children raised in dysfunctional households tend to retain the low-grade state of vigilance they experienced as a child throughout their life, and this state affects the intensity of their arousal response to all of the nuances of life experience.

The same thing may pertain to children raised in families with an alcoholic parent. Many patients have confirmed my impression that, even though physical abuse never occurred, the volatile and unpredictable behavior of the alcoholic parent was sufficient to create an environment of fear and apprehension in other members of the household. Retreating to the bedroom when daddy came home from a trip to the bar after work, or when mommy had one too many martinis before supper, represents a low-grade replication of the freeze response and dissociation in the helpless child. That child learns through a thousand tiny wounds to view the world with suspicion and fear, and he or she will carry a heritage of diminished resiliency to subsequent life traumas. Alcoholism is now known to carry a genetic propensity. If that child turns to alcohol to keep a lid on underlying anxiety, as many do, the child's alcoholism may then be attributed to genetic factors. It is likely, however, that the persistent state of threat involved in being reared in an alcoholic household contributed significantly to the activation of that genetic trait.

In Chapter 5, I explore the effect of even subtle nuances of behavior of mother rats on their newborn pups. Even slightly negative alterations in maternal behavior during the early period of infancy, including brief separation, change the state of autonomic arousal of the rat pup for life. The brain of the child is malleable and therefore vulnerable to both positive and negative life experiences, and the child's subsequent behavior, adaptability, and resiliency to stress across the life span may be determined by those experiences. Deficiencies in function and resiliency of the parent are also likely to be passed on to subsequent generations through the effect of such deficiencies on childrearing capabilities, genetic factors being otherwise equal (as, of course, they never are).

This concept challenges the hypothesis regarding the relative importance of the genetic mode of transmission of psychiatric states, and it suggests that the effect of the childrearing behavior of the dysfunctional parent is of equal or even primary importance. At a book signing I was approached by a young man who asked me if I thought that bipolar disorder might actually be due to childhood trauma. Bipolar disorder, previously called manic-depressive disorder, is believed to be due to a genetic trait. First-degree relatives of bipolar patients have an incidence of bipolar disorder of 4–24% (American

Psychiatric Association, 1994). I told the young man that bipolar disorder probably had a genetic basis, but that being raised by a bipolar parent could well be quite traumatic. The young man replied, "I'm bipolar and so was my mother. I should know, it was hell!"

As is usually the case, the truth is probably somewhere in the middle. Many psychotherapists have told me that in their clinical experience, bipolar disorder seems to have a remarkable relationship to life trauma in their patients, especially those with a history of childhood trauma. Genetic tendencies for diseases such as diabetes are known to be activated by stressful life experiences, and this also is probably the case for genetically based psychiatric disorders. It is likely that, in the absence of a dysfunctional childhood experience, the "genetically based" psychiatric disorder will never be elicited. Charles Whitfield (2003) has reviewed the available scientific literature for a genetic basis for both bipolar disorder and depression. He noted that an early study suggested a 10–20% linkage of bipolar disorder to the X (female) chromosome. This finding was not replicated, however, and further studies have been basically inconclusive, suggesting that the evidence for a genetic base for bipolar disorder at best may be limited. Studies for a genetic basis for depression have been uniformly inconclusive, most of them being based on limited family histories. Whitfield also noted that trauma in general is known to be intergenerational, reflecting the concept that the behavior of the traumatized and depressed parent is likely to traumatize the child in turn. He made a strong argument for the experiential basis for depression based specifically on a history of child abuse, a concept that is clearly supported by a remarkable body of world scientific literature.

Changing the Brain: Lessons from Brain Injury

The way that the brain operates based on the way that genes and experience alter it is much more complex than what I have thus far presented. First, we must accept the fact that mental illness, psychiatric disorders, behavioral abnormalities, or whatever you want to call them are basically selective alterations of "normal" function in specific regions of the brain. Schizophrenia, bipolar disorder, and PTSD are all associated with disordered function in specific brain regions and neurotransmitter systems, as are all of the many diagnostic categories of the DSM-IV. Because the specificity of function of brain regions is common from person to person, damage or impaired function of each region carries with it a predictable syndrome of neurological and behavioral symptoms and signs. Damage to the left side of the brain just above the temporal lobe will produce a disturbance of speech called *aphasia* in all victims (except for a few left-handed individuals). Aphasia is characterized by the inability to produce words or to understand them, or both. Damage to the posterior upper right frontal lobe will uniformly produce a left-sided paralysis, worse in the leg. These arrangements of neurons and axons that control specific functions of the body are determined by genes. In fact, similar brain patterns and functions in many cases exist genetically from the brains of reptiles to primates.

Genes therefore ensure that different parts of the brain have been designed in advance to perform specific functions. The parts of the brain that regulate emotion are also located in specific regions, and their functions are also genetically based. Impaired function due to injury to these regions may cause symptoms that we interpret as mental illness. Injury to the frontal lobes may produce a so-called frontal lobe syndrome. One of the most detailed examples of this strange and decidedly abnormal alteration of mood, affect, and behavior is that of the case of Phinneas Gage. A 25-year-old railway worker in 1848, Gage had the unique misfortune of having an iron rod, propelled by explosives, pierce his left cheek from below, traverse through the front base of his skull, and exit through the top. Accompanying the exiting rod was a substantial portion of Gage's brain, specifically the right frontal lobe. Somehow Gage survived this catastrophic accident, which led to an unusual and dramatic alteration of his behavior for the rest of his life and provided a living workshop for a study of the frontal lobes of the brain. This long and detailed study was performed by the local physician, Dr. John Harlow, who embarked on what amounted to a new career in his careful analysis of Gage. Over the subsequent century, many medical writers have referred to Dr. Harlow's findings in these studies of Gage, one of the more comprehensive and interesting being that provided by neurologist Antonio Damasio (1994). Harlow noted that, before the accident, Gage's personality was characterized by temperate habits, shrewdness, persistence, and focused energy in his work. As he recovered, friends and colleagues were shocked by what appeared to be a complete reversal of many of his positive character traits. His behavior was now characterized by impatience, irritability, and impulsivity. His speech was often profane and frequently inappropriate in content, and he had lost all social graces. He was both obstinate and capricious and was unable to attend to a task for any length of time. In short, he had experienced a complete change of personality, all of it for the worse. All of his skills and motor function, however, remained normal.

The importance of this bizarre set of behavioral changes is that it reflects a loss of the power of reasoning due to a brain injury, particularly "the ability to anticipate the future and plan accordingly within a complex social environment; the sense of responsibility toward the self and others; and the ability to orchestrate one's survival deliberately, at the command of one's free will" (Damasio, 1994, p. 10). The loss of this precious trait, believed to be unique to the human species, resulted in a complete and permanent alteration in personality to the extent that Gage's behavior, by all of the available psychological definitions, would have to be described as mental illness. For all intents and purposes, Gage, along with the rest of his human cohorts, possessed a genetically determined, hardwired set of neurons and axons in his brain that provided a standard behavioral pattern that we interpret as acceptable human social behavior. In other words, not only are the sensory and motor portions of our brain genetically determined, but the brain areas that govern appropriate adult social behavior also have a common genetic basis. In Gage's case, other properties of the mind, including perception, attention, memory, language, and intelligence, were remarkably intact, testifying to the specificity of function of the frontal lobes. Gage's case is a compelling example of the genetic basis for certain basic, archaic aspects of human personality structure.

The Shaping of Personality and Psychopathology

Don't get carried away with the idea that mental illness and personality disorders are inevitably instinctual, genetic, and predetermined. It must be evident by now that I am particularly taken by the concept of later emotional problems being shaped by the quality of early maternal/infant bonding, an event definitely on the nurture side of the nature/nurture continuum, and one that I explore in detail in Chapter 5. But negative life events that evoke traumatic stress aren't the only experiences that may cause structural alteration of the brain. If we accept this model of experience-based alterations of brain structure, we ultimately must accept the fact that all learning shapes the brain chemicals and neuronal connections of regions of the brain that were used in that process. Learning takes place through the laying down of new synapses and, in the hippocampus at least, the formation of new neurons. This process begins during the earliest phases of brain development. As I have said, brain development actually begins during the development of the fetus in the uterus; procedural learning through conditioned responses during this period has been well documented. Given these facts, we again must address the effect of the earliest of life experiences on the development of what we generally consider to be the inherited qualities of personality and character.

The nature versus nurture, genes versus experience debate continues to rage in the field of psychology. The science of genetics has literally exploded as the ability to identify minute subsets of the human genome has rapidly grown. The use of medical genetics has had its most publicized application in the ability to identify the unique genetic pattern of the individual through analysis of the most minute sample of tissue for forensic purposes, including hair, nails, skin cells, and microscopic amounts of blood. Predictably, this new science has been embraced by the entertainment media to the extent that DNA analysis as a means of identification of criminals is referred to many times on any given night on popular television shows.

We have long recognized the obvious inheritability of specific behavioral traits that define what we call personality or temperament. Studies of twins and triplets separated at birth often reveal remarkable consistency of basic preferences, intellect, academic progress and achievement, and habit patterns later in life. Very basic patterns of temperament, such as shyness or gregariousness and passivity or aggressiveness, tend to persist to a significant degree regardless of the twins' life experiences and clearly appear to be primarily genetic in origin.

Jim Grigsby and David Stevens (2000) presented a compelling case for the predominant role of life experience in shaping this genetic template. Given the examples of genetic traits previously noted, they emphasized the quality of the fit between the temperamental traits of the infant and the environment in which that infant is raised as a predominant factor in how the personality of the infant develops. They also emphasized the role of the caretaker/parent in that early environment. Within this model, the temperamental style of the parent plays a significant role in shaping the inherited traits in the infant. The authors used the obvious and common example of the fussy baby raised by the relaxed versus the anxious mother. The relaxed mother is more likely to remain calm in the face of stimulation of her own anxiety by the agitated infant. Because her general mood state is one of relaxed tolerance, she is able to remain flexible and try a variety of calming strategies with her infant without immediately entering her own state of arousal. The anxious infant therefore experiences consistent reassurance and ultimate modulation of this basic temperamental trait, which lessens the negative effect of its own anxiety on its further development. The anxious mother faced with an agitated infant, however, experiences an increase in her own baseline levels of arousal and is unable to exercise more adaptive levels of problem solving. This response in turn may aggravate and consolidate the infant's own anxious temperament. In these ways, the basic temperament of the caregiver may significantly contribute to or mitigate character traits of the infant.

The mother/caregiver may contribute to the development of personality in many other ways, creating a layered and relatively permanent structure upon the genetic template of inherited patterns of temperament. Dysfunctional patterns of the behavior of the caregiving mother are often based to a great extent on her own mother/caregiver's patterns of nurturing. This acquired dysfunctional behavior then tends to promote patterns of arousal-based personality features in her developing infant. These personality traits of vigilance and high baseline levels of arousal may progress to relatively dysfunctional traits in the older child and adult, ensuring the generational, but not necessarily genetic, passage of personality traits. Grigsby and Stevens (2000) emphasized the fact that the fit between the developing child and the environment is never perfect. This may not necessarily be a negative factor, because a less-than-perfect fit between developing child and caregiver/environment may enhance the child's underlying adaptive capacities. On the other hand, the relative fit of such a relationship, if truly negative, may actually lead to dysfunctional brain development sufficient to contribute to the development of psychopathology in the adult.

As noted, the most important factor in determining the development of adaptive and functional personality traits is undoubtedly the relationship between mother and infant, and we must consider the maternal/infant bond as a major player in this process of personality development.

How Experience Changes Genes

In his book *Nature via Nurture*, Matt Ridley (2003) explored the complex nature of the gene versus experience debate from personality structure to concepts of free will. Ridley noted a rather obscure scientific finding that a specific gene may predispose its owners to personality traits of depression, self-consciousness, anxiety, and vulnerability—traits that fall under the psychological definition of neuroticism. The degree that these traits find expression in the life of their owner, however, is specifically determined by the *life experiences of that individual*. The genes, in other words, are "switched on" by nurture. The absence of trauma even in the face of the neuroticism genetic template may minimize its expression. In the face of trauma, however, the individual with this genetic pattern may be much more likely to develop the personality traits that we associate with neuroticism, some of which correlate with the late symptoms of trauma.

Ridley provided a vast array of examples of the intimate interaction of genes and experience affecting much of animal and human behavior. In the realm of maternal/infant bonding, he cited the concept of the *window of opportunity* for genetic expression to manifest itself. This concept of a critical time for expression of an instinct to occur has been illustrated in the studies of neonatal separation of the newborn from the mother and its effects on bonding and attachment, which I discuss further in Chapter 5. This has profound implications for the removal of the newborn from the mother, even for a brief time, after birth.

The well-known studies by Konrad Lorenz (as cited in Ridley, 2003) involved the imprinting of goslings on a human being who was thereafter treated as the maternal figure by the goslings. This process required exposure of the goslings to a moving object (the experience) within an exquisitely specific timeframe of 15 hours to 3 days after birth (the genetically determined template). In the absence of the exposure during the specific time, the imprinting gene was not activated, and the gosling would never imprint on a maternal figure. As in the case of neuroticism, the goslings' gene determined their behavior but had to be "switched on" by a specific experience. Furthermore, the "switching on" had to be accomplished within a very narrow timeframe.

Scientists have also investigated the expression of genes through studies of the personality, behavior, temperament, and preferences of identical twins raised in different environments. One might think that this type of investigation would be the "purest" measure of the impact of genes versus experience, but such studies have long been a source of controversy and differing deductions, and for years the field of twin studies was in disrepute because of the theories of eugenics that were applied in a number of the great dictatorships of the 20th century, particularly in Nazi Germany. In the last 25 years, however, the study of identical twins raised apart has led to new insights into the respective roles of nature and nurture in personality. Ridley (2003) reviewed the salient literature on this subject, including the study of thousands of identical and fraternal twins. He noted that in Western cultures, identical twins raised apart were much more similar than fraternal twins raised apart. Twins raised together were obviously the most similar. Based on these studies, Ridley estimated that in a twin who is raised *with* his or her twin, about 40% of the personality traits are genetic, less than 10% are due to shared environmental experiences, and 25% are due to unique environmental experiences and measurement errors.

Ridley (2003) then presented the dilemma inherent in these twin studies: They were performed on twins raised in similar contexts, in similar cultures and societies. By exposing the separated twins to relatively constant environments and cultures, their genes were able to reach full expression, guaranteeing similar personality outcomes. The intrinsic personalities of cultures and societies surely must affect gene expression. No one has yet addressed identical twin studies where one child was raised in, for example, an American middle class family and the other in a Romanian orphanage. As Ridley (2003, p. 229) states: "Genes are cogs in the machine, not gods in the sky. Switched on and off throughout life, by external as well as internal events, their job is to absorb information from the environment at least as often as to transmit it from the past. Genes do more than carry information; they respond to experience."

Even so, can we conclude from these findings that some individuals, by virtue of their genetic inheritance, are intrinsically and instinctually likely to be more resilient to a traumatic experience than others? Is there more to resiliency to trauma and adverse life events than a well-developed right orbitofrontal cortex and a well-regulated limbic and autonomic nervous system? One would have to conclude that, all experiences being equal, individuals with an optimal genetic heritage for personality structure might indeed be less vulnerable to the neurophysiological insults that accompany the traumatic experience. Perhaps this explains one small part of the reason why some people do not respond to traumatic events with the development behaviors compatible with the posttraumatic syndromes. On the other hand, I think that we can safely assume that all experiences are *not* equal, and we would be presumptuous to deny the dual, interactive role of nature and nurture in all things behavioral.

Redemption Through Repetition

Genetic influences on personality structure and behavior would appear likely to produce a more predictable series of traits than the nuances of early life experiences, which might be subtle and difficult to detect. Irritability of the adult rat might be difficult to attribute to separation from his mother for an hour at birth if this experience was not documented. I have implied that genes produce fairly fixed and identifiable personality traits (e.g., neuroticism), whereas experience tends to promote more diffuse, global, and unpredictable abnormalities of adult behavior in stress modulation and emotional regulation. As the infant brain matures, however, the specific features of negative life events tend to be stored in procedural memory and begin to lead to more specific and less global behavior and perceptions. The genetic template for behavior will continue to be altered or "switched on" by experiences, both negative and positive, but the behavioral expression of these experiences may become more specific based on their sensorimotor components. The sensorimotor experiences of negative life events are stored as cues, most of them unconscious, that continue to shape our personalities and behavioral responses to further experience. Because this learning process tends to constrict our behavioral options, we begin to repeat certain patterns of behavior in response to new little traumas.

With the passage of time, the trauma victim may compartmentalize not only these cues but also the conscious, declarative memory of the trauma into secret little hiding places of pain, divorced from the realities and experiences of daily life. Dissociation and denial allow one to exist from day to day relatively free from the agonizing conscious perception of the repressed event. Nevertheless, these deeply buried messages remain ready to emerge in the face of environmental cues that reflect in any way the unconscious memories of the event or reflect any new traumatic event. These memories may shape our personality, our personal habits, our body postures, our sensory perceptions, and our mental health. They often determine our choice of life work, the person we choose as a mate, our recreational pursuits, and our recreational drugs of choice. Amazingly, we may also unwittingly choose activities and patterns of behavior that allow us to reenact and relive those trauma-related experiences and messages.

Why would trauma victims choose, even unconsciously, to reexperience terror and pain? What survival instinct would drive them to face the demons again and again? The occurrence of compulsive traumatic reenactment is so common and well recognized that it has been described extensively in the psychiatric literature throughout the past century. Freud (1954) attributed this compulsion to repeat the trauma to an attempt to achieve mastery over the event, a concept certainly in keeping with the important role of a state of helplessness in trauma. He ultimately admitted, however, that this type of behavior served no useful purpose in freeing the victim from the bonds of traumatic memory in the long run. Janet (1920) linked the common behavior of traumatic reenactment to his concept of "fixed ideas," a constriction of adaptive behavior that prevented the victim from pursuing more novel means of escaping from the state of helplessness.

The Role of Endorphins

Bessel van der Kolk (1989) provided a compelling rationale for the role of endorphins in perpetuating traumatic reenactment. As noted earlier, an acute state of high arousal associated with a threat results in the release of brain endorphins as a means of blunting the need for the animal to minister to painful injuries resulting from the trauma. Animals shocked and conditioned with learned helplessness will always return to the original scene of the shock rather than pursue effective escape behavior. Victims of spousal abuse will often "choose" to remain with the abusing spouse rather than seek safety in a shelter. Children who are victims of abuse by a parent will invariably choose to remain with the parent rather than accept foster placement. In all of these examples, the potential "reward" associated with the threat/arousal/endorphin cycle is activated, producing what van der Kolk referred to as an "addiction to trauma" (van der Kolk, 1989, p. 399). He specifically related this state of attraction to the perpetrator to the process of infantile bonding and attachment, an event that also is believed to be largely based on endorphinergic reward systems in the brain. The tendency to seek the reenactment of a traumatic experience is also specifically more likely to occur if the trauma was in early childhood, perhaps because of the important role of endorphins in attachment at this stage of life.

Reenactment of trauma may also occur in less obvious life behaviors. Self-abuse, including ritualized cutting of the body, is another manifestation of this type of behavior. Periodic compulsive cutting of areas of one's body with a sharp instrument is usually seen in victims of severe childhood trauma. Such self-abuse is quite typical in both male and female victims of childhood physical and sexual abuse, and it is extremely common among male prison inmates, many of whom specifically experienced such abuse as children. Cutting usually occurs in cycles. The traumatized person will experience an increasingly intense compulsion to cut himself, usually in the face of mounting anxiety and distress. The act of cutting is accompanied by an intense feeling of relief, at times associated with a definite pleasurable response, after which the anxiety and the compulsion to cut is temporarily relieved. Inevitably the cycle will recur, often enhanced by ambient life stressors that may accelerate the need to cut once again. The act of cutting is almost always described as painless, and the relief from anxiety is profound, strongly suggesting that the release of endorphins plays an important role in perpetuating this behavior, and placing it specifically in the area of traumatic reenactment. This also is an example of the fact that endorphins reduce not only pain but also anxiety.

Self-abuse as an act of trauma reenactment may vary widely based on cultural trends. Self-starvation in the form of anorexia nervosa has long been recognized as a late posttraumatic behavior, almost always in young women. Janet (1920) regarded this type of behavior as one of the major symptoms of hysteria and recognized its association in these women with childhood sexual abuse. It is likely that endorphins also play a role in anorexia/bulimia, which has many of the characteristic of self-cutting, with periods of mounting anxiety leading to an episode of binge eating and bulimia that then provides a period of endorphin-induced calming. Extravagant tattooing of the body and multiple body piercings are part of another cultural trend that I strongly suspect is a means of self-expression that is also rooted in behavioral reward systems similar to those in other forms of self-abuse. At their extreme, these cosmetic choices appear to be favored by young people who either are relatively alienated from their societal peers or have chosen to express their individuality by these means. Being tattooed or pierced involves considerable pain, and patients of mine who have indulged these habits have admitted that they think their own trauma may have contributed to their adopting them.

The Thrill of the Race, the Thrill of the Risk

The pursuit of extreme endurance sports and other sport activities associated with high risk represent another cultural trend that I believe often has its roots in traumatic reenactment and the "addiction" to endorphins. The intense somatic pain experienced by athletes in endurance sports activities has been frequently addressed in popular sports books and magazines, as well as on television. Foot races for distances of 50–100 miles test not only pure athletic prowess but also one's tolerance for extreme pain. The extreme pain and deprivation experienced in multiple-day bicycle races of several thousand kilometers certainly represent demands for unique levels of physical fitness but also rely on extreme pain tolerance. Individuals with a past history of early childhood trauma may find relief from trauma-based anxiety through the endorphinergic rewards of athleticism, mimicking the endorphinergic rewards of their dissociating in the face of stress. The recreational runner compelled to experience her "fix" by daily running, and who experiences jitteriness and anxiety without it, may well be treating the hypervigilance from her childhood traumatic experiences with the endorphin release from her compulsive running.

Participants in these types of high-level endurance activities often practice dietary habits designed for weight maintenance that border on anorexia. Problems with the anorexia in young participants in gymnastics and long-distance running have been addressed in the popular and sports medicine literature. It also is entirely possible that the brain of the childhood trauma victim, patterned to the process of endorphin release in the face of pain, makes the individual particularly adept at tolerating the pain required for such endurance activities and therefore sets the individual up to excel in performance. This, of course, is not to say that trauma and endurance athletic achievement are inevitable companions. An innate characteristic of the human species appears to be the insatiable quest for the new, the unknown, and the unique achievement. This universal trait of pushing the boundaries of achievement clearly also contributes to pursuit of achievement in athletics. Nevertheless, the incidence of childhood trauma in endurance athletics anecdotally appears to be extremely high.

This type of athletic behavior may also be an adaptive therapeutic outlet for the trauma victim who, without these culturally approved and trauma-mitigating activities at their disposal, might descend into the helplessness, dissociation, and immobility of the 19th century hysteric. Strict dieting and attaining high levels of fitness clearly represent means of achieving control over one's body and gaining power in a society that values such accomplishments. Banishing helplessness is a core goal in overcoming trauma. In a culture that increasingly traumatizes its population through institutionally sanctioned practices, the use of athleticism as an outlet for the altered brain and body certainly cannot be judged critically.

Another cultural behavior that is probably closely linked to childhood trauma but is clearly less adaptive than endurance athleticism is that of extreme high-risk sports such as skydiving, free rock climbing, extreme skiing, and extreme mountain biking, to name a few. Clearly not all individuals who engage in extreme endurance and high-risk sports do so because of childhood trauma. Having treated many victims of injuries suffered in such sports in my rehabilitation center, however, I can attest to the fact that childhood trauma and extreme sports are a common association. For example, one of my patients fell over 50 feet down a rock face while free climbing alone without ropes. He fractured his pelvis and suffered scrapes and cuts but amazingly incurred no serious injuries. He had previously suffered serious injuries in two other similar falls. Although he was unable to walk without crutches, within 2 weeks he had jerry-rigged a slinglike apparatus for one leg to allow him to resume his climbing, again unassisted. His childhood history included significant and injurious physical abuse by his father. His case is typical for a number of other patients injured in extreme rock climbing and hang gliding who also acknowledged childhood physical abuse. Most of them returned to their sport after their recovery despite having experience life-threatening injuries.

Although often referred to as "adrenaline junkies," individuals participating in such high-risk pursuits probably achieve their rewards through the endorphin release associated with intensely dangerous, often life-threatening activities. Perhaps this behavior is patterned after the similar dangers they faced in a physically abusive childhood. Compulsive recapitulation of the physical threats to life experienced at that time may well manifest in such adult risk-taking behavior. Peter Weir's movie *Fearless*, starring actor Jeff Bridges, uncannily recreates the exaggerated risk-taking behavior of one of the survivors of a plane crash. The demeanor of Bridges during these periodic dangerous activities leaves no doubt that they occurred in a state of deep dissociation, undoubtedly facilitated by endorphin release.

Although risk-taking behavior can hardly be considered adaptive, endurance sports and compulsive nonanorexic/bulimic weight control may be far more favorable to the health of society than the other dietary behavior that also may be linked to trauma: excessive food intake and morbid obesity. Feeding at the mother's breast is another prime example of an endorphinergic reward system, with its intrinsic rewards of bonding and attachment, as well as nutrition. Separation of the child from the mother at birth permanently alters the maternal/infant bond and has no doubt contributed to the decline in breast-feeding in our culture. Infant feeding and maternal attachment are therefore intrinsically linked, and they are rewarded by endorphin release.

Societal impairment of bonding due to early maternal/infant separation logically leads to maladaptive feeding behaviors in adults as a means of compensating for the maternal attachment they never adequately experienced. The fast-food athlete thereafter must unconsciously rely on food intake to achieve endorphinergic rewards that were denied as an infant through the feeding/attachment cycle. This has become a major health crisis. Obesity in developed countries is a critical and burgeoning health problem. Type II diabetes, seen primarily in adults, especially those who suffer from obesity, is now commonly seen in young children, the population where obesity is expanding the most rapidly.

It is probably unlikely that the fast food industry actually recognizes the fact that overeating in children may represent an unconscious attempt to substitute food intake for deficits in early nurturing or, for that matter, for deficits in the emotional health of the current family household. It is not at all unlikely, however, that fast food marketing directors are fully aware of the fact that advertising "super deals" that include gargantuan quantities of food for only a little more money is a terrific means of attracting feeders to the trough. One doesn't need to be a behavioral researcher to recognize a dramatic societal trend and capitalize on it though advertising.

In fact, advertising has become increasingly effective through its use of subliminal messages. Have you noticed how advertisements on television generally involve the presentation of sounds and images that each last half a second or less? In the area of food, each brief but intense composite image is far too short to be consciously processed and remembered but is filled with provocative and pleasurable images that usually contain alcohol, food, or sexual innuendos. The sexual images generally involve subtle partial nudity, the alcohol images portray laughter and "fun," and the food images feature huge portions of colorful dishes dripping in sauces that elicit almost lustful expressions of pleasure from the handsome people doing the consuming. The limbic systems in the brains of the poor victims of this sensual assault, the television viewers, don't really have a chance. Beset and besotted by images that bypass the rational brain and arouse those unconscious centers related to survival, sex, and nutrition, the victim, whose brain perceives the world as a place of emotional deprivation, is ill-equipped to defend himself against this subliminal message of nutritional plenty. Whether by chance or by design, the fast food industry has fallen upon a societal expression of traumatic reenactment as a means of powerful, effective, and very dangerous marketing.

Traumatic Reenactment and Classical Conditioning

The specific neurophysiology, as well as the behavioral basis, for traumatic reenactment is, of course, unknown. Theories of endorphinergic reward systems and trauma addiction, although compelling, are only theories. Classical conditioning clearly plays an important role in the behavioral physiology of trauma. Of course, classical conditioning is useful for survival: It is rapid, unconscious, and, with reinforcement, permanent. It also is quite adaptive in that without reinforcement, it tends to decay until it "disappears," relegated to the dustbin of obsolete survival tools.

When classical conditioning is associated with trauma, however, the freeze response and the absence of its discharge stores the association of the unconditioned stimulus and the conditioned response in survival-based, procedural memory. It also does so permanently, and the conditioned response tends to be spontaneously resurrected because of the development of the self-sustaining kindling response. Decay in the sensitivity to the conditioned stimulus (the sensory reminders of the traumatic event) does eventually occur in traumatic fear conditioning without reinforcement: If one sees enough red cars after being hit by one without experiencing another accident, the cue "red car" will gradually lose its potency. The conditioned response, however, is still relatively resistant to decay and is very prone to irradiation (spread of the conditioned response to related but not specific unconditioned stimuli). For example, the myofascial neck pain from whiplash may eventually begin to be triggered by unrelated ambient life stress without any specific cues reminiscent of the accident.

If the trauma victim's resilience to threat is reduced by childhood trauma, the conditioned response may irradiate to even distantly related stimuli or cues. This may then lead to the development of heightened sensitivity to even minimally related environmental stimuli. Physical features of the perpetrator (baldness, facial hair, tone of voice) may provoke low-grade arousal when the victim encounters random people with some of these features. The smell of volatile substances, including paint thinner or perfume, may cause anxiety or physical symptoms (nausea, shortness of breath, choking) in the person who experienced ether anesthesia several times as a child. The victim of oral rape may experience panic in the dentist's chair.

In this scenario, each new perceived threat is linked to the old, kindled conditioned response and its vast repertoire of unconditioned stimuli acquired through irradiation. Previously benign events increasingly will tend to trigger arousal. As new environmental unconditioned stimuli join the stimuli conditioned to contain the message of threat, the traumatized individual may become sensitized to a host of otherwise benign environmental cues and may experience multiple environmental allergies, chemical sensitivities, and obscure illnesses such as "sick building syndrome." Under these circumstances, traumatized people become unable to differentiate benign novel experiences from those that are actually threatening. As a result, they are prevented from continuing to develop new learned survival skills to new threats.

In the absence of any effective means of learning new, more effective conditioned responses to new threats, such individuals will "return to the scene of the crime," the old traumatic event, in order to access its conditioned response. Unfortunately, the ultimate reaction is to reexperience the freeze response, or to dissociate. Traumatic reenactment, therefore, may be viewed as an arrest of new adaptive survival learning through classical conditioning. The trauma victim is frozen in time, and the only available learned response to internal or external cues of danger is to recapitulate the failed response to the sentinel traumatic experience. Because that response by its very nature was a failure (otherwise fight or flight would have been successful), traumatic reenactment is always a failed, dysfunctional act.

PART II
The Trauma Spectrum

In the field of behavioral science, the definition of a traumatic life event has evolved dramatically over the last century. Initially, emotional disturbances following a traumatic event were acknowledged only in those exposed to warfare. After the Vietnam War era, social trauma, including rape, was added to the list, and by 1994 the DSM-IV recognized a list of largely catastrophic life events that might cause trauma, although it acknowledged that potential sources of trauma need not be limited to these events (American Psychiatric Association, 1994).

The DSM-IV, however, does not address the subtle end of the bell curve of life trauma, an area of experiences that might be called "negative life events." I propose a much broader spectrum of trauma that ranges from catastrophic events such as war and other extreme forms of violence to "little traumas" such as childhood neglect, motor vehicle accidents, and exposure to violence via the media and popular entertainment. I also include in this spectrum forms of societal trauma that are unrecognized despite their often devastating effects. One controversial but critical example of this is preverbal trauma, which includes, among other things, in utero exposure of the fetus to the stress hormone cortisol from the distressed mother, in utero fetal surgery, medicalized, technologically advanced, and intrinsically traumatic birthing procedures, and exposure of premies in neonatal ICUs to isolation and inadequate pain management. Another equally significant example of unrecognized trauma is our system of medical care delivery, which has sacrificed the concept of caring for patients in its pursuit of new technological means of curing patients, has distanced caregivers from patients primarily through the fundamentally traumatic training of its physicians, and has induced a state of helplessness in patients by viewing them not as thinking, feeling people but rather as malfunctioning bodies-as-machines that need to be "fixed." These and many other unrecognized sources of trauma—such as violence in entertainment or governmentally instilled fear in the populous to justify war or restriction of personal freedoms—are also culturally endorsed, making them even more insidious. Such "little traumas" may be experienced as an entrapment, or as approach/avoidance conflicts: The disgruntled worker cannot change jobs without losing health and retirement benefits, the anxious first-time mother wants a natural childbirth but is terrified after her obstetrician warns her about the pain.

These unappreciated traumatic events may change behavior and the brain in subtle ways that do not conform to the DSM-IV criteria for PTSD. Nevertheless, they may lay the foundation for an insidious constriction in behavioral options in response to threat, as well as contribute to a loss of resiliency, with a progressive decline in social functioning and health.

CHAPTER 5

Preverbal Trauma

As a society, we treat our infants with considerable nonchalance. We tend to assume that they are resilient and adaptable, that they should be able to handle a variety of styles of caregiving. As newborns, they seem to have only two states of being—eating or sleeping (if we're lucky). We place pacifiers in their mouths, prop them up with pillows, and let them cry themselves to sleep. Early in their infancy, we drop them off with babysitters or even at daycare centers. In the majority of cases, they are bottle-fed. At times we seem to feel that the infant should adapt to the needs of its parents. Many of these assumptions are based on the pronouncements of self-proclaimed experts in the art of childrearing, usually pediatricians or child psychologists who view the infant as adaptable and trainable and who can be "spoiled" by excessive attention to its needs. These concepts probably are rooted in medical science dogma that suggests that the preverbal infant is a nonsentient bundle of primitive reflexes.

Until the mid-1980s, medical science indeed considered the preverbal period of human development to be one of a primarily reflexive, noncognitive state of awareness of the environment. Perception of pain, storage of memory, and processing of information were believed to be limited or absent, primarily because the neural pathways serving these functions lacked myelin, the fatty sheath that ensured conduction of messages. This state therefore was felt to render the infant impervious to pain and to the effects of a traumatic experience. In addition, the infant brain was felt to be resilient and plastic: It could tolerate injury much better than an adult because it was not fully formed.

We have since found that nothing could be further from the truth. Studies now show that the fetus and newborn infant are capable of being trained and conditioned to a variety of behaviors, to recognize the voice of the mother at birth, and in many ways to show evidence of sentience. The brain of the infant and, for that matter, the fetus, is also exquisitely vulnerable not only to physical insult but also to pain, experiential trauma, and variations in the intensity of the bond between mother and infant, even the emotional equanimity of the mother while the fetus is in utero. Freedom from traumatic stress and optimal nurturing as part of the mother/infant bond are critical for the development of the brain regions in the infant that are responsible for regulation of response to threat throughout the lifespan. This chapter explores the role of preverbal trauma as being one of the usually ignored or rejected sources of societal trauma.

Preverbal Neurobiology and Trauma

There is compelling scientific evidence that the fetus and newborn infant are sentient beings, capable of processing information and learning through conditioning, perceptive of pain, and capable of interpersonal communication through behavior. This fact tends to be ignored by medical science. As a result, a major source of potential trauma at this age is the medical technology associated with prenatal diagnosis, the neonatal nursery, and the birthing process.

Preverbal Perception of Pain

As 19th-century medical scientists performed early studies of the anatomy and physiology of the human brain, they found that the infant brain was not yet fully formed. It was apparent that many neuronal pathways that connected the higher centers of the infant brain with each other and with the more primitive lower centers lacked the fatty myelin sheath around axons that was necessary for the propagation of electrical impulses along these pathways. Neurophysiologists also recognized the fact that infantile motor activity was primarily based on primitive brainstem reflexes. Very little infant motor activity appeared to be purposeful. When one turned the infant's head to one side, the infant's arm and leg flexed on that side and extended on the other. When one stroked the side of an infant's face, the infant turned its head to that side while seeking with its mouth. When startled, the infant extended its arms, arched its back, and cried. The infant was believed to be a bundle of these primitive brainstem reflexes that are genetically acquired and provide the basic core of motor behavior designed to achieve posture and mobility. This hypothesis was consistent with the infant's lack of myelin in brain pathways that incorporated the thinking, planning, and "conscious" brain.

Pathways serving declarative memory, especially those related to the hippocampus, were also not myelinated. This was believed to explain the fact that most people superficially appear to have little or no memory for the years of their infancy and early childhood. I was taught in medical school that, because most of the cerebral pathways mediating messages of pain were also not myelinated, infants probably had a markedly diminished or absent perception of pain as well. The screams of infants that I circumcised or stuck with needles to obtain blood, however, did not seem to support this medical assumption. These beliefs—that infants were not sentient, did not feel pain as much as adults, and, in any event, certainly would have no memory for negative events—permeated my early medical training.

The opinion that infants could not perceive pain actually dates back to the mid-19th century. During the first half of the 20th century, medical researchers evaluated theories that proposed that infants could not appreciate pain and were unable to establish memories. David Chamberlain (1998a) reviewed the literature related to these studies, most of which used a remarkably simplistic tool: the application of a pinprick over various parts of the body to record what the investigators interpreted as a lack of pain perception. In general, these studies were crude and scientifically meaningless, but one study suggested that there was a gradation of response to pain from birth to 10 days of life. This led the investigator to conclude that the newborn had limited pain perception, if any at all, and that there was no mental or emotional component involved in messages of pain in infants. Therefore, infants had no specific pain perception because of immature development of the cerebral cortex. This supported the already widespread belief by the medical establishment that infants were basically reflexive beings without significant conscious perception of their environment. At the time that this study was done, maternal anesthesia was routinely administered at childbirth. Chamberlain raised the important point that this exposure of the newborn to anesthesia might well explain the relatively diminished responsiveness of the infants to pinprick during the first few days of life.

The mid-20th-century medical establishment was so certain of these "facts" regarding relative analgesia to pain in infants that most surgery, even some types of open-heart surgery, was performed on infants without general anesthesia. Immobility of the infant during the surgery was assured by the use of paralytic agents. The assumption was that, because the infant had diminished pain perception and would not remember the event anyway, the surgery would not be traumatizing. The rationale for this practice was that anesthetic doses for infants were difficult to measure. By the late 1980s, research in infant neurophysiology, however, had shown that infants are indeed capable of feeling pain in a fashion comparable to adults (Salapatek & Cohen, 1987), and in 1988 the American Medical Association confirmed this conclusion in a position statement, essentially ending the practice of performing surgery on infants without anesthesia. The force of public opinion and the media also played a significant role in the ultimate acceptance of the fact that infants could feel pain (Chamberlain, 1988a).

But how could the great minds of scientific medicine have been so wrong for so long? Their sweeping assumptions regarding infant neurophysiology and perception were based on images of the infant brain under a microscope and were seasoned by a century of blind assumptions. The many studies attempting to prove or disprove these assumptions were also hopelessly flawed, leading to conflicting conclusions regarding what infants actually perceived. Physicians and researchers also probably did not appreciate the fact that intrinsically traumatic experiences (and surgery without anesthesia must certainly be considered within the realm of traumatic experiences) are processed only in part through mechanisms involving the hippocampus and declarative memory. Such experiences also involve the process of classical conditioning and procedural memory, as do all experiences that have implications for survival, as discussed in Chapter 2. And the brain pathways, centers, and mechanisms that serve intrinsic procedural memory are incredibly complex, involving systems in the brainstem that indeed are myelinated at birth. It therefore seems likely that the primary brain pathways that serve the message system related to trauma are functioning at, and probably before, birth.

Preverbal Sentience
The process of classical conditioning involves the integration of a vast array of brain regions and neuronal systems. This process depends on the nature of the conditioned stimulus, the unconditioned stimulus and the evoked response or behavior produced by each stimulus. As has been discussed, both the sympathetic and parasympathetic portions of the autonomic nervous system, most of which are myelinated at birth, participate in conditioned

responses. Pathways for all of the senses may also be involved, and we know that vision, hearing, smell, taste, and vestibular function are definitely "on line" at birth. In fact, research now indicates that most of these primary senses are functional during the first trimester of gestation. It also now appears likely that despite lack of myelination of portions of the circuits serving pain, perception of pain in some form is intact in the second and third trimester fetus (Giannakoulopoulos et. al, 1994). Implicit or procedural memory involves many diverse brain areas and circuits that do not require conscious awareness of the events involved in the process of conditioning. It is likely that brainstem centers for reflexive or instinctual processing of information play a large role in what we term procedural memory. The need for this is obvious, as demands for processing and integration of survival-based information on a conscious basis would be self-defeating and ineffectual. Initiation of survival-based behavior requires an immediate unconscious response, not conscious planning. It is very likely, therefore, that infants process a great deal of information through mechanisms involving procedural memory and begin to assemble their repertoire of survival-based learning long before conscious memory is developed through myelination of hippocampal and cortical pathways.

Declarative memory also is not solely dependant on the functions of the hippocampus. Admittedly, destruction of the hippocampus on both sides of the brain does indeed prevent the utilization of working memory or the storage of virtually all memory for facts and events. But destruction of the primary nucleus of neurons in the brain responsible for integration of declarative memory is very different from the incomplete myelination of axons. We know that axonal myelination in some parts of the human brain is not complete until adolescence, and yet children through the first decade of life establish memories, feel pain, and are sentient. The presumption that one can assess the clinical behavior and function of an infant based on the state of its myelin development has no proven basis in scientific fact.

If one accepts the likelihood that infants possess the ability to process information and store it in procedural memory, are infants therefore sentient? Sentience of course implies a level of consciousness, and consciousness is equated with acquisition of declarative memory, the ability to process information thus obtained, and to initiate behavior based on that process. However, if Pavlov's conclusions are correct, conscious behavior ultimately has its roots in the infinite combination of a myriad of experiences determined by a host of subtle learned conditioned responses. By his definition, consciousness is predicated by the sum total of procedural memories acquired through the lifespan. Damasio perhaps would also agree, although he would include the sum total of declarative memories as well—a sort of autobiographical memory structure. But, as we have noted, declarative memory is fragile, easily distorted, and subject to erosion and modification by subsequent life experiences. Procedural memory is far more hardwired, resistant to change, and accurate. It would be presumptuous therefore to assert that sentience is solely contingent upon a form of consciousness dependant on the processing of declarative memory.

In fact, there are now thousands of research studies that demonstrate without any question that newborn infants possess powers of perception, expression, and memory far beyond what has been accepted for generations. Chamberlain (1998b) reviewed a portion of this large body of international literature. Newborns have a remarkably complete visual apparatus. Physiological studies reveal excellent acuity, contrast sensitivity, depth perception, color vision, and binocular function. Perceptual studies reveal that they soon are able to selectively identify a picture of their mother from an otherwise random group of pictures. They rapidly develop the ability to imitate facial expressions, differentiate various languages spoken by the mother, and communicate by a system of "body language" that is rapidly learned and clearly not instinctual. They also rapidly learn patterns of facial expression that facilitate, and in fact condition, positive responsive maternal behavior. Within weeks of life, they have begun to actively shape their immediate environment. They selectively respond to songs that their mother sang to them before birth and to many other sensations and experiences "learned" in the uterus, including tastes, smells, musical passages, nursery rhymes, and even voices from frequently played television programs. At 2 months they can actively and accurately participate in hide-and-seek games in the same sequential manner as older children and adults. By all measures, the newborn is a sentient being.

If we can assume that infants process a great deal of information and that learning, as measured by alteration of behavioral patterns, takes place, can we pinpoint exactly when this process begins? Does the moment of birth, the taking of the first breath, or the first vocalization initiate this process of sentience? Or is the fetus also sentient, capable of learning, and subject to the neurophysiological effects and changes initiated by traumatic stress? Studies of the fetus *in utero* through imaging studies, studies of blood chemical composition, and neurophysiology have opened a window to the behavioral potential and diversity of the fetus. And the rapidly evolving science of preterm neonatology, as well as our ability to keep extremely premature infants alive, have allowed us to study the very young, relatively undeveloped fetus outside the bounds of the uterus.

As I have suggested, full-term infants possess a repertoire of skills and capabilities that qualify them as sentient beings. These infants are able to influence their environment and adapt their behavior within weeks of birth. But clearly there is nothing in the process of expulsion from the uterus that suddenly bestows sentience on the newborn: For some time before birth, the fetus possesses the same remarkable capabilities that the newborn does. As noted earlier, infant responses to different languages, poems and nursery rhymes, vocal patterns, tastes, and smells that they experienced in utero suggest evidence for fetal learning and memory. De Casper and colleagues (1994) demonstrated fetal memory by showing that infants could distinguish between different poems read by their mother while in utero. They did so by rapidly learning to regulate the reading of their favorite poem by adjusting the frequency of sucking on a device called the "suck-o-meter." Furthermore, fetuses respond physically to external stimuli by retreating and batting at intruding amniocentesis needles and by embracing or showing combative behavior toward a twin fetus. They are capable of being trained to kick a specific area of the uterine wall on verbal command by the mother and to demonstrate consistent motor behavior in response to a learned maternal verbal cue (Chamberlain, 1998b). Such skills could not be learned without a remarkably intact system of neuronal circuitry serving effective procedural memory.

One can debate about when prenatal sentience actually begins, but in the process we begin to split hairs. We know that the amygdala, the nucleus of the brain that mediates processing of arousal-based memories, reaches its critical state of development between the last trimester and the first 2 months of life and therefore establishes a timeframe for the development of procedural memory (Panksepp, 1998). Researchers in the field of prenatal child development would insist that learning and the patterning of later childhood behavior actually starts much earlier. I will address these issues more extensively as I begin to discuss the complex interactions between negative life experiences and brain development during the periods of prenatal life and infancy.

The Fetus and Intrauterine Trauma

Can the developing fetal brain be physically changed by the experience of trauma in the same manner as the brain of the child or the adult? Or does the uterus and placenta provide a protective barrier from negative or traumatizing life events? The ability of the fetus to process information from the major senses is relatively intact by the third trimester and very possibly much earlier. Therefore, one could predict that the fetal brain is capable of responding to messages of threat through activation of the sympathetic nervous system, the brain's already myelinated arousal system, and also by activation of the HPA axis, the hormonal stress-modulating system. With the advent of techniques that access fetal blood and tissue, the capacity of the fetus to respond to traumatic stress should, in fact, be easy to demonstrate. This surgical process itself of needling the infant must be considered traumatic, because the fetus should have the same capacity to feel pain as the newborn. Indeed, after needling fetuses to obtain blood, Giannakoulopoulos and his colleagues (1994) were able measure dramatic elevations of plasma cortisol and endorphins that actually persisted after the traumatic event longer than one would expect in a child or adult. Cortisol and endorphin elevation provide compelling evidence that these infants experienced traumatic stress. Because the procedure involved needling the fetus, the only logical source of this chemical stress response would be the perception of pain.

One of the expanding fields of surgery is devoted to the correction of congenital heart defects in fetuses. This is accomplished by passing a penetrating scope through the uterine wall and into the abdomen of the fetus, and then inserting a catheter with a tiny knife or balloon at the tip into a major fetal blood vessel. This catheter can then be threaded into the fetal heart, where the surgeon corrects the cardiac defect while viewing the heart under ultrasound. The technically miraculous nature of this technique distracts us from the fact that it must be done without fetal anesthesia—and must be intrinsically traumatic.

There is also evidence that the mother's stress levels have a direct and significant effect on the health and brain development of the fetus. Most mothers report increased fetal movement under stress. Studies of fetal heart rates reveal significant elevation when the mother is experiencing stress and a correlation with the mother's own levels of stress hormones (Wadhwa, as cited in Verny, 2002). Zuckerman studied over 1000 pregnant women for the presence of depression and the behavioral effect on their offspring (Zuckerman,

1990). Newborns from depressed mothers had lower APGAR scores, were more irritable, cried more, and were more difficult to console and quiet. (It's named after Virginia Apgar, who devised the score.) In other words, exposure of the mother to stress during the pregnancy contributed to changes in the autonomic status of the fetus and to behavioral abnormalities in the infant after birth.

Catalano & Hartig (2001) has demonstrated that persistent elevation of maternal serum cortisol has very significant negative effects on the outcome of the pregnancy and health of the newborn. His study was based on the concept that societal trauma could have a pervasive negative effect on societal health. Maternal cortisol levels were measured in the days and weeks after the shocking assassination of the Swedish prime minister, an event unheard of in that society. Catalano discovered a 15–20% reduction in birth weight in infants compared to controls, along with an increased neonatal death rate during the months following this societal shock. These findings correlated with the elevated levels of serum cortisol in mothers of the infants with poor gestation outcomes. Spikes in maternal cortisol are also correlated with increased miscarriages in early pregnancy. In this study, maternal stress due to a societal trauma resulted in elevated levels of stress hormones, which in turn induced sufficient fetal distress and contributed to increased miscarriages and infant death at birth. One wonders what similar effects the 9/11 terrorist attacks may have had on American mothers.

Finally, exposure of the fetus to the stress-related hormones of the distressed mother is likely to alter the infant's adaptive capacity to further life stress through sensitization and reprogramming of the fetal HPA axis. As we know, this phenomenon has been demonstrated in adults exposed to traumatic stress and suffering from PTSD. Programming the fetus in this manner has been studied in laboratory animals and more recently applied to the study of the human fetus. Nathanielsz (1999) reviewed the findings in the field of fetal programming and concluded that exposure of the fetus to stress, including that derived from the mother, is a significant factor in the susceptibility of the infant to the later development of many diseases, especially heart disease and diabetes.

Neonatal Intensive Care

The same concerns regarding the vulnerability of the fetus exist in the rapidly emerging field of neonatal intensive care for the markedly premature infant. Medical science has developed techniques to prolong and in many cases save the lives of premature infants as young as 24 weeks of gestation and as small as 1.2 pounds. These "micropreemies" have profoundly immature brains and lungs and require massive and continuous total care for months in order to mature sufficiently to survive. The life-saving techniques involved are extremely invasive and include insertion of numerous catheters and tubes in veins, arteries, bladder, lungs, and stomach to breathe, feed, provide intravenous fluids and calories, measure lung function, and extract blood for measuring blood chemistries. These infants are so fragile that they must be kept in hi-tech incubators to maintain body temperature. In many cases, they cannot be held or touched and must remain in almost total isolation. The primary sensations that they experience are generally painful or noxious.

There appears to be an increasing awareness in neonatal ICUs that isolation and exposure to constant pain are exceedingly negative factors in the survival, well-being, and ultimate health of these infants. Based on the expanding literature on the negative effects of pain on infant development, greater efforts are being made to provide analgesia when possible for painful procedures in these infants. These efforts, however, run up against the problems presented by the unpredictability of preemies' ability to metabolize narcotics and analgesics due to the infants' diminutive size. Systemic painkillers can induce paralysis of breathing and circulatory collapse in preemies. Thus, most efforts at blocking pain involve local anesthetic, including creams (EMLA cream) and local injections at the site of surgery. Despite these laudable efforts, relief of pain remains a huge issue in management of the care of the preemie, and pain itself remains a major source of traumatic stress for these infants.

Isolation and lack of tactile and vestibular stimulation of the preemie in the isolette are also major concerns, in this case with regard to brain development. The uterus is an environment rich in sensory stimuli that are important to brain development. The fetus is exposed to the rhythmic sounds of placental circulation and the heartbeat of the mother, as well as to the muted sounds of the external environment, including the mother's voice. The fetus receives vestibular stimulation triggered by the movement of the mother and the wavelike patterns of amniotic fluid, and it is exposed to the smells and tastes of a myriad of chemicals released in the amniotic fluid and based on the diet of the mother. This rich sensory environment contributes to the development of brain centers that mediate the specific sensory information that is provided in the uterus. It creates sensory learning as a reference point for the fetus to evaluate its environment after birth and desensitizes the infant to the relatively sudden onslaught of sensory information confronting it from the moment of birth. The sensory experiences in the uterus gradually "prep" the fetus for exposure to a host of new sensory experiences at birth.

The isolative neonatal ICU certainly has its own menu of intense sensory experiences, many of them painful, threatening, and alien. The nature of these stimuli is likely to be traumatic and therefore not conducive to learning appropriate behaviors that are related to the development of the necessary sensorimotor responses that contribute to brain maturation. In addition, chronically elevated levels of serum cortisol, instigated by the preemie's response to threatening and traumatizing sensory experiences, are likely to produce the same deficits in development of the hippocampus that we see in childhood and adult victims of trauma, resulting in long-term deficits in declarative memory mechanisms.

This combination of traumatic sensory overload and deprivation from the ordinary sensory experiences associated with later intrauterine development in many cases appears to be catastrophic. Outcome statistics that are emerging from research on preemies during their first years of childhood are demonstrating a host of neurological deficits that are disabling to varying degrees. These deficits may well be caused by physical or chemical damage to the brain, such as abnormal development due to lack of sufficient oxygen or glucose for the brain during the more critical phases of ICU treatment. On the other hand, the deficits may also be partly due to the damaging effects of the hormones of stress and of overwhelming traumatic experience. Many scientific studies of the epidemiological outcomes of treatment of preemies in neonatal ICUs have shown significant and persisting impairment and disability in the infants studied. In one of the largest studies, Vohr and colleagues (2001) from the National Institutes of Health studied 1151 24- to 28-week preemies at 15 to 22 months of age. Of these, 25% showed abnormal neurological functioning; 25%, impaired mental development; and 37%, abnormal psychomotor development. Neurological disabilities were common and severe. Nine percent had visual impairment and 11% demonstrated severe hearing loss. One wonders how many of these deficits were related to actual physical injury and how many related to impaired development from the somatic effects of trauma. Vohr and colleagues (p. 1225) concluded that "extremely low birth weight infants are at significant risk for neurological abnormalities, and developmental and functional delays."

One must conclude that in the specialty of neonatal care, science may have outstripped our society's ability to deal with the complications and negative outcomes created by its expertise. And much of this dilemma may be due to our inability to avoid the horrible trauma inflicted on preemies by the techniques that are saving and prolonging their lives.

The American Way of Birth

The history of the process of birthing, or assisting the mother in the delivery of her child, has been consistent across many cultures for many millennia. Typically, the infants were born in their homes, whether that home was a tent, a hut, a house, or a palace. The mothers were attended to and assisted by other women, whether relatives, midwives, or members of the tribe or society experienced or trained in assisting with the birth. Even in residences of the wealthy or of royalty, assistance with delivery was usually provided by a midwife.

In Western Europe during the mid-19th century, however, the birthing process was moved into to the setting of large hospitals, some of them designated specifically for childbirth. This move was seen as a symbol of medical progress, and it laid the foundation for a new, "technological" birthing process that, although still widespread in Europe, has been embraced most fervently by the United States.

One of the earliest legacies of this symbol of medical progress was the establishment of an often-fatal maternal illness termed "childbed" or "puerperal fever." One of the pioneering researchers of infectious disease, the mid-19th-century physician Eric Maria Semelweiss discovered that these infections appeared to be associated with the frequent practice of surgeons' moving directly from the autopsy rooms to manual examination of women in labor. For his efforts, Semelweiss was castigated and rejected from his academic post.

Fortunately, with the discovery of the germ theory of disease, the practice of hand washing was introduced into hospital-based birthing practices, virtually eliminating puerperal fever. As with most institutions, the birthing process became associated with time-honored yet often scientifically unproven rituals that became standard procedure in the obstetrical hospital theater. The infant's heel was punctured with a lancet for its first blood count. An ocular instillation of a solution of silver chloride, a caustic and painful compound, was begun to prevent gonorrheal infection of the infant's lining of the eyes, and it persisted for many decades. In the erroneous belief that the newborn could develop pneumonia (sterile amniotic fluid fills the lungs of the fetus up to the moment of birth, as it does in all mammals), the obstetrical nurse provided vigorous suction of the mouth and of the upper bronchial airways through a tube passed through the nose, as well as suction of the nostrils with a bulb syringe. To promote cleanliness, the protective waxy material that coats the skin of the newborn was vigorously washed off. Other traditions of cleanliness pertaining to the mother were also introduced despite having no real scientific basis. These include emptying the mother's urinary bladder with a catheter in the late stages of labor, giving the laboring mother an enema in order to prevent fecal contamination of the sterile field of delivery, and shaving the mother's perineal hair on admission to the birthing unit. As noted, there are no scientific statistics validating the usefulness of these procedures, and they have largely been abandoned.

The discovery of ether and other forms of inhalation anesthesia allowed physicians to provide the laboring female with relief from the pain of childbirth. Because anesthesia often slowed or even stopped the natural course of uterine contractions and labor, techniques for assisted extraction of the newborn had to be developed, leading to the introduction of mechanical devices (forceps) that were designed to grasp the infant's skull within the birth canal and drag or twist the head out of the vagina. A variety of forceps designs were developed during the early 20th century. More recently manual assistance to delivery of the newborn has involved suction devices that are placed on the top of the head of the infant.

Until the early 1980s, narcotics often were used to ease the later stages of the mother's pain. Meperidine, or Demerol, was generally the drug of choice, but it carried significant risks. Because the fetus receives a significant dose of the narcotic through the umbilical cord during the labor, great care had to be taken not to administer the Demerol too close to the actual time of delivery. Narcotics suppress the respiratory drive, and delivery of a narcotized newborn could lead to apnea (arrest of breathing), with the associated risk of anoxic brain damage.

The use of caudal or epidural anesthesia was also introduced. These techniques involved introduction of local anesthetic through a needle in the lumbar spine, into the space through which the spinal nerves travel to provide sensation to the mother's lower body and the legs. This technique paralyzes and removes all pain sensation from the legs, bladder, uterus, vagina, and perineum, and provides a conscious but anesthetic birth. Emptying the bladder with a urinary catheter was necessary because of bladder paralysis. Epidural anesthesia slows the normal course of labor as well as the ability of the laboring woman to push during the final stage of delivery, once again usually requiring the use of forceps or suction for extraction of the infant.

Driven by a number of factors, including an increasingly litigious medical-legal climate in obstetrics, the fear of harming the newborn began to assume overwhelming importance in the hospital birthing theater. Although some complications are inevitable in the most normal of births, the specter of an infant suffering injury as part of the birth process has become totally unacceptable in current society. The process of giving birth, although a totally natural part of the cycle of life, is not without some risk of complication, as are most of life's processes. Our society, however, has come to expect that its institutions are responsible for providing a risk-free environment. As a result, a burgeoning technology has arisen to meet the demands for delivering an undamaged newborn.

One can hardly argue that this goal is anything but laudable. But the burden of expectation that is thus placed on the medical obstetrical system is so great that any complications in the birthing process, however unavoidable, predictably lead to a lawsuit. Societal and legal pressure to deliver the perfect newborn have become so intense that state-of-the-art techniques are routinely applied in the birthing process despite the fact that they have no proven benefits in the average delivery and may even carry added risks. If they are *not* used and a complication occurs in the birthing process, a lawsuit is very likely to occur because "usual and customary" medical practices were not followed. "Usual and customary" is a phrase applied to the prevailing practice habits of physicians in the regional medical community and has nothing to do with a scientific basis for that practice or even with customary practice on a national basis. As a result, the "science" of obstetrics in recent decades has been characterized by the sequential introduction of new technologies specifically designed not only to ensure the birth of an undamaged infant, but also to ensure the protection of the obstetrician from litigation. Unfortunately these techniques remain largely unproven, but now that they are standard procedure, the fear of litigation perpetuates their use.

Birthing Technology

Amniocentesis (the obtaining of amniotic fluid for analysis through a needle passed through the abdominal and uterine wall) was initially developed to detect Rh blood type incompatibility but now is used to detect so-called congenital neural tube defects, such as spina bifida, as well as many other metabolic and genetic defects. The procedure undoubtedly has a traumatic effect on the fetus, and medical complications include a slight increase in fetal death or injury to organs of the fetus. Ultrasound of the fetus and uterus accompanies this technique. Significant exposure to ultrasound has been demonstrated to fracture or alter DNA, with potential effects on gene transmission.

For many years, the fetal heart rate and tone were monitored by the obstetrical nurse by auscultation (listening to the fetal heartbeat through a stethoscope applied to the abdomen of the laboring mother). Alterations in fetal heart rate, especially slowing, are believed to indicate the likelihood of fetal distress. In the 1950s, electronic monitoring of the fetal heartbeat (EFM) was introduced, initially conducted externally with electrodes over the maternal abdomen and later internally with needle electrodes implanted into the scalp of the infant through the mother's vagina. This procedure allowed alterations in fetal heart rate to be monitored continuously. The introduction of any new technology requires the medical profession to redefine what is normal and what is abnormal based on an entirely new set of information. EFM was introduced and utilized based on existing information about the implications and relationships of fetal heartbeat with distress. In a review of the newborn literature, Verny (1986) showed that the introduction of EFM in a number of large scientific studies has resulted in no improvement in incidence of fetal death, brain damage, health, APGAR scores, or blood gas levels in the umbilical cord.

Application of EFM, especially the internal variety, requires that the mother remain relatively immobile, which prevents the accommodative movements and positions that she would normally make to achieve comfort and slows the normal progression of the labor. It also introduces a new source of pain to the fetus and increases levels of stress hormones. Furthermore, EFM was found to double the incidence of C-sections, and it tripled the rate of postpartum maternal infections. Despite these statistics, EFM is now considered to be standard procedure in most deliveries. To refrain from its use and then have a birth complication virtually guarantees litigation. Additionally EFM is another example of a culturally induced and endorsed source of trauma, in this case to the newborn and possibly to the mother.

New birthing technologies have also slowed the natural course of labor. Narcotic analgesics, anesthesia, immobilization, and the stress of a new and frightening environment have all been noted to slow the course of labor and delivery. In response, obstetrical science has had to find means to intervene and speed up the course of labor and the vigor of uterine contractions. The earliest technique was that of amniotomy (artificial rupture of the amniotic membranes), a technique that indeed seemed to induce more vigorous uterine contraction. If labor was prolonged, however, this procedure increased the risk of infection through repeated vaginal examinations and in some cases prompted intervention through a C-section. The introduction of pitocin, a synthetic form of the pituitary hormone that specifically stimulates uterine contraction, became standard in cases of slowed labor. The contractions produced by pitocin, however, are often violent and painful, requiring more analgesia and a cycle that also often may lead to a C-section. In many cases, the use of pitocin and the vigorous contractions that result lead to slowing of the fetal heart rate and evidence for fetal distress. As is often the case, the introduction of new medical technology led to the need for additional new technology to deal with its complications, and so on.

As one can see, the move of the birthing process from the home to the institution drastically changed the laboring mother's experience: She was forced to relinquish control, acquiesce to authority, and undergo exposure to a new, strange, and frightening environment in the name of pain relief. Technology introduced a host of new information and data to the caregiver, most of it designed to warn of impending danger to the fetus and much of it unsupported by scientific fact. This made for apprehensive physicians and nurses in the delivery room, which inevitably was a source of further anxiety and apprehension for the mother and, by its hormonal implications, for the newborn. At the end of an often painful and emotionally harrowing experience, the mother could only be eternally grateful to the caregiver for escorting her and her fortunately healthy newborn through the obstetrical minefield—and also confused about why she felt so badly about her birthing experience.

The healthy newborn had shared that harrowing journey, both through the chemical storm created by the increased levels of cortisol and the hormones of arousal that it received from its traumatized mother and through its own experience of pain from the scalp needles, the crushing force of the forceps, the tube thrust into its lungs, the burning fluid in its eyes, and the lancet stick of its heel. Its brain was irrevocably modeled by this experience, its survival-based procedural memory acquired a new set of cues and memories on which to rely in the face of further such experiences, and it learned perhaps for the first time what a terrifying and dangerous place its new world was going to be.

Some might argue that I have overdramatized the traumatic nature of hospital-based birthing. But given the compelling evidence for the sentience of the fetus and newborn, I believe that an element of hyperbole is justified. Medical science continues to view the human brain and body in a Cartesian, mechanistic manner, assessing health and disease only by objective measures that show alterations from the statistical bell curve of normality. It also discards evidence, such as that for the state of fetal sentience, that conflicts with established opinions and perceptions, especially evidence suggesting the need for a paradigm shift in usual and customary traditions, practices, and rituals. The field of trauma highlights these problems in that evolving concepts of trauma continue to run up against established cultural rituals that, though accepted as appropriate, are nevertheless insidious sources of life trauma.

Bonding, Nurturing, and Brain Development

The role of maternal/infant bonding in the healthy development of the infant has been the subject of scientific study and conjecture since the mid-1970s. Studies by Bowlby (1976) and Klaus and Kennel (1976) emphasized the critical role in the development of the brain and behavior of the infant through face-to-face and skin-to-skin contact of the infant with the mother. Animal studies in rats and primates demonstrate the pervasive effects of even subtle interruption of the contact between mother and infant on long-term development and lifelong resilience to stress. Increased understanding of the physiology of the brain in bonding and trauma provide compelling evidence that impairment of nurturing is a significant source of societal trauma.

Animal Studies

At the 2002 annual meeting of the International Society for Traumatic Stress Studies (ISTSS), Rachel Yehuda and Charles Nemeroff chaired a special satellite meeting titled *Biologic Concepts Related to the Etiology, Pathophysiology and Treatment of PTSD*. Several of the presentations addressed animal models of brain development and subsequent adult behavior that provided dramatic and compelling evidence for the importance of the earliest and most intimate maternal/newborn interactions.

Paul Plotsky addressed some of these issues in his presentation *Early Adverse Experience as a Developmental Risk Factor: Evidence for Rodent and Primate Models*. He reported studies of neonatal separation of the rat pup from the dam (mother) for varying periods of time and the effect of this separation on the pup's physical and cortisol response to a startle stimulus (an air puff). During a critical period within the first few weeks of life, separation of the pup from the dam resulted in a lifelong enhanced startle response, an altered HPA axis with excessive cortisol response to stress, and diminished formation of new neurons in the hippocampus. Some of these adverse responses could be reversed by increased contact with a foster dam or by postnatal sensory enrichment. In other words, separation of the newborn from the mother in the first moments after birth led to permanent changes in the brain and endocrine system that we equate with PTSD in humans. Fortunately, enhanced nurturing could undo some of the damage.

In primate studies, neonatal isolation or neglect resulted in altered cortisol levels with exaggerated response to a startle stimulus, as well as impaired cognition, locomotion, and social function. What our human culture might consider to be trivial variations in the earliest experiences of the newborn infant in fact have significant implications for tuning of the infant to an exaggerated fear response and for inhibition of the development of areas of the brain critical for memory and cognition.

At the same symposium, Michael Meaney presented a session titled *Maternal Care and the Development of Individual Differences in Vulnerability for Anxiety and Trauma Related Disorders*. Studies in rats involved variations in licking/grooming (L/G) behavior in dams and their effect on infant development. Licking and grooming of the infant rat by the mother are manifestations of instinctual maternal nurturing. As one might expect, this nurturing maternal behavior varied considerably among rat dams and followed a fairly typical statistical bell curve of distribution. Dams who exhibited high levels of L/G behavior reared pups that subsequently showed decreased cortisol and HPA sensitivity, and this high L/G trait was passed on through several generations of rat dams. Dams exhibiting low L/G behavior reared pups with increased fear behavior, increased startle response, and high cortisol/HPA responsiveness. Remarkably, stressing a high L/G dam changed her behavior to that of a low L/G dam, with negative consequences for her offspring dams for several generations. And switching a pup from one dam to another changed its behavior and hormonal responsiveness based on the new dam's L/G traits.

In other words, subtleties of maternal nurturing during the earliest phases of newborn life may tune the infant's autonomic and hormonal responses to stress for life, for better or for worse. In addition, not only is instinctual maternal nurturing behavior impaired by stress, but the change in nurturing behavior also may be passed down through several generations. This study also implies that abnormal social behavior seen in several generations is not necessarily a genetic phenomenon.

These simple but elegant studies of maternal/newborn interactions tell a dramatic and critically important tale that relates to the welfare of mankind. We ignore the relevance of such studies in animals to the human experience at our own peril. These studies yield an inescapable conclusion: In animals and humans, early separation of the newborn from the mother and even subtle variations in the quality of maternal care have a profound effect on the emotional and cognitive development of infants and on their resilience to subsequent ambient life stress throughout the life span. Infant/mother bonding changes the infant's brain and ensures its ability to deal effectively with subsequent life stress and trauma.

Studies in Bonding
An equally remarkable fact is that these findings have been documented in the medical pediatric literature since the mid-1970s. Veronique Mead (2003) provided a comprehensive review of the literature on maternal/infant bonding and attachment theory. She reviewed much of the pertinent literature in this field, particularly the work of Klaus and Kennel in the early studies of bonding. In their landmark book *Maternal and Infant Bonding: The Impact of Early Separation or Loss on Family Development*, Klaus & Kennel (1976) presented results of their own findings, as well as those of other researchers, on the effects of early maternal/newborn interactions on subsequent behavior and well-being in both mother and infant. In addition to offering an immense amount of data regarding the critical importance of bonding during the newborn period, their book provides an uncanny endorsement of the findings of the animal studies described in the previous section, studies that took place 25 years later.

Klaus & Kennel (1976) noted that the mother's capacity to bond with her newborn depended to a great degree on her own prior life experiences and on the events that occurred during the pregnancy, especially the levels of ambient life stress to which she was exposed. Her caretaking skills and her ability to bond with her infant were affected, for example, by the way that she was raised as a child, whether her pregnancy was planned, stress during the pregnancy, the labor and delivery experience, and the occurrence and length of maternal/newborn separation after birth. Klaus and Kennel defined a "sensitive period" during the first hours and days of the newborn's life, when physical contact with the mother lays the seeds for maternal-infant attachment. Skin-to-skin contact during this critical time clearly established persisting patterns of maternal/infant interaction that easily can be compared to the high L/G behavior exhibited in rat dams in the animal studies. Infants raised in this close tactile environment cried less, laughed more, and predictably showed higher IQ and language scores compared to control subjects at age 5. Infants separated from the mother at birth manifested elevated cortisol levels that subsequently dropped with resumption of skin-to-skin contact (Anderson et al., 1995). The "primitive" L/G behavior of rats and other animal species has its correlates in human mother/infant physical interactions that have been largely forgotten and ignored by our society.

Mead (2003) noted that hormones released during the infant's delivery (and subsequently released under the influence of touch), the interactive gaze between infant and mother, and especially breast-feeding enhanced the maternal/infant bond. The pituitary hormone prolactin promotes mobilization of breast milk, and the hormone oxytocin facilitates contraction and shrinkage of the uterus after birth to its size before pregnancy. Both hormones are considered critical to the development of the emotional state between humans that we describe as "love," and they facilitate social affiliative behavior (Klaus & Kennel, 1976; Porges, 1998). Hormones such as oxytocin and prolactin also act as neurotransmitters, agents for transmission of messages between selected brain areas. Enhancement or inhibition of neurotransmitter access to neurons affects the function of those neurons and therefore permanently affects the behavior of the animal or person. Their presence in the mother and infant creates permanent patterns of behavior, such as in the high or low L/G maternal behavior of the rat dam, and enhances or impairs the behavioral and cognitive heritage of the nurtured or separated infant. In addition, the intrusive interventions in the childbirth process have been documented to interfere with the capacity for maternal/infant bonding. These practices include the use of synthetic oxytocin (pitocin) to speed delivery, anesthesia, use of forceps and suction extraction, the application of electronic fetal monitoring, the performance of C-sections, and the separation of the newborn from the mother at birth (Verny, 2002, as quoted in Mead, 2003).

Having traversed the minefield of a medicalized and technological pregnancy and birth process, the new mother and newborn infant hopefully will proceed on an intense and intimate process of mutual attunement to the behaviors and responses of the other. Optimally this process of mutual and dynamic interaction results not only in bonding but also in a more complex affiliative process of attachment that has lifelong implications for the maturation and development of the nervous system of the infant. As noted earlier, early separation of the newborn infant from the mother results in subsequent long-term vulnerability to stress and arousal-based life experiences, manifested by exaggerated startle and cortisol responses. John Bowlby (1976), the founder of attachment theory, believed that infants possessed instinctual behaviors that stimulated their caregivers to meet their needs. This mutually reinforcing behavior led not only to emotional attachment but also to physiological self-regulation of the infant.

The Physiology of Bonding

Allan Schore (1994) presented an exhaustive and comprehensive review of the literature on the effects of attachment through the maternal/infant dyad in his book *Affect Development and the Origin of the Self: The Neurobiology of Emotional Development*. In Schore's model, the infant presents at birth a plastic and malleable unfinished genetic template on which life experience will build a behavioral structure. The critical element for development of this structure is the bonded pairing of the infant with the caregiver, a union that Schore and others termed the *maternal/infant dyad* (two-as-one). The most important mutual behavior that facilitates this dyadic attachment is the early face-to-face and eye-to-eye connection of the mother and infant, which has been termed *gaze interaction* or *transaction*. The importance of this visual/facial interaction in maternal/infant bonding has been noted by many researchers and is believed to facilitate the normal development of the right cerebral hemisphere. As you will recall, the processing of emotion and threat is specifically relegated to the right cerebral hemisphere, as is the response of the autonomic nervous system and its hormonal counterpart, the HPA axis. The optimal distance between the faces of the infant and the mother based on the developing visual system of the infant is approximately 10 inches, the distance that is associated with gaze interaction during breastfeeding and cradling the infant in the arms (Mead, 2003). Breastfeeding, and the tactile/visual interaction associated with it, initiates the hormonal release that facilitates bonding. It starts the rhythmic cycle of homeostasis that begins the process of self-regulation of the infant brain.

Ashley Montagu (1986) addressed the critical importance of the sense and experience of touch in the development of the newborn. He noted that the face, especially the mouth and tongue, is represented in the cerebral cortex by a huge area, many times that of any other part of the body. Sensory input from lips, mouth, and tongue are therefore obviously the most important sources of information to the brain. In the newborn and infant, human skin-to-skin touch in general represents the most critical means of stimulation and development of the infant brain. Oral/skin contact is the most important means of promoting infant brain development. Combined with maternal/infant gaze transactions, oral stimulation lays the seeds for optimal brain function in the adult. Breastfeeding clearly provides the best environment for this process.

Gaze transactions are associated with finely modulated shifts in the facial expression of the mother and her infant that clearly reflect shifts in the autonomic state of the mother and infant. This period of intense interaction has its most important effect during the period of birth to 8 months of age. Schore (1994) noted that the early stages of maternal/infant facial attunement are associated with a progressive modulation of arousal and withdrawal responses. Initial visual contacts between infant and mother are associated with sympathetic arousal and excitement, with widening of the eyes and dilatation of the pupils. As arousal becomes uncomfortably intense, the infant will avert its gaze, unconsciously lessening the arousal as the parasympathetic nervous system is brought on line. The mother responds in kind with a lessening of her state of arousal until gaze interaction is again restored, and the cycle of attunement returns.

This gaze-determined dance of rhythmic autonomic cycling begins the process of self-regulation by the infant. The theoretical means by which this occurs is far too complex for this discussion, but it largely involves the development of neurons and synapses in the parts of the right frontal lobe that thereafter modulate the infant/child/adult's autonomic response to arousal and threat. This process of self-regulation fosters the development of the right orbitofrontal cortex (OFC), which, as noted earlier, is the area of the brain that functions as the master regulator of the limbic system, the autonomic nervous system, and the HPA axis in processing arousal-based information. The repetitive facial and gaze-based interaction between mother and infant literally promotes growth of neurons and synapses within the OFC and its connections to other brain regions. This critical period of brain development eventually provides for the developing infant a consistent means of modulating its own response to arousal as a child and adult.

This process of brain maturation proceeds through stages where the infant begins to separate intentionally from the mother. The first of these stages, between 10 and 12 months of age, includes the period of early development of mobility through crawling and walking. During this stage, the infant often is in a high state of positive sympathetic arousal, as manifested by elation, excitement, and laughter. Sympathetic arousal may indeed be a positive experience associated with pleasure, as in athletic and play behaviors.

As the 16- to 18-month-old infant's increasing mobility requires maternal controls for purposes of safety, the mother will initiate limit-setting behavior that elicits a negative response in the infant, with behavior characterized by withdrawal and shame, a state of parasympathetic dominance. If bonding has been successful, this limit-setting behavior and the infant's withdrawal response will continue to foster the development of the reflex regulatory skills that control the infant's ability to handle arousal and stress in an appropriate, healthy fashion. It will also foster the growth and development of the OFC and its neuronal connections and facilitate the development of internal autonomic control that will eventually occur automatically in the infant in the absence of input from the mother.

Shame by itself is a regressive phenomenon, one that correlates in part with the parasympathetic state associated with the freeze response. In a well-modulated and attuned maternal/infant relationship, shame is a necessary tool for the infant to begin to experience modulation of states of excessive sympathetic arousal and to find a place of safety where it can regroup its resources for another venture in exploration and the arousal associated with new experiences. Schore (1994) has referred to this period of parasympathetic retreat as "conservation-withdrawal." During this state, the infant averts its face, hangs its head, and becomes relatively immobile. Blushing is also characteristic of shame. If maternal/infant misattunement is present, especially in the case of the mother's excessive use of shame-inducing limitations, the infant will begin to retreat more frequently into the state of conservation-withdrawal and may develop lifelong behavioral patterns that mimic this state when stressed. These parasympathetic dominant habitual responses to stress are just as dysfunctional as the behavior of the misattuned infant who develops habitual states of intolerable arousal under ambient life stress. Conservation-withdrawal is the earliest manifestation of dissociation, which if perpetuated becomes a lifelong tendency in the face of threat or stress. In the day-to-day life of the child, repeated retreat into states of shame presents as repetitive dissociative symptoms, including tics, stuttering, poor eye contact, and persistent childhood somatic symptoms, including headache, backache, and stomach pain.

This whole process of infant development has remarkable implications for all facets of a person's life. To use a trite metaphor, the flap of a butterfly's wings in Mexico affects wind patterns over the Gobi desert—similarly, the nuances of gaze transactions in the newborn infant may affect the cholesterol level and dose of Prozac for depression in the middle-aged adult. There is compelling evidence that the physical and chemical changes in the brain that result from inadequate maturation because of inadequate bonding and nurturing are relatively hardwired and permanent. The female infant who has experienced misattunement with her mother will also have difficulty providing optimal attunement with her own infant as a new mother, having never developed her own internal system of modulation of arousal. Schore (2002) postulated that this process of early traumatic attachment involves the storage of traumatic memories, just as the adult stores all of the cues of an unresolved trauma in procedural memory, leading to persistent maladaptive behavior and symptoms of PTSD. He considered these earliest negative experiences of infancy to be traumatizing and to predispose the affected infant to vulnerability to further life stresses and to PTSD. In fact, he cited evidence that affect dysregulation is now seen to be a fundamental mechanism of all psychiatric disorders (Taylor, G. et. al, 1997, in Schore, 2002).

The misattuned child will experience exaggerated responses to otherwise tolerable life stress, resulting in excessive sympathetic arousal on a repetitive basis. He or she also will experience chronically elevated levels of serum cortisol associated with these frequent states of inappropriate fight/flight responses. Once again, elevated levels of cortisol have been associated with atrophy of the hippocampus, the center for declarative memory. This could well account in part for the impairment in cognitive function that has been documented in primates exposed to maternal separation as infants, as well as account for similar cognitive deficits in adulthood in neglected human infants. Persistent arousal states in the misattuned child would be expected to interrupt ordinary processing of verbally based information, potentially leading to interruption of attention resulting in attention deficit disorder (ADD). Combined with impaired attention, the exaggerated motor expressions of persistent arousal could lead to behavior that meets the criteria for hyperactivity in the affected child. Conversely, the child tuned to respond to stress with conservation-withdrawal may manifest dissociative symptoms throughout childhood and be diagnosed as suffering from somatoform disorder.

Our society is currently experiencing a remarkable epidemic of what has been considered to be a genetic disorder: attention deficit/hyperactivity disorder (ADHD). It should be obvious that one does not experience "epidemics" of genetically based disorders or diseases. Gene mutations require generations to manifest their changes in structure, function, and disease. Episodes of epidemic gene alterations, of course, may be induced by overwhelming exposures to toxins that have the potential to alter DNA, such the nuclear radiation at Hiroshima, Nagasaki, and Chernobyl, which produced birth defects. It is remotely possible that our current ADHD epidemic could be due to some subtle neurotoxin affecting the brain development of many of our infants, but the occurrence of the epidemic across the geographical span of our nation makes this explanation extremely unlikely. The tendency for a culture to search for mechanistic explanations for such negative trends in health and disease is not surprising. As I propose in Chapter 5, our entire healthcare system's approach to diagnosing and treating disease is founded the perception of the patient as a machine. Even when a disease presents as an aberration of normal behavior in children, a culture will seldom look at its own accepted behaviors, rituals, or standards as a potential cause. Instead, the culture will search for some tangible external agent that must be to blame for what might actually not be a disease at all but rather a detrimental societal change in customs, habits, or rituals. For example, our current epidemic of obesity has been blamed on the rampant abuses of the fast-food industry. This ignores the fact that not everybody overeats, and that the amount of calories consumed in morbid obesity is so large as to indicate an unmet need. I would propose that the unmet need is often deprivation of oral stimulation as an infant based on cultural patterns of nursing and nurturing our infants.

Let us assume that behavior, not just in infancy but through childhood and adulthood, is patterned at least partly by prenatal experiences, maternal/infant bonding, and infant attunement, and that this patterning affects the lifelong capacity of the infant to modulate arousal and to promote homeostasis. Given that premise, if a society experiences an epidemic of childhood behavior that typifies poor arousal modulation, wouldn't you think that the society might want to look at how it manages the first days and months of the lives of its children? As I have noted, numerous scientific studies have documented and supported the risks and predictable negative behavioral outcomes that derive from inadequate maternal/infant bonding and attunement. This literature addresses numerous causes and factors that may impair bonding and attunement, including prenatal factors, events surrounding the birthing experience, and the influence of prior life trauma and current stress that may affect the mother. Unfortunately, these studies have been relegated to the dustbin of pediatric medical science and to the few societies, such as the Academy of Pre- and Perinatal Psychology and Health (APPPH), that continue to serve as spokesmen for the welfare of the fetus and newborn infant. In the words of Michel Odent (2000), this body of scientific literature is referred to as *cul-de-sac epidemiology*. Such medical literature, although significant and topical, is generally shunned by the medical community and ignored by the media. "Cul-de-sac" studies are never referenced by other medical articles, and no attempt is made by other medical researchers to replicate or, for that matter, disprove them. Odent referred to such epidemiological literature as usually being "politically incorrect," accounting for the banishment of this otherwise significant scientific data. I would suggest that a more appropriate term might be "culturally unacceptable."

Evidence suggesting that adult mental and physical health is rooted in the intrauterine experience of the fetus, the nature of the birth experience, and the bonding experience of the infant is, in some circles, culturally taboo. It threatens many of the standards of care in the pediatric and obstetrical specialties. It challenges cultural assumptions regarding the emancipation of women and their right to pursue professional goals. It defies the culturally accepted belief that prolonged nursing, maternal/child contact, and avoidance of daycare creates "dependency" in children. However, as is discussed later in the book, patterns of childcare throughout the millennia have varied widely in different cultures and have often clearly determined the nature of those cultures, specifically with regard to tendencies toward pacific or warlike behavior.

When presenting these concepts in workshops and lectures, I have understandably been challenged at times by women in the audience, many of whom are working mothers. In these instances, I try to present myself as the messenger, not the judge. There is no doubt that the entry of women into areas of the workplace formerly occupied by males has provided many positive benefits for our society. One can only look at this trend as cultural progress. The dilemma lies in the irrefutable evidence that face-to-face, skin-to-skin nurturing of the newborn and developing infant is not only beneficial, but also essential for optimal brain development.

The studies in rat pups and dams that have been presented also show that adequate nurturing can be achieved through a substitute or surrogate dam. In the case of licking/grooming (L/G) behavior, the high L/G surrogate dam in fact is more effective than the low L/G natural dam. The mother who carried the infant in her womb is obviously the optimal caregiver, but one can reasonably assume that the presence of a constant, nurturing figure such as the father, a nanny, or wet nurse could provide many of the benefits of the maternal presence. Whether this is possible in a cash-strapped, two-parent-working family is of course problematical. One often has to weigh what is optimal and what is possible, and try to find the best compromise. Since daycare is often the only means available to allow the mother to work, the most desirable feature that one should look for is the presence of a consistent and nurturing daycare worker who can provide the most one-on-one care for the infant. Because the most critical changes in brain maturation occur in the first months of life, the longer one can wait before introducing the surrogate caregiver, the better for the infant's development.

CHAPTER 6

The Spectrum of Societal Trauma: From Neglect to Violence

Our brains and bodies are designed to adapt and cope with a world that is full of danger. The concept of survival of the fittest implies that species are designed to prey on each other. All plant and animal species compete for territory with relentless and implacable purpose. Carnivores are common to most animal species and serve an essential purpose in the survival of their prey, culling the old and weak from the herd and preventing their eventual demise from overpopulation and starvation. In animal populations, the unrestricted relationship of predator and prey is necessary for their mutual survival.

In primitive man, the same relationship with other animals and other members of his species existed. The hunter/gatherer would move on when the population of prey had diminished through his hunting or through that of competing tribes. Territorial battles between tribes were common. Certainly they were exposed to forms of traumatic stress—from animal predators, intertribal warfare, illness, and severe injury. Life was brutal and short. Sources of trauma were also explicit, simple, and often overwhelming.

As the human species grew and expanded, tribe members congregated into increasingly large communities that ultimately evolved into defined and socially structured centers of population. Simple early tribal institutions, such as defense and raising and hunting for food, expanded into institutions such as religious practice, governance, laws and law enforcement, and the military. The concept of survival of the fittest continues to apply to present-day institutions within cultures, and survival is basically based on power. In the wild, power is wielded through physical strength and weapons of predation—the tooth and the claw. In institutions it is wielded through the weapons granted by the mantle of authority. At least part of the exercise of that authority is directed toward control of a particular behavior of the populace, whether pertaining to religious expression, the limits of the law, or the use of their own and the society's financial resources.

The concept of "control" in this sense intrinsically implies a reduction in options and a subtle movement away from empowerment and toward helplessness. Such controls, of course, are allegedly necessary for the orderly management of a given population and are of universal benefit to the welfare of that populace. A populace that has ceded control of its behavior, however, has also ceded some of the behavioral options necessary for what it (unconsciously) perceives to be survival. For example, governments of nations at war, especially those that are authoritarian, often disseminate messages of danger to the populace in order to unify and control that populace through instillation of fear. In this state of compromised control and relative helplessness, the seeds are sown for traumatization by little experiences that might appear to be trivial but for their unique meaning to the well-being of the individual—a meaning that is based on the person's cumulative life experiences. A case in point: The news and entertainment media has found through trial and error that the populace/audience tends to watch television shows that feature societal mayhem—scenes of battle on the news, graphic depictions of disfigured human bodies on crime shows, and bullets passing through bodies. By inducing traumatic recapitulation in an already traumatized populace, they improve their "ratings" and therefore their profits.

A spectrum of societal trauma exists, but it is invisible to the eye of the citizen because the sources of that trauma are accepted as "normal" and endorsed by their parent institution. As a society and its cultural norms evolve, increasing extremes of experience may be deemed benign or acceptable as intrinsic and important parts of cultural ritual, such as the carnage of the Roman games or the human sacrifice in ancient Aztec games and religious practices. The acceptance of these societal traumas occurs through a process of numbing on the part of the populace and a collective dissociation driven by the cumulative effects of little traumas.

The Trauma of Societal Rituals

It would also be hard to deny the fact that the two universal goals of attainment of power and money sometimes play a role in the process of societal control through the subtle application of little traumas. Because the needs of a society are a constantly changing affair, the shaping of beliefs by institutional leaders also needs to be fairly flexible. In a remarkable number of instances, fear and shame are the primary underlying emotions evoked in members to ensure their acceptance of cultural beliefs and rituals. Fear is the emotion produced by threat, and it is associated with the incipient fight/flight response, a function of the sympathetic nervous system. Shame is associated with blushing, a parasympathetic system response, and is the earliest infantile response to negative disapproval expressed in the mother's face. Shame can be considered to be the first expression of the freeze response. Institutional leaders often establish societal rituals and standards in societies through the subtle application of methods that incorporate exposure to traumatic stress, specifically fear and shame. This means of shaping a society has been a common practice for millennia in many various cultures, but its application has been greatly enhanced by the current technological explosion in techniques of instant communication. News travels fast, and bad news travels the fastest, because, after all, bad news is important for our survival. Why do we remain fixated on grisly murder trials, television shows based on crime and justice, and medical shows with graphic depiction of horrors inflicted on the human body? When a culture is shaped by its little traumas, we remain on the alert for messages of danger—and we unconsciously seek to recapitulate the trauma through daily experience.

Fear is instilled through societal rituals in many ways. Some religious institutions preach that pain, anguish, and misery in hell will occur after death if the tenets of the religion are not followed during life. As I discuss in depth in chapter 7, our current system of healthcare fosters a pervasive sense of fear through medical rituals and procedures that don't always benefit the patients subjected to them. The American insurance industry has achieved vast corporate success through advertising that emphasizes the threat of financial ruin from almost any imaginable negative life event. The plaintiff's bar in particular has fostered the success of the insurance industry by frightening virtually every service industry with horror tales of financial ruin from lawsuits for perceived negligence. Governments of all types have used the method of instilling fear in the general populace to justify wars, destruction of literature, pogroms and genocides, and the restriction of personal freedoms. In these cases, the pervasive nature of this fear may result in a frozen, dissociated society numb to the aggressive excesses of its leaders and pathologically bonded to them, just as the abused child is bonded to its abusing parent. The reign of the German Third Reich is the most recent and horrific example of the traumatization of a society—it used terror to "inspire" passionate loyalty to its leaders and blindness to their brutal excesses. Nazi Germany is an extreme case; subtler examples are more common. The United States government justified the invasion of Iraq by claiming it was a necessary means of combating terrorism, and this justification was backed by the fear-based rationale that the invasion would help deter further attacks on the homeland.

This definition of trauma falls far short of the DSM-IV criteria for an event sufficient to cause the syndrome of PTSD. Studies in PTSD, however, are beginning to document and recognize an increasing spectrum of life events that may be traumatizing based on their cultural meaning. They also are beginning to address a host of emotional responses and behaviors in trauma victims that are more pervasive and subtle than the symptom complex required to make the diagnosis of PTSD.

Jerome Kroll (2002) reviewed five articles in *The Journal of the American Medical Association* that studied trauma in a variety of social contexts. He noted that "the particular psychological reactions to trauma are influenced by cultural norms of how individuals are expected to respond to threat, injury, and loss" (Kroll, 2002, p. 667). Kroll documented the lack of association between the severity of the trauma and that of subsequent posttraumatic symptoms, as well as the fact that symptoms of depression rather than PTSD may predominate. The scientific literature on trauma is beginning to acknowledge the increasing complexity not only of what we define as traumatic stress, but also the physical and emotional symptoms and illnesses that may result from it. It is beginning to recognize that exposure to trauma is basically a universal experience, that trauma may constitute more subtle and culturally defined experiences, and that its effects on mental and physical health may be more insidious and pervasive than we currently acknowledge. When one takes a medical history from a patient whose clinical symptoms suggest a traumatic basis, one must consider the societal and culturally based rituals and experiences that may be contributing to the texture and meaning of that person's reservoir of life trauma.

Little Traumas

Traumatic experiences by the fetus and infant must be "little traumas": After all, they happen to little people. These little people, however, are the least resilient members of society. If neonatal separation for an hour in the rat pup can determine its autonomic vulnerability for life, 6 weeks of isolation in the preemie isolette must have a devastating effect on right orbitofrontal cortex development and therefore on lifelong autonomic stability. The experience of abandonment in the infant and young child must be overwhelming. Three of my four children managed to cut their foreheads at play when they were under the age of 4. On two of these occasions, when we arrived at the hospital, our child was separated from us, wrapped up in a sheet for purposes of immobilization, and sewn up in the emergency room. One child had night-mares of the hospital for months; the other still has the indelible memory of the nurse "sticking a needle into my brain." The third had her head sutured while she sat in my lap and was none the worse for the experience. The trauma in my first two children was more about the abandonment than the injury.

Abandonment and neglect occur in many subtle contexts in childhood. The emotional absence of the alcoholic parent has been noted as an ongoing source of trauma even in the absence of physical abuse. Our materialistic, work-oriented culture has made the chronic absence of family intimacy a societal norm. The disappearance of family congregation at breakfast and supper due to the 10-hour workday of the commuter employee has been accepted as the price of the cost of living. "Latchkey kids," who let themselves into the house at the end of the school day, fix themselves a snack, and then settle down with their video games until Mom or Dad gets home, are consid-ered normal. The placement of infants younger than a year in daycare centers where a single worker cares for a large group of infants clearly constitutes abandonment, but it is a necessary routine for the young family that cannot make ends meet on one income. As a culture, we have been sold the sublim-inal message that we deserve a standard of living and material possessions that demand dual incomes in a family. The result is a widespread abandonment of our children. The institution served by this message is the vast for-profit corporate structure.

Most American families live under a dark umbrella of personal debt. The nation has bought the concept that we can purchase everything from clothes to cars to houses on credit, and this has been a wildly successful means of controlling our behavior by encouraging us to enter into a state of helpless-ness over the control of our financial resources. The result is a mountain of personal debt, with the victims facing terror at the beginning of each month as they slip inexorably into bankruptcy. The perpetrators of this cultural trauma are the vast banking and financial institutions of our society.

The Spectrum of Societal Trauma

The mayhem on our highways has been mitigated somewhat by advances in car design and safety devices—the glaring exception, of course, being the behemoth of the highway, the sports utility vehicle. Horrific auto accidents are, naturally, universally accepted as a source of trauma. What we don't understand very well, however, are the intrinsic implications of driving a car and the threat that is implicit in that act. Maneuvering a 3-ton steel machine around at 35 miles per hour seems like a fairly benign undertaking until one is involved in their first auto accident. Even in a 10-mile-per-hour fender-bender, the noise, the smell, the sensation of violent and wrenching movement, and the sense of helplessness are enough to permanently and traumatically change one's perception of invulnerability in a car. The realization that one is *completely helpless* in that environment creates the ideal milieu for traumatization. Individuals who have experienced prior developmental trauma or other sources of major life trauma may be shattered by even a minor accident. Those who are more resilient may do well in the wake of their first MVA, but after a series of accidents (which is not uncommon) they may be severely traumatized by a trivial accident. In the long run, no one comes away totally free from trauma in a car accident.

If the accident victim is injured, another source of societal trauma comes into play. Our tripartite system of medical care is divided into general healthcare, care for the injured worker, and care for the MVA victim. In the latter two cases, the system is biased: suspicious of *secondary gain*, the benefits that one can achieve through a specific outcome, in this case validity of the injury. Because injury in the workplace and in car accidents has significant monetary implications in addition to treatment and healing, the goals of the patient are immediately suspect. The injured MVA victim must face a gauntlet of insurance company personnel whose sole focus is to ferret out the patients motivated by secondary gain. This creates an immediately adversarial relationship between the insurance company and the patient. If that patient's physical symptoms are amplified by the more unusual symptoms intrinsic to the trauma itself, they are even more suspect. Already traumatized by the accident, the patients are now compromised by their own healthcare providers, which expands the field of traumatic stress. Finally, the process of litigation that inevitably seems to accompany injuries suffered in car accidents provides another source of societal trauma. The tort system is intrinsically adversarial, and the process of independent medical examinations, discovery, deposition, and trial testimony can be quite traumatic to the car accident victim.

As a physician who served on a panel of specialists as an impartial arbiter regarding the claims of injured workers, I observed the cumulative opinions of my medical peers who treated these patients. The suspicious, often derisive tone of these physicians' reports left no doubt that they believed the injured workers' complaints were based on malingering and secondary gain. Even claims that I felt were totally justified were generally universally rejected and dismissed. All of these people's physical symptoms were amplified by the helplessness and trauma of their treatment within the system. Ironically, the institution creating this insidious source of trauma is the very healthcare system designed to ameliorate it.

Almost any social setting where control is lost and relative helplessness is part of the environment can easily progress to a traumatic experience. Perhaps the most obvious and pervasive source of this insidious societal trauma is in the workplace. The relationship between employee and superior is a fertile ground for insidious trauma and depends primarily on the good graces of the superior. Not surprisingly, the generous or mean nature of the superior may well be based on his or her own positive or negative childhood experiences. Women are more vulnerable to trauma: Roughly three quarters of PTSD victims are female. Excluding warfare, they are also more frequently exposed to it. Gender discrimination is a reality. However, whatever the gender, the abused employee is often helpless to change the circumstances of his or her employment, and when deliberate abuse occurs, it constitutes a life threat associated with the loss of income and health and retirement benefits. For example, one of my female patients was exposed to unreasonable performance demands by a male superior in a workplace known for its gender discrimination. On a trip to another city, she physically collapsed and was taken to the hospital. No cause for her illness was found, but subsequently she remained physically disabled by recurrent weakness to the point of collapse. Her response to sustained "little traumas" at her workplace was to freeze/dissociate in the face of helplessness in that environment.

These examples of trauma inherent to the structure and function of many cultural institutions are largely unrecognized and unappreciated by their victims. Many adults who grew up in pathologically dysfunctional family environments have no real appreciation of the fact that this experience was traumatic. After all, it was the only reality they knew. They have no concept that this experience has irrevocably changed their brains and behavior, created their personalities and preferences, influenced their choice of spouse and career, and rendered them increasingly vulnerable to further life threats and stresses. In the same manner, institutionally endorsed societal rituals that are intrinsically traumatizing eventually tend to be accepted as the lesser of a variety of alternative evils and are perceived as necessary to protect society from danger. Helplessness in the face of these insidious rituals and standards of behavior ultimately leads the society to accept them.

Violence and Society

Man is a violent creature. I need no references to statistics to make this assertion. One only needs to look at the newspaper, magazines, or television for any given 24 hour period in the past century to be convinced of the validity of this statement. Of course, warfare is violence at a national level, and war has been a unique behavioral practice of the human race since we banded together enough to form rudimentary communities or tribes. Wars on a national level have occurred for thousands of years, in all parts of the globe, throughout most nation states, and usually for reasons that seem to defy any rational justification. The territorial imperative may be invoked in many of these conflicts, but murderous crusades in foreign lands, apparently solely for the purpose of furthering the spread of monotheistic religions, certainly go beyond the territorial rationale.

War, however, is not the topic of this discussion, although the tendency of our species to wage war must reflect the prevalence for violence within societies. Almost without exclusion, wars are waged by males, and the overwhelming majority of societal violence is also committed by males. If we go back to the nature versus nurture dilemma, we might suggest that the chromosomal heritage of the male must dictate aggressive behavior and a tendency to provoke combat with other males, not to mention violence toward susceptible females. Matt Ridley (2003) maintained that this indeed is the case. Females possess two X chromosomes, males one X and one Y chromosome, and it is one tiny gene on the tip of the Y chromosome, called SRY, that is responsible for the very focused role of masculinizing the body of the male. This gene is switched on in the brain and in only one other body tissue, the testis, on the 11th day after conception. Ridley also noted that, after late adolescence (when the release of testosterone from the testis is initiated), the well-recognized tendency for males to die prematurely begins, and most of this mortality is due to violence—homicide, suicide, and accidents. Heart disease, a condition correlated in some studies with repressed rage, is the fourth most common cause of male deaths. So at the least, there is a genetic marker that contributes to a predisposing template that provides the potential for the male member of the human species to be prone to violent behavior. The fact that all males do not exhibit violent behavior during their life is quite in keeping with the concept of "switching on" the SRY gene through early childhood experience.

Van der Kolk (1989) noted numerous studies that relate male adult violent criminality to childhood physical and sexual abuse. We know that not all males exposed to personal violence in childhood go on to become violent themselves, but they do so far more often than females. Abused female children are more likely to dissociate, experience symptoms of PTSD, and demonstrate internalization of traumatic behavior. Bruce Perry (1995) provided a logical rationale for this gender-based dichotomy, in part based on the anthropological work of Leakey (1994). In primitive hominid tribes, raids were common between male members for the purpose of killing other males and abducting females and children. Males who were attacked were killed if they did not exhibit an aggressive response, whereas females who were abducted were more likely to survive if they adopted a more dissociative or helpless form of adaptive behavior. Their passivity in response to threat had a survival benefit: They were enslaved by the victorious tribe and allowed to transmit their genetic heritage to subsequent generations. The role of males in the tribe, however, demanded a capacity for violence. This tendency for females to freeze/dissociate in the face of a life threat may also explain in part the predominance of women with symptoms of PTSD and other syndromes of late trauma.

The Epidemiology of Violence in America

In her review of violence portrayed in popular entertainment in the United States, Sissela Bok (1998) noted that we have the highest levels of homicide of any advanced industrial democracy in the world. Other countries, specifically Russia, South Africa, and Columbia, lead the world in the frequency of homicide. In addition, the homicide rate in the United States has fluctuated rather dramatically over the decades; it fell by nearly half between the years of 1946 and 1962, and it more than doubled between the years of 1962 and 1991. After 1991 it again began a significant decline.

But homicide rates are not the only benchmark for societal violence. Violent treatment of our children arguably represents an even more meaningful measure of societal violence than homicide. James Prescott (2002) reviewed the Third National Incidence of Child Abuse and Neglect Executive Summary (NIS-3) from 1986 through 1993. This report addresses levels of childhood endangerment as well as the number of children who were subjected to risk of maltreatment and actual injury. Between 1986 and 1993, the number of children endangered rose from 254,000 to 1,032,000—an increase of 306%. The number of children actually injured increased 298%, from 143,000 to 569,900. The number of children who were sexually abused (girls three times more frequently than boys) rose from 119,200 to 217,700, an increase of 125%. Studies of causes of death due to injuries in infants suggest that infantile homicide is the most common cause, accounting for almost one-third of such deaths (Overpeck et al., 1998). Violence toward our children and infants has especially grim implications for societal health. One might expect that these disturbing statistics would have equally disturbing implications for the mental health and social behavior of our adolescents and young adults. Suicide and depression might be considered to be fairly representative measures of mental health in segments of society. Prescott noted that suicide in the 15- to 24-year age range was the third most common cause of death between 1979 and 1993, and the sixth most common cause in ages 5–14. Suicide in the 5–14 age range jumped from 0.4 to 0.8 per 100,000 during the same time period. Comparable, and sometimes more dramatic, suicide statistics are noted in other Western countries.

Statistics documenting the use of psychotropic medications during the past decade also reflect the dramatic increase of use of drugs, primarily stimulants (Ritalin, Adderal) for attention-deficit hyperactivity disorder (ADHD) in the 5–14 age group and antidepressants (particularly the serotonin reuptake inhibitors) in the 14–19 age range. More recently, studies have shown a trend for increased use of these classes of drugs even in preschoolers (Prescott, 2003). These statistics may represent a significant increase in depression and ADHD in our young children during the past 10–15 years, a finding that may correlate with other measures of societal distress noted earlier, including abandonment and neglect as infants. They may also represent the current insidious marketing of prescription drugs by the pharmaceutical industry in a manner that instills fear of disease as well as entitlement to perfect, pain-free health. Finally, childhood depression in some cases may be related to the unreasonable expectations of excellence and demands for unattainable levels of performance by parents who themselves were never nurtured or rewarded as children.

Why do we seem to be hurting our children more, and why are our children showing increasing signs of deep emotional upset? Epidemiological studies are always subject to sources of error that can skew their findings in any number of directions. The more intensely that one studies behavioral trends, the more abnormalities one may find. The increased use of pharmaceuticals in any condition or population may be more due to marketing than to the increased incidence of a disease. I would maintain that the best way to address these findings is to identify core causes of abnormal behavior and emotional distress.

Cross-Cultural Studies

If one accepts a Darwinian theoretical approach, the male tendency for violence doesn't make much sense if it leads to premature death. Surely there must be a better way of getting through life than killing and therefore being prematurely killed. The study of the social behavior of indigenous tribes suggests that violent behavior may be unique to specific tribes, especially those with hunter-gatherer traits (Ridley, 2003). In some Amazon tribes, the death rate by homicide in males exceeds 50%. In other tribes, the number of sexual partners that a male member is able to attract is proportional to the number of men that he has killed—the more violent the male, the more women he is able to impregnate, and the more genes he is able to pass on (Chagnon, 1992).

Despite increasing the likelihood of early death, does the skill of killing attract the sexual interests of females in the tribe? Certainly it may be a measure of power within the tribe, and power may well be a universal aphrodisiac, just as the length of the tail of a male peacock may facilitate the number of hens that he impregnates. So violent males are able to beget more violent males. Violence exhibited by the male members of such tribes may therefore represent a measure of *sexual selection*, a means of guaranteeing that violent, homicidal behavior is passed on through subsequent generations. As presented in this scenario, then, violent behavior in the human species is genetically designed to ensure the reproduction of the fittest members of the species at the expense of long-term survival of the violent males (Ridley, 2003). Perhaps this correlates with insect behavior, where the female black widow spider consumes the male after copulation, or where the male honeybee drones' sole purpose in their short lifespan is to impregnate the queen. Premature death may be the price of sexual selection.

As with every other example, however, it's never that simple. Many indigenous tribes are remarkably peaceful and nonviolent, with virtually no waging of tribal wars and negligible crime and homicide within the tribe.

Could it be that the male members of these tribes have developed a mutated SRY gene by virtue of their environmental isolation that has less of a masculinizing effect and therefore does not equate the trait of violent behavior with power and sexual attractiveness? Theoretically, this could be the case, but again, the assumption is too simplistic. Prescott (2002) reviewed a number of studies in different indigenous societies that tried to assess reasons for the prevalence of violence within them. These studies evaluated a number of cultural characteristics of these societies, most specifically their childrearing practices. Throughout multiple analyses of tribal behavior, utilizing the data resources of Textor (1967), Prescott presented compelling evidence for the relationship between violence in a society and the relative absence of nurturing behavior as part of its childrearing practices.

For example, mothers in many indigenous societies carry their young children in slings or packs on their backs as they attend to their daily tasks, including tending to crops, walking from village to village, preparing food, and the like. This behavior correlates with other forms of high physical affection between mother and infant, including breastfeeding beyond 2.5 years of age. Conversely, torture, mutilation, and killing of enemy tribesmen captured in warfare is felt to be a particularly potent measure of violent tribal behavior. Using the data from Textor (1967), Prescott (2002) showed that carrying of infants by a tribe's mothers correlated highly with high infant indulgence, low child anxiety, low theft, and virtually absent torture, mutilation, and killing of tribal captives. High infant physical affection, including carrying the baby and nursing over 2.5 years, also correlated with a low suicide rate within the tribe. Interestingly, tribal characteristics that correlated with high violence included male dominance, punishment of adolescent premarital sexual activity, and belief in an aggressive/violent god.

Making assumptions about the relationships of cause and effect in this type of data analysis is obviously risky. Perhaps breastfeeding and carrying infants is a common genetically based feature of maternal, pacific societies rather than a cause of this type of societal behavior. *Low* physical affection of infants, *ignoring* of infant pain, *lack* of touch and carrying, and *brief* breastfeeding, the opposite societal behavioral traits to those associated with a pacific society, not surprisingly tend to be seen in tribes with greater measures of violence. Is this coincidental or due to different genetic dispositions within these societies? Or do high levels of infant nurturing and maternal/infant bonding simply *mitigate* the expression of the universal genetic propensity for violence in males?

Providing the proper nutrients for brain development may influence the expression of a gene. Prescott (2002) made the case for the roles of tryptophan and serotonin, important chemicals found in high amounts in breast milk but not in infant formula, as important determinants of brain development. Tryptophan is a precursor, or required element, for the formation of dopamine, an important neurotransmitter in the brain. Dopamine mediates pleasure and maternal/infant bonding. Its lack is associated with drug addictive behavior and a variety of emotional and behavioral disorders. Tryptophan also is a precursor for serotonin, a brain neurotransmitter that promotes calming, intensity of social interaction and maternal/infant bonding. Lack of brain serotonin may be associated with depression, aggressive behavior, impulsivity, and impaired social relations. Prolonged breastfeeding may therefore have a specific effect on brain development by promoting the formation of critical neurotransmitters that may mitigate the propensity for violence associated with the SRY gene.

As I have noted, tribes that are characterized by aggressive and warlike behavior tend to be associated with more punitive and less nurturing practices of early infant rearing. I believe that it is reasonably apparent now that this variation in tribal societal behavior is not primarily related to differences in tribal social instincts. Given the vast differences in environments in which various tribes live, one could well imagine that warlike behavior might provide an advantage for survival in some instances. For example, an island environment containing several competing tribes, some agrarian and others hunter-gatherers, might well lead to territorial competition that would enhance the survival value of aggression toward competing tribes. Under these circumstances, the leaders of the aggressive tribe would probably soon discover that restrictions placed on the nurturing behaviors of mothers tended to produce male children and adults who manifested higher levels of aggression and were more prone to violence. These "negative" behavioral features could have positive consequences for the survival of that tribe. By fostering adult aggression, relative deprivation of infant nurturing would predispose deprived male infants to become effective warriors, and would enhance the strength and success of the tribe in defending and expanding its territory. The warlike nation of Sparta in ancient Greece epitomized these methods of creating a warrior nation through the practice of self-deprivation beginning in childhood. The leaders of societal institutions tend to be the shapers of beliefs, rituals, standards of behavior, morality and ethics, cultural tastes, and all of the other subtle benchmarks of behavior that form the weave and texture of a society. These benchmarks tend to be established based on the needs of the leaders, who may be both self-serving and altruistic. Manipulating childrearing practices in order to shape adult behavior for the perceived benefit of a society is an example of the endorsement of standards of societal behavior by its leaders in order to meet their needs for power and control, in this case the creation of warriors.

In referring to studies of indigenous societies I by no means am attempting to glorify the status of primitive societies as the "noble savage." Violence in indigenous societies is as varied and disparate as it is within other social groups. Perhaps such studies are particularly useful because isolated societies present a "purer" distillation of behavioral trends, divorced from the intrusive influence of a world that is enhanced (or contaminated) by widespread and rapid means of communication. At any rate, I would maintain that such studies remain a valuable window through which we can observe the roots of our own behavior. After all, we are all one species.

Lessons from Primates

Just as we can learn a great deal about the implications of human behavioral habits from the licking/grooming behavior of rats, we can also learn more about human behavior from our closest species relatives. Not only can we observe them in their natural state in the wild, but we can also expose them to varying environments in the laboratory. Predictably, the anthropological approach of observing unimpeded animal social behavior in their natural habitat should give us a picture of their instinctual—and therefore genetic—behavioral heritage. The shaping of their behavior by an alien laboratory environment provides a means of studying the varieties and subtleties of life experience and their effects on behavior. The shortcomings of both of these approaches are probably obvious, but the results are still worth exploring.

The earliest and most compelling studies of primate behavior in the wild are probably those of Jane Goodall (1990), who studied the common chimpanzee (*Pan troglodyte*) in Gombe, Africa, beginning in 1960. Goodall's perhaps most important findings had to do with the remarkable complexity of the social behavior of chimpanzees, their ability to fashion and use tools from basic environmental materials, and their ability to teach their offspring acquired skills. Interestingly, Goodall was also able to document that chimpanzees are inherently homicidal. The male members of the troops that she lived with would periodically raid the territories of other troops in the regions, do battle with the males, and usually kill them of they were victorious. Perhaps warfare and selective male violence is not unique to the human species.

The bonobo, or pygmy, chimpanzee (*Pan paniscus*), however, presents an entirely different social and behavioral model. Prescott (2002) reviewed the social behavior of the bonobo in detail, and the differences between them and the common chimpanzee are striking. Bonobos are part of a basically matriarchal society; the females of the troop bond strongly with each other and the male -members exhibit passive and generally nonviolent behavior. Male warfare between adjacent troops is almost nonexistent. Female bonobos bond strongly with their infants, carrying them until about 1.5 years of age. Infanticide by males, common among gorillas and other apes, is virtually absent among bonobos. Like humans, female bonobos do not experience the estrus cycle and remain sexually active at any time. As a result, female bonobos copulate freely with other males throughout the troop. One might speculate that this expression of sexuality itself might contribute to the harmony between the sexes in this species, as well as account for the absence of warlike instincts in bonobo males. In other words, bonobos appear to make love, not war.

Can these dramatic differences in what appears to be innate societal propensity for violence both in humans and primates lead us to any useful conclusions regarding human societal violence? Differing human tribes are born with the same genetic template that may be altered and shaped by experience. It would not be surprising that behavior of a tribe that is isolated from outside influence would be perpetuated by the commonality of generational tribal experience, associated with gene transcription secondary to that experience. Cultural isolation would probably perpetuate specific genes and their expression. We know that the introduction of alien cultures to isolated indigenous tribes rapidly contaminates behavioral traits that have persisted for generations, even without intermarriage and the introduction of new genes. After only one generation of contact with the outside world, some Amazon tribes now routinely wear Western-style clothes and use firearms for hunting as opposed to blow darts and curare. New Guinea headhunters have given up intertribal homicide and cannibalism within a generation of exposure to a more Western culture.

The more radically different genetic templates between species, however, suggest that societal behavior is more hardwired and resistant to change induced by altering the environment: One cannot elicit bonobo behavior in a common chimpanzee by placing it in a bonobo family. It is clear that certain aspects of a tendency toward violence are genetic and instinctual. Nevertheless, is experience a sufficient stimulus to instill violence in the absence of such a genetic trait? Can we blame human violence on our genetic heritage, or might it be specifically the product of early childhood experience? Finally, can we temper the genetic expression of violence through higher levels of infant nurturing? To even attempt to answer such questions, we must continue to use all techniques at our disposal, both in the native environment of a variety of mammalian species, as well as in the laboratory.

Lessons from the Laboratory

Harry Harlow (1958) performed some of the first laboratory experiments on primates, studying the effects of varying degrees of absence of maternal contact on infant behavioral development. These studies involved raising infant rhesus monkeys in a variety of states of isolation, including sensory isolation in a darkened pit for long periods, as well as raising infants with a mother figure made out of a wire cage and with a figure made of padded cloth. All of these levels of maternal deprivation were associated with dramatic abnormalities of social behavior as the monkeys matured, including depression, compulsive rocking, head banging and self-mutilation, and pathological violence. Abnormal sexual activity was also noted. Most monkeys exhibited severe sensitivity to touch, responding violently to the approach of other monkeys, especially if touched. These violent and abnormal behaviors persisted through life, despite efforts to reintroduce them into rhesus society. Interestingly, the severity of this social deprivation syndrome was somewhat reduced in monkeys reared with the surrogate mothers made of padded cloth. These infants routinely clung to these maternal figures throughout their childhood, suggesting that the sensory experience afforded by a surrogate that *felt* somewhat like a natural mother played an important role in the process of nurturing.

Mason and Berkson (1975) extended this research by providing isolated infant monkeys with a padded surrogate mother that moved in a rhythmical pattern through a series of ropes and pulleys. They found that maternal deprivation syndrome diminished even more significantly with this addition of movement that produced vestibular-cerebellar stimulation. The vestibular system connects to balance centers in the middle and inner ears and helps control balance and movement through our relationship with gravity. The cerebellum also is related to control of balance and coordination, but additionally has links to memory and emotional control. The compulsive rocking universally seen in the severely deprived monkeys clearly represents an attempt at vestibular and cerebellar self-stimulation, an experience that seems to be necessary for normal infant brain development. The need for and usefulness of such movement stimulation are certainly reflected in routine practices of infant care. Rocking chairs and baby rockers to calm the infant are taken for granted and have been used for centuries. Movement intrinsically calms infants, perhaps through cerebellar stimulation. It also probably is necessary for normal cognitive and emotional development in the brain of the infant.

Prescott (2002) again reviewed the literature on brain development in the absence of such stimulation, and he documented strong evidence that development of critical areas of the brain, particularly the cerebral cortex and cerebellum, is significantly impaired without such sensory stimulation as part of infant rearing. He defines a somatosensory affectional deprivation syndrome (S-SAD) resulting from lack of body touch and body movement sensory stimulation in the developing infant. This syndrome is defined by the experimental studies in primates noted above, but it also applies specifically to human infants reared in an environment lacking adequate somatosensory stimulation. The clinical features of this syndrome in both the primate laboratory and in human society include depression, impulsivity, sexual dysfunction, and violence. In humans, excessive alcohol consumption and drug use are also frequent in somatosensory deprivation.

These particular behaviors are, as noted earlier, associated with impaired functions in the neurotransmitter systems involving dopamine and serotonin. Like tryptophan, 5-hydroxyindoleacetic acid (5-HIAA) is another precursor of serotonin, and the level of 5-HIAA in spinal fluid is a useful measure of brain serotonin activity. Prescott (2002) noted several recent studies that document low levels of 5-HIAA in the spinal fluid of primates with the S-SAD syndrome, as well as the spinal fluid of children with behavioral traits of hostility toward parents, aggressive behavior, and cruelty to animals. It appears that tactile and movement stimulation of the infant facilitates the functions of brain neurotransmitters that are calming and promote optimal mood and effective bonding and social behavior.

Societal Implications

So we now have come full circle in exploring the fact that the early life experience of the infant defines later adult social behavior, that specific types of experience (somatosensory stimulation) are critical for development of normal behavior, that brain chemicals (dopamine and serotonin) may contribute to this process of normal brain development, and that obtaining these brain chemicals may be achieved by administering a readily available product (breast milk) to the infant. As we are beginning to see, the neurophysiological process involved in bonding and attachment involves specific exposure of the infant to sensory stimulation, and it is mediated by chemicals that are available in the environment and directly affect brain development. All of these factors may affect adult behavior and the degree of violence in a society.

Somatosensory stimulation may be best provided by the practice of carrying the infant wherever the mother goes and by the act of nursing. These maternal behaviors in the tribal mother may be rooted in genetic instinct, but they also may have evolved simply as a means of childcare that allows the mother to continue to pursue activities that are essential to her family and to the tribe. As evidenced by Harlow's (1958) monkeys mothered by cloth surrogates, simple body-to-body contact of mother and infant clearly promotes the brain development that leads to more normal social behavior as an adult. Marsupial mammals have the advantage of a natural maternal pouch in which to accomplish this process, hence the current concept in mothering circles of "kangaroo mother care." Charpak et. al (2001) exposed premature infants to "skin-to-skin" holding and contact with exclusive breastfeeding by the mother for the first 3 months of life, and found remarkably better measures of development and maturity in these infants at a year of age compared to preemies that received standard neonatal ICU care. Primate mothers in most species carry the infant and nurse on demand throughout their early childhood. I would suggest that this very simple behavioral trait is genetically hardwired and provides part of the universal template for fostering optimal adult mammal behavior across the species. The process of acculturation, with the institution of societal rituals and demands on the mother, has suppressed this universal maternal trait in more "advanced" societies. The result appears to be a heritage of impaired social behavior characterized by impulsivity, hostility, aggression, drug use, aberrant sexual behavior, and violence in childhood and ultimately in adulthood. The roots of societal violence therefore probably lie to a significant extent in: (1) the genetic heritage of the male members of the species, and (2) the molding of that genetic heritage through suppression of practices of childrearing that promote optimal infant brain development.

Of course, the modern, acculturated mother is no more to blame for this process than is the low-licking/grooming rat dam who was raised by a similar low-nurturing mother. Genes are transcribed and switched on by experience, and behavior is determined by exposure to intense cultural norms of behavior as much as it is by the original genetically based instinct. The habits and rituals of a modern urban society are probably more powerful than the impetus provided by much of our genetic endowment, as evidenced by our ability to rapidly change our preferences in food, dress, jobs, cars, and entertainment, to mention only a few examples.

Violence in Entertainment

Our current exposure to increasingly graphic and extreme images of violence in our popular entertainment media is a topic of great concern to many people and a dilemma for which we have found few solutions. The dilemma, however, brings up numerous questions. Does the exposure to scenes of gratuitous and vivid physical violence influence our young children to commit violence themselves? Is exposure to such stimulation a source of vicarious trauma—one of those subtle traumatic experiences that are endorsed by our culture? Despite protest from certain sectors, we have embraced violence-as-entertainment as a desired and valued (at least financially) societal norm. Is this trend yet another measure of our increasingly "sick" and degenerate society, or is it simply another manifestation of our basic instinct for violence as a species? Finally, are we so traumatized as a society that we are drawn to images of violence as part of traumatic recapitulation?

As a society, we certainly have tried to answer these questions. Numerous scientific studies have attempted to correlate increasing violence in entertainment with behavioral trends in our society. They have attempted to identify causes for the almost universal popularity of violent entertainment, as well as identify undesirable societal behavior that may be resulting from it. Answers to these questions are clear in some cases and uncertain in others. I will not try to document the statistical bases for these answers but rather summarize what we know and don't know about the causes and effects of violence in entertainment.

When one approaches this topic, one must understand that the derivation of pleasure from the vicarious experience of violence goes back to the origins of recorded human history. Bok (1998) provided a detailed and engrossing history of perhaps the most graphic, well documented, and prolonged experiment with violence-as-entertainment in human history: the Roman "games" from 264 B.C. to 483 A.D. Of course, the Roman games were not filmed or computerized "make believe," as are contemporary video games, television shows, and movies. They were the "real thing"—the intentional and violent death of human beings and animals at each other's hands or claws. Slaves and prisoners were "thrown to the beasts" and slaughtered; warrior slaves, known as gladiators, were set upon each other or wild animals, armed with a variety of lethal weapons. The games of the gladiators ended with the victory of the blood-soaked "last man standing." Roman society endorsed the system that supported the games with gambling, feasting, and the sponsoring of favorite gladiators. The universal response to the overwhelming cruelty, suffering, and bloodshed that characterized the entire experience of the games was pleasure—not disgust, horror, or revulsion.

It comes as no surprise that the society that endorsed this ritualistic violent entertainment was brutal, autocratic, and militaristic. This "culture of violence" permeated daily life and customs. It affected the treatment of its infants, its children, its slaves, and its underclass of "noncitizens," to whom it subjected the infamous practice of crucifixion as a means of torture/execution. In this climate, any criticism or debate about the excesses of the games was impossible and probably punishable by imprisonment or death. During their most popular period, the games represented a large part of everyday conversation, and the populace seemed immune to the concepts of basic inhumanity or cruelty in their favorite pastime. Eventually, however, distaste and revulsion surfaced, leading to the decline in popularity and ultimate abandonment of the games in the 5th century.

Do the Roman games have any corollary in 21st-century Western society's entertainment? The pleasure that the Roman audience experienced when viewing of graphic violence and slaughter may well represent the extreme of an instinct that we still express two millennia hence. In the interim, we have experienced public ceremonies of the burning of witches and heretics in the Inquisition, the beheading of traitors on the guillotine in the public square during the French revolution, and the public hanging of criminals in the American frontier, to mention a few examples of popular forms of capital punishment that generated public excitement. Our current Western sports of boxing, American football, and wrestling may represent vestiges of such public brutality as pleasure, although televised wrestling probably falls more into the category of video games. And even though we have substituted violent images for reality, we continue to derive real pleasure from the experience of violent entertainment.

In many cases, violence in entertainment media incorporates plotlines where an obvious protagonist avenges a criminal perpetrator. As such, it appeals to the possibly overdeveloped Western obsession with justice and vengeance. Violence as vengeance also tempers the sense of helplessness and horror that may accompany "senseless" violence and may provide a different source of pleasure, the sense of justice completed. The many forms of lethal blood-letting inflicted on the bevy of villains in the *Rambo* movie series carried a significantly diminished shock value compared to the gratuitous violence and bloodshed graphically presented in Quentin Tarantino's *Pulp Fiction*. One can perhaps justify the violence in *Rambo* as a form of catharsis, a release of anxiety through acting out fear, rage, or vengeance in imagination. However, as Bok (1998) noted, most media scholars dismiss the notion of violence's having cathartic value for children, adolescents, or adults who admit to experiencing aggressive thoughts in the context of such forms of entertainment. So what negative effects resulting from exposure to violence-as-entertainment can we identify with reasonable certainty?

Jeffrey Goldstein (1998), editor of *Why We Watch*, noted that every study in every nation shows that boys are far more attracted to violent entertainment than girls. Not surprisingly, more aggressive boys are also more drawn to violent sports and entertainment. This especially applies to groups of males, incorporating concepts of bonding, rites of passage, and associated group aggression, as in youth gangs.

Bok (1998) noted that, based on available statistics, there is absolutely no doubt that high levels of viewing television violence correlate specifically with acceptance of violent behavior and increased aggressiveness. Viewing of violence at an early age in children predisposes them to increased aggressiveness, both short- and long-term, including subsequent serious violent behavior and spousal abuse. Viewing violence begets violence.

Viewing violence also increases fear. Fear may be induced more by news coverage of real societal violence and crime than by fictional violence, however graphic, although both forms may enhance a sense of helplessness and victimization. The graphic and repetitive coverage of the 9/11 World Trade Center terrorist attacks clearly created a climate of national fear, insecurity, suspicion, and mistrust that has lead to a host of emotional and physical symptoms, not only in people who witnessed the scene but also to the larger television audience across the globe.

Both enhancement and suppression of sensation may be the goal and effect of high exposure to entertainment violence. High-sensation seekers like horror movies more than low-sensation seekers. One might venture to say that such individuals may be analogous to general risk takers who crave traumatic recapitulation and completion. If so, the amount of pleasure an individual experiences with exposure to media violence would reflect a significant past history of trauma.

The flip side of sensation seeking in exposure to violent images is the process of desensitization. Bok (1998) described what appears to be the development of immunity to shock and horror after viewing vast amounts of violent entertainment material. She noted that some movie and drama critics seem to develop such an immunity to shock with such exposure. The same phenomenon in children may present as loss of empathy, or the ability to identify with the suffering of others. Bok called this a state of "numbing" and raised the issue of chronic dissociation as a response to exposure to entertainment violence, especially in children and victims of prior life trauma. Endorphinergic reward in these cases may explain the popularity of television violence, while simultaneously suggesting that people who derive pleasure from violent entertainment do so on the basis of traumatic reenactment.

Grossman (1994) notes that in all wars prior to Vietnam there had always been a remarkably low rate of firing to hit a target and a high rate of purposely firing *over* the heads of the enemy. Firearms training by the armed forces prior to Vietnam had routinely consisted of target practice. In the United States, training for Vietnam and other wars began to incorporate the use of pop-up targets depicting actual soldiers in camouflage, experienced in a mock combat environment. The result was the effective use of conditioning to develop instant and reflexive firing at the enemy, which effectively and dramatically raised the incidence of lethal firing. In the process, remarkable desensitization occurred, similar to that which occurs in repeated exposure to media violence. Desensitization, however, offers no protection from traumatization, and indeed, the incidence of PTSD in Vietnam veterans may well have its roots in part in the guilt of doing the unthinkable— killing of another human being.

Goldstein (1998) noted that media experts believe that violence on television may also serve as a means of social control. Nursery rhymes, many of them written in the 19th century, are often remarkably graphic and violent. The plotlines of many children's fables and fairy tales include threats of violence for minor misbehavior. Many children's poems were written with the same goal of social control of children's behavior. Goldstein also noted that the watching of media violence may be a means of expressing emotions that might otherwise be suppressed, leading to pleasure and excitement. He supported this contention by calling attention to the fact that in theaters showing horror films, the audience usually is quite verbal in expressing disgust and excitement during the presentation. Because violence in movies is often more graphic and intense than what can be seen in real life, pleasure may primarily be based on the universal appeal of fantasy. The line between excitement, fear, and terror, however, can be quite blurred, and the same images may produce excitement in one person and terror in another.

So what meaning does our society attribute to the violence we experience vicariously through our entertainment industry? Clearly the phenomenon is driven by the male members of our society, especially those who already possess aggressive behavioral tendencies. It may, in fact, be "addictive"—based the real satisfaction that is experienced with exposure to certain sensations—and it may mimic risk-taking behavior as a means of trauma reenactment. It also may lead to an increase in aggressive behavior to the point of criminal violence in some males who are exposed to it. It also can lead to fear and a sense of loss of safety in some individuals. But is it yet another example of culturally endorsed trauma?

The answer to this question in the end must be based on relatively informed speculation. We have presented evidence that the commission of violence by male members of our species has at least a partly instinctive, genetic basis. The expression of that genetic behavioral substrate clearly is affected by the nature of the nurturing of the male infant within the context of the social/cultural standards of its tribe, society, or nation. A warlike, violent culture will foster the development of warlike violent males within that culture, enhancing the pleasure they experience from violent life experiences, including the waging of war, violent social behaviors, and violence in entertainment. Violence begets violence, as well as the pleasure derived from it. Violent entertainment both reflects our culture and, to a lesser extent, perpetuates violence.

As I have noted, violence directed toward male children in the form of abuse is reflected in their violent behavior as adults. As such, our warlike behavior and our taste for violent entertainment are both direct manifestations of male childhood trauma. Thus, our lust for viewing violent fictitious images may indeed constitute a "compulsion to repeat the trauma," as defined by van der Kolk (1989). And as in the whole cycle of traumatic recapitulation, reexposure to the trauma heightens its negative effects on brain structure and function and increases the likelihood of its reexpression. The "pleasure" that we paradoxically achieve through this type of vicarious exposure to violence is probably mediated by the same endorphins that we savor with risk taking, extreme sports, and self-mutilation.

The decline and death of the Roman games occurred at a time when the Roman Empire began its centuries-long decline and fall. It had achieved its truly remarkable level of influence and power at the expense of the human spirit. Great city-states in general have been built by warrior cultures that by definition must inflict societal trauma as a means of establishing social control, a prerequisite for governance. If so, the popularity of violence in entertainment may be not only a byproduct but also a symptom of that society's traumatic cultural base. It also may be a symptom of its ultimate demise.

The Cultural Cage

We have traced the tortuous path of the spectrum of societal trauma from its subtlest of beginnings in the lack of touch and movement stimulation in the newborn infant to the violence of entertainment, crime, and war. Neglect and subtle abandonment of the child, standard medical procedures, gender and job discrimination, the use of images and violence in the news and entertainment media—these are but a few examples of often insidious but also often purposeful fostering of sources of trauma in a society by its institutions. Some might take issue with this concept of a seemingly "grand conspiracy." I would maintain that this societal behavior has been evident throughout the history of mankind, as long as groups of people have banded together to form a critical social mass. Social control through the establishment of institutions is necessary to prevent chaos and to protect the well-being of its citizens. But that control is inevitably corrupted in the process, leading to the subtle spectrum of societal norms that create helplessness in the face of everyday conflicts. The result is the inevitable traumatization of members of the society through "little traumas."

I have noted that the freeze/dissociation response and its discharge are the core prerequisites for an experience to be traumatizing. I have also noted that animals in captivity are generally unable to initiate the freeze discharge, a trait that is also shared by humans. Entrapment and helplessness are the key elements in this equation—the metal cage in animals and the cultural cage in humans. It may not be that it is "unseemly" for humans to relinquish control to the instinctual but messy behavior of freeze discharge. It may also be that discharge simply does not occur in humans because they are in a continuous state of helplessness due to their entrapment by the little traumas inherent in an organized society.

CHAPTER 7

The Trauma of Illness and Its Treatment

Being diagnosed with a life-threatening illness is acknowledged by the DSM-IV to be an experience that may be sufficient to cause PTSD (American Psychiatric Association, 1994). Other related events also must be considered, including the diagnostic tests that were performed before and after the rendering of that diagnosis, the exposure to the hospital environment that was associated with the testing and subsequent treatment, the experience of the treatment itself, including pain, side effects, and surgery, and the loss of control and decline in quality of life that the illness creates. Relatively few scientific studies have explored the relationship between PTSD and exposure to life-threatening illness. Not surprisingly, dramatic medical illnesses and events such as heart disease with coronary artery bypass graft surgery (CABG), treatment for breast cancer, and awakening under anesthesia are associated with moderately high incidences of PTSD based on DSM-IV criteria. More often, however, late symptoms that might be attributable to illness and surgery occur, including depression, insomnia, persistent pain, and a variety of seemingly unrelated physical symptoms and complaints. Such complaints are invariably attributed to the patient's normal response to illness or to an underlying neurosis, rather than specifically to the physiological changes associated with trauma.

As I have already said, the spectrum of posttraumatic symptoms goes far beyond the rigid criteria of the DSM-IV, and these somatic symptoms are red flags for the occurrence of a past traumatic experience. The acknowledgment by the medical profession that circumcision might be traumatic to an infant was based solely on the increased pain sensitivity demonstrated by circumcised boys in response to subsequent immunization shots (Taddio et al., 1995). This finding indicates that trauma may manifest itself through more subtle, delayed somatic symptoms. The major studies that have linked the occurrence of PTSD with the major illnesses just noted have attributed the trauma to the intrinsic life-threatening implications of the disease itself. No one, however, has attempted to study the nature of the medical experience alone as a source of trauma. Some patients after relatively minor surgery and illness develop late somatic symptoms of trauma—chronic pain, depression, sleep disturbance. This suggests that the experience implicit in the treatment process may have been a source of trauma. In order to adequately address trauma in the medical experience, we need to try to separate the intrinsic trauma related to the life-threatening implications of the illness from the trauma that may have been induced by the "care" provided for the patient—the whole experience of diagnosis and treatment.

An Abbreviated Autobiographical Account of the Making of a Doctor

In order to make sense of the therapeutic environment in clinical medicine that has evolved over the last half of the 20th century, one must understand how doctors are created and what they are taught to think and to feel. Practicing medicine is endlessly fascinating, seldom boring, inherently stressful, and not infrequently frightening. It may be tremendously demanding, frustrating, and exhausting. The demands of the profession cause the breakup of many marriages and can destroy the relationships between physicians and their children. Constantly dealing with people in distress or crisis requires physicians to distance themselves from the illness, unfortunately often at the expense of distancing themselves from the patient. Empathy can be incredibly difficult to acquire and maintain. Physician's incomes are among the highest of all professions, but the demands also are among the highest. The greatest and most difficult of these demands may be to deal effectively on an interpersonal level with patients, many of whom are in great distress.

When I entered medical school, I believed that at last I was entering the really critical part of my long training. Instead, I instantly became immersed in the mind-boggling volume of names, terms, facts, and images that a first-year medical student must memorize and be able to regurgitate on command. All of these endless and arcane facts were taught in a vacuum, generally with no application to the ultimate skills that we were expected to attain, which primarily were diagnosing and treating diseases.

We participated in lectures and labs 8 hours a day and studied in the evening for 6. Competition was fierce, and so were we. We became irreverent, cynical, and sarcastic, making fun of the quirks of the professors who held our fates in an iron grip, while simultaneously respecting and fearing them. Although we frequently questioned the actual importance of the vast volume of data we were accumulating, we were terrified of failure, because if we didn't know *everything*, the next test might consist of the very subject that we had neglected. The preclinical years were just the first of many rites of passage and the start of an education that had many of the features of boot camp, hazing, and even brainwashing.

I had the unique benefit of attending a medical school that was the first to introduce a biopsychosocial model of medical education in the years of actual clinical training, the third and fourth years of medical school. Led by one of the nation's first psychosomaticists, Dr. George Engel, my clinical training started with learning to do a clinical history and physical exam with a patient-oriented history. The patient was encouraged to tell his whole story without interruption, down to the minutest detail. We were taught that the story of the illness would provide us with more vital information than any diagnostic test. Of course, at that time we had none of the sophisticated scanning and imaging techniques that we do now. I also know that anything like this approach has largely been lost in the face of pressures of cost containment, managed care, and the idea that we literally cannot afford to spend this kind of time with patients. Patient interviews are increasingly being relegated to computerized data entry points, symptom checklists, and automated patient histories into which names, words, and phrases are inserted.

The intense demands on us in terms of time and the pressure to perform at the highest level persisted through the clinical years. We were taught that medicine was a sacred profession, that personal sacrifice was expected, and that our calling took precedence over all other functions in our lives. Spouses and families must be aware of this. Although the financial reward would be substantial, the hours would be long and the stress great. Practicing medicine was not for the weak of heart. Presumably in an effort to convince us of this, the faculty saw to it that the clinical training years were associated with endless hours in the hospital, little sleep, and almost no recreation. We "learned" the laboratory sciences by performing blood counts, bacterial microscopic exams, and urinalyses on our patients—work that saved the hospital countless dollars and was called "scut work."

These demands became even more intense during internship and residency training. I was fulfilling a time-honored tradition of self-sacrifice that each generation of doctors demanded of the group of young interns following them. The slow and tedious climb up the ladder of respectability in medical training reflects the hierarchical structure of other male-dominated organizations, including the military services. Young doctors are taught that only through self-sacrifice and pain can one be toughened enough to succeed. The process works well in forming tough soldiers, but it also produces tough doctors.

The Cultural Anthropology of Medical Training

Robbie Davis-Floyd and Gloria St. John (1998) assessed the cultural aspects of medical training through their own research and through interviews with 40 physicians who had evolved into what they termed "holistic" practitioners. They related the features of medical training that I have described in part to the evolution of what they called the "technocratic" model of medicine that is practiced in the United States today. As I have, they concluded that medical training consists of an initiatory rite of passage. They noted that a rite of passage entails three stages: (1) social isolation and separation of the initiate from his or her previous social status, (2) a period where the initiate is in social limbo, belonging to neither social status, and (3) a period of ritualistic incorporation into the new status. Within this process of separation, transition, and integration, three ritual techniques are practiced: hazing, strange-making, and symbolic inversion. Hazing, as practiced in fraternity rites and military basic training, involves "wearing down and disorienting the initiate through exhaustingly repetitive activity." Strange-making involves making the routine and common become strange while accepting the strange as normal. Symbolic inversion involves disrupting the order of one's everyday life in order to break up one's usual pattern of thinking and instill new concepts and ways of thinking (Davis-Floyd & St. John, 1998, pp. 49–51). The social and intellectual isolation, ritualistic memorization of vast amounts of focused and esoteric information, sleep and recreation deprivation, and denigration of one's sense of self-worth that are experienced in medical training more than fulfill these definitions.

The Trauma of Illness and Its Treatment

These ritual techniques are even more pronounced during internship and residency. Social isolation and sleep deprivation are so extensive that health-care analysts have raised concerns about patient injuries caused by mistakes made by interns and residents so overwhelmed with work and deprived of sleep that they become incompetent. These interns and residents, also known as "house officers," are required to do vast amounts of scut work, such as drawing blood for lab tests, delivering lab specimens, passing catheters, starting IVs, and even delivering patients to X ray or the operating room, duties that may occupy a quarter of their time. The only rationale for such activities, which could be handled by aides or other hospital assistants, is the continued instillation of a lack of self-worth and the acceptance of self-sacrifice that is intrinsic to the medical training process. The cognitive overload and physical exhaustion that accompany everyday life prevent house officers from assessing the preposterous circumstances of their existence and instill the belief that this is the norm and that practicing medicine requires suppression of one's own basic needs. Having undergone such extraordinary duress during medical training, many physicians develop a sense of entitlement and even superiority over those who have not endured this rite of passage. The result is an underlying egotism, at times bordering on arrogance, that typifies the behavior of many physicians in their dealings with colleagues, patients, and even the general public.

Another common result of this process is a state of remarkable detachment from the patient, a separation of the individual from his or her disease, where the disease becomes the patient's identity. Young doctors in training, demonstrating the "humorous" cynicism that becomes their armor against anxiety, often refer to patients as, for example, "the gall bladder in room 12" or "the mastectomy at 10 o'clock." The patient as a person becomes a secondary or nonexistent consideration in the process of evaluating and treating the medical condition. In the process of making "rounds" on patients in the teaching hospital, the attending physician, resident, intern, and medical student travel from patient to patient, often discussing the patient's medical history, lab, and X ray tests without addressing the patient except in a cursory fashion. In this process, the patient's body is viewed as a machine made up of potentially defective parts that must be repaired, removed, or replaced. The means of diagnosing the defective parts of the machine usually involve the use of other technical machines that measure and image the patient's body. The parts of the body/machine that cannot be measured or imaged are thought to be of no importance to the process, and any attempt to introduce these unquantifiable and therefore unknowable entities into the healing process is immediately suspect as being nonscientific. Symptoms not associated with a measurable defective part of the machine are thought to be "psychological" and are therefore relegated to the dustbin of psychosomatic disease. The patients' minds, emotions, and lives are basically irrelevant to the process. The physician has indeed adopted the technocratic model of medical practice.

However, in many cases, addressing the immediate problem with this level of detachment is not easy. The doctor-in-training is exposed daily to new experiences that are shocking, frightening, and tragic—the dissection of the human body in the first year of medical school, the first spillage of blood in surgery, the shattered bodies of accident victims, the physical evidence of the ravages of severe illnesses, the unspeakable tragedy of the death of a child, the emotional expressions of grief of bereaved families. The doctor is exposed to shock, fright, and pain, all of which are consistent with a personal trauma. Many, perhaps most, physicians unconsciously learn to distance themselves from their emotions, cutting themselves off from their own shock, pain, and grief. Medical training does not specifically help doctors deal with such issues. This process of desensitization on the part of physicians contributes to the suppression of their ability to deal with emotional and stress-related issues in their daily life. There are many reasons why the incidence of depression, suicide, and substance abuse are so common in the medical profession.

In essence, the limbic system and right brain, the areas that mediate emotions and the response to threat, are gradually suppressed in the evolving physician as a means of self-preservation, much as the soldier in combat becomes desensitized to the horrors of battle. The process is physiologically the same as that seen in threat, entrapment, and helplessness, with a resulting freeze/dissociation that creates learned helplessness. The physician in training periodically "escapes" from this state of entrapment and threat as he ascends the hierarchical ladder of educational promotion, only to be trapped again by the new layers of the bureaucratic system above him. In essence, the roller coaster of empowerment/disempowerment results in a state of fragmented and fragile self-perception. Beneath physicians' façade of arrogance and cynicism is often a pervasive sense of inferiority, vulnerability, and even incompetence. This basic fear of exposure, the revelation that the "doctor has no clothes," is seldom expressed in the doctor's lounge or at cocktail parties. Doctors are generally unable to admit to this basic sense of insecurity within

their profession. Admittedly, this emotional dichotomy within pl
not universal. But the frequency of patient reports of physicians'
distance, lack of communication skills, and condescension attests to the
schizoid nature of the medical training experience.

Empathy inevitably is lost in a system of education that preaches self-
sacrifice and normalizes self-abuse. When physicians do not meet their own
emotional needs, they cannot do so for people who are dependent on them.
Certainly some distancing is needed if the physician is to deal with the
extreme human pain, terrible injuries, illness, disease, and tragedy inherent in
the medical profession. But when physicians-in-training are treated by their
superiors with derision and lack of respect and are subjected to the elements
of a painful rite of passage, they become unable to develop the self-awareness
that is required to form empathy for others. I was very specifically taught that
sympathy toward the patient invited involvement and emotional entangle-
ment that would destroy my ability to remain objective in medical decision
making. *Empathy*, however, involves the ability to understand and acknowledge the patient's distress without taking on the emotional burden of
sympathy. This is an exquisitely fine line to walk, but it is essential if physicians are to provide treatment effectively while still remaining humanists.
Unfortunately, our American system of medical education, increasingly
devoted to science and technology and driven by a system of training that is
basically punitive, has increasingly distanced itself from this philosophy.

In defense of the efforts of the many fine medical academic institutions
and the dedicated physicians who teach there, other trends in medical education have moved toward the early exposure of medical students to clinical
experience. This has been done in the hope that the dry, esoteric information
learned in the first 2 years of basic science might be integrated with actual
disease in live patients. Davis-Floyd and St. John (1998) noted that a number
of medical schools have initiated these approaches to teaching. Some schools
have instituted tutorial-style teaching, with small groups of students replacing
the large, full-class lectures. Other schools have begun exposing their
students to "live" cases for diagnosis and treatment at the same time that
those students pursue study of the basic sciences. This trend may account for
the growing interest in general practice.

Some schools have also begun to introduce what are called "complementary medical techniques." These relate to alternative medicine and in many
ways reflect a return to the relatively nonscientific medical sects of homeopathy and osteopathy. Examples include acupuncture, yoga, massage, and the

use of supplements and dietary measures to facilitate healthy habits and behavior. The introduction of spirituality into medical training has also emerged, and the importance of the interaction between patient and physician in the healing process is being emphasized. Considering that these changes have occurred in the face of an unprecedented burgeoning of technology in medicine, the implications are at least somewhat heartening. Unfortunately, these positive trends are more than balanced by the explosion of technology and drug development, which further distance the patient from the primary medical caregiver. This trend toward high-tech medicine has its roots in the unique history of the development of American medicine.

The Evolution of the American System of Medical Practice

American medical education in the 18th and 19th centuries was one of basically learning by apprenticeship, combined with a stint at one of the few regional medical colleges (Starr, 1982). Physicians applied poultices and routinely used bloodletting as a universal treatment. Surgeons comprised a lesser class of medical practitioners, setting fractures and lancing boils. Pharmacists operated relatively independently, prescribing a variety of compounds, some based on native Indian preparations. This system of giving substances that would create new symptoms or changes in the body that would then combat the disease was termed *allopathy*. There was little in the way of licensure, and medical societies had little success in establishing routine and accepted standards for medical practice. With the advent of the germ theory of infectious disease, the age of the application of science to medicine was introduced. Allopathic medicine adapted itself well to this theory.

Other theories of disease treatment also arose during the 19th century, forming medical philosophies sometimes termed "sects," such as homeopathy and osteopathy. At least a portion of the training in these modes of practice was devoted to the basic medical sciences of anatomy, physiology, pathology, and chemistry. The remainder of the education was based on the sect's basic theory of disease treatment, theories that had not been exposed to the new mantra of scientific scrutiny.

At the turn of the century, an obscure private school headmaster, Abraham Flexner, was commissioned by the Carnegie Foundation and the U.S. Congress to perform an evaluation of the medical colleges in the United States (Flexner, 1910). In a remarkably exhaustive study, Flexner demonstrated that there were far too many schools of medicine, that most schools were underfunded and basically inadequate, and that standards of excellence were routinely absent. He was also sharply critical of the "medical sects" of homeopathy and osteopathy, as well as of the eclectics and the physiomedicals, two smaller and relatively inconsequential fields of practice. Based on the recommendations in his "muckraking" report, an era of educational reform took place, resulting in the shutting down of many medical schools, the association of medical schools with established universities, and the institution of more rigidly defined curricula. Medical licensure was solidified, and, in the process, the validity of the medical sects was vastly diminished. By the 1920s, the American system of medicine and of medical education had fully embraced the concept of allopathy and was acknowledged to be the best in the world.

In this process, hospitals were transformed from places of dubious cleanliness and disorganization that were built primarily to house the poor to "awesome citadels of science and bureaucratic order" (Starr, 1982). They became an integral part of medical practice and of medical training. As such, they actively participated in the burgeoning field of medical scientific research.

Through the later years of the Roosevelt administration, the move for the development of a system of national health insurance gained impetus. During the Cold War, periodic efforts to develop such a system were systematically rejected, primarily through the vigorous efforts and considerable financial resources of the American Medical Association (AMA), industries, and pharmaceutical firms. Nevertheless, medical cost coverage was increasingly provided through private health insurance policies that were often sponsored by employers or by unions. During the 1940s, the American Hospital Association (AHA), in concert with selected states, instituted plans for state-sponsored hospital insurance, termed Blue Cross, in a number of states. Blue Shield, an additional system for payment for physician services, followed soon thereafter despite the vehement opposition of the AMA, who feared that hospitals themselves would begin to practice medicine. Under the liberal democratic Johnson administration, a new plan for medical care of the elderly and indigent, linked to Social Security, was passed. Medicare and Medicaid also were strongly opposed by the AMA and Republican party, but they soon became entrenched, despite many difficulties at the onset. The financial engine that was primed by these policies contributed to a dramatic increase in the cumulative costs of medical care.

By the 1970s it was becoming apparent that the escalating costs of medical care were not associated with improving quality of health of the American medical consumer. Patient dissatisfaction and the increasing burden of cost borne by the federal government demanded intervention. The first reference to a "crisis in healthcare" appeared during the Nixon administration. This was a crisis not only of cost but also of distribution of care. Many segments of the U.S. population lacked access to general practice physicians, a declining group because of the rapid influx of specialists into the medical field. This trend was driven by the increasingly complex scientific knowledge generated by research, which had greatly outstripped the capacity of the generalist to master it all. It was also driven by the perception that technological knowledge and expertise of the specialist merited a higher income than did the "cognitive skills" of the generalist. At the same time, studies of disease and mortality revealed that many smaller European nations had much better health than Americans.

By the 1980s, the federal government had introduced increasingly stringent methods of oversight of hospitals and physicians for Medicare patients. Certificates of need (CONs) were required for most expansions of technology and new services by hospitals, as increasingly advanced technology was seen as a major contributor to medical costs. After less than a decade, however, the government found that the CON process cost more than it saved, and it was abandoned. A dramatic proliferation of new techniques and machinery followed, along with the profit that derived from their use. At one point, there were more CAT scans in Los Angeles than in the entire United Kingdom.

The American hospital system was developed specifically as a voluntary, nonprofit industry exempt from federal taxes. In the 1980s, hospital bureaucrats discovered that certain profit-making activities could be pursued without incurring a taxable status. Partly because of this, profitable corporate hospital chains, which purchased and consolidated existing voluntary hospitals, were developed. The 1980s and 1990s also saw the emergence of health maintenance organizations (HMOs)—private corporations that provided managed delivery of medical services, often within their own hospitals and by their own physician employees. Viewed as a means of containing ever-expanding hospital costs, the federal government gave lip service to this trend. With the dismal failure of the Clinton administration's attempt to institute universal healthcare, the door was left open for the rapid and unregulated expansion of the for-profit corporate HMO.

Such organizations expanded rapidly, deriving huge profits by "cutting the fat" out of hospital costs. This was usually accomplished by denying medical services for patients and by downsizing, or reducing the number of salaried medical personnel. HMO CEOs were paid outrageous salaries, and corporate profits soared. Medicine is not a growth industry, however. Early profits had resulted from reducing the costs of supposedly unneeded clinical personnel as well as access to care. But after this early profit had been taken, the huge administrative costs involved in supervising the vast amounts of paperwork required to "manage" the care began to outstrip the profits. The late 1990s and early 21st century has seen the decline, consolidation, and death of many of the early HMOs.

Nevertheless, the "crisis in health care" continues unabated, with costs increasing inexorably, with increasing physician and patient dissatisfaction, and with no sign of improvement is U.S. health statistics. A major part of this cost lies in the burgeoning expansion of research and development in diagnostic and therapeutic technology. New types of imaging scanning techniques, new forms and means of performing microsurgery, new combinations of radiology (involving imaging and operating through catheters threaded up arteries), and new and complex drugs are just a portion of a list of developments that changes so quickly that many of the state-of-the-art procedures addressed in this book will be commonplace or even obsolete by its publication.

Compounding this problem has been a crisis of costs of physician and hospital malpractice insurance based on an increasingly dissatisfied and litigious society. Skyrocketing malpractice costs are forcing large groups of physicians, especially obstetricians, to leave certain states where insurance premiums are in excess of $100,000 per year. This is clearly not due to incompetence on the part of physicians, as the complication rates in childbirth have not shown a dramatic upswing. Pursuing litigation for perceived wrongs is certainly as American as apple pie, and it constitutes enough of a problem in the malpractice field that many people, including our current president, have pushed for tort reforms.

But why does our crisis of healthcare coincide with a crisis of malpractice litigation? Atul Gawande (2002) quoted Troyen Brennan, Harvard professor of law and public health, who noted that studies routinely show that malpractice litigation does not reduce rates of medical error. Brennan also noted that less than 2% of patients who clearly received substandard care file lawsuits. On the flipside of the coin, only a small minority of malpractice suits are actually based on demonstrated medical negligence. Finally, most suits that are successfully litigated are based on bad outcomes that are due to unavoidable risks and intrinsic qualities of the illness, not on whether negligence occurred. Malpractice litigation at least in part appears to be due to a relatively small number of patients' *expectations* of the outcome of their care.

These expectations have been generated to a great degree by the extensive marketing efforts of the pharmaceutical and technology industries. Television commercials touting the effectiveness of prescription drugs are an insidious means of solidifying patient expectations, and they often lead to patients' demanding these drugs, which are usually prohibitively expensive. Dramatic new techniques for treating a host of diseases are routinely reviewed in the lay press long before their effectiveness has been proved by objective studies. Exaggerated claims for their effectiveness set the climate for malpractice litigation in the event of their failure, again based on unreasonable expectations generated by marketing.

Whatever the factors that are contributing to the malpractice crisis, it appears at least in part to represent a loss of trust and faith on the part of the U.S. patient population. The scientific revolution that produced the best system of medical care in the world has been subverted by the forces of profit and control, which have greatly contributed to our current healthcare crisis. Along the way, the emotional well-being of the patient has been lost in the shuffle. The patient not infrequently participates in the process as a helpless cog in a vast, impersonal, and at times terrifying machine. The structure of this machine seems intrinsically designed to create a state of helplessness and isolation in the patient. Often distanced from social supports within the medical system, ill-informed, and exposed to frightening machines and painful, invasive tests, the patient is set up to emerge from the process in a state of trauma and dissociation, manifested primarily by new and unexplained physical symptoms that are considered to be psychosomatic.

Science, Technology, Economics, and Trauma

There are many reasons why it makes perfect sense for a culture to isolate, ignore, and suppress information that has the potential to significantly improve the quality and, for that matter, the length of life of members of that culture. In their book *From Doctor to Healer: The Transformative Journey*, Davis-Floyd and St. John (1998) addressed what they perceived to be the core values of American society and specifically noted how those values pertain to the American system of healthcare. Davis-Floyd, a cultural anthropologist, outlined the core values of our American society as science, technology, economic profit, and institutions governed by a patriarchy. Regardless of gender, age, or political leanings, one would find it difficult to challenge these designations. There are few exceptions to the patriarchy as the defining social structure that characterizes institutional governance in societies worldwide, and there are essentially no exceptions in developed countries. The role of the patriarchy in the perpetuation of traumatizing cultural customs and rituals is already the topic of many books and papers and understandably will not be addressed here, although it is quite in keeping with the thesis of this book.

The other major values—science, technology, and economic profit— define America as the premier first-world society. In fact, these values are precisely the sought-after values of most emerging countries. Science and technology are such tightly intertwined concepts that they are often confused with each other. Technology is specifically based on scientific study and design, and for this and other reasons it is considered to be "scientific." For example, we may discover a new star or solar system through the application of mathematical calculations and imaging techniques. This ultimately yields what we usually call a new "scientific discovery." But this discovery has not been "proved" by a scientific study—many other facts must come together over time to provide a sufficient weight of evidence to corroborate that star's existence. When a new technology is developed, there is no doubt that we consider it to be a scientific achievement. The development of this technology, however, in no way proves its effectiveness or worth—or, for that matter, its benefit to mankind. Nevertheless, the development of technology in American society is rooted in our passionate acceptance of science as the ultimate means available for the human species to attain its highest achievement. As such, our society considers technological achievements automatically worthwhile simply because they are seen as "scientific."

So pervasive is this American devotion to science, and therefore technology, that any opinion, conclusion, or behavior that relies on experience, intuition, or emotional intelligence is automatically considered suspect, if not automatically invalid. Science abhors subtleties, enigmas, and the color gray. The "meaning" of a piece of information only has significance within the central area of the bell curve. So pervasive is our society's slavish devotion to the mantra of technology/science that the leaders of institutions routinely used it to support their preconceived agendas, while dismissing and suppressing "bad science," most of which is perceived as dangerous to their agendas. In point of fact, "good science" is a distinct rarity, even in the best of scientific journals. Scientific studies that support the important agendas of institutions are routinely repeated over and over, a phenomenon that Odent (2000) termed "circular epidemiology," the tendency for "good scientists" to obsessively repeat scientific studies that have positive institutional implications.

These institutional implications relate to the core value of American society—namely, economic profit. One of the wonders of Western capitalism is the theoretically boundless opportunity for any given individual to "make it" in American society. This concept of infinite economic opportunity continues to bring thousands of immigrants from less economically advantaged societies to our shores to share in our bounty, which is linked specifically to our other core values, science, and technology.

Finally, the technology revolution fits exactly with the current system of medical training, which values technology rather than intrinsic *care* of the patient. In addition, the technology revolution further distances the body of the patient from the person, and the person from the physician, resulting in the patient's being treated as a body, a disease, and a defective machine. Machines are intrinsically helpless, relying on the operator to turn them on and run them. Feeling like a helpless, defective machine while in a state of arousal and fear constitutes the definition of a traumatic event. It is no wonder that our system of healthcare delivery may intrinsically be a poorly recognized source of trauma.

Science and Technology: Our Cultural Holy Grail

Technology now pervades virtually aspect of our daily life. Data acquisition, analysis and storage, communication systems, entertainment, banking and handling currency, travel, warfare—the list is endless and expanding rapidly. Interestingly, technology during its infancy was primarily touted as a means of achieving time efficiency, with the golden promise of increased leisure time, the opposite of which has occurred. Technology now demands a newly defined behavior: multitasking. Much of this trend is due to the ratcheting up of the speed of communication through electronic techniques. Recent studies now show that when tasks are performed to completion one task at a time, they are achieved more accurately and faster than when multitasking has been done. The "rewards" of technology include machines of communication that bypass face-to-face conversation, and the written letter is analogous to the pony express. The technology of entertainment has progressed to the point that American's can recapitulate their personal trauma with images that are far more "real" than reality. The computer screen and work station have generated a whole new field of diseases of cumulative trauma involving the neck, arms, and hands that no one thus far has recognized as representing reenactment of old dissociative defensive patterns of motor behavior unearthed by compulsive repetition of movements. The "convenience" of computers, emails, faxes, and cell phones has introduced such increased efficiency that it has allowed institutions to downsize, hire temporary workers, avoid paying benefits, and further prime the economic engine through the implementation of a culturally endorsed trauma.

It is hardly surprising that the application of a technological, mechanistic model on the complex, infinitely variable, and ultimately unknowable physiology and behavior of the human animal would present dilemmas. The scientist assumes that with enough knowledge, we can solve anything. The technologist assumes that with enough science, we can rebuild or replace anything. The medical scientist/technologist assumes that we can image, discover, alter, and repair any disease or injury, given enough scientific/technological studies and money. In this process, the scientist/technologist assumes that he is dealing with a machine whose structure and function will be solved through science. What he has ignored is the fact that the structure and function of the human body is not merely a tangible image, a damaged organ, or an abnormal blood test. It is also a set of complex, ever-changing, and as-yet barely measurable states of brain function that we might call "emotions" for want of a better scientific term. What the behavioral scientist is beginning to recognize is that these complex, labile, and unpredictable states of brain function have everything to do with producing the images, organ damage, and abnormal blood tests that the scientist/technologist is attempting to work with or repair. And these altered states of brain function are produced by negative life experiences, the most important of which are those that occurred in the early stages of brain development in infancy and early childhood. The moral, ethical, legal, economic, and just plain practical dilemmas that have resulted from ignoring this fact have significantly contributed to an impending collapse of the American system of healthcare, and to a massive and unacknowledged source of ongoing societal trauma.

The Problems of an Imperfect Science

At the completion of medical school, internship, and specialty training, young doctors have at last completed their formal training and are prepared to enter private or institutional practice or begin as instructors in teaching hospitals. They no longer must face the burden of being at the bottom of the pecking order and are no longer subjected to personal criticism. They are ready to live by their own merit as well as their mistakes. They at last are on top of their own little world—but the top of any world is also a dangerous place. Whatever its negative consequences, the nagging criticism that doctors-in-training are subjected has its purpose. Successful medical practice requires a state of continued vigilance. Each new technical advances in medicine carry with them the ever-increasing risk of human error, always at the relative expense of the patient.

Gawande (2002) explored the imperfect science of medicine with admirable and at times almost shocking candor. A surgical resident at a Boston hospital, he presented the case that human error in medicine is as common as in any other human endeavor, and perhaps more so than most because of the incredible complexity of the effort. He described in graphic detail the trial-and-error process of learning of young physicians, who practice their limited skills often on a portion of the patient population who are uninsured and disadvantaged. He made the obvious point that this is the only way for young doctors to learn new skills, but he also acknowledged the risks to the patient that this presents. He presented cases of his own early in his training in which his naiveté resulted in frightening, although not life-threatening, complications in his own patients. Every doctor, including me, has committed similar errors that constitute frank negligence. Gawande's point is that even very good doctors make very bad errors.

On the other hand, there also are a small number of doctors who are bad doctors, and as a group, they make bad errors more commonly. One risk factor for performance of substandard medicine is the use of addicting self-medication, including prescription drugs, street drugs, and alcohol. Statistics suggest that physicians are just as likely as members of other professions to abuse substances and are probably more likely than most. Physicians are also quite prone to emotional disorders, most specifically depression. State medical associations and boards of medical examiners have fortunately become increasingly active in policing this segment of the physician community, but this requires reporting these errant physicians, an act that other physicians avoid at all costs. As Gawande (2002) noted, all doctors are keenly aware that they also have made terrible mistakes at some time during their career. The persisting fear and guilt associated with that fact not only inhibits them from turning on one of their incapable or guilty peers, but also unconsciously affects all of their decision making.

The Trauma of Illness and Its Treatment

As I have discussed, the training to which doctors have been exposed often has also been traumatic, leaving them to practice medicine in a subliminal state of perceived inadequacy and fear of failure that compounds the fears generated by their latent sense of the imperfect science that they embrace. This low-grade sense of vulnerability virtually locks them into the rigid model of conformity that is demanded in medical training. Deviation from what they perceive to be scientific objectivity is both dangerous and unethical. To such physicians, by far the majority of medical practitioners, the avowedly holistic physician is looked upon with derision and even contempt. In many cases, attempts to establish programs in hospitals based on alternative or complementary medical practice concepts that incorporate holism are met by vigorous opposition by the medical staff as a whole. Making changes in any institution shakes the intrinsic power structure, and in the case of many physician-based institutions, holism challenges the entire basis of their medical education. Fortunately, as I have noted, cracks appear to be developing in the century-old edifice of modern allopathic medicine, as evidenced by the popularity of alternative medicine outside of care that is covered by insurance companies.

The Doctor-Patient Relationship

I once had a conversation with a colleague regarding the role and relative importance of the physician in the healing process of the trauma victim. He insisted that the physician role was defined by the techniques that he or she used, and that their basic *presence* in the process was generally irrelevant. I disagreed, insisting that the basic presence of the physician caregiver actually involves the complex and almost indefinable role of a *healer*. By healer, I meant one whose social, emotional, and empathic presence with the patient/victim involves a personal interaction that actually contributes to changes in the internal environment of the patient. This healing, empathic presence affects and alters the parts of the brain that process pain, fear, anxiety, and distress. It provides an environment of safety rather than threat. By modulating these negative emotions and the resulting cascade of neurotransmitters and hormones, this personal interaction literally enhances the body's potential to heal.

This *presence* is both tangible and intangible. Many features of social interaction are nonverbal, consisting of subtle variations of facial expression that set the tone for the content of the interaction. Body postures and movement patterns of the therapist or physician also may reflect emotions such as disapproval, support, humor, and fear. Tone and volume of voice, patterns and speed of verbal communication, and eye contact also contain elements of subliminal communication and, along with the other physician/therapist behaviors just noted, contribute to the unconscious establishment of a safe, healing environment. These attributes of the caregiver, of course, have their deepest roots in the maternal/infant facial attunement and bonding process. We have a sense of how these processes of social interaction are handled in the brain. They involve the limbic system, the part of the brain that also processes messages related to threat and survival. Maternal/infant bonding, social relationships and support, and physician/patient interaction involve the parts of the limbic system that modulate the basic response to threat and inhibit fear conditioning. The behavior of the body indeed contains important messages that determine the nature of the interaction between physician/therapist and the patient.

The nature and content of the verbal interplay between the physician and patient obviously also play a role in maintaining a healing environment. The content of ideas, explanations, interpretations, challenges, and reassurances—all elements of talk therapy and patient education—contribute greatly to the way patients interpret their own thoughts and symptoms. Healing is fostered when physicians/therapists provide a meaning that defuses the thoughts and symptoms that kindle a state of fear within the patient. The tangible and intangible environment in which the physician/patient interaction takes place is critical to the healing of the patient.

Healing is a physical process within the brain that produces a physiological pattern of function that in turn promotes homeostasis and optimal autonomic function. To play the role of a healer, one must believe that the brain indeed is plastic and adaptable and that experiences create long-lasting changes in brain structure and function. One must accept the fact that human beings are social beings, and that they derive their strength and health from positive interactions with their social peers. Conversely, their strength and health are also vulnerable to impairment by negative interactions. If one's health is impaired, one is uniquely vulnerable to further physical insult in the face of negative experiences. Thus, the physician/therapist healer holds the key and therefore bears the burden of responsibility for providing a social environment within the system of care that is as free as possible from fear and negative experience. Numerous scientific studies show that having a strong social support system from family and friends is associated with less likelihood of dying from a disease and more likelihood of healing. The absence of a positive social environment inhibits patients' sense of safety and control and increases the likelihood that their medical experience will be traumatic. And that environment begins with content of the initial and subsequent interaction between the patient and the physician.

Davis-Floyd and St. John (1998) discussed the humanistic and holistic models of medical practice as compared to the allopathic, technological model. Humanism implies a departure in part from the technological practice of medicine by incorporating the concept of a mind/body connection and viewing the body as an organism rather than a machine, with the patient's being a relational object. Humanistic physicians emphasize the connection and compassionate caring between the physician and patient, and they incorporate the patient in the clinical decision-making process. Other alternative treatment approaches are viewed with an open mind. Disease prevention is stressed, and death is viewed as an acceptable outcome. The needs of the patient and the medical system and institution are balanced. The role of a healing environment is accepted. Humanism also accepts the concepts of allopathy that relate to healing diseases through intervention from the outside in.

The holistic physician perceives mind, body, and spirit as one entity. One cannot approach healing without addressing all entities, and one must address the patient's whole life in the process. The patient and physician must function as a unit, and the ultimate authority is in the hands of the patient. Science and technology do not dictate the course of treatment but rather are at the service and disposal of the patient. The patient's body is part of a universal energy system, linked to others, and death is a step in the process. Healing is the primary focus and takes place from the inside out, not solely due to interventions based on the allopathic model. Maintaining health and well-being is a primary focus.

As you can see, humanism and holism are quite similar, but with notable differences. They clearly represent two points on a continuum that places the allopathic, technological approach at one extreme. Most importantly, however, both recognize the physician-patient relationship as a critical part of the healing process. They also emphasize empowerment of the patient and tacitly acknowledge that one cannot heal in a state of helplessness. Being informed rather than blindly reassured and sharing medical decisions rather than being dictated to are means of empowerment. Allowing unlimited

..ιτη family support systems even if it "interferes" with hospital protocol creates safety, diminishes fear, and enhances one's sense of control, especially in children. Both humanism and holism recognize the critical importance of the nature of the medical experience in facilitating—or, for that matter, impairing—the process of healing. And the primary physician should assume the role of conductor of the medical orchestra in achieving an experience that allows healing instead of causing trauma.

When a physician tells a patient that testing technology is needed to diagnose the condition, the fight/flight response is immediately initiated. Virtually everyone has had this experience in seeking medical care. Whether the patient freezes and is traumatized or is able to maintain autonomic equilibrium depends primarily on the environment provided by the physician at that moment. The physician skills involved in maintaining that equilibrium require: (1) empathy regarding the effects of the recommendation on the patient's mind/body, (2) educating the patient regarding the rationale for the testing, as well as offering all alternative approaches, (3) incorporating the patient in the decisions regarding the use of alternative therapeutic approaches, (4) providing assurance that the patient will be informed immediately at each step along the way, and (5) educating and recruiting support from the patient's particular social support systems. This process may have to be repeated at each step along the path of diagnosis and treatment.

When technology is involved, the patient must know in advance the possible nuances of the experience. Many tests and treatments that involve technological intervention are by nature frightening to varying degrees. MRIs are shockingly noisy and claustrophobic. Angiograms (blood vessel studies) are noisy, uncomfortable, and sometimes painful. Spinal taps may be painful, and bone marrow aspirations are almost invariably extremely painful. Entering the cold, stark surgery room, strapped to a table, blinded by bright lights, and surrounded by masked apparitions who are talking to each other and not to you can be a terrifying experience.

Trauma takes place when fear is aroused in a situation where the patient has relinquished control to the institution and the unexpected occurs. Patients are frequently immobilized in the process of diagnosis and treatment—strapped to a stretcher, attached to electrodes on their skin, and penetrated by tubes and needles that prevent their free movement. Being immobilized immediately produces a state of helplessness, making the patient extremely vulnerable to trauma. Strapping a patient to a board during the ambulance trip to the hospital may convert a trivial rear-end fender bender to a full-blown traumatic experience. In that state, even passing comments by the attendants may elicit terror. Wrapping a child in a sheet in preparation for surgery or suturing in the emergency room, especially in the absence of the mother, the primary social support system for the child, is a recipe for trauma. Covering the eyes in the process adds to the state of helplessness. When the patient expresses fear or anxiety in these situations, angry responses by the caregivers either enhance the anxiety or, more likely, trigger freeze/dissociation, virtually ensuring that that experience will remain with the patient for life as yet another "trivial" traumatic event.

Unfortunately, many physicians trained in the allopathic, technological model of medical practice have long ago been desensitized to the frightening nature of the system in which they operate. Frankly traumatizing experiences such as those just discussed are considered routine. Perhaps these physicians expect patients to be as adaptive and tough as they have had to be. They tend to assume that anyone can tolerate a certain amount of pain if it is necessary for their treatment. Cartesian dualism and the concept of the body as a machine has allowed physicians to separate their patient's expressions of pain and grief from the illness or medical procedure at hand, and to attribute "excessive" expressions of distress to emotional instability or neurosis. The concept that a psychological problem can produce physical changes in the body was considered to be heresy and is still considered to be so by many physicians. The notion that a simple negative life experience may also produce physical changes is inconceivable.

Changing the System

In the late 1970s, Angelica Thieriot was hospitalized for a series of medical problems. These experiences were very traumatic for her. Although she was impressed by the efficiency of the high-tech environment, she was appalled by the virtual absence of anything resembling personalized care. The nurses who attended to her needs always seemed to be in a hurry. None of them seemed interested in her as a person, and many seemed oblivious to her needs. More disturbingly, some of them appeared not even to be familiar with the medical aspects of her case. She was left alone for hours, and the whole experience left her feeling alone, helpless, and afraid.

Rather than accepting her experience as inevitable in this rapidly changing world of medical technology, she realized that, if her upsetting experiences were representative of the hospital environment for every patient, great harm could come to many people. After her last hospitalization, she formulated her ideas into a plan for restructuring the whole concept of hospital care to address the personal needs of the patient. This would be accomplished by staff support of the patient at all levels of treatment, creating an intrinsically healing environment. She approached the chief of medicine at the hospital with her ideas, and they were eventually accepted. In 1985, Planetree, a conceptual model for a system of hospitals and care centers was created. A 13-bed medical/surgical unit was established in a large San Francisco hospital. In the ensuing 25 years, over 40 hospitals and care centers have joined the Planetree system, adopting their philosophy of holistic care in a fashion that meets each of their unique needs.

I doubt the Planetree founders were versed in concepts of traumatic stress and its behavioral physiology. Yet they seemed to sense the basic tenets of the roots of trauma in their theory and philosophy of medical care. They addressed many of the concerns that I have raised here regarding the frequently traumatic environment created by our current system of high-tech medicine. Most specifically, their philosophy addresses the concept of the healing environment in many ways.

Planetree emphasized the need for human interactions in the healing process. As I have noted, the social environment and relationships with other persons may be the most critical element in healing from trauma. Many scientific studies in PTSD have documented this fact. The Planetree philosophy not only emphasizes personalized attention and care for patients and their families, but also addresses how staff members take care of themselves and how the organizational structure of the institution can create such supportive structures. Care Partner programs enlist family and friends in providing care services while the patient is hospitalized and trains them in home care service. Trained volunteers also participate in these services.

Empowerment of the patient and the patient's family through information and education is provided. Information packets, care conferences, an open-chart policy, video- and audiotapes, and computer-based information resources are provided. Bedside self-medication programs provide a renewed sense of control where appropriate.

Attention is devoted to spirituality and the healing aspects of human touch. Chaplain services, meditation spaces, and natural gardens, as well as special attention to a physically healing environment, are provided. Therapeutic massage is available, and friends and families are taught to give massages for loved ones. Proper nutrition and the use of complementary therapies play an important role in the therapeutic process.

I do not mean specifically to endorse the Planetree hospital system. Other hospitals have adopted philosophies of care that reflect many of the concepts of the Planetree system. Changes in philosophy of this type are usually made after patients like Angelica Thieriot have had the courage and intelligence to speak up about their unpleasant hospital experiences and advocate change. I am sure that many similar suggestions for change have been met with strong resistance from hospital administrations and medical staffs, with the most powerful objections being based on concerns for quality of care, additional cost of care, and the risk of exposure to malpractice suits based on the use of "unscientific" practices. Resistance to holistic practices in hospitals is deeply rooted in medical training, and it is usually based on good faith on the part of medical staffs based on their medical training. What is usually required to make such changes is the dreaded "paradigm shift"—one that has deep ethical and financial implications in our current medical system. It is also very difficult to make changes in an institution when fear plays a role in the decision-making process.

Nevertheless, the power to effect change in institutions basically comes from within, specifically from the consumers of goods and services provided by them. Examples like that of Angelica Thieriot provide compelling evidence for the opportunity to make changes within our system of health-care delivery. And institutions in distress, like our present system of health-care, often present the best opportunity for concerned consumers and citizens to influence such changes.

PART III
Trauma in Health and Disease

There is no question that stress and trauma are ultimately bad for your health. Our brains and bodies are quite efficiently designed to deal with these negative life experiences on an emergency basis. But prolonged stress and the process of traumatization cause changes that outstrip our intrinsic capacities for adaptation. The result of this is a group of widely varied diseases, medical syndromes, and clinical conditions, many of which are chronic, poorly understood, and ineffectively treated. They are so varied in their clinical presentation that one would have difficulty at first glance relating them to a common pathological process. But an understanding of the myriad effects of trauma on the brain/body provides a cogent rationale for these diseases of trauma.

A logical entry point for the study of trauma-based disease is a review of a unique and peculiar group of symptoms first studied in Europe in the 1800s. Called "conversion hysteria," this bizarre cluster of neurological symptoms and behaviors included paralysis, ataxia, collapse, convulsions, and anesthesia of parts of the body. Conversion hysteria was generally attributed to malingering, and physicians and society treated victims of the condition (which were usually women) with disdain, derision, and rejection. Although researchers in Paris in the late-19th century made the remarkable discovery that conversion hysteria was associated with childhood sexual abuse, these findings were suppressed by society and the diagnosis as such does not exist in the DSM-IV.

I propose a physiological rationale for conversion hysteria that is based on the concept of the brain/body continuum. I believe that the parts of the body that provided sensory information to the brain during the traumatic event become dissociated in victims of conversion hysteria. Those body regions reflect the neurological deficits of conversion hysteria, but they also are physically changed by the process of dissociation. I have called this phenomenon somatic dissociation, and I relate it to a cluster of perplexing symptoms and diseases, including stigmata and reflex sympathetic dystrophy. Of course, the hypothesis that a supposedly psychological process could actually alter a specific region of the body in a predictable way contradicts usual medical dogma.

The full spectrum of the diseases of trauma is, as noted, quite broad, but they share a common theme of exaggerated and dysfunctional autonomic cycling. Many of them are characterized by predominant parasympathetic and vagal tone, as in the freeze response, but most also have symptoms of increased sympathetic tone, including vasoconstriction, arousal, and rapid heartbeat. Most fall into the category of diseases that defy explanation, have no definitive associated laboratory or imaging abnormalities, and have no discernable cause. Many fall into the category of psychosomatic or somatization disorders.

Because the importance, and even the existence, of some of these illnesses are dismissed by many in the medical profession, patients have formed advocacy societies to validate their condition. These diseases are chronic and resistant to specific treatment but are the source of more physician prescriptions—analgesics, anti-inflammatory agents, and medications for gastric reflux—than any other diseases. They also generate over half of all complaints seen by primary care physicians. Although genetics and lifestyle undoubtedly contribute to the development of many of these diseases, I maintain that their major cause is the cumulative effect of negative life events in the face of helplessness, a manifestation of the trauma spectrum.

CHAPTER 8

Somatic Dissociation: Conversion Hysteria, Stigmata, and Reflex Sympathetic Dystrophy

Dissociation is basically a subjective experience, a continuum of abnormal perceptions and behaviors that occur in people subjected to a traumatic event or even to an intense period of stress. It is a disruption of consciousness, memory, identity, and perception of the environment, and it may alter any of these states and functions. The combination of alterations in cognition, memory, and perception that define dissociation leads to a remarkable array of seemingly bizarre states of feeling, thinking, remembering, and functioning. The subjective sensation of dissociation may be characterized by a feeling of detachment or disconnection from the event or from one's perception of one's immediate surroundings. Subsequent memories of the episode of dissociation reflect this feeling of strangeness, as well as an alteration in one's sense of time and continuity of events. Clearly one's perception of reality in this peculiar state is distorted and fragmented. Dissociation is frequently associated with amnesia for some or all of the events that have triggered it, but the fact that memories of the event may be recovered later with fair accuracy suggests that they remain tucked away in unconscious memory. The dissociated person's sense of self and identity may be altered (feelings of unreality or familiarity) or fragmented (separation of one's sense of self into separate, isolated parts). For example, many of my patients have had out-of-body experiences after a car accident, where they perceived themselves and the car from above, viewing the events literally as a third person.

I have suggested that sensory perceptions, pain, and motor behavior related to physical experiences during a traumatic event are stored as procedural memories in the survival brain. In fact, many of these sensorimotor experiences retained in memory fall under the category of dissociative phenomena. For example, the patient who fractures his arm in a very traumatic car accident may experience persistent chronic pain in the arm that does not remit despite complete bone healing. At the same time, the arm may feel numb, clumsy, and like it is not part of him. The pain represents procedural memory for the sensory experiences of the traumatic event; the numbness and clumsiness reflect dissociation or "rejection" of the body part that provided the sensory information of the traumatic event to the brain and now represents an ongoing threat. The concurrence of numbness and pain—two opposing perceptions—is not unusual in a dissociated body part.

This is an illustration of what I call *somatic dissociation*. This concept is different from the very similar term *somatoform dissociation*, coined by Ono van der Hart and colleagues (2000). Van der Hart described a series of motoric and sensory manifestations of dissociation, such as paralysis, tremors, and sensory loss that correspond in part to the signs of conversion hysteria that I discuss later. These in fact are the manifestations of procedural memory for the experiences of the trauma. *Somatic dissociation* refers to actual physical and pathological changes that occur in the tissues of these dissociated body parts and that correspond with a number of poorly understood disease states. This will be discussed in detail.

Although a critical part of the entire syndrome of traumatization, dissociation is also a universal and frequently benign experience common to all people and societies, frequently culturally dependent, and not always of pathological significance. Terms such as "daydreaming," "wool gathering," and "spacing out" reflect relatively benign states of dissociation. Feelings of déjà vu represent a dissociated perception of reality, as do out-of-body experiences and the perception of the slowing of time that is often experienced during traumatic events. Even the transient amnesia associated with stressful intrusive thoughts and the transient confusion experienced after a particularly demanding day of multitasking are at least in part dissociative experiences. We all, at one time or another, have experienced similar phenomena in situations of stress without going on to develop chronic states of PTSD or a dissociative "disorder." Some cultures actually seek to achieve states of dissociation through the use of hallucinogenic plants in order to access deeper states of primordial consciousness. The shamanic trances of indigenous healers probably fall into this category as well.

The Pathologic Spectrum of Dissociation

On the pathological end of the spectrum, dissociation is indeed a state of profoundly disordered brain function associated with a severe degree of fragmentation of perception. People experiencing pathological dissociation are unable to view the world in a way that conforms to the perceptions of those around them. Consequently, that person's response to events is based more on distorted perceptions than on reality. The person's social behavior is often inappropriate and dysfunctional with respect to the limits of approved societal behavior because it is dictated by these distorted perceptions. Because mental illness is basically defined by societal norms of "appropriate behavior," the person suffering from a dissociative disorder may be unable to perform the normal activities of daily life, many of which are dictated by these very societal norms.

Although dissociation is often described as a numbing of emotions and perceptions, it is anything but a state of pleasure. Dissociation is often associated with *anhedonia*, a state of complete inability to achieve or experience pleasure, and *abulia*, a state of profound apathy and inability to make decisions or initiate movements or actions. Repetitive movement patterns, paralyses, tics, and areas of anesthesia are related to impaired body perception and may cause significant physical impairment. Periods of amnesia interrupt perception of daily events. In addition to emotional numbing, episodes of spontaneous violent emotion that are often personally and socially disabling may occur. Currently termed *dissociative identity disorder*, severe fragmentation of the sense of self with a variety of states characterized by different personality traits may present. The most severe end of the dissociative spectrum therefore represents perhaps the most disabling result of complex life trauma.

The neurochemical and neurophysiological states associated with, and perhaps causing, dissociation are only partially known. What is fairly certain, however, is that dissociation is associated with numbing, in terms of both acute pain perception and clarity of thought, both of which are criteria for the diagnosis of PTSD in the DSM-IV. Indeed, many people who have experienced dissociative episodes have used the word *numb* to describe the state, particularly with regard to the sharpness of their perceptions and their ability to think clearly and remember things that have occurred during this state. Victims have also described this state as "the fog"—a feeling of heaviness of the body and a slowing of their general mental processes. During this state, the dissociated person may indeed be unaware of minor injuries and may ignore them. Similarly, states of arousal, anxiety, or panic may be inhibited. These features of numbing of arousal and analgesia suggest the influence of endorphins on the subjective experience of dissociation, a relationship that I will address. In personal contact, the person in this state may appear to be confused but certainly not hypervigilant or aroused. In other cases, the dissociated patient may cycle rapidly between arousal and numbing and between hypervigilance and confusion, which is not surprising in light of the fact that trauma is associated with abnormal cyclical autonomic regulation. As a result, panic and arousal may be hard to distinguish from the numbing of dissociation.

The dissociated victim may stumble over his words, stutter, and repeatedly ask the person with whom he is speaking to repeat what was just said. Word finding, comprehension of speech and words, and enunciation may be impaired. This occurs because the left side of the brain, especially Broca's area (the region that controls speech), is "shut down," with less blood flow and metabolism during arousal (Rauch et al., 1996). This physical impairment of speech in arousal and dissociation is therefore not "psychological." In fact, it may account for the common association of *alexithymia* (the inability to find

Figure 8.1
"*Babble*," images of dissociation, alexithymia (Caroline Douglas).

words for emotions) with traumatic stress. One of my patients, a gifted ceramic sculptor, promoted her own healing after a very emotionally traumatic head and facial injury by representing her perceptions through her art. Figure 8.1 vividly illustrates her frustrating experience with the structure of words in trauma and dissociation. Persistent cognitive complaints are also common with dissociation and are usually manifested by distraction, impaired attention, and problems with short-term memory. These cognitive problems may be partly related to distraction by repetitive intrusive thoughts, as well as to a general dulling of awareness. The sculpture in Figure 8.2 dramatically illustrates this state of perception, as if the mind were full of holes. Dissociated people often experience sudden "blocks" in thinking, losing track of the content of their thoughts in the middle of speaking, blocking on familiar words and names, and then experiencing anxiety over their cognitive failures. Many of us have experienced such frustrating episodes when we have been under undue stress, illustrating the fact that transient episodes of stress-related dissociation are not uncommon.

As I have said, I believe that dissociation is clearly linked to the freeze response, so it is not surprising that brain endorphins are specifically linked to the experience of dissociation. Analgesia (impairment of pain perception) is produced by an acute stressful experience, probably so that the animal or person does not have to

Figure 8.2
"*Blind,*" images of dissociation, cognitive impairment with somatic dissociation (Caroline Douglas).

deal with pain or nurse the wound, behaviors that might interfere with fight or flight behaviors. This state of analgesia persists in the event of a freeze response, again to allow the animal or person to maintain immobility. The clinical effects of endorphins, of course, are similar to those of synthetic narcotics such as morphine, heroin, or the codeine derivatives, and the alteration of perception, impairment of cognitive function, and numbing of pain perception experienced with these drugs are in many ways analogous to the numbing experienced with dissociation. Dissociation is at least in part clearly mediated by the presence of elevated levels of brain endorphins. In fact, synthetic drugs that block the effect of morphine on the brain, including naltrexone, have been used to diminish the numbing effects of dissociation.

I believe that much chronic, unexplained pain has its basis in the procedural memory for pain associated with a threat to life. This may be because the pain patient has a life history of severe trauma that has left him vulnerable, hypervigilant, and susceptible to kindling. It may also be associated with a painful injury linked to severe traumatic stress, such as an injury in warfare, a catastrophic accident, or a personal assault. Under these circumstances, the victim of such a traumatic event may freeze and incorporate the messages of

181

Figure 8.3
"*Stigmata*," images of dissociation, somatic dissociation (Caroline Douglas).

pain in procedural memory along with other sensory messages of the trauma. Phantom limb pain is a good example of this phenomenon. There is also solid evidence that inadequate analgesic control of terrible pain may allow the pain itself to be traumatizing; cases of PTSD associated with and caused by severe, untreated pain have been reported. Victims of this type of chronic pain often find no relief without the use of high doses of narcotics, which mimic the effects of brain endorphins. Once again, severe pain may accompany dissociation of a body part. The patient may report that the limb does not feel that it belongs to him and is numb while at the same time experiencing excruciating pain. Figure 8.3 illustrates this state of loss of perception of a body part in dissociation, in this case both hands, which at the same time were lacerated and painful.

If one explores the emotional state of such chronic pain patients, one finds high levels of anxiety, vigilance, and fear of the pain. There is often clinical evidence for a dissociative disorder as well. These patients have remarkable tolerance for extremely high doses of narcotics with relatively mild side effects. They will also tell you that even doses of morphine that would cause coma in other individuals still don't actually kill the pain. Further exploration of their symptoms usually reveals that the prospect of weaning them from the narcotics is terrifying and, in fact, that the narcotics serve as much to allay anxiety as to remove pain. Chronic pain in this circumstance represents a procedural memory for pain in a dissociated part of the body, and no amount of external synthetic narcotics will ever totally relieve it. Only by extinguishing the conditioned association of the pain message with the unresolved traumatic experience will pain relief be achieved. In addition, because the numbing effect of endorphins and synthetic narcotics also dulls arousal and anxiety, one must be aware that the use of narcotics in this type of chronic pain is treating patients' terror as much as it is their pain.

I have introduced somewhat of a paradox into the concept of dissociation. If dissociation is mediated at least in part by endorphins and is a state of relative numbing, how could chronic pain be a manifestation of the dissociative process? The phenomenon of conversion hysteria helps to solve this riddle. Conversion hysteria is one type of dissociative symptom that specifically involves altered sensory perception and motor function of a part of the body. That part of the body is not perceived normally and does not function normally. It may be overly sensitive to pain, insensitive to pain, paralyzed, or weak. And inevitably it is associated with procedural memory for a traumatic event that involved sensory information coming from that very body region. Dissociation therefore plays a part in the persistent somatic symptoms that represent procedural memory for a traumatic event, such as those of whiplash syndrome.

Shellshock and Somatoform Dissociation

Onno van der Hart and colleagues (2000) addressed varieties of this type of dissociation in World War I combat soldiers. They described *somatoform dissociation* as sensory, perceptual, and motor symptoms that reflect the body's dissociative response to an unresolved threat. The World War I physicians who cared for these patients made the remarkable observation that the paralyses, contractures, and tics that they observed invariably replicated the body position or defensive movements that occurred at the moment of trauma.

Ferenczi (1919, 1921) described such a condition in shellshock, referring to the defensive body position as a *tic*:

> . . . an unexpectedly powerful trauma can have the result in *tic*, as in traumatic neurosis, of an over-strong memory fixation on the attitude of the body at the moment of experiencing the trauma, and that to such a degree as to provoke a perpetual or paroxysmatic reproduction of the attitude. (as quoted in van der Hart, 2000, p. 11)

Ferenczi (1919, p. 62) also gave an example of this. In one patient, the peculiar contractions of the man's shoulder and elbow had probably mimicked the position of his arm at the moment of trauma:

The man whose right arm is contracted at an obtuse angle, was concussed by the shell just as he was sliding *his rifle into the "stand easy" position.* This position corresponds exactly with that imitated by the contracture. (as quoted in van der Hart, 2000, p. 13)

These movements were stored in conditioned procedural memory because the victims dissociated at the time of the trauma and were unable to complete the act of survival defense, thereby imprinting these movement patterns in memory, to be replicated time and again under conditions of stress or with cues from the old trauma. Van der Hart and colleagues (2000) also noted that helplessness typified the trench warfare at that time and the syndrome that resulted from this state was shellshock, a condition that was specifically dissociative in nature. Confined to the inescapable prison of the trenches, any attempt at fight or flight was useless, and freeze/dissociation was the only available survival response. As a result, soldiers in this environment manifested relatively pure dissociative symptoms rather than the arousal, startle, and panic symptoms of PTSD. Shellshock was a relatively pure dissociative disorder.

After the war left the trenches, the threat to life persisted, but the state of helplessness diminished with the reduction in enforced immobilization, resulting in a dramatic decrease in the unique dissociative syndrome of shellshock. Shellshock as manifested in victims of trench warfare in World War I has seldom been seen in subsequent armed conflicts on a similar scale. Van der Hart and colleagues (2000) made the important observation that the DSM-IV has totally ignored these very important manifestations of dissociation and proposed that posttraumatic syndromes indeed are primarily syndromes of dissociation rather than of arousal or PTSD per se.

The bizarre movement patterns, tics, and fixed postures of the victims of shellshock served only as a symbolic and repetitive attempt to avoid the life threat that was never resolved. Conditioned responses are meant to protect against future threats of a similar nature, not to defend against a past threat that is only real in memory despite its perception as being real in the present. The spontaneous and involuntary appearance of inappropriate movement patterns from procedural memory is not limited to the extreme case of shellshock. It occurs to a lesser extent in many victims of lesser trauma. The continuing elicitation of archaic patterns of reflex movement in the face of ongoing life stimuli will disrupt, abort, and distort the normal reflex patterns of movement that are required for the unconscious skillful performance of everyday activity. It is no wonder that victims of trauma complain of clumsiness and loss of coordination and suffer repetitive mild injuries—they are prone to bumping into obstacles in their environment, such as doorjambs, curbs, cupboard doors, and countertops. Their body's responses to the demands of navigating through their environment are determined primarily by conditioned reflexes designed to protect them from unconsciously perceived imminent danger. These dysfunctional reflexes interfere with the normal motor skills required for the simple passage through a seemingly benign space. Based on the burden of unconscious trauma-based cues in their immediate environment, and on their current burden of nonspecific life stress, the dissociated person may be more or less clumsy, distracted, and uncoordinated.

These patterns of persistent impaired motor function are actually examples of somatoform dissociation like that seen in shellshock victims. Shellshock, in fact, is part of a continuum of sensorimotor disability, from the clumsiness of the whiplash victim to the helpless, paralytic, and anesthetic state of disability seen in conversion hysteria. I believe that somatoform dissociation in fact is defined by the sensory and motor manifestations that were first described by Breuer, Freud, and Janet in the victims of hysteria that they evaluated at the end of the 19th century.

Conversion Hysteria

The study of dissociation by the neuropsychiatric profession flourished throughout the 19th century, reaching its peak in Paris in the 1880s. For centuries, dissociation was defined by the term *hysteria*, a state of rather stereotyped alteration of behavior that was believed to be unique to women. By the 20th century, however, it was clear that this strange phenomenon did not spare the male gender. Several authors have provided compelling reviews of this forgotten history (Herman, 1997; van der Kolk, Weisath, & van der Hart, 1996). The champion in the resurrection and study of hysteria in the late-19th century was the famous French neurologist Jean-Martin Charcot. Combining the medical disciplines of psychiatry and neurology, Charcot embarked on an intensive study of the strange condition of hysteria. This was a disease characterized by the bizarre alteration of consciousness, perception, and physical function in young women that for years had been attributed to malingering or a weakness of the mind. Society treated many of these patients with scorn and derision. The persisting and disabling changes in behavior associated with hysteria were often attributed to accidents, which could be emotionally or physically traumatic events. In some patients, disabling symptoms of hysteria arose from railroad accidents and were attributed to a syndrome called "railroad neurosis" (Janet, 1920). This early version of what ultimately became known as whiplash syndrome was apparently recognized 150 years ago. Even then it was attributed to neurosis and malingering.

The term *hysteria* derives from the Greek word for the uterus, *hystera*, and actually appears in the medical literature in Hippocrates's 35th aphorism, referring to displacement of the uterus in labor (Didi-Huberman, 2003). This suggested that the uterus could actually move—be displaced from its designated position at the very base, or seat, of womanhood. Hysteria became associated with base, animal energy, deep and impenetrable passions, and behavior that implied animal sexuality as well as madness or insanity. It was a state solely attributed to women. In 18th- and 19th-century France, hysterics were often confined in chains in great institutions, along with classes of women that included the insane, sufferers of degenerative and infectious neurological illnesses such as syphilis, and even paupers and whores. Confinement was usually associated with horrific filth, disease, and early death.

The Salpêtrière, a venerable asylum for the indigent and the insane in Paris, was just such an institution. In this madhouse, Charcot became fascinated with the behavior of hysterics, noting a consistent behavioral theme in these women that suggested a common cause. As a neurologist, he was fascinated by the fact that the symptoms of hysteria were primarily neurological. These symptoms included disorders of sensation, motor function, memory and consciousness, and collapse or seizures. Charcot discovered that many of these neurological symptoms or events could be triggered by various forms of physical or emotional stimuli that often were unique to the individual patient. In his studies, Charcot documented and categorized in writings and photographs the varied signs of hysteria (Didi-Huberman, 2003). He also lectured and presented his cases of hysteria in his Tuesday lectures at the Salpêtrière, demonstrating signs and behaviors typical of hysteria in his patients by eliciting them in front of the assembled physicians and dignitaries (Figure 8.4). Clearly Charcot's passionate study of hysteria was driven by curiosity rather than empathy.

Charcot achieved considerable fame as a result of his studies, and his work attracted the attention of other pioneers in the emerging field of neuropsychiatry, including the physician and philosopher Pierre Janet, as well as the

Figure 8.4
Brouillet, *A Clinical Lecture by Charcot* (Didi-Huberman, 2003).

Austrian psychiatrist Joseph Breuer and his student Sigmund Freud. Freud and Breuer collaborated in an intensive study of hysteria, and they, along with Janet, eventually concluded that hysteria was almost invariably associated with a history of emotional trauma. They began to explore the life histories of their patients before the event that seemed to have triggered the hysterical symptoms, and they found that almost universally these patients had experienced severe childhood sexual abuse (Breuer & Freud, 1957; Janet, 1920). The shocking nature of these findings initially generated skepticism in these early pioneers despite a long historical association of sexuality with the origins of hysteria. Despite these reservations, they persevered in their clinical research through exhaustive patient interviews.

In 1893, Breuer and Freud published *Studies in Hysteria*, a series of case studies and papers providing their early insights into this perplexing condition. The introductory paper, "The Mechanism of Hysterical Phenomena: Preliminary Communication," outlined their theory of the psychical mechanism of hysteria (Breuer & Freud, 1957). In this paper, Breuer and Freud presented concepts that with uncanny accuracy reflect current concepts of dissociation and the manifestations of old traumatic experiences stored in procedural memory as sensations and motor behaviors. Indeed, they asserted that "hysterics suffer mainly from reminiscences" (Breuer & Freud, 1957, p. 7). They noted that these sensorimotor symptoms of hysteria actually reflect the physical experiences of an old, suppressed original trauma rather than the physical experiences of the new "accident" or traumatic event that seemed to trigger the hysteria:

> The symptoms which we have been able to trace back to precipitating factors of this sort include neuralgias and anaesthesias of various kinds, many of which have persisted for years, contractures and paralyses, hysterical attacks and epileptoid convulsions, which every observer regarded as true epilepsy, *petit mal* and disorders in the nature of *tic*, chronic vomiting and anorexia, carried to the pitch of all nourishment, various forms of disturbance of vision, constantly recurrent visual hallucination, etc. . . . The memory of the trauma acts like a foreign body which long after its entry must continue to be regarded as an agent that is still at work. (Breuer & Freud, 1957, pp. 4–6)

Breuer and Freud noted that bringing the memory to consciousness—and, more importantly, giving words to it and describing it in its minutest detail—often promoted the disappearance of the hysterical symptom or manifestation. Putting the associated emotion into words also was uniquely therapeutic. Both of these features of therapeutic success are quite compatible with extinction of the memory/symptom association through conscious expression of the events of the trauma, which before the therapy had been largely unconscious.

More specifically, Breuer and Freud (1957, p. 8) also addressed the concept of discharge, which they referred to as an "energetic reaction to the event that provokes an affect." Phrases that described these energetic reactions included "to cry oneself out," "to blow off steam," or "to rage oneself out" (Breuer & Freud, 1957, p. 8). They stated with unique insight that "if the reaction is suppressed, the affect remains attached to the memory" (Breuer & Freud, 1957, p. 8). They also maintained that language is a substitute for the "reaction" in therapy (Breuer & Freud, 1957, p. 8). Thus, Breuer and Freud recognized that trauma causes the imprinting of the emotions, perceptions, and physical experiences of the traumatic event in unconscious memory. Thereafter, the memories of this trauma were likely to resurface in the form of "hysterical" perceptions, emotions, altered states of consciousness, behaviors, and physical symptoms in a fashion that replicated the traumatic experience.

Finally, Breuer and Freud recognized the critical role of helplessness at the moment of the traumatic event as a requirement for the establishment of the hysterical state. Factors that might prevent the "energetic reaction" from occurring at the time of the trauma included social circumstances that might block the reaction, such as intentional repression, severe paralyzing affects such as fright, and states of altered perception, such as daydreaming or hypnoid (dissociative) states (Bueuer & Freud, 1957, pp. 10, 11). They referred to this energetic reaction as *abreaction*. They also noted that psychical trauma might *produce* such an altered state, which in turn would make the reaction impossible. In other words, the occurrence of dissociation at the time of a traumatic event would predictably lead to the establishment of the hysterical state by suppressing the reaction. I would suggest that the "energetic reaction," or abreaction, to which Breur and Freud were referring was in fact the discharge of the freeze response and dissociation.

It is quite clear that Breuer and Freud considered hysteria to be the ultimate manifestation of the emotional response to trauma, just as we tend to consider PTSD to be the definitive diagnosis for the spectrum of behavior and altered emotional states related to trauma. During the 19th century, hypnosis was widely felt to be the treatment of choice for hysteria, and Freud embraced hypnosis as a therapeutic tool. Breuer and Freud recognized that the hypnoid state produced by clinical hypnosis and the altered perceptions of hysteria had much in common. The splitting, or dissociation, of consciousness in hysteria was in fact a "hypnoid state" and was the basic phenomenon of hysteria. Many people were prone to such states of altered perception and were believed to be uniquely vulnerable to the development of hysteria as a result either of traumatic events or of more minor social conflict, the latter being associated with a syndrome they referred to as *dispositional hysteria*. Finally, they recognized that hysteria, despite its bizarre alterations of perception, which often verged on hallucination, was not a psychosis. These remarkably altered states of perception were in fact state-dependent and were initiated by predictable triggers that usually contained cues to the original trauma. Hysterics often were "people of the clearest intellect, strongest will, greatest character, and highest critical power" (Breuer & Freud, 1957, p. 13).

Following the publication of *Studies in Hysteria* in 1893, Freud pursued the thread of the theory of early sexual trauma in hysteria to its ultimate conclusion, which he addressed in his seminal article "The Aetiology of Hysteria" in

1896 (Freud, 1962). Unfortunately, the social implications of this concept made it difficult for even Freud to sustain this line of inquiry. Hysteria was a relatively common condition in Parisian and Viennese society at that time, and the concept of underlying sexual trauma in its victims had scandalous implications for all classes of people, especially as many of Freud's hysterical patients came from the upper tiers of Viennese society. Beset by his own inability to accept these implications, and increasingly rejected by his psychiatric peers, Freud was forced to recant his theories of sexual abuse and incest in hysteria, ultimately rejecting them totally. In the process, he developed his theory of repressed infantile sexuality, attributing his prior patients' stories of sexual abuse to fantasies based on their own sexual attraction to the perpetrating adult. In essence, he "shot the messengers." The resulting theory of childhood psychosexual development laid the groundwork for his psychoanalytic theory (Freud, 1938).

Although they had arrived at conclusions that have withstood a century of controversy and rejection and are finally emerging as bedrock concepts in the brain's response to trauma, Breuer and Freud mutually abandoned these concepts by the turn of the century. Breuer had always accepted these conclusions with reluctance, and had frustrated his younger colleague with his vacillation. As noted, Freud also eventually rejected his earlier linking of hysteria with trauma for more pragmatic reasons. As he revised his writing to accommodate his new theories, he continued to give lip service to his theories in his chapter on "preliminary communication," while simultaneously rejecting many of the bases for these theories. The crucial link between trauma, procedural memory, and the clinical manifestations of hysteria was relegated to the back burner in psychiatric theory, although references to these concepts emerged again in studies of shellshock during World War I.

Despite almost universal rejection by his peers, Janet, however, persevered in his insistence that the tales of horror related to him by his "hysterics" were indeed accurate and that the roots of hysteria lay in the history of childhood sexual trauma (Janet, 1920). He defined in detail the clinical state of hysteria, referring to "fixed ideas," which constituted the entire spectrum of symptoms—sensory, emotional, visual, auditory, and perceptual—that were associated with the traumatic event that triggered the hysterical condition. Symptoms of hysteria included loss of sensation, blindness, deafness, muteness, and stupor as part of sensory or perceptual dissociation of specific parts of the body. Disorders of sensation were referred to as "anesthesias" and could include blindness, deafness, or complete loss of sensation of a body part. Fixed ideas also included the frequently bizarre aberrations of behavior that accompanied these sensory symptoms. Motor behaviors included convulsive attacks, paralysis, loss of balance, sleep-walking (somnambulism), stuttering, and complete loss of speech. Symbolic involuntary movements included tics (habit spasms) and choreiform (twisting) movements, as well as complex and more organized movement patterns. Contractures included peculiar sustained flexion contractions of body parts, primarily the extremities (Figure 8.5). Tics that he described involved compulsive repetitions of stereotyped movement patterns, often twitches or brief muscle contractions, especially

Figure 8.5
Hystero-epilepsie, contracture
(Didi-Huberman, 2003).

involving the head, neck, and face (Figure 8.6). "Somnambulisms" were states if amnesia often associated with strange and pointless behavior similar to fugues. Sudden fits of sleep or physical collapse were also noted.

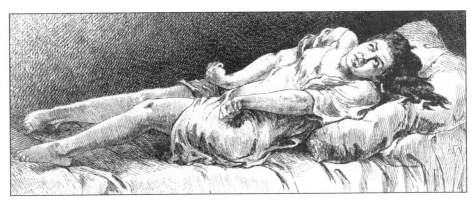

Figure 8.6
The "phase of tonic immobility or tetanism" (Didi-Huberman, 2001).

I suspect that these fixed ideas in fact were the procedural memories for the sensory experiences of the trauma. The stereotyped and ineffectual defensive behaviors, which were aborted by the victim in a state of helplessness at

191

the time of the abuse, were thereafter triggered repeatedly by these "fixed ideas" throughout their lives, producing inexplicable complaints and bizarre neurological disability. They were also a repetition of the failed motor attempt at self-defense stored in procedural memory.

Janet (1920) proposed a number of general concepts in hysteria as *stigmata*. One of these stigmata involved the retraction of the field of consciousness, a state of lowering of the mental level, with cognitive impairment that he called "absent-mindedness." This state of mental regression was also associated with *abulia*, the loss of will or ability to initiate action. He described in detail the progressive narrowing of behavioral options with the passage of time in trauma victims, which was associated with the insidious incorporation of ambient life sensory cues into the spectrum of perceived threat. Janet recognized that hysteria was a disease of the mind that affected all of its functions, and he specifically noted that late trauma was associated with changes in intellect and cognitive performance. Whereas Freud, as a neurologist, continued to maintain that alterations in brain physiology would ultimately be found to underlie all psychical disorders, Janet continued to relate the processes of hysterical dysfunction to disorders of the mind and consciousness. Nevertheless, his work presents a comprehensive categorization of the widely diverse but nevertheless closely connected symptoms of hysteria. Both Freud's early work and Janet's voluminous publications have been in large part vindicated by the emerging studies of the images and physiology of the brain in trauma. As is frequently the case, the seekers of truth in a culture are rejected for their impertinence, and several generations may pass before the truth once again emerges.

Somatic Dissociation: The Body in Hysteria

Janet's, Breuer's, and Freud's descriptions of how trauma-related somatosensory information is stored as memories that are later replicated in perception and behavior are uncannily similar to current descriptions of whiplash syndrome. Or perhaps I should say that we have developed a theory of whiplash syndrome that is uncannily similar to what they wrote over a century ago. If one accepts the concept of the brain/body continuum, one must assume that if trauma can induce relatively permanent structural and functional changes in the brain, it might also do so in the body itself. I have already established that a traumatic event in which the freeze response is never completed leads to retention in procedural memory of the *physical* behaviors and experiences of the trauma. These behaviors, and the sensory and perceptual experiences associated with them, are then brought forth by subsequent exposure to cues of the old trauma.

To revisit a previous example, if an MVA victim suffers a broken arm, that region of the body played a major role in providing the sensory information to the survival brain during the trauma. Thus, the likelihood of the victim's experiencing dissociation of that body part would be relatively high. If the person was traumatized by the event, the pain and proprioceptive messages provided by the injured arm will thereafter also persist in procedural memory. That part of the body will then continue to contribute to messages of threat and therefore to recurrent states of arousal, as was the case with the patient who had been hit on the back with a switch by the nuns in her grade school. In her case, back pain from an MVA replicated back pain in the same region as the pain from the childhood trauma. In response to intolerable arousal, the trauma victim dissociates; the same process of dissociation applies specifically to the parts or regions of the body that provided the physical messages of that unresolved threat: That body part is subjected to specific regional dissociation.

I believe this type of regional somatic dissociation is the same clinical syndrome has been described in historical psychiatric literature as conversion hysteria. Janet and Freud both noted that the hysterically paralyzed body parts had often been those that experienced the physical elements of the abuse. In a sense, the brain has literally disowned the body part that provided the bad news. Janet and Freud felt that these neurologically based impairments of regions of the body served to protect the victim from memories of the experiences of trauma and therefore from anxiety. The resulting detached and diffident behavior of the hysteric, freed from the burden of the terror of her memories, was referred to as *la belle indifférence* (Janet, 1920).

I have always been fascinated by the fact that the neurological signs of conversion disorder, although far from typical of the patterns of motor and sensory impairment due to disease and damage of the nervous system, are nevertheless quite similar from person to person. The sensory loss is mild to complete and involves the numb extremity in a stocking and glove distribution, a pattern that might include numbness and loss of sensation to pinprick of the entire arm below the elbow or the entire leg below the knee. This is not consistent with any examination findings from physical injury to the spinal cord or brain. Sometimes the sensory loss involves one entire half of the body to the midline. In contrast, when structural damage to the brain or spinal cord has occurred, sensory loss will spare about an inch of the body short of the midline due to reduplication of sensation at the midline by both sides of the brain. The weakness in conversion hysteria is characterized by a give-away, or ratcheting quality, as if the person were alternately contracting and then voluntarily releasing the contracted muscle. Clumsiness, such as when attempting to touch the nose with the eyes closed, is often exaggerated and inconsistent from test to test. These clinical features, although remarkably consistent among patients with conversion disorder, are attributed to malingering or emotional distress, probably because they don't make sense according to what doctors are taught about "real" neurological findings on examination. Somehow I doubt that this patient group devised an underground communication network to ensure the consistency of everyone's neurological signs in a grand conspiracy to dupe the medical profession. It seems more likely that there is some tangible neurophysiological mechanism underlying these unusual but strikingly similar physical/neurological manifestations of hysteria.

Evidence that conversion hysteria indeed involves functional alteration in parts of the brain that process sensory information and control motor function is just beginning to emerge. If the paralysis and numbness of the body part in conversion hysteria were solely "psychological" or malingering, one would expect to see no change in the region of the brain that regulates that body part. If, however, the paralysis or numbness *were* due to a change in function of that specific area of the brain, brain imaging techniques would presumably be able to measure it. Mailis-Gagnon and colleagues (2003) studied four patients with chronic pain and "hysterical" anesthesia of a body part. Using a brush and a painful stimulus to stimulate the anesthetic area, they performed fMRI studies of the brain and compared the patients' response to the stimulation to their response to similar stimulation of a corresponding intact area on the opposite side of the body. On the normal side, skin stimulation produced activation on the fMRI in expected areas of the opposite side of the brain, especially the parietal cortex, insula, and thalamus, the areas that process sensory information. On the anesthetic side, however, stimulation did not activate the corresponding areas on the opposite side. Although preliminary, these findings strongly support the idea that the impairment and deficits in function in conversion hysteria have a neurological basis and may be due to an abnormality of message transmission within the brain itself.

Somatic Dissociation

Janet, Freud, and Breuer noted that dissociation in trauma is characterized by a variety of stereotyped neurological symptoms affecting specific regions of the body. However, they did not address the possibility that the dissociated body part might not only participate in and experience the hysterical symptom but also actually be changed in the process. If the brain is altered in this psychological condition, as recent studies have documented, could the actual tissues of the body part experiencing the hysterical symptom also be altered?

Drawing on the concept of somatic dissociation, I would make the case that the region of the body manifesting the hysterical symptom (the area of regional somatic dissociation) indeed is altered by this process—in a way that affects regional blood flow and nutrition of the involved tissues. Circulatory control of blood is determined by the nutritional needs of specific regions of the body at any given time. If the muscles are being used, the blood vessels supplying those muscles dilate to provide more blood carrying oxygen and glucose. When one has eaten food, the blood vessels supplying the digestive organs are dilated for the same purpose.

This regulation of regional circulation, a process called *vasomotor* control, is governed by reciprocal alternating dominance of the sympathetic and the parasympathetic parts of the autonomic nervous system. As discussed earlier, a state of normal, stable cycling between sympathetic and parasympathetic dominance is called *homeostasis*. The autonomic nervous system of the trauma victim, however, is characterized by a state of instability, sensitivity, and a cyclical abnormality of its normal state of regulation. Homeostasis may be disrupted by excessive and disproportionate stimulation by one limb of the autonomic nervous system, a state that is characteristic of the trauma victim. Assaulted by internal cues of threat, the victim experiences repetitive episodes of sympathetic arousal that in turn reflexively trigger deep parasympathetic dissociation. The trauma victim lives in a state of involuntary and disruptive autonomic instability and cycling.

This state not only produces alternating bouts of anxiety and numbing of perception but also alternating physical symptoms. Sympathetic arousal is experienced as palpitations, tremor, muscle spasms, hyperventilation, perspiring, and cool, pale skin. Parasympathetic symptoms may include bowel cramps, indigestion, nausea, diarrhea, generalized weakness, and warm, red skin. These symptoms may cycle so rapidly that the victim is unable to differentiate the two types of experiences. I maintain that this pervasive state of vasomotor instability in the trauma victim may selectively and more severely affect the regions of the body that experienced the sensory messages of the traumatic event or that were selectively involved in the complex pattern of defensive motor behavior. In other words, the regions of the body that were dissociated and therefore more likely to manifest the syndromes of hysteria might also experience vasomotor instability. Dissociated parts of the body may cycle between states of cool, pale, sweaty skin to warm, red, dry skin. Most importantly, this state of poorly modulated circulation might actually cause abnormal physical and pathological changes in the dissociated region of the body.

The Stigmata Enigma

Stigmata are physical changes in the body (usually wounds) that defy rational scientific explanation. For centuries they have been associated with specific religious experiences and largely relegated to the realm of the supernatural or, in Christian terms, the miraculous. Consistent documentation of stigmata and similar phenomena appears in the historical literature of the Catholic Church, with stories of ecstatics (persons who have manifested stigmata) developing wounds that replicated the wounds on the feet, hands, brow, and side of the body that Christ suffered during the last days of his life. Not only were the "wounds" quite obvious, but they also were usually associated with intense suffering of the ecstatic, replicating the suffering of Christ as described in the Bible. Michael Freze (1989) provided a comprehensive review of the literature, gleaned from the writings of observers going back to the 12th century, on the unique mystical experiences of the 320 reported cases of stigmata in the Catholic literature.

Of these 320 cases, 41 were men and 62 were canonized by the Catholic Church as saints. The first was St. Francis of Assisi during the 12th century. As noted, all of them were called "ecstatics" because they manifested altered states of consciousness that primarily involved religious ecstasy. Other descriptions of these altered states include rapture, mystical flights, visions, supernatural communions, inedia (lack of nourishment), transverberation (a wound of the soul), divine union, and mystical marriage. In many cases, these periods of ecstasy and the appearance of stigmata occurred on Thursdays and Fridays, the days of Christ's Passion. Descriptions of the wounds have been meticulous and usually note reddening, occasionally actual wounds or breaking of the skin, and frequently the exudation of a clear red liquid thought to be blood. With the advent of the microscope, examination of this liquid proved that in fact it contained no blood cells and was simply a clear liquid.

Physiologists have tried to explain stigmata as actual physical changes in the body induced by a vivid imagination coupled with powerful emotions. The Catholic Church has countered this argument by noting that medical treatment has no effect on healing of the wounds. It has also been noted that the stigmatic wound is stable, does not become infected or suppurate, and gives off no foul odor. Other scientists have attempted to discredit stigmata as being self-inflicted. To this end, ecstatics have been observed day and night, and the spontaneous appearance and remission of stigmata have been exhaustively documented. The limbs have been wrapped in cloth to prevent self-mutilation. Janet himself was fascinated with stigmata and even devised a copper shoe with a window over the area of stigmatic change to prevent the person from self-inflicting the wound. In numerous cases, the spontaneous appearance of the stigmata has been documented (Freze, 1989). The actual appearance of wounds remains controversial.

What does a discussion of religious miracles have to do with a supposedly scientific discourse on the neurophysiology of trauma and the body? It has everything to do with concepts of procedural memory, classical conditioning, dissociation, and abnormal vasomotor regulation of regions of the body. Bob Tinker, a colleague and friend of mine and the coauthor of a book on eye movement desensitization and reprocessing (EMDR) in children, told me about a remarkable case of his that explains the phenomenon of stigmata (Tinker & Wilson, 1999). During a session of EMDR, a client who had been severely physically abused by her husband recovered a conscious, declarative memory of a particularly violent beating that she had received. As she burst into tears, a vivid, red blush appeared on the left side of her face: the complete and unequivocal imprint of a right hand, the fingers extending toward her ear. Procedural memory for the pain of that blow to her face, resurrected during a session of EMDR, had induced autonomic regional changes in the body part that had processed the sensory information of that traumatic event. The resulting autonomic changes replicated the stigmata with dilatation of blood vessels and redness of the skin in the exact pattern of that sensory input, a hand striking her face. In somatic dissociation, the initial manifestation of abnormal vasomotor control of the body part is usually parasympathetic, with vasodilitation. She also was aware at the time that the left side of her face had felt strange, disembodied, and not quite part of her. The combination of trauma, procedural memory for the somatic elements of that trauma, and dissociation of the area of the body that experienced the somatic elements of the trauma had physically changed that body part. It was now subject to alteration of circulation in the face of a traumatic cue (memory for the traumatic event), producing a visible change in the tissue in the form of a stigma. The redness of the stigma in fact represented a distinct regional episode of dilatation of blood vessels of the face in the exact pattern of the "wounding" by the hand of her abuser.

The process of dissociation is intimately intertwined with the entire experience of ecstatics who have been documented to manifest stigmata. All have experienced altered mental and emotional states that accompanied the stigmatic changes in the body, which strongly suggests a state of dissociation. These altered perceptual states closely mimic many of those described by Janet in his discussions of hysteria and clearly prompted him to pursue the study of patients manifesting stigmata. Immersion of the religious ecstatic into the existential suffering of Christ during his Passion would certainly be sufficient for the student of Christ's doctrine to incorporate that suffering into procedural memory as a conditioned experience and response. Thereafter, in the face of conditioned cues (the days of the week that Christ suffered) the ecstatic would predictably manifest the physical changes linked to that memory as part of ecstatic dissociation, the timing based on traumatic recapitulation. The stigmata would appear as visible changes in autonomic vasomotor control of the dissociated areas of the body. These visible changes in autonomic control would manifest as localized reddening (vasodilatation) and perhaps release of perspiration in the regions of somatic dissociation—the hands, feet, brow, and side.

In deference to the religious implications of stigmata within the Catholic Church, this speculative attempt to explain what has been considered a miracle in no way lessens the miraculous and spiritual content of the phenomenon of stigmata in those few who have experienced it. Indeed, the Catholic Church feels that religion or mysticism is not dependent on a scientific solution that either proves or rules out a rational scientific explanation. The Church in fact maintains that in the process of canonization, stigmata are not considered to represent uncontestable miracles (Freze, 1989).

Stigmata in Clinical Practice

Like Bob Tinker, I have seen local skin changes in many of my patients who have suffered physical trauma and have been traumatized by the experience.

These changes are usually associated with fluctuating mild redness (erythema) in the area of the body that received a blow or experienced pain in a traumatic event. This erythema is usually accompanied by mild but definite puffiness (edema) of the affected area. These changes are clearly not representative of actual residual effects of the injury, as they persist for a long period of time after the injury, often for months. Almost invariably, close questioning reveals that the patients are quite aware that the area of skin involved feels strange and different than the skin around it or the skin on the opposite side of the body, and they often perceive the affected area as being "not quite part of them." In addition, the tissue changes clearly fluctuate in appearance and even disappear at times, usually in relationship to the degree of emotional distress that the patient is experiencing.

Examples of this type of stigmata in my professional experience include the areas around an abdominal surgical scar in a patient who awoke under anesthesia, the side of a woman's face where it struck the window of a car, the forehead of a man who was struck there in an unprovoked assault, and the area on the neck of a woman who was struck there by lightning. In all cases, these changes recurred intermittently for many months after the original injury. All of these patients experienced periodic changes in color and skin temperature in the area of their body that experienced physical sensations during the traumatic experience. In many cases, these stigmata visibly changed in appearance during my sessions with the patients, usually based on the emotional content of the discussion. In most cases, the stigmata eventually disappeared with successful therapy for PTSD. All of these patients had baseline numbing of the affected area and, despite the numbing, several had pain.

In other cases of somatic dissociation, the regional autonomic alterations noted in stigmata blended with the development of what can only be called *dystrophic* changes in the affected body part. Such changes, as the term implies, were associated with evidence for loss of tissue nutrition and were characterized by hair loss, thinning of the skin, and slowed growth of the nails, often with ridging, splitting, and thinning. Many of these patients complained of hair loss, and on several occasions, selective loss of hair was evident on one side of the scalp, usually the side where other dystrophic skin changes and sensory symptoms were noted.

My first such case occurred in a woman with the neurological signs of conversion hysteria. She suffered hysterical sensory loss and clumsiness on the right side of her body—the side on which she perceived an oncoming car that broadsided her car. When she told me that her hairdresser had mentioned that the hair on the right side of her head was growing more slowly than on the left, I examined her scalp and indeed noted obvious thinning of the hair restricted to the right side. I have subsequently documented this remarkable phenomenon in numerous patients, all of them with dissociative symptoms and neurological signs of conversion in the affected body part or on the symptomatic side of the body.

In addition to these signs of actual atrophy of skin structures, many patients complained of coldness and skin discoloration in the affected extremity. It appeared that the hand or foot was actually not receiving normal circulation, and usually it was quite obvious that there was indeed a difference in skin temperature, the affected side being cooler than the opposite side. At its worst, the skin of the affected extremity also appeared paler, with a strange mottled appearance in a spider web pattern. Vasoconstriction and diminished blood flow could certainly explain the dystrophic changes noted in hair, skin, and nails. The same changes in skin nutrition may also be seen in patients with inadequate blood flow to an extremity due to diabetes or atherosclerotic narrowing of arteries. Of course, none of these patients suffered from these conditions.

With further questioning, some of these patients noted that earlier in the course of their problem, they had actually experienced redness and warmth of the extremity, at times with remarkable increase in growth of the hair and nails. This indicates an abnormal cycling of autonomic regulation of a part of the body that was affecting its basic circulation and nutrition. This cycling also represented the extremes of sympathetic and parasympathetic control of circulation to that part of the body. In fact, these were classic signs of a well-known but poorly understood disease called *reflex sympathetic dystrophy* (RSD), a disease that in my patients appeared to be linked to conversion hysteria, dissociation, stigmata, and a history of traumatization.

Reflex Sympathetic Dystrophy: The Pathological Extreme of Stigmata

RSD (also called complex regional pain syndrome) was initially described by neurologist S. Wier Mitchell and colleagues (1864) in their documentation of injuries suffered by soldiers in the American Civil War. Some of these gunshot victims developed exquisite, burning pain and sensitivity to any touch stimulus in the injured extremity, accompanied by coldness and atrophy of the limb and clawlike flexion contractures. Mitchell named the condition *causalgia* after the Greek word for burning, *causus*. Subsequent physicians recognized that there were varying degrees of severity in RSD, that it was often associated with a phase of excessive warmth, redness, and increased growth of hair and nails, and that it occasionally remitted or disappeared altogether. Because one of the major manifestations was coldness and vasoconstriction, a property of the sympathetic nervous system control of peripheral arteries, the name *reflex sympathetic dystrophy* was given to the condition, recognizing its most disabling manifestations. Treatment for this condition involved attempts to block what was believed to be excessive activation of the sympathetic autonomic control of the affected limb by blocking the sympathetic ganglia (nerve bundles) that controlled the limb. Sympathetic nerve blocks also have been used as a diagnostic test in therapy, but they are quite unpredictable in both modes of application. For the most part, therapy for RSD has produced unpredictable results at best, although spontaneous improvement and remission is fairly common. Unfortunately, most of the therapy for RSD, involving painful, invasive, and intrinsically threatening procedures, is almost guaranteed to traumatize the patient further and worsen the condition.

I believe that RSD is a syndrome of procedural memory and brain-based abnormal regulation of cycling of the autonomic nervous system, a condition that is the basis for all posttraumatic syndromes and diseases. In presenting this theory, I am, in a sense, challenging the basic approach of medical science, as "behavioral problems" such as PTSD can't really cause specific physical diseases in the allopathic system of medicine. Unfortunately, nonacademic physicians who have not traversed the gauntlet of obtaining grants and publishing medical scientific studies are not allowed to speculate about the nature of disease based only on their personal anecdotal medical experiences. Medical science consists of a rigidly defined hierarchy of institutions that control the flow of information within the field. One ascends this hierarchy by discovering and proving scientific theories through a carefully proscribed process of application for grant monies to support experimental studies. These studies must prove something and be published and acknowledged by the medical academic community. With the accumulation of successfully published studies, the medical academic may gradually ascend the hierarchical ladder of success in medical science. Only then may that scientist be allowed to speculate about his own theories beyond the bounds of his existing scientific data. Of course, although this process may inhibit the development of possibly valid theories, it also is a reasonable and necessary contingency if the flow of knowledge within the medical field is to be validated.

Nevertheless, I have felt compelled to pursue the concept of somatic dissociation, and the consistent though subtle manifestations of autonomic dysregulation associated with it, in greater detail because of its regular appearance in so many of my patients. I have realized that these clinical signs and symptoms form a continuum of regional abnormalities of vasomotor regulation of tissues, ranging from subtle stigmata to dramatic and disabling RSD. In presenting these findings and theories to groups of mental health professionals, I have discovered that many nonmedical psychotherapists have observed similar clinical manifestations in many of their patients, from the common occurrence of RSD in their patients to the incidence of hair loss and bald patches in specific areas on the scalp. Their anecdotes combined with my experiences form a compelling litany of tales supporting these concepts of disease and dissociation

During a break in one of my workshops, an attendee approached me with the story of one of her patients—like many, a tale of unspeakable tragedy. The attendee's patient, a 19-year-old woman, had experienced a kidnapping and ritual rape, sodomy, and fellatio at age 15. Being forced to perform fellatio on her perpetrator was particularly traumatizing. Predictably, she developed severe PTSD that evolved into anorexia, bulimia, and an unremitting dissociative disorder. Multiple suicide attempts required repeated hospitalizations. She developed interstitial cystitis, a condition of inflammation and ulceration of the bladder, and irritable bowel syndrome. Most dramatically, however, after one terrible exacerbation of panic and dissociation, she developed extreme pain in her throat and was found on examination through an endoscope to have severe ulceration of her throat and upper esophagus, for no apparent reason. The physician noted that this finding was something that he had never seen before. This unfortunate woman had developed inflammatory and dystrophic (ulcerative) changes in the dissociated parts of her body that had experienced the most intense somatic sensations of the traumatic event.

A patient of mine developed RSD in her right hand that was believed to be secondary to repetitive overuse tendonitis of the hand due to performing data entry in her job. During trauma therapy for a subsequent car accident, her memory went back to a prior abusive marital relationship, one in which she recalled repeatedly defending herself with her right arm from blows by her left-handed husband. After describing these experiences, she experienced significant emotional release and, as her right hand warmed perceptibly, the pain of the RSD diminished.

A colleague in the field of trauma therapy practicing somatic experiencing showed me a video of a therapy session involving a patient who had been struck by lightning at the base of the right side of her neck. That side of her neck remained numb thereafter. Interestingly, her clinical presentation was not for symptoms of PTSD but for a manic disorder that caused her friends great distress. After about 15 sessions, she had a dramatic breakthrough during which her body recapitulated the violent movement patterns caused by the lightning strike, thereby completing the defensive response that had been truncated by her freeze at the moment of the electrocution. At the completion of the session, the right side of her neck and throat was asymmetrically bright red, and normal sensation had returned to the skin.

I am certain that many of you readers who have a clinical psychotherapy practice will have similar tales and experiences with some of your patients. You probably have also puzzled at the strange and sometimes even bizarre nature of these stories. Patients themselves at times seem reluctant to tell me about such experiences, probably because of the skeptical response they may have received from other physicians. As I have noted, deriving conclusions from anecdotes is strictly forbidden in the medical field. Nevertheless, the bizarre and arcane in both medicine and life itself, including such mystical phenomena as religious stigmata, almost by definition have a plausible explanation, unless one simply accepts the indefinable laws of religion and spirituality. The truth indeed may be found in the detailed telling of stories by patients, as well as in the careful search for the minutia in clinical findings.

The primary barrier to accepting this non-Cartesian model of disease goes back to issues presented at the beginning of the book. We still struggle with the idea that the brain, body, mind, spirit, and self may be an indefinable whole rather than separable entities. To consider the mind as a special, separate entity from specific brain processes defies what we know about the neurophysiology of thought. But to assert that the mind and its creative thoughts and perceptions are simply based on a fluid combination of declarative and procedural memories robs us of such sacred concepts as free will and our ability to create entirely new concepts. To relegate the spirit to our imagination layered over existing instincts and memory systems is to lose many of the glorious intangibles of our existence. In the end we must accept the existence of a vast and humbling unknown in the processes of the brain, mind, and body, even in the most rigorous fields of science. We probably will also have to accept a vast and imponderable *unknowable* as well. Far greater minds than mine have written brilliant treatises on these topics. Nevertheless, in the infant field of medical science, we must continue to pursue a melding of brain processes and body changes that occur, not because of some external influence, but because of internal, learned information that may physically change the body and cause physical, tangible disease.

CHAPTER 9

Diseases of Stress and Trauma

Stress and trauma have much in common as bad things that happen to a person during the course of his or her life. I have basically defined trauma as an experience that involves a threat to life while the victim is in a state of relative helplessness. By now it should be clear that trauma itself exists on a continuum and that many events that ordinarily would not be considered life-threatening can be traumatic depending on their meaning within the context of the victim's prior life experiences. Stress, as we know, is any force of nature or experience that disrupts the physiological equilibrium (homeostasis) of an animal or person. Because trauma disrupts homeostasis, it falls under the category of stress, but obviously not all stress is traumatic. Basically, the two states, like most everything else, form a continuum. Stress may become traumatic if it occurs in the face of helplessness or lack of control, especially if features of the stressful experience contain cues related to past life trauma. Thus, the female corporate executive who is subjected to undue duress by her male superior may respond to that stress with symptoms of trauma if she bears the burden of the effects of an abusive and traumatizing father.

Nevertheless, both types of experiences potentially impair one's health. *How* they impair it (and how they differ in the process of doing so) is important to understand. Most researchers consider many of the medical syndromes covered in this chapter to be psychosomatic in nature. Some physicians believe that stress produces symptoms that may in a sense be real but don't actually constitute a disease. Others think that stress-related symptoms are largely imagined. I believe that the symptoms of these diseases and disorders are the very real consequences of the effects of traumatic stress on the body.

As this chapter illustrates, diseases of stress have much in common with the diseases of trauma. Although they overlap a great deal, and although both represent disruption of autonomic homeostasis, stress-related diseases are associated more with chronic low-grade fight/flight, sympathetic arousal, whereas trauma-related diseases are more associated with the parasympathetic physiology of the freeze response.

The Diseases of Stress

Stress-related diseases, as described by Hans Selye (1956), are based on the basic hormonal changes in the body during the fight/flight response. Noted earlier, these hormonal changes are primarily the result of activation of the sympathetic nervous system. In the face of a perceived threat or danger, the animal must mobilize the body's access to sources of short-term energy, primarily for the brain and musculoskeletal system, in the form of glucose. The animal must have its wits about it and must be swift and powerful. It must be prepared for a short-term energy crisis caused by the immediate critical needs of the brain, the skeletal muscles, and the heart.

Of course, in most cases evolutionary survival is based on the animal's capacity for speed. Generating speed demands an immediate increase in blood flow to the organs that move the body, the skeletal muscles, as well as to the organ that controls them, the brain. The instinctual arousal response of the brain discussed in Chapter 2 reflexively triggers the release of adrenaline (epinephrine) from the medulla, or center of the adrenal glands, two small, quarter-sized glands that perch on top of each kidney. Adrenaline stimulates the heart to beat faster and stronger, immediately increasing the amount of blood that is pumped throughout the body. To allow this blood to reach the correct organs to enhance strength and speed, adrenaline dilates the blood vessels that feed the brain and the skeletal muscles. It simultaneously constricts the blood vessels that feed the organs of digestion, including the liver, pancreas, stomach, and intestines. One doesn't need to digest food when immediate survival is at stake. One does, however, need immediate access to glucose, the primary source of energy for the brain and muscles. The major storehouses for glucose are the muscles themselves as well as the liver, where glucose is stored in the form of a chemical called *glycogen*. Adrenaline stimulates the liver to break down its stored glycogen into glucose and to release that glucose into the bloodstream for immediate energy utilization. The brain needs more blood, oxygen, and glucose to direct this process, and it receives them through the dilating of its blood vessels. This whole process basically sets up the animal for a limited period of sustained arousal, as well as muscular and cardiovascular effort in the interests of survival.

The same process that sets up adrenaline release also influences the pituitary gland, the master gland of the endocrine system, to release a hormone that specifically influences the adrenal cortex, or outer layer of the adrenal glands. Through secretion of adrenocorticotrophic hormone (ACTH), the pituitary influences the release of cortisol by the adrenal cortex. Cortisol has several different functions that basically prepare the threatened or stressed animal to tolerate and manage a threat or stress if it persists for very long. Selye (1956) called this response to prolonged stress the "general adaptation syndrome" (GAS). The GAS consists of a number of unusual changes in organ systems of the body resulting from excessive and prolonged exposure to the effects of cortisol and its related steroid compounds produced by the adrenal cortex. Chronic stress or threat no longer demands the immediate and maximal cardiac and muscular response that is associated with an imminent life threat. It basically requires that the animal's body be prepared for a period of chronic readiness for danger and potentially higher demands for energy (Selye).

In order to prepare the animal for such a state of affairs, cortisol and related adrenal cortical steroids promote retention of salt and, therefore, of body water. This allows the animal to sustain a high blood volume to promote blood pressure and blood flow in the face of potential physical injury. It also increases levels of blood glucose for potential energy demands. Cortisol stimulates brain activity and increases alertness, leading to insomnia, one of its bothersome clinical side effects. It also increases serum lipids, raising triglycerides and cholesterol levels in the blood. Cortisol promotes the storage of ingested calories as fat for long-term access to energy, usually distributed in the abdominal region. In the interests of efficiently storing calories, it effectively promotes obesity. As one of the predictable consequences of their exposure to trauma in an auto accident, most of my patients gained 10–20 pounds during the first few months after the accident without any perceived increase in caloric intake.

Unfortunately, animals are poorly designed to deal with this costly state of stress adaptation for very long. Cortisol has a long laundry list of adverse side effects, many of which contribute to the diseases of stress described by Selye (1956). In addition to obesity, prolonged exposure to abnormally high levels of cortisol promotes diabetes (sustained increased blood glucose), hypertension (increased blood volume), and atherosclerosis (elevated serum lipids). Because cortisol suppresses the inflammatory response in the body, synthetic forms of cortisol have been extensively used for suppression of the inflammatory manifestations of such diseases as asthma, rheumatoid arthritis, lupus erythematosis, and soft-tissue inflammations. Patients treated with steroids of this type are prone to developing the abnormal glucose tolerance typical of diabetes, as well as elevated blood pressure. Prolonged treatment carries the risk of premature development of atherosclerosis and heart disease.

High levels of cortisol suppress the immune system and cause atrophy and shrinkage of lymph nodes and the thymus gland, rendering the stressed animal vulnerable to infections. In the early days of organ transplantation, synthetic forms of cortisol were given to these patients to intentionally suppress their immune systems to prevent rejection of the transplanted organ. These patients were extremely sensitive to bacterial and viral infections, including so-called opportunistic bacteria, microbes that usually are benign members of our bacterial environment. They also were vulnerable to certain kinds of cancer, another complication of immune suppression. With the current world epidemic of AIDS, we now have a fairly pure model of a disease characterized by severe suppression of the immune system. AIDS patients, of course, usually die from rare and opportunistic infections. Notably, they also develop rare forms of cancer, including Kaposi's sarcoma. A more mundane example of stress-related immune suppression, of course, is the tendency for "cold sores" (Herpes simplex viral ulcers, usually on the mucous membranes) under conditions of heightened stress, such as minor viral upper respiratory illnesses or even sun exposure.

Many of the stressed rats studied by Selye (1956) manifested these disease states. Selye's rats also developed ulceration of the linings of their intestines, partially due to the fact that cortisol also increases the release of peptic acid in the stomach. Gastric acid reflux, or indigestion, is a common symptom of stress and is associated with the development of peptic ulcers, although a bacterium, *H. pylori*, has also now been implicated in ulcer disease. It is also possible that the relative immune suppression associated with stress might allow *H. pylori* to exert its damaging effect on the lining of the stomach and duodenum.

Selye (1956) speculated about a great many other diseases or conditions that he felt might be due to stress. He noted that exposure to cortisol and its steroid relatives sometimes seemed to exert a paradoxical effect, at times suppressing inflammation and at other times promoting it, and at times suppressing experimental types of epilepsy and at other times worsening it. His work led to the general understanding that hypertension, diabetes, atherosclerosis, heart disease, and peptic ulcer disease could be precipitated by stress. Because steroids such as cortisol increase arousal and affect mental function, stress as a disruption of normal hormonal balance might well contribute to disordered mental and emotional functions of various types. This may account for the fact that physicians usually blamed life stress as the primary cause for emotional distress in patients. It would appear, then, that the diseases of stress probably relate primarily to heightened levels of serum cortisol as a result of the brain's adaptation to a relatively sustained state of preparation for defense against an ongoing but relatively low-level threat.

Clearly this is a simplistic description of the physiology and diseases of stress. The continuum between an acute life threat, a sustained exposure to danger that is just short of being potentially mortal, and a persistent conflict that impedes normal function and homeostasis but does not threaten existence may be subtle indeed. All of these examples, however, certainly would fall under the definition of stress, and all of them to some degree would produce the hormonal changes and complications that have been described. In fact, stress by this definition is inevitable, and our bodies are designed to respond to these experiences in a quite functional fashion. It is only when stress achieves a degree of intensity or continues for a sufficient duration that we begin to see adverse effects on the body's organ systems. Selye (1956) even recognized that the presence of subtle but normal levels of stress, or *eustress*, might even enhance the animal's basic level of function. Like every facet of the body's physiology, the continuum between optimal, normal, and impaired function is subtle. So too, the line between health and disease is a fine one.

The Diseases of Trauma

Not surprisingly, the diseases that may be attributable to traumatic stress also form somewhat of a continuum with the specifically stress-related diseases just described. Scientific research has shown that childhood life trauma may contribute significantly to an adulthood susceptibility to many of the diseases that are attributable to stress. In a massive study of 13,494 adults, Felitti and colleagues (1998) documented a close and proportionate relationship between a variety of types of child abuse, from a simple dysfunctional family life to outright physical and sexual abuse, and many of the major causes of death in adult life, including heart, lung, and liver disease. Many of these diseases may well have been related to the fact that those exposed to child-hood trauma were more prone to use alcohol and tobacco excessively. Never-theless, it was clear that even low levels of stress and trauma in childhood led to increased health-risk-taking behavior, increased use of mood-modifying substances, and stress-related disease in adulthood. The diseases of trauma, however, are often believed to be "functional," or psychosomatic. Conse-quently, few of the diseases of trauma discussed in this chapter were addressed in Felliti's study, except for the use of alcohol and street drugs.

The relationship between early negative life experiences and the propen-sity for diseases of stress throughout the life span is not surprising considering the fact that victims of trauma experience exaggerated and cyclical abnormal regulation of the autonomic nervous system, a significant part of which is associated with elevated levels of serum cortisol. Part of the legacy of child-hood trauma is the resetting of the arousal response to a higher, more sensi-tive level, as well as the inability to regulate the arousal response once it has been produced. In addition, childhood trauma victims are aroused by a broader spectrum of environmental events, many of which would probably be well tolerated by the person blessed with a life relatively free from traumatic stress. In fact, there is no doubt that the increased use of tobacco and alcohol in this group of people is for the purpose of dampening their heightened arousal response.

Studies of wartime veterans and former prisoners of war also show an increased incidence of peptic ulcers, hypertension, and atherosclerotic heart disease, the classic diseases of stress (Beebe, 1975; Friedman & Schnurr, 1995). Many of these veterans also suffered from PTSD. Tobacco and alcohol use were also more prominent. Although child abuse was not an issue in these patients, it is clear that traumatic stress sufficient to cause PTSD may also independently predispose victims to the stress-related diseases associated with chronic exposure to increased levels of serum cortisol.

Chronic stress is associated with a low-grade state of activation of the fight/flight response, with its association with release of norepinephrine in the brain, epinephrine (adrenalin) by the adrenals, and cortisol. At some point, however, the stress either subsides (at which point homeostasis returns and healing begins to take place) or persists to the point where the animal can no longer sustain its cortisol-based adaptive response (at which point the body begins to deteriorate with the diseases of stress). On the other hand, the stress may escalate and assume the implications of a life threat. Under these circumstances, the animal has no choice but to gather its resources for full-blown fighting or fleeing, the last-ditch effort for survival. If the animal's effort is successful, the stress may be resolved and homeostasis once again may be recovered. Unfortunately, in many circumstances, the animal is not able to control the threat through fight or flight, and the freeze response occurs. As discussed earlier, if the freeze response is not resolved and completed with a discharge, the animal is subjected to chemical changes in its brain and body that determine a whole different group of conditions, syndromes, and diseases that, unlike stress-related diseases, are not cortisol-driven. Because helplessness is a state of reality or perception that is essentially required for the freeze response, one might also classify these medical syndromes as diseases of helplessness.

Thus, diseases of trauma basically fall on a continuum, with those related to the fight/flight response (which usually are the same as stress-related diseases) on one end of the continuum and those related to helplessness, the freeze response, and dissociation on the other end. Of course, no creature is entirely immune to states of helplessness. Furthermore, helplessness has many meanings and at times remarkably subtle criteria: Entrapment, imprisonment, disempowerment, defenselessness, vulnerability, and weakness, for example, could all be considered forms of helplessness. Each of these states implies a relative lack of control, but by itself would not necessarily be considered a risk factor for trauma. Nevertheless, as I have repeatedly noted, the events that may be considered traumatic also form a continuum. Trauma to a great extent is dependent on the meaning of the event to the individual based on the person's cumulative burden of negative life experiences and on the similarity of the event to any of those experiences. Where the person falls within the spectrum of states of relative helplessness is also determined by this cumulative burden of prior negative life experiences. Helplessness, therefore, is contingent upon the individual's relative state of resiliency or vulnerability, both of which are determined not only by the "real" effects of prior negative life experiences but also by the person's *perception* of those experiences.

One of the most common sources of life stress in an urbanized, acculturated society is the approach/avoidance conflict, in which one's options have both positive and negative implications for one's sense of well-being. Obviously, the greater the intensity of these implications, the greater the conflict will be and the greater the intensity of ambivalence. It is not uncommon that one must make life choices that have actual implications for survival. Decisions regarding marriage or divorce, vocation, employment, major moves, or treatment for a serious illness are all examples of life-changing decisions that we make many times during our life. Persecution by one's superior in a job that one cannot leave because of financial needs is a rather common example of an approach/avoidance conflict. Unfortunately, in some situations, all the possible options have potentially life-altering or life-threatening implications. Under such circumstances, the intensity of one's perception of helplessness increases as the deadline for making a decision approaches. The case of the man described in Chapter 2, who abruptly collapsed and died when he was faced with an unbearable social dilemma in one city and then was thwarted in his attempt to escape to a new social setting, illustrates the profound effect that helplessness can have on an individual. His death is quite analogous to the fatal effects of the freeze response in wild animals immobilized in the alien setting of the scientific laboratory or the captured wild animal that "inexplicably" dies on its trip to the zoo. They have experienced the ultimate expression of the freeze response in the face of overwhelming helplessness.

The approach/avoidance conflict typifies the basic state of helplessness in the face of threat that is the precursor of the freeze response. The human victim of this state of behavioral immobility enters a state of physiological collapse and withdrawal that is characterized by many of the features of the freeze response. As I have said, I associate the human experience of dissociation with the perceptions that occur during the freeze response. The unique alteration of the physiology of the brain and body in the freeze is quite distinct from the alteration caused by the low-grade arousal associated with sustained stress and the diseases related to it. Once the condition of helplessness has emerged in the face of an ongoing threat, the brain's response changes, and the diseases of trauma begin to emerge along with the diseases of stress. And these related disease states are really quite different from those related to Selye's GAS.

It is important to reiterate that the cascade of abnormal events that follows a traumatic event sufficient to trigger the freeze response occurs because the freeze has not been discharged or completed. Once again, the freeze discharge extinguishes most of the *meanings* of the multiple internal and external cues associated with the trauma. Completion of the aborted motor act of survival through the freeze discharge also stores the details of the event as a *past* memory, not as an ongoing threat. The autonomic nervous system is allowed to revert back to the gentle and rhythmic cycle of homeostasis. Inhibition of the freeze discharge appears to be related to a sustained state of helplessness, entrapment, or disempowerment. In animals, this state of sustained helplessness may be exemplified by capture, caging, or domestication. In humans, it may be related to certain aspects of acculturation, and it may be more or less prevalent based on behavioral threats and limits associated with the particular culture. In other words, the cage in this case is cultural.

Given this state of culturally determined physiological inhibition, humans are likely to freeze/dissociate fairly frequently. This tendency to freeze occurs not only during major traumatic events, but also with the experience of unavoidable and irresolvable conflict. If the person is the victim of accumulated complex trauma, the freeze may occur with "trivial" life events whose *meaning* is sufficient to represent a life threat. If the person is unable to routinely and effectively discharge the freeze, the physiological events that occur in the brain and endocrine and autonomic nervous systems associated in response to trauma and freeze will occur repeatedly. The intensity of this response will be proportionate to the intensity of the threat or conflict. It obviously will also be cumulative, with the freeze tendency increasing in proportion to the degree of exposure to past threat or conflict. The progressive loss of resiliency that one experiences in this scenario would indicate that the diseases of freeze/dissociation would probably begin to appear during the middle decades of one's life, again based on the volume of accumulation of negative life experiences.

These diseases have their pathological roots in the autonomic and endocrinologic alterations that result from the lack of discharge of the freeze response, which I described in Chapter 2. This state is one of dramatic increase in the oscillation of rhythmic systems of autonomic regulation. At times, the autonomic nervous system may manifest marked accentuation of activity in *both* the sympathetic and parasympathetic systems, as when the prey has frozen after a failed attempt to flee. As a result, one may see diseases and conditions with symptoms that appear diametrically opposed to each other, at both ends of autonomic function, in the same patient. For example, many of my patients with RDS have first experienced redness, warmth, and increased hair and nail growth of the dissociated limb—parasympathetic symptoms. This is then followed by pallor, sweating, loss of hair, and breaking of nails—sympathetic symptoms. Patients with irritable bowel syndrome usually experience alternating constipation and diarrhea.

Because these regulatory systems affect every organ system in the body, the patient may present with disabling symptoms affecting multiple organs and regions of the body, a condition that defies the allopathic system of concepts of disease. Because these diseases are in part associated with the perceptual phenomenon of dissociation, their severity may be associated with prominent emotional symptoms and may also be increased by emotional arousal. Finally, the region of the body that is the source of the primary complaint often played a role in the unconscious procedural memory for a traumatic event. As a result, the complaint often can't be linked to any obvious event (who would guess that the back pain experienced by an MVA victim who suffered no appreciable physical injuries was actually caused by the trauma of being hit in the same place with a switch during grade school?) and therefore it won't make sense. It is no wonder that the diseases of freeze/dissociation are perplexing and are often considered to be the result of hypochondria or psychosomatic or somatization disorders.

For purposes of discussion, I have divided these diseases into categories based on the predominant feature of their abnormal function. These categories are as follows:

- Diseases of abnormal autonomic regulation
- Syndromes of procedural memory
- Diseases of somatic dissociation
- Disorders of endocrine and immune system regulation
- Disorders of cognition and sleep

As with any categories related to a common cause, the conditions addressed in part will fall along a continuum. Consequently, virtually all of these disease categories contain some similar clinical characteristics and symptoms and a similar basic physiology.

Diseases of Abnormal Autonomic Regulation

The most prominent feature of altered autonomic regulation in trauma and dissociation is a dramatic and abnormal enhancement of the normal oscillatory cycling of homeostasis. Antelman and colleagues (1997) presented a physiological model for PTSD based on this concept. Many of the systems of the body, including the endocrine and autonomic systems, manifest such oscillatory cycling, a process that by definition promotes flexibility and adaptability for the system. Providing a strong input to either the upward or downward limb of that cycling process tends to drive both limbs to an increased level of cycling. With continued abnormal input, the process of oscillation may then increase to the extremes of tolerance of the system. In PTSD, of course, the two limbs of the cycling are sympathetic/parasympathetic, fight/flight or freeze. Input of even a minor threat response in the traumatized victim of PTSD will therefore elicit an extreme sympathetic response, or panic, followed rapidly by an extreme parasympathetic response, or dissociation. This response is based on a sensitized, already abnormally oscillating autonomic nervous system that is primed for an extreme oscillatory response.

With the passage of time, however, the cardinal symptoms of PTSD tend to subside, and a group of secondary symptoms and conditions, which probably correlate with a significant change in the way that the autonomic nervous system now functions, begin to appear. Although the victim of late PTSD continues to experience heightened levels of arousal to stress, that arousal tends to be relatively transient, moving more readily into symptoms of dissociation. It is as if the late-trauma victim is programmed to freeze at the slightest hint of a threat. The model of learned helplessness in animals typifies this response. This pattern of response is especially common in PTSD victims who have had childhood trauma or have suffered exposure to many episodes of traumatic stress, a condition now referred to as *complex trauma*. Such persons may be said to be primed to dissociate, and they may intermittently experience many different perceptual states that are typical of dissociation, such as episodes of depersonalization, amnesia, altered sense of time, and feelings of unreality. With this degree of sensitization to threat, the freeze response occurs frequently and persists for longer periods of time. Such a person will therefore spend a great deal of time with the perceptual symptoms of dissociation and will experience a state of chronic and heightened parasympathetic autonomic tone, alternating, of course, with briefer periods of arousal, or sympathetic tone. This state of sustained freeze/dissociation is also associated with persisting abnormally low levels of serum cortisol.

When the parasympathetic nervous system is operating in a healthy fashion, the animal is at rest, often having eaten or procreated. Food is actively being digested, glucose stores are being accumulated in the form of glycogen in the muscles and liver, the muscles are resting and replenishing energy. Much of this activity is driven by impulses from the vagus nerve, discussed in Chapter 2 in the context of its relationship to energy conservation and the mediation of the freeze response. Located in the brainstem medulla, the vagus nerve also regulates the parasympathetic activity of the viscera of the thorax and abdomen. In a parasympathetic dominant state, the digestive organs are quite active, with the stomach and intestines contracting in peristalsis and the glands of digestion secreting enzymes in the process of digesting food and storing energy. The heart and respiration are slowed, and blood pressure is lowered. The skeletal muscles are relaxed and immobile.

In the freeze response, however, this "vegetative" state may be exaggerated. In a state of terror, which implies extreme fear combined with helplessness, it is not uncommon for a person to involuntarily vomit, lose control of their bowels or bladder, or faint. These visceral responses are due to excessive contractions of the gut, slowing of the heart, and lowering of the blood pressure based on excessive influence on these organs by the vagus nerve. The muscles may be relaxed to the point of paralysis, as in being "paralyzed by fear." It is in this very pathologic vegetative state that the frozen mammal may die due to slowing and stopping of the heart. In addition to abnormally increased parasympathetic tone, the freeze response is associated with numbing, not only of pain but also of cognition. Numbing is related to high levels of endorphins that are first released in response to threat and then released as part of the freeze response. In dissociation, the perceptual component of the freeze response, perception and cognition are altered, distorted, and impaired due to excess endorphins, with amnesia being the most prominent cognitive symptom.

The freeze response, however, may also contain elements of marked autonomic cycling and exaggerated levels of both sympathetic and parasympathetic activity. When the prey animal has been run to the ground in a failed flight response, it has experienced high levels of cardiac, brain, and skeletal muscle activity, along with the high levels of norepinephrine and adrenaline driving these responses. When it literally crashes into a freeze, both autonomic states remain in a paradoxical high level of activity. No wonder that this is a state of real danger to the health of the animal!

The diseases discussed in this section of the book are primarily parasympathetic in dominance and are related to freeze and dissociation. However, one must remember that these conditions also may be with manifestations of exaggerated sympathetic tone, causing a perplexing fluctuation of symptoms. In fact, most of the diseases of trauma are characterized by this vexing tendency for bimodal and unpredictable symptoms.

I believe that a number of well-known but perplexing diseases are prototypes for abnormal function of the parasympathetic/vagal nervous system in freeze/dissociation. These diseases are characterized by fatigue and weakness, as well as by hyperactive function of the viscera controlling digestion and excretion of wastes (stomach, intestines, bladder, digestive glands). Cognitive symptoms, emotional symptoms, and sleep disturbance combine with these visceral problems to form a group of symptoms that suggest an abnormal state of function of the parasympathetic nervous system and brain endorphins. Abnormal control of the regulation of the heart and of circulation (vasomotor function) is often a prominent problem. Abdominal visceral symptoms accompany many of these syndromes. Symptoms of allergies or hypersensitivity are common. As with all of the diseases of trauma, pain is an almost constant companion.

Fibromyalgia and Chronic Fatigue Syndrome

Fibromyalgia is a well-known syndrome, constituting about 5% of the general medical population and about 20% of the population seen in rheumatology clinics. If you ask rheumatologists about whether there really is such a disease, they will invariably agree that it indeed exists but scratch their heads in frustration about its unpredictable nature and resistance to treatment. Many physicians will deny its existence as a true disease.

Chronic fatigue syndrome (CFS) is so commonly associated with fibromyalgia that many physicians describe them as one syndrome. However, debilitating chronic fatigue may occur independently of the diffuse skeletal pain of fibromyalgia, and many researchers have chosen to separate the two syndromes. Nevertheless, because CFS is associated with many of the diffuse and separate conditions linked to fibromyalgia, I feel that it is appropriate to consider the two syndromes as parts of a continuum rather than as separate conditions.

The primary symptoms of fibromyalgia are diffuse skeletal pain, widespread points of tenderness over the surface of the body, morning stiffness, daytime fatigue, and interrupted, nonrestorative sleep. Common symptoms also include scattered areas of numbness and tingling, hypervigilance and emotional instability, cognitive impairment, and dizziness. Other common conditions linked to fibromyalgia include a strange spiderweb mottling of the skin called *livido reticularis*, Raynaud's phenomena (cold sensitivity) in the extremities, sicca phenomena (dry mouth and eyes), irritable bowel syndrome, gastroesophageal reflux disease, interstitial cystitis (pain and inflammation of the urinary bladder), multiple chemical sensitivities, and mitral valve prolapse/dysautonomia syndrome. I will discuss these syndromes individually later in this chapter. As with all of the diseases of trauma, the rather remarkable variety and breadth of symptoms in fibromyalgia strongly suggest that this is a disease of regulation, leading inexorably back to the brain as the seat of the problem.

Seventy-five percent of fibromyalgia patients are female (curiously roughly the same gender ratio as in PTSD), and onset of the disease usually occurs between the ages of 20 and 40. It has been noted to follow physical injuries and illnesses and at one time was linked to the Ebstein Barr virus, the viral cause of mononucleosis. I personally have seen several dozen cases of fibromyalgia develop during treatment for delayed recoveries from MVA-related whiplash syndrome.

The primary symptom is diffuse musculoskeletal pain especially affecting the axial (core) part of the body, associated with a gluelike stiffness of movement. Fibromyalgia also involves exquisite tenderness over specific points over the body, and the only remotely objective test for the syndrome is to document tenderness in at least 10 of the 18 prescribed tender-point areas. This skeletal pain is cyclical and unpredictable in nature, although it is generally made worse by emotional stress, physical activity, and cold or wet weather. It is often improved, although not abolished, by local heat.

Virtually all fibromyalgia patients experience daytime fatigue and weakness. This is specifically associated with awakening feeling stiff, tired, and unrefreshed, although insomnia per se is not a primary problem. Nevertheless, many fibromyalgia patients experience delayed sleep onset and multiple awakening episodes, often due to skeletal pain. Fatigue is severe enough to result in almost involuntary "collapse" at times. I have treated a number of patients for dramatic symptoms of collapse, during which they suddenly lose all strength and literally sink to the ground, lying there for long periods of time and unable to force themselves to get up and go to a couch or bed. All of these patients have had significant recent trauma, and the collapse is in the context of other trauma-related symptoms. Most have experienced a state of entrapment or irresolvable approach/avoidance conflict. Several have had concomitant visceral hyperactivity symptoms, and several definite fibromyalgia. I believe that the weakness and collapse that is seen in fibromyalgia and other posttraumatic states relates to the parasympathetic immobility of the freeze response.

Interestingly, the phenomenon of awakening with pain in fibromyalgia and other trauma-related skeletal pain syndromes is linked to, I believe, a symptom of muscular bracing combined with abnormal vasomotor tone during the dream—or rapid-eye-movement (REM)—cycle of sleep. As I have noted, one of the roles of dreams is to integrate the day's stressful or threatening experiences with past procedural memories of threat and trauma in order to replenish and expand the survival brain's storehouse of remembered survival skills. In the victim of complex trauma, this storehouse is overflowing with memories of danger. Accessing these memories at the onset of dreaming sets off muscle bracing in patterns of learned attempts at failed self-defense from old traumatic experiences. The muscle bracing reenacts what the body did during the traumatic event. It also sets off activation of autonomic cycling that causes abnormal patterns of constriction and dilatation of blood vessels, primarily in the regions of the body that were involved in these old traumatic experiences. Constriction of blood vessels in muscles that are contracting causes severe pain, as in a heart attack. This leads to immediate awakening with pain, often in the core of the body—the head, neck, or back—which must be braced before any other self-protective behavior can begin. Therefore the symptom of awakening with pain is, at least in part, related to arousal, or the sympathetic limb of the exaggerated autonomic cycling in trauma.

The other major problem associated with this symptom is interruption of the dream process. Because dreams are aborted before they are able to complete, the patient with fibromyalgia is in essence dream-deprived, a condition that is known to cause fatigue, irritability, and emotional and cognitive impairment. This abnormal sleep cycle has been demonstrated with elecroencephalograms (EEGs) in patients with fibromyalgia. In fact, some researchers have suggested that the sleep disturbance itself may contribute to many of the secondary symptoms of fibromyalgia (Reynolds et al., 1991).

Fibromyalgia is so inclusive of many separate syndromes that it may be considered to be the prototype for posttraumatic autonomic illnesses. Although there is really no solid scientific literature that addresses these issues, I have a strong sense that fibromyalgia may well be based on extremely early and probably preverbal trauma that often is difficult to document in a patient's clinical history. The presence of complex trauma beginning in child-hood, with resulting vulnerability to subsequent relatively minor life trau-matic events, would certainly be in keeping with the well-recognized association of the onset of fibromyalgia with viral illnesses, medical proce-dures, and often minor physical injuries. We will have to see whether this hypothesis survives the test of time.

A review of the laundry list of apparently varied conditions linked to fibromyalgia reveals a subtle but distinct thread of continuity. Most of them are associated with abnormal function of the organs and glands of digestion, elimination of waste, blood circulation, and control of the peripheral blood vessels. In most cases, these conditions are associated with abnormal parasym-pathetic activity, including excessive secretion of stomach acid and increased contraction of smooth muscles in the stomach, small intestine, colon, and bladder. Some are also associated with symptoms of abnormal *sympathetic* tone (dry mouth and eyes), and some with exaggeration of abnormal cyclical sympathetic/parasympathetic activity (Raynaud's, livido reticularis, mitral valve prolapse). In Raynaud's phenomenon and livido reticularis, the small blood vessels of the skin are specifically affected by excessive autonomic cycling, leading to alternating states of dilatation and constriction. In general, however, there is a universal pattern of a parasympathetic dominant disruption of the rhythm of autonomic homeostasis consistent with the freeze response.

A vast body of scientific literature on the topic of fibromyalgia has accumulated over the years, and much of it is contradictory, speculative, and controversial. However, rather than referring readers to a long list of scholarly articles on the subject, I suggest referencing a self-help book by Devin Starlanyl, a physician and victim of fibromyalgia. This comprehensive and reader-friendly survival manual addresses virtually every facet of fibromyalgia symptoms and modes of treatment (Starlanyl & Copeland, 1998). Treatment of fibromyalgia has perhaps been the most frustrating aspect of this frustrating disease, both for caring physicians and their patients. Starlanyl addresses treatment options more comprehensively than most authors, making her book a particularly valuable resource. The one consideration that is not addressed is the treatment of the primary cause of fibromyalgia: the dysregulated mechanisms of autonomic homeostasis associated with unresolved trauma. Starlanyl does acknowledge the increased incidence of prior trauma and abuse that has been documented in fibromyalgia, as well as the role of trauma in triggering the onset of the disease. It is clear that fibromyalgia appears to be a prototype for the vast array of somatic syndromes that may accompany and result from the late effects of life trauma on homeostasis. A basic tenet of trauma treatment must be extinction of the links between the somatosensory messages of traumatic experiences that have been stored in procedural memory and the arousal/freeze responses. Somatically based trauma therapy would therefore appear to be a primary and necessary process for resolution of the abnormal autonomic function in fibromyalgia. To this end, I discuss models of treatment for trauma in the conclusion of this book.

Irritable Bowel Syndrome

Irritable bowel syndrome (IBS) is a condition affecting the large and small intestines. It is characterized by alternating constipation and diarrhea, associated with bouts of cramping abdominal pain. Bloating, flatulence, and increased mucous in the stools may also occur. The pain often is relieved by a bowel movement, and the consistency of the stool and frequency of bowel movements vary considerably. Anxiety and depression, fatigue, headache and backache, sleep disturbance, heart palpitations, and urinary symptoms accompany the bowel symptoms in many cases.

Two-thirds of patients with IBS in the United States are women, although this ratio may vary in other cultures and countries. X-ray studies, direct examination of the large bowel (colonoscopy), as well as blood tests are normal. It almost always appears before the age of 40. Development of symptoms of IBS after the age of 40 should prompt one to look for another cause. The consensus of medical opinion is that IBS is a disorder of the regulation of muscle contractions of the bowel, characterized by periods of increased contractions, with diarrhea and cramps, alternating with decreased contractions, with constipation. Many physicians relate the syndrome to stress, and some studies of IBS have documented improvement with antianxiety and antidepressant drug treatment. Others recommend medications that inhibit contractions of the bowel or high-fiber diets.

As with virtually all of the conditions discussed in this category, there is an increased incidence of childhood trauma and abuse in the IBS population of patients. Additionally, even in the absence of fibromyalgia, IBS is often associated with many of the same general symptoms, including emotional symptoms, fatigue, sleep disturbance, soft-tissue pain, and bladder symptoms. As with most of these conditions, IBS manifests with symptoms that suggest abnormal autonomic cycling, specifically predominance of abnormally high parasympathetic tone. In the absence of tissue damage, it appears to be a syndrome of disrupted homeostasis, and it is consistent with other manifestations of the effects of a persisting freeze response on a vulnerable system of the body.

Gastroesophageal Reflux Disease

Gastroesophageal reflux disease (GERDS) is a common condition known to be associated with stress. As mentioned earlier, stomach and intestinal ulcers were one of the conditions that Selye (1956) was able to link to the adaptation syndrome related to chronic, sustained exposure to stress and persisting elevated levels of serum cortisol. In GERDS, however, the problem is related to a more complex situation in which stomach acid backs up into the esophagus and causes local irritation. This produces the burning pain in the upper abdomen and lower chest that we usually call "heartburn." The sphincter muscle that closes the far end of the esophagus to prevent acid from refluxing from the stomach usually closes when the stomach contracts during digestion. In GERDS, this sphincter becomes incompetent. The cause for this is not apparent, leading some to suspect that GERDS may be caused by impaired or abnormal messages to the stomach and esophagus from the brain through the autonomic nervous system.

GERDS is also commonly associated with many of the other diseases of autonomic regulation, and the paradoxical impaired coordination of the stomach and esophageal sphincter could represent another example of disrupted homeostasis, with both sympathetic and parasympathetic symptoms. The incidence of past life trauma is certainly elevated in GERDS, and the disease is extremely common in patients with fibromyalgia and in populations of trauma patients.

Mitral Valve Prolapse/Dysautonomia Syndrome

The mitral valve controls blood flow between the left-sided chambers of the heart, the atrium and ventricle. It has two leaflets, or cusps, attached by cord or tendons to the wall of the heart. These cords prevent the leaflets from flopping (prolapsing) into the atrium when the ventricle contracts. In mitral valve prolapse (MVP), the cusps of the valve tend to prolapse with each contraction of the heart. This may lead to backward leakage of blood with each contraction of the heart. When a physician listens to the heart in these cases, he may hear a subtle murmur that sounds like a click over that region of the heart. In many cases, however, no abnormalities are actually found on various tests of heart imaging and function. MVP may also occur as part of an actual or anatomical distortion of the heart valve, a condition that is distinct from the syndrome of dysautonomia that I am describing here.

Actual symptoms of MVP are usually not cardiac in nature, and, conversely, many patients who have anatomical MVP have no symptoms. The symptoms of MVP are primarily autonomic in nature. The most common symptom is panic attacks associated with palpitations and chest pain, although it is not known whether the panic attacks cause the MVP or vice versa. Most physicians feel that MVP is actually a secondary manifestation of a generalized abnormal regulation of the autonomic nervous system, or dysautonomia. Although the primary symptoms are indeed sympathetic in nature, as evidenced by the occurrence of panic attacks, it is clear that dysautonomia is actually a syndrome of exaggerated autonomic cycling usually triggered by stress and arousal. I believe that it is distinctly possible that the irregular heart beat and actual prolapse of the mitral valve are caused by impaired synergy of atrial/ventricular contraction due to disrupted homeostasis in late trauma. In this sense, it may be analogous to the abnormal esophageal/gastric synergy of GERDS, with "prolapse" of acidic gastric juices into the esophagus. Both diseases involve abnormal regulation of the passage of fluids from one chamber of the body to another.

As with all of these conditions, patients with MVP are predominantly female. MVP/dysautonomia also is associated with many of the common conditions described earlier, including dizziness, sleep disturbance, cognitive symptoms, balance disturbance, exaggerated startle, numbness and tingling, IBS, and chemical sensitivities. These allied symptoms also reflect disordered homeostasis, with both sympathetic and parasympathetic manifestations. Kristine Scordo (1996) provided an excellent overview of MVP/dysautonomia, including many therapeutic recommendations that reflect the need for stabilization of autonomic regulation. This may be achieved in part through avoidance of stimulants (such as caffeine), practice of various forms of relaxation, medications, and diet.

Multiple Chemical Sensitivities

Multiple chemical sensitivities (MCS) is the most emotionally charged and controversial of the syndromes involving sensitization and regulation. MCS is so closely allied with fibromyalgia and CFS that approximately two-thirds of patients with these syndromes suffer from MCS, and vice versa. Like fibromyalgia and CFS, MCS is not associated with any objective abnormalities on any tests for disease or abnormal function of the body, including tests for immune function or allergies. Brain imaging studies have been performed, with varying and inconsistent results.

As with all of these diseases, a number of patient advocacy organizations have been formed to support victims of MCS, and there is a remarkable body of information on their Internet websites. Most of these sites present the lengthy list of symptoms that may accompany MCS, as well as a variably objective assessment of the medical scientific literature supporting the syndrome. Physicians who support and treat the disease call themselves "clinical ecologists," although many medical organizations do not support MCS as an established organic disease. Articles in the medical literature vary in content from empathic and caring support for the treatment of MCS victims to overtly angry and sarcastic discussions that frame MCS in terms of a hysterical epidemic. A number of governmental organizations have recognized MCS as a valid source of disability, including the Americans with Disabilities Act in 1991.

The primary symptoms of MCS involve progressive sensitivity to a variety of environmental "chemicals," usually after moderate exposure. Thereafter the degree of sensitivity increases and the breadth of agents incorporated in that sensitivity spreads, with incorporation of multiple symptoms involving multiple organs, multiple senses, and multiple chemicals. The olfactory sense is probably the most common initiating exposure, and everyday volatile chemical sources, such as perfume, tobacco smoke, and paint are often the offensive agent. Symptoms include irritation of skin and all of the mucous membranes, associated with impairment of breathing, sleep, and cognition. Fatigue, joint and abdominal pain, impaired balance, and diffuse sensitivity to any or all environmental stimuli often develop. Patients with MCS frequently meet DSM-IV criteria for depression, anxiety, somatization, and PTSD. Several studies have suggested a higher rate of childhood stress and abuse in MCI victims, but no solid documentation of this relationship has been attempted. Matthew Friedman (1994) postulated that MCS, like PTSD, might represent a model for neurobiological sensitization.

Following the 1991 Gulf War, an epidemic of symptoms that mimicked MCS syndrome appeared in over 20% of its U.S. veterans. Symptoms included chronic fatigue, headache, muscle and joint pain, sleep disturbance, cognitive dysfunction, IBS, and sensitivity to multiple chemicals and environmental stimuli. Many Gulf War veterans with this symptom complex were also diagnosed with fibromyalgia/CFS. The bitter controversy between proponents and detractors of the Gulf War syndrome mimics the controversy over the validity of MCS as a unique disease process. Brain imaging results, as with MCS, show inconsistent abnormalities that allow different interpretations by proponents and detractors. Toxicology studies have also been inconclusive. Several studies have documented an increased association between PTSD and Gulf War syndrome, but none have explored the incidence of adverse childhood experiences. In all respects, Gulf War syndrome replicates the syndrome of MCS.

I agree with Friedman (1994) that MCS is almost certainly a syndrome of brain sensitization, or kindling. It is acquired predominantly through the olfactory system, the most primitive and sensitive of the primary senses. Of all the senses, the olfactory system has the most direct and intimate access to the amygdala, the primary center in the limbic system for processing threatening sensory information. Victims of prior trauma with already sensitized limbic pathways in the brain would be far more vulnerable to developing MCS with relatively minor subjection to noxious odors. Because this trauma may be subtle or preverbal, trauma histories in these patients may be "negative." The spread of symptoms to multiple systems and multiple stimuli is virtually diagnostic for brain sensitization, linking somatic symptoms of autonomic dysregulation to a traumatic event. One might predict that an identical sensitization syndrome epidemic with the same varied complex of physical symptoms will, after a latency of several years, follow the traumatic terrorist-attack event experienced by many people in New York City on September 11, 2001.

The entire group of diseases that I have just discussed represents a continuum of illnesses along a spectrum of neurosensitization and autonomic dysregulation. To only a slightly varying degree, each illness contains features of the others. This fact leads to the inevitable conclusion that this group of diseases represents an innate response of the brain to the exposure to a specific noxious and traumatic stimulus. The common history of life trauma, the physiology of the brain's and body's response to trauma, and the nature of the symptoms in all of these illnesses form a unique confluence that suggests a powerful link to trauma physiology. This combination forces one to consider them as a continuum of states of autonomic dysregulation and sensitization that has developed from the unresolved freeze response.

Migraine

Migraine is an extremely common syndrome, occurring in about 1 in 10 people, two-thirds of whom are female. It clearly has a strong genetic basis, and although stress is known to be perhaps the most potent trigger for migraine, it is a bit of a stretch to include it specifically under diseases of post-traumatic autonomic dysregulation. The physiological mechanisms for migraine continue to be studied, but its clinical symptoms provide a remarkable model for very specific abnormalities of the regulation of autonomic function. In migraine, that abnormality primarily affects the blood vessels of the head and brain. Based on recent findings and theories, migraine is probably a disorder of abnormal neurotransmitter function, especially involving norepinephrine and serotonin. It also involves specific brain centers, most prominently the locus ceruleus, which initiates the arousal response (see Chapter 2).

In classical migraine, clinical symptoms are characterized by a period of constriction of blood vessels in the head and brain, with abnormalities of brain function that cause symptoms reminiscent of a stroke. These symptoms are usually one-sided and may include numbness, clumsiness, bright visual flashes with visual impairment (scotoma), impaired speech, and confusion. After 15–20 minutes, the patient usually experiences a headache, sometimes relatively mild but often excruciating, that is commonly on the opposite side of the body's neurological symptoms. Nausea, vomiting, diarrhea, and physical debility are the general rule, with debility lasting from hours to days. Migraine, then, is a dramatic example of marked autonomic dysregulation, involving both sympathetic and parasympathetic clinical manifestations and presenting primarily with symptoms arising from cyclically altered blood circulation of the head and brain.

Migraine victims may find that their headaches are precipitated by certain foods, such as cheeses, nuts, and alcohol (especially red wine), many of which contain a substance called *tyramine*, a chemical related to serotonin. Sleep deprivation, stress, physical exertion, altitude (low-oxygen tension), and the menstrual cycle in women are predictable migraine triggers. Periods of relative relaxation after a period of stress seem to be times of risk as well (e.g., Saturday-morning or holiday migraines).

Although a number of studies have noted an increased incidence of childhood physical and sexual abuse in migraine, one really cannot categorize this common condition along with the regulatory syndromes that we have just discussed. In part, trauma in some people may represent a switching on of the migraine gene in childhood, but a more likely explanation would be that the intrinsic autonomic dysregulation of trauma activates the genetically determined autonomic dysregulation of migraine itself. On the other hand, in treating thousands of migraine sufferers in my career, I have noted hundreds of patients with no family history of migraine who, after a severe life trauma, especially a car accident, have developed typical common or classic migraine. (Common migraine basically is the headache without the neurological symptoms.)

Based on the incidence of vascular headaches in trauma victims, it would appear that virtually anyone can develop migraine under sufficient stress. I personally have no family history whatsoever of migraine, but during a uniquely stressful period in my professional career, I experienced two episodes of migrainous scotoma, one with a mild headache. They have never recurred in the subsequent 15 years. I have had many patients with similar stories. Many of my patients traumatized in motor vehicle accidents have experienced similar events, and some have gone on to develop intractable migraine as one of their primary disabling symptoms. The migraines eventually subsided with their treatment, in some cases rather dramatically with the use of somatically based trauma psychotherapy. Posttraumatic migraine may indeed be another primary illness of disrupted autonomic regulation.

Syndromes of Procedural Memory

In Chapter 2 I discussed in some detail the clinical syndromes of abnormal movement and sensation that reflect procedural memory in trauma. These conditions are extremely common in the practice of the psychotherapy of trauma, and they often represent some of the most perplexing aspects of the case. Numbness, tingling, clumsiness, spasms, pain, tremors, twitches, stutters, hoarseness or cough, impaired swallowing, choking, dizziness, tinnitus, blurred vision, and localized weakness are typical examples of sensory and motor symptoms that may be based on traumatic procedural memory. Many psychotherapists have told me that when they consult their medical colleagues about these cases, the unusual physical symptoms are usually attributed to "psychological" processes or somatization, or simply don't make sense. They are usually dismissed as irrelevant because these symptoms and behaviors don't seem related to any recent or past event that conceivably might have caused them. They also may be shaped and distorted by the emotional content of the event that caused them and consequently may appear strange or exaggerated. With a painstaking and thorough history of the patient's life experiences, one often finds that the particular symptom is clearly related to an obscure traumatic event. In all of these cases, the symptom is not imagined or pretended but rather represents a physiologic change in the areas of the brain that processed and stored in procedural memory the experiences of a specific area of the body during that traumatic event. In other words, syndromes of procedural memory are defined by their *meaning*.

Whiplash Syndrome

Whiplash syndrome provides the rationale for the traumatic basis for virtually all of the symptoms that usually accompany syndromes of procedural memory. In my long rehabilitation-based practice of neurology, I had the opportunity to evaluate and treat over 5000 cases of MVA-related whiplash. All of the patients eventually experienced most of the cluster of symptoms that we relate to whiplash. The scientific literature on whiplash syndrome demonstrates a virtually universally appearing cluster of symptoms that involve many systems of the body. The fact that this set of symptoms appears so consistently in almost all of these patients demands that we consider the validity of their complaints despite many doctors' doubt of the validity of the whole syndrome.

It is known that the severity and duration of whiplash symptoms have nothing to do with the speed of the accident, the violence of the crash, or the damage to the cars. Most significantly, studies of racecar and demolition derby drivers document a modest incidence of neck pain but virtually none of the other varied symptoms of whiplash. These factors have cast doubt in the minds of insurance adjustors, defense attorneys, and many doctors about the validity of physical causes for whiplash complaints. I realized in the late 1990s that childhood trauma was a constant feature in the history of my chronic pain patients. Based on this, I began to do trauma histories on all of my patients. Eventually I did a retrospective chart study of my 250 whiplash victims for the incidence of life trauma and its relationship to the severity and duration of their symptoms. I found that childhood physical and sexual abuse were the most powerful predictors of the number, severity, and duration of post-whiplash complaints. At that point, I pursued an extensive study of the scientific literature on traumatic stress. There I found what I became convinced was a plausible explanation for the entire group of symptoms of whiplash based on procedural memory.

Many patients who have been in an MVA experience some or all of a stereotyped groups of symptoms. Pain symptoms involve spinal pain and headache, numbness and tingling of the arm or arms, and ear and jaw pain. These are attributed to strained ligaments in the neck and spine, spasm of spinal muscles, impaired circulation to the arms due to this spasm, and jaw clenching, or TMJ (temporomandibular joint syndrome). Neurological symptoms include dizziness, blurred vision, numbness about the face, ringing in the ears (tinnitus), and problems with memory and concentration. These symptoms are usually attributed to a brain concussion, and the entire group of symptoms is called the postconcussion syndrome. Psychological symptoms include anxiety and panic with driving or exposure to any cues of the accident, nightmares, hypervigilance, irritability, startle, and stimulus sensitivity—in other words, symptoms of PTSD. On many occasions, physicians attribute emotional symptoms in these cases to preceding neurosis, and the physical symptoms to somatization. The real dilemma presented by these symptoms is that they often take days or weeks to develop and get worse over time in some patients. Delay in onset and spontaneous worsening of symptoms are characteristics that are certainly not typical of most physical injuries. It should be noted that less than 25% of MVA victims have this group of multiple symptoms that persist for a prolonged period of time. Most patients recover in 4–8 weeks. The MVA victims that I am talking about here are the minority of patients who suffer from a large spectrum of symptoms and experience a delayed recovery. As I have said, most of these patients have a history of significant life trauma.

This concept of whiplash syndrome as a somatic expression of traumatic stress is based on the presumption that the severity of the syndrome correlates with the amount of prior life traumatic stress that the victim brought to the MVA. MVA victims with a history of complex trauma arrive at the accident experience in a state of vulnerability to traumatic stress and therefore are likely to dissociate, or freeze, in the face of threat. The unpublished chart study that I mentioned earlier, and the trauma histories that I received from hundreds of MVA victims over the past 8 years, bear this fact out with uncanny accuracy. In this process, of course, I took into account such life experiences as an a difficult birth, alcoholic parent, exposure to medical treatment in childhood, and other generally unappreciated or ignored sources of societal trauma.

This theory is based on the physiological model of how the brain processes trauma as discussed in Chapter 2. The most critical part of this model involves the storage in procedural memory of the sensory information that was accessed during the MVA through the process of kindling for the purpose of future survival. This process in turn depends on the fact that the MVA victim arrived at the moment of the accident in a helpless state. In this state, the only option was to freeze, or dissociate. Careful histories taken from such patients at the moment of impact often reveals a perceptual state of stunning, shock, time distortion, or confusion—in short, dissociation. Virtually all of my patients with delayed recovery from whiplash experienced elements of this altered perceptual experience at the time of the MVA. These victims then did not discharge the freeze response.

We don't tend to recognize the fact that the power and control we often feel behind the wheel of a car is largely a delusion. Being a victim in an MVA shatters the myth that we have control, and even without a history of significant prior trauma, the victim of an MVA may never feel in control in an automobile again, especially after multiple accidents. Conversely, demolition derby and racecar drivers are predators in a game, and therefore are not helpless. Once again, helplessness and lack of control are required elements for trauma to occur. Perhaps this explains the very rare occurrence of PTSD in even serious competitive sports injuries: Whiplash is essentially absent in the violent game of football—the players are also predators.

At the moment of impact in an MVA, the head, neck, and spine are subjected to rapid and violent movement in a variety of directions. The arms and legs may be subjected to a variety of forces, such as bracing the right foot on the brake pedal, stiffening the arms, and gripping the steering wheel with the hands. All of these forces cause bracing of the affected muscles as part of the stretch reflex, as typified in the simple testing of the knee jerk. The messages sent to the brain from the receptors in the tendons and muscles are stored in procedural memory in the form of movement patterns linked to the parts of the brain that process danger. In future experiences of stress or threat, especially those that have anything in common with the MVA experience, these movement patterns and reflex bracing of muscle groups are replicated as part of the repertoire of remembered survival skills. This process then leads to strange and unexplainable habits of movement, problems with coordination, and localized painful muscle spasms.

In the process of somatic dissociation, the parts of the body that sent the sensorimotor messages related to the threat to the brain are subsequently specifically dissociated. They thereafter experience abnormal regulation of blood supply in a cyclical fashion, as in the production of stigmata. This abnormal regulation of regional blood flow in the specific muscles that were recruited in defensive movement patterns results in relative ischemia, or impaired local circulation, leading to myofascial pain, the typical muscle pain and spasm of whiplash. One type of myofascial pain in whiplash involves the jaw muscles. As explained in Chapter 1, the jaw muscles are derived from embryonic gill arches and therefore are intimately linked to survival instincts, in this case killing, defense, and chewing. Jaw clenching, a common nighttime event that is related to life stress, can lead to problems with injury to the teeth and morning headaches, an extremely common problem in MVA victims. I will discuss myofascial pain in more detail later in this chapter.

As the head is involuntarily thrown about during an MVA, the patterns of movement will activate the vestibular (balance receptors) in the inner ear. Procedural memory for this pattern of head movement may then cause the patient to experience vertigo or dizziness with head movement in the future. This vertigo is a very real symptom based on procedural memory, despite the inevitably negative tests for vestibular function done in the laboratory. At the time of the impact, the fight/flight response is activated, affecting the reflex positioning of the eyes. Like all predators, humans have eyes situated in the front of their head to enable binocular vision that may fine-tune distance cues. Prey animals tend to have eyes on the side of their heads in order to allow for a wider field of vision for self-protection. In the whiplash victim, the eyes enlarge the field of vision, because the traumatized human predator has, figuratively, now become the prey. This reflex is also stored in procedural memory, leading to subsequent eye divergence (outward-turning) and the perplexing symptom of blurring of vision under stress because the brain can't process binocular vision unless the eyes move as one. The behavioral optometrist will then diagnose *convergence insufficiency* and *binocular dysfunction*, usually attributing this problem to a brain injury, when the problem is really a conditioned posttraumatic reflex involving the eye muscles and stored in procedural memory.

PTSD and dissociation are characterized by the rather specific pattern of cognitive impairment that I discussed in detail in Chapter 3. Deficits in declarative and working memory, attention and concentration, divided attention, and multitasking skills are often documented in neuropsychological tests in whiplash victims, and they are often attributed to a minor traumatic brain injury. Although a number of whiplash victims indeed may have suffered a cerebral concussion based on the impact and the rapid movements of the brain within the skull, these cognitive problems often occur in MVA patients who have experienced only low-impact injuries that were insufficient to damage the brain. The presence of prominent emotional symptoms, dissociation, and especially a history of past life trauma make it very likely that cognitive symptoms in whiplash are related to impairments due to traumatic stress, specifically to the high endorphin state of the freeze/dissociation response.

That said, physical injuries of course may also occur, even in relatively minor MVAs. Of the thousands of cases I have seen, I have diagnosed and treated three to four patients with acutely ruptured cervical discs and nerve root injuries, and several with documented significant ruptured ligaments in the neck. All were involved in MVAs over 30 mph. In general, these patients recovered rapidly with no long-term disability. The red flags for traumatic stress include a delayed onset of symptoms, worsening over time, a combination of spinal and neurological symptoms, and the presence of the typical emotional symptoms suggestive of trauma, dissociation, and PTSD.

Myofascial Pain

Myofascial pain may well be the most common condition for which patients seek medical attention. It is the painful spasm of muscles that causes tension headaches, chronic pain and spasm in the neck, and shoulder-girdle and low-back pain. Indeed, the vast majority of cases of low-back pain, one of the major dilemmas of the workplace, suffer primarily from myofascial pain. Many physicians attribute spinal pain in general to degeneration of spinal discs and arthritis of the spinal joints. Extensive studies of MRIs of the cervical and lumbar spines, however, show no consistent relationship between abnormalities of the spine on the MRI and the pain complaints by the subjects of the studies (Borenstein et al., 2001; Breslau & Seidenwurm, 2000; Krappel & Harlands, 2001). Just because one can see an abnormality on an imaging study does not mean that the abnormality must be the cause of a symptom. Furthermore, we now know that disc degeneration may start in the first decade of life and as an aging process is probably as inevitable as facial wrinkles; there is basically no proof that degeneration of the spinal discs is intrinsically painful.

Although myofascial pain may affect any muscle in the body, it primarily causes spasm and pain in muscles of the axis of the body—the head, entire spine, and shoulder and hip girdles. The role of these muscles is to position the body for almost any functional activity; consequently, these muscles are in almost continuous use except when the person/animal is in the recumbent position. Therefore, in any behavior involving self-defense, the muscles of the core are intensely activated. The pattern of their contraction and movement in a threatening situation will therefore be stored in procedural memory if the act of escape is never completed because of helplessness and freeze.

Repetitive muscle contraction by itself need not be painful. In a high-intensity learned athletic activity, the precise repetition of patterns of skilled movements is basic to success in the sport. Generally this occurs without disabling muscle pain. In myofascial pain, however, the patterns of muscle contraction are associated with procedural memory for a threat. They therefore are also linked to the autonomic dysregulation of trauma, associated with variable dilatation and constriction of blood vessels, especially in the body parts involved in the traumatic experience. Calling for the contraction of muscles that once participated in a failed defensive act activates abnormal autonomic cycling, leading to periodic constriction of blood flow to those muscles, with resulting reactive ischemic pain and spasm. This process explains why myofascial pain is a uniquely stress-related problem. It also tends to reoccur in the same muscle region because it replicates patterns of procedural memory with uncanny accuracy. So the persistent left-sided pain at the base of your neck and shoulder blade that always pops up under stress reflects an old and forgotten defensive use of those muscles in a physical event or injury where you had no control over the situation and experienced a subtle freeze.

The piriformis muscle in the buttocks participates in the Kegel maneuver to contract the floor of the pelvis and clench the buttocks. The piriformis is unusual in that it is pierced by the sciatic nerve as it proceeds through the pelvis on its way down the back of the leg. Patients with *piriformis syndrome* experience spasm of the muscle, associated with leg pain typical of sciatica. The symptoms are often precipitated by a minor injury and then persist under stress or with any activation of the muscle itself. Pain with sexual intercourse virtually always occurs, because the piriformis passes closely behind the vagina. When I began to take trauma histories in my patients, I accumulated a consecutive series of 31 patients (30 females and one male) with piriformis syndrome, all of whom had experienced sexual trauma with penetration, including incest, molestation, and rape. Their myofascial pain represents a dramatic example of the storage in procedural memory of the defensive activation of a particular muscle group in a failed attempt at self-protection. Spasm and pain subsequently occurred with any stress or activity involving the use of this muscle. Piriformis syndrome basically is a metaphor for all examples of regional myofascial pain based on procedural memory.

Cumulative Trauma Disorder

I noted earlier that repetitive use of muscle groups in athletics generally is not associated with myofascial pain. That doesn't mean that repetitive use of muscles in some activities under certain circumstances does not sometimes lead to chronic pain. One of the banes of our current sedentary forms of employment is the perplexing chronic upper extremity pain that seems to accompany repetitive use of the arms and hands, a syndrome that has come to be known as *cumulative trauma disorder* (CTD). Typical activities that seem to precipitate this syndrome in a significant number of people include building small objects such as microcircuits in assembly lines and using keyboards in data entry and word processing. Other examples include repetitive sewing, butchering meat, delicatessen food preparation, and carpentry. All of these activities entail using the upper extremities in a repetitive fashion, with manipulation of the fingers and the maintenance of sustained postures in the head, neck, and shoulders. Much of this activity also occurs in an environment that places time-contingent demands on the worker.

Because most of these activities select for the preferred upper extremity, CTD most often affects the dominant hand. Symptoms usually start with vague, intermittent cramping pain in the fingers and hands, sometimes associated with numbness of some or all of the fingers. Occasionally the diagnosis of carpal tunnel syndrome (compression of the median nerve at the wrist) is made. Tendonitis of the wrist is often implicated. With time, however, the symptoms seem to march inexorably up the arm, first to the elbow, where the diagnosis of epicondylitis (tennis elbow) is usually made. Gradually the shoulder becomes involved, with the diagnosis of shoulder impingement syndrome or rotator cuff syndrome becoming the next culprit. Increasing numbness of the hand then may lead to the diagnosis of thoracic outlet syndrome. Spasm of the muscles of the neck and shoulder girdle is attributed to myofascial pain, clenching of the jaws to TMJ syndrome, and intractable one-sided headaches to migraine. Emotional symptoms usually accompany the problem at this point of its progression. Joints are injected with cortisone, anti-inflammatory medicines are prescribed, and median nerves, elbows, and shoulders are surgically decompressed and released. The success rates of all of these medical and surgical interventions are abysmal.

The problem constitutes another of our medical "epidemics," sufficiently severe in scope that then-President Clinton proposed a massive public health program to investigate and find a treatment for CTD as part of the great flurry of legislation passed at the end of his presidential tenure. For better or for worse, this grand project was vetoed by President Bush as one of his first acts as president. The problem remains an enigma, with its bizarre but predictable progression of symptoms that often worsen long after the offending repetitive use of the hand and arm has ceased. In this respect, CTD also rather strikingly resembles its cousin, whiplash syndrome.

Patients with a life history of multiple traumas, particularly childhood trauma, live a life of low-grade sustained vigilance, sensitive to the sensory nuances of their environment, especially those derived from their own internal body sensations. If a sensory message is repeated often enough in this group of people, the message itself is likely to kindle and become incorporated into the vast assembly of procedural memories of body movements, sensations, and experiences that are linked to threat. Any repetitive movement of the body that is similar in any way to past thwarted defensive body movement will be especially likely to trigger reflexive bracing. The preferred upper extremity is the body part most likely to have participated in such aborted attempts at self-defense. If the victim of complex trauma engages in such repetitive activities, it is only a matter of time before the movement pattern of that activity will elicit patterns of defensive myofascial spasm and pain. These patterns include bracing of arm, shoulder girdle, neck, and head muscles, with each pattern of learned spasm progressing to a higher level, perpetuated by ongoing kindling. This sequential and progressive spread of regional pain, with each region being recruited by the past one, is an absolute prototype for the characteristics of chronic pain in the victim of complex trauma. This unique but common syndrome constitutes a vast misunderstood population of treatment failures, especially in the fields of worker compensation and MVA-related injuries.

Unfortunately, until the medical profession is able to consider behavioral factors in the generation of physical syndromes, the scientific epidemiological investigation of the incidence of past trauma in CTD and related syndromes is unlikely to be pursued. Complicating this problem is the rigid attention to causation of an injury by our dysfunctional system of medical care reimbursement. Attributing a current medical problem to past injuries or illnesses relieves the medical care payer from the responsibility of paying for the care because the illness therefore must have preexisted the terms of the insurance policy. In addition, an experiential, behavioral cause for the physical symptom suggests that it is not "real" and therefore falls under psychological services, the benefits for which are generally limited or nonexistent under managed healthcare payment systems.

As a consultant for the state Workers Compensation Division for 10 years, I evaluated over a dozen cases of failed treatment for CTD. All the patients were women, and all had a substantial history of complex life trauma. This type of anecdote of course has no scientific validity and technically does not prove that CTD is yet another syndrome of traumatic stress. Nevertheless, all science begins with the presentation of unique single-case observations. The intrinsic pattern of symptoms that characterize CTD once again compels one to relate this condition to other somatic expressions of traumatic stress in procedural memory.

Tics (Habit Spasms)

As I have already indicated, the strange, stereotyped, and repetitive body movements that are designated as tics represent fragments of old, conditioned, and kindled sequences of failed defensive motor behavior that was generated in response to a perceived life threat. The elegant description of the phenomenon of tics provided by Sandor Ferenczi (1919) in World War I victims of shellshock (see Chapter 8) is another example of a piece of wisdom that was forgotten under the influence of societal dogma. Tics, and their extension into basic patterns of learned posture, movements, and body asymmetries, represent perhaps the purest expression of traumatic somatic procedural memory. Not surprisingly, they usually affect the muscles of the head and neck, which are connected most closely to the early warning systems of the brain. Facial twitches, especially those about the eyes, are probably the most common tics. Except for olfactory messages from smells, visual messages are probably the primary source of threat-based information. Blinking, and therefore protecting the eyes in response to seeing a sudden threat, is as basic as a knee jerk.

Tics involving vocalization and respiration are also extremely common, for obvious reasons. Repetitive "clearing the throat," coughing (nervous cough), and expectoration of phlegm represent failed attempts at expelling a foreign object that has been thrust into the throat, especially during childhood. These kinds of tics often follow ether anesthesia. Intubation of the trachea by passing a tube to assist respiration as an emergency medical procedure also may result in this type of respiratory tic. If the initial induction of anesthesia with the drug pentathol was sufficient to block declarative memory but not the centers of the brain that process procedural memory, the patient may develop respiratory tics as a result of the traumatic nature of the semiconscious experience of intubation. Choking as part of an assault, choking on food, or traumatic dental procedures are other examples of causes for throat or respiratory tics. Partial asphyxiation by a cord around the neck at birth is another candidate.

Tics of vocalization and speech are also common. The classic *stutter* is clearly an acquired habit spasm involving the muscles of speech. Typically persons who stutter do so especially in selective situations that are stressful, such as speaking in public. Speech pathologists in my rehabilitation center suggest that punishment or abuse by parents that was prompted by a child's attempts at verbal expression is a common life experience in chronic stutterers. I have had a large number of MVA patients with PTSD and delayed recovery that also have developed a rather dramatic but atypical stutter that eventually disappeared as the emotional symptoms of PTSD and dissociation cleared with therapy. I suspect that these patients had also experienced emotional abuse associated with their "talking back" as children, with the stutter released by the later adult traumatic stress of the MVA.

The well-known condition of *spastic dysphonia* is another type of habit spasm that clearly is related to early trauma, appearing in adulthood as strained, painful vocalization. Spastic dysphonia is generally considered to be related to stress, and it is often precipitated by a traumatic event, such as a death of a loved one, a job loss, or an accident. It is characterized by a strained, hoarse, and harsh vocal quality that often follows a prolonged period of excessive talking. Once established, any speaking will trigger the abnormal vocal quality which then by itself will be a source of anxiety and will cause worsening of the basic problem, again suggesting the process of kindling. The condition therefore mimics many of the motor problems related to procedural memory of trauma that in general are triggered by stress in the victim of complex trauma and, once established, become self-perpetuating and worsen. Viewing the body as a defective machine, surgeons have devised operations that alter the anatomy of the offending part of the body, in this case the vocal cords and folds of the larynx. Follow-up of such patients shows an extremely high rate of recurrence of the dysphonia.

Spasmodic torticollis is another well-known condition involving a repetitive localized pattern of involuntary movement, in this case a persistent turning of the head to one side. Torticollis may be congenital, and in this case is associated with a small mass in the sternomastoid muscle of the neck in an infant. The sternomastoid runs from the back of the skull to the top of the sternum and, when operating alone on one side, turns the head to the opposite side. In the congenital condition, torticollis indeed is a mechanical problem due to shortening of the muscle, presumably due to injury before or at the time of birth.

Torticollis may also be acquired, however, and in this condition the cause is unknown. Some physicians believe that it is an example of a *dystonia*, or an abnormal and uncontrollable muscular contraction due to some abnormality in the basal ganglia, the part of the brain that controls complex sequences of movements. Emotional factors in torticollis have been suggested but never proven, although the involuntary head movements worsen under emotional stress. Interestingly, placing one finger on the side of the chin that tends to turn will usually inhibit the turning itself. The traumatic origin for torticollis is certainly less clear, but I have documented the development of clinically true torticollis in several patients as part of their treatment for the persistent neck pain of whiplash. I have postulated in the past that torticollis may actually be an aborted orienting reflex, where the instinctual head turning that occurs with the evaluation of a potential threat becomes fixed due to the subsequent traumatization that occurred in that victim. Indeed, Sa and colleagues (2003) presented a series of 16 patients who developed torticollis after automobile and work related injuries. Psychological factors were implicated in all cases, and the diagnosis of "posttraumatic painful dystonia" was suggested. The association of a traumatic experience with these cases, as well as those I've observed, would again suggest that traumatic procedural memory is a likely cause of torticollis.

Phantom Limb Pain and Other Forms of Chronic Pain

Chronic pain is one of the primary complaints that prompt patients to consult physicians. The recent flooding of television networks with advertisements touting the effectiveness of prescription drugs certainly reflects this fact. Most of these ads recommend the use of a variety of medications called nonsteroidal anti-inflammatory drugs (NSAIDs). Usually this recommendation is for the "pain of arthritis," an allegedly ubiquitous source of discomfort associated with aging. If one considers the frequency of a particular ad as a measure of societal distress, the other major source of pain in our society would be for the pain of "indigestion" associated with GERDS. Based on my conclusions regarding myofascial pain, I would venture to propose that the majority of what we consider to be arthritis pain in the neck and back is in fact myofascial pain associated with our own particular societal stress and trauma. If so, most of the low-grade chronic pain syndromes that we see represented on television in drug ads are in reality based on the mechanisms of life trauma presented in this book.

This conclusion may or may not be presumptuous. The forms of chronic pain that I discuss in this section, however, are generally at the high end of the pain intensity spectrum. They constitute pain in the participants in the hospital-based chronic pain program that I once directed, the patients who are felt by some physicians to be candidates for maintenance narcotic treatment, and the patients for whom the medical profession has exhausted attempts at finding a cause or effective pain treatment. The lives of these patients have usually been pared down to the bare essentials with regard to financial security, family and social relationships, and employment potential. Their needs are such that they have usually been reduced and compartmentalized by the social systems that they need the most. Most of them carry a

DSM-IV psychiatric diagnosis and are on psychotropic medications. The average chronic pain patient probably takes between four to six different medications at any given time. As in all such groups, however, these patients still vary in severity of symptoms and disability along a typical bell curve from mild to severe.

Phantom limb pain, like reflex sympathetic dystrophy, was recognized and described as long ago as the late-19th century. Phantom limb sensations occur in almost all victims of limb amputation and usually mimic the perception of how the limb felt before the amputation. These relatively benign sensations generally fade and disappear with time. However, 5–10% of amputation victims experience the onset of pain in the amputated limb, sometimes immediately and sometimes after a period of variable latency. The pain may be described as cramping, squeezing, shooting, stabbing, or burning. It is often associated with the sensory perception of the limb being in a twisted, distorted position that by itself would be painful. It usually is aggravated by ambient life stress and sometimes by exposure to cold. Phantom limb pain is definitely more likely to occur if the amputation has been associated with a traumatic injury or if severe pain in the affected limb preceded the amputation. Unfortunately, phantom limb pain tends to be chronic and persistent.

Theories of the cause of this condition include peripheral physical changes in the stump, such as formation of neuromas (nerve-end scarring). Sensitization of nerve messages through pathways that transmit pain messages at the level of the spinal cord has been postulated. Alteration of pain pathways in the areas of the brain that processes pain messages has been suggested, and indeed anticonvulsant drugs for epilepsy have proved to be helpful. As noted, psychological causes influence the severity of the pain. Treatment has included medications, nerve blocks, surgery for removing neuromas, electrical stimulation and physical therapy, injection of spinal steroids, and narcotics. Some neurosurgeons have even performed surgical removal of regions of the spinal cord and brain. As one might expect, none of attempts at treatment, including the surgical heroics, has been consistently successful.

The reader by now may have recognized that the basic symptoms of phantom limb pain beg to be related to memory mechanisms that we have discussed. The relationship of the development of phantom limb pain to the experience of severe pain prior to the amputation, as well as to a traumatic origin for the amputation, suggests a rationale for the storage of the painful sensory experience in procedural memory. Accentuation of the pain by stress is common with many forms of pain but suggests a learned process. The quality of the pain, which includes memory-based perception of painful postures, strongly suggests a central, or brain-based, origin for the experience, again involving intrinsic memory.

The reader will also probably not be surprised that the rapidly emerging science of brain imaging is indeed proving that this concept is probably correct. PET and fMRI studies of the brain show that the parts of the brain that process pain messages have become reorganized and changed in patients with phantom limb pain, but not in amputation patients who are pain-free (Flor, 2002, 2003; Melzack, Coderre, Katz, & Vaccarino, 2001). The behavioral experience of phantom limb pain, like all behavioral experiences, causes structural alteration in the brain regions that processed that life event. These regions include those that are associated with procedural memory, and also involve their links with the emotional brain, the limbic system. Intractable pain itself constitutes a traumatic experience and has been documented as being sufficient to lead to the symptom complex of PTSD (Schreiber & Galai-Gat, 1993). In phantom limb pain, the perception of a distorted, painful posture of the amputated limb probably relates to postural sensori-motor messages that the brain received from the limb before the amputation and that were also stored in procedural memory.

In this respect, phantom limb pain is a prototype/metaphor for all forms of chronic pain in the patient population that I have described. The linkage of pain messages with a traumatic event that caused them is a logically obvious recipe for incorporating those pain messages within the kindled circuitry of traumatic stress. This is especially likely in the already kindled victim of past trauma, where the pain itself may assume the role of the traumatic event. It should not be surprising that the findings of brain reorganization on imaging studies has also been documented in a variety of chronic pain syndromes, including fibromyalgia, low-back pain, and other forms of myofascial pain (Flor, 2002, 2003; Melzack, Coderre, Katz, & Vaccarino, 2001). One would predict that patients with a life history of complex trauma would be much more vulnerable to the development of phantom limb pain, as they are for all types of chronic pain. As in phantom limb pain, the region of the body that experiences other types of chronic pain by definition has *meaning* for the original source of that pain, suggesting that most cases of unexplained chronic pain may well have a posttraumatic basis in procedural memory.

Clearly not all forms of chronic pain are caused by brain reorganization by the pain experience, due to a traumatic event, or as part of the past experience of complex life trauma. Cancer pain, the neurogenic pain of a chronic neuropathy, the intractable postherpetic pain of shingles, or the facial pain of cluster headaches and trigeminal neuralgia (tic douloureux) all are examples of the unfortunate reality of often disabling chronic pain unrelated to life trauma. In these syndromes of severe chronic pain, however, it is likely that the very experience of unremitting pain recruits the brain pathways that participate in the generation of the response to traumatic stress. The chronic pain itself may then be incorporated as a kindled internal cue, leading to the inevitable posttraumatic emotional component to the pain that all of these patients experience. As I noted, the group of drugs with anticonvulsant properties that may be useful in PTSD and other syndromes involving brain sensitization or kindling may also be useful in not only traumatically based chronic pain, but also in these examples of primary intractable pain. A warning that I must include in this discussion is that the physician must always search diligently for a physical, structural source of persisting pain, such as cancer, before finally concluding that the pain may be indeed based on traumatic procedural memory.

Premenstrual Dysphoric Syndrome and Postpartum Depression/Psychosis
Both premenstrual syndrome (PMS) and postpartum depression are well documented as being more common in female victims of childhood sexual abuse. Abuse victims quite obviously would be more vulnerable to arousal and dissociation with exposure to any cues related to these traumatic experiences. Traumatic cues may be internal as well as external, and the normal processes of the female body that relate to the pelvic organs certainly might be expected to activate trauma-based experiences and behavior, based on the somatic sensorimotor procedural memories of the trauma. It would be inappropriate, however, to attribute the cause of these syndromes in all cases to trauma. Clearly not all women who experience PMS or postpartum depression have suffered sexual abuse.

The childbirth literature contains many references to dissociation at the time of birth in mothers who were victims of childhood sexual trauma. Interestingly, this documentation is primarily in the nursing and midwifery literature, not in standard medical texts. Dissociation often is then associated with the arrest of labor in these cases, leading to a high incidence of Cesarean sections. Prematurity and childbirth complications in general are more common in these patients, and the institution of breast feeding is predictably more difficult. So-called postpartum psychosis is probably related to profound dissociation due to the overwhelming assault of the female victim of childhood sexual abuse by internal somatic procedural memory cues during the delivery and postpartum period. Although adequate studies have not been done to prove an association, postpartum psychosis is often a red flag for a history of sexual abuse in the affected mother. Awareness of the likelihood of this experience occurring in maternal victims of early sexual trauma should prompt prophylactic psychotherapy during and after the pregnancy.

Diseases of Somatic Dissociation
As described earlier, somatic dissociation involves abnormal physical changes that may occur in a region of the body that is dissociated, specifically when the perception of that region has been altered because the sensorimotor messages from it contained information regarding a life-threatening traumatic stress. That region is distanced from the normal awareness of the conscious brain and perceived as "different." Some people report that the region or body part "does not seem like it belongs to me." Others note altered sensation, such as pain, numbness, or tingling. Still others are totally unaware that the dissociated region feels any different from other regions of the body. Measurement of the functional properties of that region on a neurological exam might show alterations in normal perception of sensory stimuli, such as touch, pain, or identification of temperature. One might find stiffness, weakness, tremor, or impaired coordination when testing motor function. All of these findings would vary from time to time and be accentuated under stress. And the pattern of these findings wouldn't quite fit with the patterns of neurological disability that might be produced by actual brain damage. In fact, they would be more typical of the findings that one might document in conversion hysteria. The neurologist might then attribute such symptoms to "psychological causes."

Nevertheless, when one evaluates the autonomic regulation of these dissociated regions of the body, or body parts, one might find a rather disconcerting and variable alteration in skin temperature, color, sweat production, and health of the hair and nails. The findings might be quite subtle, such as the changes in skin color that I discussed under stigmata. The regulation of circulation to that region of the body would appear to be altered, but in a variable fashion. Sometimes a predominantly sympathetic influence would be apparent, with coldness, pallor, and sweatiness; other times parasympathetic dominance would prevail, with redness, dryness, and increased warmth. In other words, the normal *vasomotor regulation* of that region would be abnormal in a cyclical fashion, associated with excessive constriction and dilatation of the small blood vessels. Impairment of blood flow in these regions would adversely affect the nerve supply of that region and the organs of the skin by depriving the region of adequate blood supply and oxygen, leading to atrophy of the tissue. The dissociated region of the body would reflect the intrinsic cyclical autonomic dysregulation that is a hallmark of the brain kindling seen in PTSD and the physiological spectrum of posttraumatic states.

I have discussed in detail the disease prototype for somatic dissociation: *reflex sympathetic dystrophy*. RSD can affect any area of the body based on the region that participated in the trauma experience, as in the tragic case of the young woman in Chapter 8 who experienced throat ulcerations long after her oral sexual trauma. Like all diseases, it may vary from mild to severe, from subtle stigmata to the full-blown syndrome of excruciating pain, exquisite sensitivity to touch, contractures, and atrophy of a limb. The phenomenon of regional constriction of small blood vessels that is typical in somatic dissociation may play a part in a variety of syndromes, and it probably accounts for the muscular pain associated with the spasms and trigger points of myofascial pain because it produces periodic muscle ischemia (impaired blood flow and oxygenation). In this context, myofascial pain might be designated as RSD of muscles. Because these changes affect the region of the body that participated in and experienced a traumatic event, procedural memory obviously also participates in incorporating the body area and the specific muscle group into the cycle of autonomic changes that occurs in somatic dissociation.

Chronic pelvic pain is extremely common in victims of past sexual trauma, and it probably has its origins both in procedural memory and somatic dissociation. The piriformis syndrome, or reactivation of a defensive Kegel maneuver to tighten the pelvic floor in sexual assault, is one example of this.

Interstitial cystitis (IC) is a chronic disorder of the bladder characterized by pain in the bladder and surrounding region of the pelvis, associated with an urgent and frequent need to urinate and pain with urination (dysuria). Pain increases as the bladder fills and worsens with menstruation in women, who constitute 90% of the cases. Pinpoint areas of bleeding (glomerulations) and small ulcers (Hunner's ulcers) may be seen on cystoscopy. The cause of IC is a mystery, although, like irritable bowel syndrome, it is one of the conditions often seen in fibromyalgia and is also associated with chronic fatigue and sleep impairment. Although several studies have looked at the incidence of childhood sexual abuse in IC, no consistent relationship has been found. The combination of regional organ pain with evidence for tissue inflammation, as well as the fact that there is absolutely no definable cause for the problem, also make IC a candidate for a disease of somatic dissociation. This association is clearly speculative, however, and won't be clarified until further studies addressing sexual trauma epidemiology in IC patients have been conducted.

Disorders of Endocrine and Immune System Regulation

The endocrine and immune systems are intimately related to brain processes, especially those that process and regulate the body's response to stress. This interaction is so complex, however, that defining diseases that may be specifically attributable to the physiological changes in trauma is especially difficult. Still, the brain/endocrine/immune linkage is so critical to survival that changes in each of these systems have direct effects on the others.

The cyclical rhythm of autonomic homeostasis is directly mirrored by the rhythm of regulation of the endocrine system. As noted in Chapter 2, the baseline state of arousal is ultimately controlled by the right orbitofrontal cortex, which in turn influences the hypothalamus to prepare the body for the appropriate endocrine response to stress or threat through the HPA axis. The brain's arousal response is ultimately modulated by the adrenal cortical hormone cortisol, which also prepares the body for adapting to exposure to prolonged stress, if necessary. Exaggerated hormonal cycling in any of these systems would potentially be expected to produce abnormalities at both ends of the functional spectrum in any of these endocrine glands. We do know that the control of the adrenal glands through the HPA axis is associated with quite significant normal variation in cortisol levels throughout the 24-hour (diurnal) cycle in perfectly normal individuals. Consequently, it is hard to pin down a specific tendency for sustained abnormally high or low levels of hormones from any of the endocrine glands as a specific response to traumatic stress. Nevertheless, we do recognize the contribution of stress-related elevation of cortisol to the diseases described by Selye (1956), mentioned earlier in this chapter.

Of course, the adrenal gland is not the only endocrine gland to be affected by this process, because the pituitary gland regulates all of the endocrine system. The thyroid gland is also regulated by the pituitary gland, and its main function is the regulation of metabolism in the body. The metabolic rate, in turn, is governed by the needs of the body for expenditure of energy, a process that obviously is intimately related to the fight/flight/freeze response. It is well known that *hyperthyroidism* (chronic overactivity of the thyroid gland) frequently has its onset in the face of acute and severe life threat. Components of thyroid hormone also tend to be elevated under similar stressful conditions. Although I have seen a few unexplainable cases of the development of thyroid deficiency in cases of PTSD, there is really no evidence that endocrine gland failure may be a result of trauma. Traumatic stress does not appear to contribute to other specific abnormalities of thyroid function, unless it does so through alteration of the immune system, as there are diseases based on immune reactions that cause both hyperthyroidism and thyroid damage.

The act of mating is, of course, one of the last behaviors that one might engage in while defending against a life threat. The endocrine glands that regulate sexual behavior, the ovaries, and the testes, are also controlled by the pituitary gland, and activation or suppression of their function would be expected to vary with the absence or presence of threat. Temporary *suppression of function of the sex glands*, with interruption of menses in women during periods of extreme stress, is a fairly common and well-known phenomenon. Temporary stoppage of menses has been typical for many of my female MVA victims with PTSD, but all were temporary symptoms.

Finally, the islet cells of the pancreas produce insulin, which controls entry of glucose into cells of the body to provide energy. The release of insulin is therefore intimately related to subtle shifts of hormonal balance. The use of synthetic cortisol preparations in a variety of diseases can trigger the clinical onset of latent *diabetes*, because cortisol enhances blood glucose elevation. The onset of diabetes may also be triggered by acute or sustained stress in susceptible individuals by the same mechanism. In fact, Felitti and colleagues (1998) found that diabetes was one of the diseases that were more common in his groups of patients with childhood trauma.

Mead (2003) presented a review of literature addressing pre- and perinatal risk factors implicated in *Type I (juvenile) diabetes*. These include prenatal maternal stress, preeclampsia, maternal infection, cesarean section, amniocentesis, and labor complications. She noted that one animal study related perinatal separation of the infant with high rates of diabetes. Although genetic factors clearly contribute to a propensity for this disease, traumatic stress may also be a common denominator in the development of Type I diabetes.

The *autoimmune diseases* are a more intriguing and likely candidate for the category of diseases of trauma. These diseases, among others, include *rheumatoid arthritis, systemic lupus erythematosis, Sjogren's syndrome, Grave's disease, Hashimoto's thyroiditis, multiple sclerosis*, and *Type I diabetes*. All of these diseases are associated with the body's developing abnormal antibodies to its own tissue, with resulting inflammation and damage to that tissue. Except in lupus (where multiple organs and tissues are affected), in most of these diseases a specific tissue seems to be singled out for rejection by the immune system. Rheumatoid arthritis affects the tissues of the joints of the body, Sjogren's syndrome primarily affects the glands of the eyes, mouth, and upper respiratory tract, and Grave's and Hashimoto's diseases affect the thyroid gland. Multiple sclerosis affects myelin (the fatty covering of axons, or nerve pathways in the brain and spinal cord), and diabetes affects the insulin-producing islet cells of the pancreas.

Many of these diseases have been found to be associated in part with the presence of specific genes in susceptible people. All of these diseases involve an allergic inflammation and damage affecting specific organ systems, except for lupus. Antibodies to the affected organ tissues may be found with appropriate testing. The immune system is closely linked to the endocrine system, with cortisol playing a significant role in immune regulation. High levels of cortisol inhibit immune responses, and low levels enhance or release them. Synthetic compounds related to cortisol have routinely been used to treat the autoimmune diseases and to inhibit the tissue damage caused by them. The period of chronic or late PTSD has been shown to be a state of relatively enhanced immune function, consistent with findings of relatively lowered serum cortisol level in these patients. Blood studies in late PTSD have indeed also demonstrated elevations in T-cells, the white blood cells that regulate immunity, suggesting that the victim of complex trauma might well be susceptible to autoimmune diseases (Wilson et al., 1999).

In addition to the endocrine system, the immune system is also independently closely linked to brain receptors and mechanisms, as well as to the genetic heritage. The incredibly complex interplay between these related systems makes theories of more specific causation extremely difficult. Levels of hormones and activity of message receptors in the brain constantly change and reset themselves based on messages from both the body and the environment. Current theories suggest that rheumatoid arthritis and Sjogren's syndrome may develop because of deficiencies of production of adrenal and gonadal (sex) hormones, and in the case of Sjogren's syndrome, thyroid hormone (Johnson, Skopouli, & Moutsopoulos, 2000). By this definition, one could well consider the immune disorders to be diseases of altered homeostasis.

I have seen two intriguing cases of Sjogren's syndrome that may illustrate the complex interaction between genes, trauma, procedural memory, and altered homeostasis. Both of these patients were born with strabismus, or crossed eyes, and both underwent multiple eye surgeries under ether anesthesia as early infants. Both developed Sjogren's syndrome in their 30s after stressful life events, and one went on to develop fibromyalgia after another adult surgical procedure. The regional areas of the body that experienced the sensorimotor messages of a traumatic threat in infancy were the eyes, the mouth, and the throat, the latter through the ether anesthesia. Is it possible, then, that the peculiar regional autonomic and dystrophic symptoms of Sjogren's syndrome are, at least in part, due to regional somatic dissociation of the eyes and throat? A study addressing the incidence of ocular trauma and anesthesia in infancy in patients with Sjogren's syndrome would certainly be of interest.

Most of the diseases of abnormal immune function are remarkably linked to psychological stress and even perhaps to personality types. There have been many studies attempting to define the "rheumatoid personality," based on nuances in the behavioral traits of victims of rheumatoid arthritis. Although a few traits appear to be more prevalent, studies have been unable to tell whether this was due to the stress of the illness or represented a risk factor for it. In addition, studies of early childhood trauma do not reveal consistent prevalence of childhood abuse in the immune disorders, as they do in fibromyalgia. The role of life trauma in the generation of immune disorders therefore must still remain an intriguing but speculative hypothesis. Clearly one of the problems with proving or disproving this relationship is the definition of which "negative life experiences" in childhood are actually traumatic. Pre- or perinatal trauma, including abnormal maternal/infant bonding with resulting inadequate modulation of autonomic functioning, remains an intriguing possibility. Autonomic dysregulation, with abnormal cycling and disordered homeostasis, is the prototype for most of the diseases of trauma. Early childhood and complex trauma appear to be the primary causes for this state of chronic altered homeostasis. The resulting activation of latent genetic tendencies for these immune disorders ultimately might place them under the umbrella of diseases that are linked to early life trauma.

Disorders of Cognition and Sleep

In Chapter 2 I reviewed the changes in brain function that occur with traumatic stress. Victims of trauma who have developed the syndromes of PTSD

247

and dissociation have permanent deficits in verbal memory retention that are measurable on neuropsychological testing for cognitive deficits (Bremner, 2002). This deficit in cognition is related to demonstrable atrophy of the hippocampus, the brain region that is intimately related to the function of declarative memory. In many cases these cognitive deficits are also associated with the basic symptoms of PTSD, including agitation, hypervigilance, and stimulus sensitivity.

Attention deficit/hyperactivity disorder (ADHD) is a disorder of cognition and behavior that is characterized by distractibility, impaired attention span, and hyperactivity, or pathologic restlessness. The syndrome may occur without specific hyperactivity, in which case it is called *attention deficit disorder* (ADD). It affects about 4–6% of the population. ADD/ADHD appears in childhood and often persists throughout adult life. Studies of families suggest, but do not prove, a genetic link. Many studies of other factors, such as allergies, excess sugar intake, too much television viewing, and a poor home life, do not correlate with ADHD.

However, a large number of studies of ADD/ADHD do reveal a significantly increased incidence of early childhood physical and sexual abuse, and, similarly, studies of children who are victims of sexual abuse reveal an incidence of ADD far higher than the general population. This finding is certainly not surprising, as the basic cognitive deficits and hypervigilance seen in PTSD might well contribute to substantial attention deficits. The overlap between ADHD and PTSD therefore presents a real diagnostic dilemma.

We are seeing a minor epidemic of ADD/ADHD in the current school population, something that really cannot occur in a condition with purely genetic roots. It seems unlikely that the incidence of physical and sexual abuse has suddenly increased, although one cannot rule this out. However, the possibility of a traumatic source for this increase in a behavioral/cognitive syndrome is intriguing. The principles of neonatal brain development discussed in Chapter 5 raise some important concerns in this regard. The increasing application of technology in the birthing process, the dramatically escalating Cesarean section rate, the declining rate of breast feeding, and the increasing use of daycare for infants during the first year of life are current statistical facts in our society. All of these cultural trends would be predictive of impaired maternal/infant bonding and therefore of arrested development of the right orbitofrontal cortex, the area of the brain that modulates autonomic regulation and homeostasis. This developmental process also promotes cognitive and emotional regulation, and impaired attention and impulse control would certainly be among the predictable outcomes of deficits in these processes.

ADD/ADHD is not specifically a disease, but rather a syndrome—a cluster of often-related symptoms. As such, it probably has the potential to be produced by any process that results in abnormal development of specific brain regions that modulate emotional states and homeostasis, whether acquired from genes or experience. In fact, one possibility is that the societal habits mentioned earlier are switching on a greater number of existing ADD/ADHD genetic traits in our societal gene pool. Regardless of the specific source, ADD/ADHD almost certainly represents in many cases a posttraumatic behavioral syndrome in both children and adults.

Sleep disordered breathing (SDB) and *sleep apnea* are disorders of respiration during sleep that are associated with insomnia, especially repetitive nighttime awakening, a sleep problem that is extremely frequent in chronic PTSD. Obstructive sleep apnea is related to collapse of the soft tissues of the pharynx during certain stages of sleep, especially during REM sleep. It is much more common in patients who are obese, and weight loss often leads to relief from the sleep apnea. Sleep apnea is associated with chronic, severe daytime sleepiness, fatigue, and significant cognitive impairment. Over the long term, it is associated with development of hypertension and cardiovascular disease.

Virtually all patients with PTSD suffer from sleep disturbance, including nightmares, repeated awakening, and nonrestorative sleep. Early studies of the physiology of sleep in victims of trauma with and without PTSD were relatively inconclusive. These studies utilized polysomnography, which documents abnormalities of sleep structure and measures the EEG, heart rate, EKG, breathing rate, and throat muscle contraction during sleep. It also measures the incidence of normal REM sleep during the sleep cycle, as well as the autonomic and somatic regulation of the heart and skeletal muscles. More recent studies show that victims of earlier trauma with PTSD have an extremely high incidence of SDB, including sleep apnea (Krakow et al., 2002). I have had several patients with sleep apnea that began during the year after a major trauma, with no obesity or other life factors that might have accounted for their developing this condition. This association is not surprising in patients who intrinsically suffer from abnormal autonomic regulation. Although SDB cannot to attributed to trauma in all cases, it may well represent another condition that may be triggered by traumatic stress. Studies of SDB in trauma victims are currently in the very early stages.

Narcolepsy is a remarkable syndrome of disturbance of normal sleep that is characterized by a cluster of four quite different groups of symptoms. *Daytime somnolence* is associated with attacks of profound sleepiness so compelling that the person will fall asleep during routine activities that usually sustain one's attentions, such as eating, conversing, or even such stimulating activity as playing games. *Cataplexy* is another strange symptom involving complete and sudden muscular collapse in response to any emotional expression or experience. The person may literally fall to the ground when laughing at a joke. *Hypnogogic hallucinations* involve experiencing dreamlike visual and auditory images, often on awakening, while the person is actually awake and aware of their surroundings. *Sleep paralysis*, also occurring on awakening, is characterized by complete immobility although the person is fully awake.

The four features of narcolepsy do carry a common thread of the physiology of the REM cycle of sleep, which is characterized by dreams and loss of muscle tone. The syndrome suggests the occurrence of the REM cycle during the waking hours. As I have noted, dreams are intimately related to the process of processing traumatic memories, and nightmares represent storage of traumatic experiences in procedural memory. Cataplexy and sleep paralysis have uncanny similarities to the weakness, fatigue, and even collapse that is characteristic of dissociative states.

There is no question that there is a very specific genetic tendency for narcolepsy, and several specific genes have been identified that predispose one to this condition. On the other hand, there are many reports of the onset of narcolepsy with a variety of sources of damage to the brain, including head injury, stroke, brain tumor, multiple sclerosis, encephalitis, and so forth. In addition, several reports describe head-injury patients who had no genetic markers but nevertheless developed narcolepsy (Maeda et al., 1995). Clearly genetic narcolepsy may be triggered by neurological insults, and on rare occasions these insults may trigger the syndrome in the absence of a genetic tendency. At one of my workshops, an attendee asked me if he thought trauma alone could cause narcolepsy. He had several patients with the syndrome who suffered from PTSD. Obviously, any conclusions in this area would be speculative. But considering the close relationship between the neurophysiology of trauma, memory, and sleep, the switching on of the narcolepsy gene in a traumatizing event is more than plausible.

Implications

The diseases, syndromes, and health risks associated with traumatic stress discussed in this chapter represent problems that account for the majority of visits to doctor's offices. Admittedly, not all of them can be attributed solely to abnormal brain physiology based on trauma. However, I believe that diseases of freeze/dissociation, procedural memory, and somatic dissociation are directly associated with and caused by trauma-based alterations in brain function. In saying this I am effectively throwing down the gauntlet into the field of allopathic medicine. Of course, because many of the scientific rationales for these conclusions are speculative and theoretical, their validity may or may not stand the test of time, and many may never be tested.

The contribution of trauma physiology to the activation of gene expression in other syndromes, such as the immune diseases, is easy to argue but difficult to document or test. The burgeoning study of the human genome in disease and the increasing evidence for the effects of experience on gene expression may well shed light on this process. As in most situations of this sort, I suspect that we will ultimately be faced once again with the dreaded continuum of cause and effect.

Nevertheless, I also believe that we must continue to pursue vigorously such subtle leads in the search for the interaction of experience, behavior, physical illness, and disability. Chronic diseases currently represent the most important area of treatment failure in modern medicine, generate the greatest costs, and are treated the least effectively. We know that many of these diseases, such as obesity, diabetes, hypertension, and heart disease are in part products of a lifestyle that fosters excessive eating of the wrong foods and inadequate exercise. However, I maintain that a major cause of many of these chronic conditions is an alteration of brain and body physiology by the accumulation of negative life experiences from birth, many of which are fostered and endorsed by our cultural institutions.

Healing Trauma and the Power of the Human Spirit

One can't begin to address the topic of healing trauma without dealing with the fact that trauma is an aberration of memory. It freezes us in a past event that thereafter dictates our entire perception of reality. The past event is ever-present, awaiting its chance to intrude on our daily life based on the subtlest of cues. Locked in the crucible of terror created by the traumatic experience, we dance like a puppet on strings controlled by a manic and repetitive puppeteer. Our thoughts, our choices, our values, our behavior, even the control of our bodies seem to be governed not by conscious intent but by some inner tyrant that operates with an unknown and sinister agenda. The messages provided by our very thoughts are alien, nonsensical, and divorced from the events around us and from our moment-to-moment perceptions. Our storehouse of old memories on which we base the perception of our identity is fragmented, distorted, at times terrifying, at times confusing. We respond to events in our daily life with emotions that seem to arise spontaneously with a degree of intensity that alone is terrifying. Deep in our hearts we recognize that our inner life makes no sense, and overlying it all is a deep sense of shame. Seeking safety, we find ourselves shrinking into a smaller and smaller space until there is no space at all around us that we can call ours. And still the world seems able to assault us with messages that somehow instill fear.

Clearly this is only one way to describe the perceptions of the victim of traumatic stress. Surely not all individuals who have experienced significant trauma live in a volatile haze of unpredictable emotions, constricted and sensitized to their own thoughts, the sensations of their bodies, and every nuance of stimuli from their environment. Many survivors of even severe traumatic stress, of course, appear to cope quite well with the demons of their past and lead fruitful and productive lives. In fact, they often seem driven to excel, to achieve the pinnacle of their sport or profession, to possess unique powers of focus, drive, and achievement. On the other hand, this success often occurs at the expense of noncompetitive self-gratification and intimate human relationships. And the seemingly solid yet actually fragile underpinnings of their life force are remarkably prone to disintegrating under the strain of a new, often relatively trivial life trauma—if that trauma contains a *meaning* based on their troubled past. For no person who has apparently overcome past trauma through sheer force of will is ever free from the vestiges of that past and the procedural memories associated with it.

This brings us to an important question: Is the trauma victim frozen in the past, or is the past a persistent and inappropriate intruder on the present? Or, do the past and the present coexist, with no perceptual boundaries separating them? I'm not sure that it is really necessary to make this distinction, but I suspect that in trauma, perceptions of the past and present are indeed distorted and intermingled in a way that at times profoundly distorts one's sense of reality. Wisdom, as I will discuss, is in short supply when one has been traumatized. In the best of all worlds, we use the past and the lessons learned from it to face the perils of each day with a continually expanding repertoire of skills that allow us to learn, adapt, excel, and survive. This acquisition of skills, of course, occurs through memory, whether conscious or unconscious, verbal, semantic, perceptual, proprioceptive, visual, auditory, linked to or free from emotional content, trivial or profound. Memories linked to emotions, both present and past, tend to stick with us, to pop up apparently unbidden at times, and to color our perception of seemingly unrelated events, because such memories have *meaning* for survival. Derived from past experience, they have both a pleasurable and, at times, nasty tendency to *become* part of our present existence. If a memory linked to a negative emotion was also associated with life threat, the memory will become a life threat whenever it is resurrected. And it will usually be resurrected by a new life event that contains a *meaning* based on the content of that traumatic past memory. The past will become the present, and the present will recapitulate the past. The schematic content of memory in the trauma victim indeed seems to lack past/present perceptual boundaries.

Is this obsessing on traumatic memory really necessary for the consideration of healing trauma? I believe that it is. Healing the wounds of trauma inevitably demands altering the meaning of memories and thereby altering the memories themselves. It involves disconnecting the elements of these memories—separating the component parts, including those linked to conscious, declarative processes and those contained in conscious and unconscious somatic perceptions. It requires restoration of the subtle and automatic perception of what is past and what is present. For healing to take place, the tangled, kindled, and expanding web of learned associations must be teased apart and broken. If one attends only to the verbal and visual content of the traumatic event, the unconscious procedural matrix of body-based memories will continue to intrude and resurrect the trauma. Unless one extinguishes the automatic response of freeze/dissociation in the face of subtle arousal states, the trauma will inevitably and progressively express itself in the somatic symptoms, syndromes, and diseases of trauma, even in individuals who have "dealt with" their traumatic past.

I do not intend to present a laundry list of therapies for PTSD. There are dozens, perhaps hundreds, of books in the recent psychotherapy literature with the words "healing" and "trauma" in their titles, many of them by authors with far more experience than I have in treating victims of trauma. I would rather like to apply the theoretical considerations that I have addressed in this book to the basic concepts of therapy for traumatic stress. In so doing I hope to establish a foundation for the unique, and I believe imperative, use of somatically based therapeutic techniques in healing trauma.

Desensitization, Completion, and Extinction

If trauma begins with a conditioned response, surely we must try to end the symptoms that represent this conditioned association through the process of extinction. We must separate the elements of this tangled matrix of conditioned linkages—cognitive and somatic, conscious and perceptual, cortical, limbic and autonomic, neuronal and synaptic—and make them meaningless to each other and to survival. In the victim of complex trauma, the brain has erected a structure that is hardwired, connecting the diverse elements of the traumatic experience. Over the passage of years, this structure grows in size and complexity and incorporates new elements based on the accumulation of life experiences that possess meaning subtly related to old portions of that structure. With continued reinforcement, the dog will eventually learn to salivate with any musical tone and ultimately with any similar sound. Because the reinforcement in trauma is also from internal messages through the process of kindling, the brain's internal trauma structure will expand slowly but exponentially by itself. Ultimately it will direct every facet of perception and behavior, leading to the state of behavioral constriction that I described earlier. Cognitive processes no longer present an avenue for access to the structure of trauma at this point. Although cognitive processes ultimately must play a role in the healing process, they will never dispel the tyranny that the messages of the body exercise over the mind until the body is brought out of dissociation and into consciousness. I believe that at some point in the therapeutic process of healing trauma, one must address the conditioned links between states of arousal and the sensory experiences and motor responses of the body that remain as sources of kindling.

Ultimately somatically based therapy must establish a safe and secure place for the patient, find the subtle body sensations that are linked to the trauma, and elicit those sensations in this environment of perceived safety. The motor responses to these sensations must be slowly and incrementally brought out. Only then can their traumatic link be extinguished. Initially those sensations will inevitably elicit arousal. The degree of arousal must be tempered by *titration*, the interweaving of subtle transitions back and forth between the "safe place" and the experiencing of the sensory perception. In a sense, this is a type of exposure therapy, but because the sensations are usually subtle, the risk of flooding, which is substantial with most types of exposure therapy, is significantly mitigated. In somatic experiencing (SE), access to trauma-linked sensations is attained through guided exploration of the "felt sense," the subliminal sensations that are constantly screened out by our conscious brain as being trivial or nonessential to the task at hand. In the hyperaroused victim of trauma, very few sensations are screened out, and this person will be exquisitely sensitive to *all* internal and external sensory messages. The severely dissociated patient, on the other hand, may lack any sense of body awareness and may have great difficulty accessing any felt sense whatsoever. Special techniques to bring the body back into conscious aware-ness must be applied in such cases.

In SE, successfully accessing the felt sense will usually bring forth a subtle sympathetic arousal response, with a sense of constriction in the chest or pit of the stomach, shallow breathing, rapid pulse, and muscle tenseness. These are the sensations that occur in frightening social situations. In many trauma victims, the onset of these sensations in the face of a meaningful cue has the capacity to initiate the kindled response of anxiety that then may progress to a panic attack. In therapy, sequentially and gradually exposing the patient to self-awareness of these sensations in a safe setting will gradually extinguish their meaning so that the basic somatic sensations of fear no longer trigger further fear. As in all psychotherapy, the demeanor of the therapist and the trust developed with the patient are critical to the success of extinction techniques.

One may then progress to enhancing the perception of somatic sensations that are more specific to the traumatic event itself. Accessing the felt sense can be facilitated by body scanning assisted by subtle suggestions. This is often done in conjunction with asking the patient to assume different postures (such as lying down), usually with the support of pillows or even the subtle support of a hand under the head, shoulder, or feet. The perceptive therapist can observe the subtle alterations of posture, movement, and facial expression that accompany traumatic stress and represent its somatic remnants. The patient is encouraged to report the perception of subtle sensations as well. Using these cues, the therapist provides suggestions that guide the patient in the process of uncovering these memory-linked subtle sensations. The use of any form of touch, of course, raises issues that are unique to the practice of psychotherapy, and this must be approached based on standards of psychotherapy practice within the community and state. Under certain circumstances, gentle and completely benign touch may be able to elicit sensory experiences that significantly facilitate the therapeutic process.

The following description of the therapeutic response in SE is based on my own personal observations and those of Peter Levine. For a more detailed description, refer to Levine's (1997) book *Waking the Tiger*. As one accesses the felt sense, progression of the therapeutic response may be associated with involuntary and self-perpetuated movement patterns that proceed without the will or intent of the patient. These movements may be simple tremors, twitches, or muscle fasciculations (muscle twitches, most commonly seen in the eyelids, that occur spontaneously and are usually associated with muscle fatigue). One may also see subtle turning movements of portions of the body, especially the head and neck, which replicates the orienting reflex discussed earlier. Movement patterns that emerge virtually always have a meaning in the context of the cumulative traumatic experience. They almost invariably replicate the aborted or truncated defensive movement patterns that were never completed as part of the fight or flight response. As such, they also replicate the tics, body postures, and patterns of muscle tension stored as part of the freeze response that was not completed or discharged. Often the stereotyped patterns of movement brought forth in therapy go far beyond the partial and incomplete movements that occur in tics and in fact probably represent *completion* of the act of defense or escape. As such, they specifically serve to extinguish the internal somatic sensations that are associated with those movements and that perpetuate kindling. It may take many sessions of this type of somatic extinction to quench the conditioned associations of the varied sensory experiences that are linked with the event, as well as the autonomic and limbic fear-based response. A useful benchmark for success in the therapeutic process is the disappearance of tics and postures that characterized the patient's former response to ambient life stress. The archaic and instinctual head-forward, rounded-shoulder posture that represents self-defense, helplessness, and aging may also relax into a more upright stance.

It is quite tempting to consider that an involuntary motor response that arises during therapy is basically a dissociative phenomenon. In fact, one of the primary abnormal behaviors of the patients studied by Charcot and Janet in the late-19th century was a pattern of stereotyped postures, pseudoseizures, tremors, and dystonias. Charcot actually used to elicit these movement patterns by touching specific sensitive points on the bodies of his patients during his lectures. Another example may be the elicitation of similar involuntary movement patterns as part of trance states associated with societal rituals in indigenous societies, a practice that almost certainly has its roots in induced states of dissociation. Similar involuntary motor behavior may be elicited by shamanic healing rituals in such societies and are also considered to represent dissociative states. What is the difference between inducing a pattern of movement stored in traumatic procedural memory in a therapeutic setting, and doing so as a 19th-century theatrical showpiece in the Salp trière? Are all of these examples based only on truncated procedural memory and dissociation? If so, how could some be a symptom of unresolved trauma and others be part of the process of healing?

The interpretation of events must always take into consideration the context and environment in which they occurred. Although we write about dissociation as one of the cardinal states we see in trauma, we also see it in subtle form in daily life in many individuals in the absence of trauma. As I have noted, in some societies it is an accepted or even sought-after state that may be used to achieve enlightenment. Or it may be used to accomplish a healing of the spirit and therefore of the body

The prey animal enters and exits the freeze response to varying degrees on dozens of occasions throughout its life span without untoward effects. Dissociation as a neurochemical state per se is not the disease, the villain, or the perpetrator of the sustained trauma response. It is the perpetuation of freeze/dissociation through lack of completion of the traumatic experience that creates the pathology. The fine line between a dissociative posture and a movement pattern that represents completion and extinction probably therefore depends on the safety of the therapeutic setting. The tic or dissociative, hysterical posture is a product of a threatening environment and represents incompletion of the freeze discharge. A similar movement pattern in a successful therapeutic environment is not aborted and repetitious, but rather is able to proceed to its natural completion, often with the accompanying autonomic discharge (perspiration, deep breathing, profound relaxation).

What about the traumatic experience that occurs in the absence of a sensorimotor experience? The death of a spouse, child, or parent may be traumatic. Being an uninvolved spectator at a shocking and terrifying event may be associated only with the somatic sensation of vision and not with movement or somatosensory cues. Would somatic psychotherapy techniques be useful in quenching body responses that may be implicated in perpetuation of the trauma reflex in such instances? The answer, of course, is that the body participates in all traumatic events with the autonomic sensations of fear and threat that I have already discussed, such as the "pit of the stomach" sensation. In addition, the relatively permanent and instinctual somatic postures of fear, rage, shock, terror, and helplessness are also induced by exposure to a life threat without the need for a defined motor response. These archaic postures occur in all species. They include anterior rotation of the shoulder girdles, flexion of the neck, and curvature of the thoracic spine, the posture of "aging." Physically shrinking from the horror of mangled bodies at the sight of an explosion elicits variations of this instinctual posture that subsequently are incorporated into our basic unconscious posture.

An example is a case mentioned earlier: the woman who was struck in the right side of her neck by lightning. After the event she developed symptoms of mania, along with a clumsy, uncoordinated gait. Ultimately she underwent a lengthy series of SE sessions, during which involuntary movement patterns associated with a stereotyped flinching of her head to the left emerged. After about 20 sessions, the movements progressed to a rhythmic jerking of her entire body, with her arms and hands tightly flexed against her body and her legs and feet rigidly extended. This posture reflected an instinctual, universal posture called *decorticate rigidity*, which is seen in mammals whose cerebral cortex has been destroyed or disconnected from the brainstem. It is most commonly seen in victims of a severe stroke or brain injury or during an epileptic seizure. Because electrocution selectively first shuts down the cerebral cortex and may produce a seizure, it is also the posture seen with overwhelming electrical stimulation of the brain. In this patient, the movement pattern reflective of the trauma indeed was an instinctual brainstem-controlled posture, and not associated with a more complex attempt at defense or escape that was organized by the more conscious motor cortex. Nevertheless, allowing this posture to occur to its full expression in a safe and therapeutic environment "completed" the act of escape, extinguishing the link between the trauma-based arousal and the involuntary instinctual posture associated with it. The patient's symptoms of mania and PTSD, as well as the debilitating clumsiness, thereafter abated. As noted earlier, at the end of the session a bright red area of skin, an unmistakable stigmata, appeared at the right base of her neck where the lightning had struck her. It is quite unlikely that effective healing of the traumatic experience would have occurred without extinguishing these latent somatic messages retained in her brain.

Certain types of trauma seem to be more likely to be traumatizing. Personal trauma inflicted by another human being seems to be tolerated less well than trauma associated with environmental events, such as acts of nature. This is especially true if the person inflicting the trauma is socially related to the victim, particularly if the perpetrator is a caregiver. The emotional content, the duration, and the replication of the trauma are also important factors in the severity of the traumatic response. It is interesting to speculate whether the association of the trauma with a great deal of movement and sensory experience will increase the severity of the dissociation and PTSD. I would argue that this is indeed the case. The trauma-related somatic memories serve as internal cues on which the trauma structure is built. These cues perpetuate kindling, which is dependent on the number and intensity of the cues. Without extinction of somatic cues, the trauma structure will never be completely dismantled. Once again, these "radical" concepts may simply be a resurrection of theories that emerged over a century ago. Breuer and Freud (1955, p. 8) addressed modes of therapy in their hysterics that involved an "energetic reaction to an event that provokes an affect" as a distinct and necessary therapeutic goal. If this is not achieved, they said, "the affect remains attached to the memory." How better can one describe a somatic "discharge" as a means for extinguishing the relationship between a somatic procedural memory linked to a trauma and the associated state of emotional arousal?

There are probably many means to this end. The literature related to the treatment of PTSD offers a number of therapeutic modalities in addition to Somatic Experiencing (SE) that approach the problem at least partially from a somatic base. Eye Movement Desensitization and Reprocessing (EMDR) involves the use alternating eye movements from side to side, or alternating auditory or touch stimuli while imagining a troubling or traumatic event. Visual Kinetic Dissociation (VKD) and Traumatic Incident Reduction (TIR) both use variations on guided stereotyped and sequential visual imagery to extinguish associations between traumatic memory and emotions, including their somatic feeling states. Thought Field Therapy (TFT) and Emotional Freedom Therapy (EFT) use a combination of visual imagery, self-affirming spoken statements, and ritualized tapping on acupuncture meridian points to reintegrate a disrupted "energy field." In general, the somatic approaches to healing trauma all involve somehow accessing body awareness as part of the process, and they often also involve some form of movement or sensory input, although touch by the therapist is generally not a necessity. Guidance of the patient in imaging the traumatic event is a common feature of most of these techniques. Accessing the felt sense, whether autonomic or somatic, is also frequently used. Eliciting a physical "discharge" is not a universal goal, although such a somatic event may occur with any of these techniques, as it may with almost any type of cognitive behavioral or exposure therapy. Emotional abreaction is certainly not a goal, although emotional expression, especially crying, is an extremely common accompaniment. A number of the more esoteric types of therapy that might fall under this category, such as TFT, are based on theories of body "energy" that relate in part to Eastern theories that underlie acupuncture. Such techniques are not well accepted in Western academic centers. Nevertheless, they have achieved remarkably wide acceptance and application in the basic psychotherapy of trauma at the community level.

The category of somatically based therapy for trauma continues to be quite controversial within the group of behavioral scientists who devote their careers to the study and treatment of traumatic stress. The teachings of Freud, his disciples, and other theoreticians in the field of psychiatry over the past century primarily dealt with changing abnormal functions of the mind and spirit through mindful, not physical, processes. Most of them endorsed the important role of the "unconscious" in the perpetuation of psychopathology but approached the unconscious through processes of the mind. The practice

of introducing stereotyped forms of physical behavior to access the unconscious and to change it seems alien and primitive by accepted psychotherapeutic standards. Not surprisingly, there continues to be a great deal of
resistance in traditional circles to the introduction of this class of therapies.
One of the major objections to their current application and burgeoning use
is the lack of testing to prove their effectiveness.

In the case of some of the therapies used for PTSD, such as critical incident debriefing, the technique has seemed so logically useful that it has
achieved widespread use, only to be found to be relatively useless. It took a
long time to discover this with critical incident debriefing, probably for the
reasons just noted. Except for EMDR, none of the somatic psychotherapy
techniques for PTSD have been subjected to legitimate studies measuring
their effectiveness. EMDR is now perhaps the most common and widespread
technique used in the treatment of PTSD. Hundreds of books and articles
have been written about its effectiveness. But it has taken over a decade for
sufficient documentation in clinical scientific studies to establish its now
well-accepted efficacy in PTSD.

For a variety of reasons, proving the effectiveness of behavioral therapy in
general is extremely difficult. The reasons for this are fairly obvious. The
distinct boundaries between different psychiatric disease classifications are
based on the consensus of experts who periodically convene to amend the
DSM. The frequently drastic overhaul of diagnostic categories that we see
with each new edition of the DSM shows how difficult it is to separate psychiatric syndromes. One problem, as I have noted, is placing accurate boundaries
between disease definitions that often have much in common, such as anxiety
disorder, panic disorder, and PTSD. Because symptoms frequently overlap, it
is very hard to find a pure sample of patients with a specific diagnosis. As a
result, treating a group of patients supposedly with the same disease with a
specific treatment tends to show variable results. Perhaps the most notable
example of this problem is the fact that Freudian psychoanalysis has never
been scientifically proven to be effective.

The mode of action of these techniques or, for that matter, any form of
psychotherapy, is basically theoretical and unproven. It is tempting to work
backward from the theoretical brain abnormalities in a syndrome and try to
figure out how one type of therapy might change them. For instance, we know
that during arousal the right side of the brain is overactive and "on line" while
the left side is relatively shut down. Based on this fact, many researchers feel

that EMDR may be effective because moving the eyes from side to side or presenting alternating clicking sounds in each ear may stimulate both sides of the brain. Thus, EMDR may bring the left brain on line and abolish arousal. Because PTSD is associated with abnormal autonomic regulation, regaining homeostasis should help. Unfortunately, biofeedback and acupuncture do not seem to help. Reducing or abolishing limbic kindling would seem to be a universal and necessary goal of any trauma therapy. Medication management has increasingly addressed these goals, with variable results. Most therapists would agree that abolishing internal trauma-linked cues is probably the key to mitigating kindling. If so, techniques that somehow extinguish this link are ultimately necessary. Exposure therapy meets this theoretical basis for therapy, and it has been found to be effective. In fact, all of the physiological abnormalities of the trauma response, from inhibition of the left brain to autonomic dysregulation, probably have their origin in sustained and kindled internal arousal mechanisms. Thus, healing would seem to be dependent upon our success in quenching this self-perpetuating process.

Dissociation as a Therapeutic Barrier

One of the primary barriers to therapy is the prevalence of dissociation. Dissociation, of course, is always part of the clinical picture in victims of trauma. Cycling between arousal and freeze defines the syndrome. The very factors that tend to determine whether a person is likely to be traumatized by a specific event are those that also predispose the victim to tendencies to dissociate in the first place. Prior childhood trauma is the most important factor predictive of dissociation with trauma later in life. This is probably due to the fact that childhood is the life period of greatest helplessness. Children are too slow to flee and too small to fight. In addition, if the trauma is perpetrated by a caregiver or family member, the source of safety is also the threat, and there literally is no place for the child to go to find safety. As a result, children inevitably dissociate in the face of traumatic stress. Even nonpersonal trauma, such as multiple medical/surgical procedures or car accidents in childhood will elicit dissociation. Multiple events and multiple forms of trauma in childhood lead to complex trauma, which is associated with many of the complex posttraumatic syndromes that are seen later in life. These syndromes include conversion, somatization, and dissociation, as well as borderline and narcissistic personality disorders. All of these conditions are intimately associated with dissociation.

Conclusion

We have discussed the fact that adults who have been traumatized in childhood seem to retain the basic maturational social coping skills that were common around that age. Having incorporated the traumatic experience in survival-based memory, they are destined to be "stuck in the past," with not only the experience of the trauma, but also with the maturational survival skills that were available to them at that time. Their coping skills with new stresses are therefore relatively ineffectual and often may seem inappropriate and repetitive. They often just don't make sense in the light of the new experience. To the victims of complex trauma, however, they *do* make sense, because they reflect the only means of survival that really is at their disposal—the means that they learned at the time of their initial traumatic experiences in childhood. These failed survival behaviors indeed represent traumatic repetition or recapitulation, a process that basically is based on dissociation. They usually make sense only in light of the original trauma.

Obviously, verbal interpretation of the patient's primitive attempts at self-preservation by the therapist will be ineffectual, because the reasons for repeating the behavior are unconscious. Challenging patients' maladaptive behavior will probably produce panic because it takes away their one means of self-protection. One way to approach this dilemma is through the back door, so to speak, by gradually instilling other means of empowerment that don't relate to the original trauma but ultimately may provide the victim of complex trauma with additional survival skills to supplant the archaic repetition. Extreme athletes who find the pain of training and competition so effective in keeping their trauma-based arousal and anxiety at bay may train and compete not only for the endorphin reward, but also for the acquisition of new means of empowerment. In the end, however, the endorphin reward of dissociation may continue to present a real barrier to treatment.

As van der Kolk (1989) noted, many trauma victims seem to be "addicted" to the trauma. This addiction is metaphorical, but also probably has some basis as an unconscious reward stimulus. The actual druglike alterations in perception that we associate with dissociation are probably chemically mediated by the neurotransmitters associated with it, especially endorphins. Drugs that block the effects of narcotics, and therefore endorphins on the brain, seem to have some effect in lessening dissociation. Dissociation clearly is associated with decreasing pain perception as part of the freeze response. It also probably lessens anxiety, arousal, and the physical sensations associated with these states. As such, it may well represent a state of perception that is preferable to the patient compared to the very painful opposite state of the arousal/dissociation spectrum.

The problem is not that this state of altered perception is "desirable." In fact, it is automatic, a reflex response that is predictably produced in the victim of complex trauma by any state of arousal. I have seen many patients who cannot tolerate any elevation of heart rate and blood pressure as part of a gentle aerobic exercise program to supplement their rehabilitation. The subtle physical sensations associated with an increase in heart rate sufficiently mimics the sensation associated with fear-based arousal to produce anxiety, usually followed by the weakness and collapse of dissociation. The arousal is so brief that it is almost inconsequential, whereas the dissociation is debilitating. Perpetuation of dissociation in this circumstance is not a matter of choice, but one of inevitability.

Somatic dissociation renders the dissociated part of the body unavailable for effective functional use. It also renders it unavailable for conscious perceptual access through the felt sense. If childhood trauma has been multiple or severe and has involved many parts of the body, dissociation may be so complete that the adult trauma victim may have virtually no accurate, conscious sense of their whole body. Obviously these victims are quite clumsy. Cutting and self-mutilation are also common. They often have little if any sense of personal boundaries, and boundary testing in any capacity and any region is usually frightening and uncomfortable. Patients with this degree of dissociation obviously have great difficulty accessing or tolerating the somatic psychotherapy techniques. The differences between a purely dissociative postural response and a therapeutic somatic discharge may be difficult to determine. Arousal may be produced very easily, and the accompanying tendency toward profound dissociation may be countertherapeutic. Even when trust has been established, the patient may become "stuck" at some point in the process of quenching critical somatic cues. This may be due to an intrinsic inability to access the felt sense in parts of the body that retain somatosensory cues to the trauma, making the body unavailable to the therapist. Under these circumstances, a number of options, detailed in the following section, are available.

Resolving Dissociation

The judicious use of *touch* may be quite useful. This may involve holding or assisted movement in the dissociated body region, or nonspecific touch, including acupressure or craniosacral techniques that are related to the region of somatic dissociation. Although the psychotherapist may be constrained from touch by standards of practice, the use of ancillary touch-based therapy by a bodywork practitioner experienced in dealing with victims of trauma may be extremely useful. If done carefully, and with knowledge of the areas of the body that might be most sensitive to proprioceptive input, gentle bodywork may ultimately bring the dissociated patient "back into their body" without eliciting the arousal and fear that are linked in procedural memory to sensitive regions. The process must always be a carefully balanced approach. Input that is too intense may suddenly access declarative memory of the trauma if the specific region or muscle group that is touched is closely linked to the traumatic experience. Recovered memories of remote, severe trauma during physical therapy and massage reflect this risk. Severe panic, followed by debilitating dissociation, may occur under these circumstances. Applying touch stimulation that is too vigorous to a body region that has contributed messages of threat from past trauma may also result in reflexive spasm in muscle groups or precipitate pain that is stored in procedural memory related to the trauma. This phenomenon often explains why some types of physical therapeutic body work that appear to be appropriate may actually make the pain worse in some patients. Thus, vigorous massage, neuromuscular therapy, trigger point injections, or acupuncture may substantially accentuate pain in these patients. Many of my complex trauma patients with chronic myofascial pain have experienced marked worsening of pain in the hands of too vigorous manual treatment of muscle spasm. A basic understanding of the concepts of the trauma-based physiology of myofascial pain is important in such cases. As with all types of touch-based therapy, balance and proportion, as well as constant feedback from the patient, are critical.

Another important avenue to accessing the globally dissociated body is carefully induced *movement*. Carl Jung, early in his psychiatric career, explored the relationship of the body and the psyche. He also connected the bizarre, stereotyped, and repetitive movements of some of his psychotic patients to past conflicted and traumatic experiences. In identifying the source of these movements, he found that they had a very specific meaning based on these experiences (Jung, 1965). He recognized that these meaningful movements comprised part of the unconscious. In this process, he speculated about the use of artistic media such as painting, drawing, sculpting, and dance as means for accessing the unconscious (Jung, 1916). He was far ahead of his time, and these speculations were never introduced into practice.

Jungian analyst and dance therapist Joan Chodorow (1994) reviewed the use of dance therapies in psychiatric disorders. Drawing from both disciplines, she encouraged patients to access movement patterns in the form of "dance" while she bore witness as the observer, guide, and interpreter. Although she couched her descriptions and interpretations in analytic terms, she described movement themes and patterns from the "primordial and cultural unconscious" that I believe represent procedural memory, some skill-based, some instinctual, and some traumatic. Chodorow noted that encouraging patients to focus on a body part or somatic symptom could cause the emergence of an "idiosyncratic movement pattern." This pattern is often was associated with an emotion that, when it emerged, represented a reversal of denial and repression. This process may bring a somatic symbol out of the unconscious into a conscious state that may be understood, thereby eliminating the symbol as a source of conflict. For example, the rape victim whose body defensively braced against the assault but then froze might replicate this bracing movement as part of a guided movement theme, allowing it to move past the immobility response and into the natural completion of the defensive pattern. I believe that Chodorow has described precisely the process of completion of a truncated traumatic movement pattern that is elicited by somatic techniques.

Suppression of movement patterns that reflect failed attempts at escape is linked to the freeze response and therefore is a dissociative phenomenon. Although the procedural memory for that pattern persists, it is isolated from consciousness and therefore from intent or *will*. Replicating the movement is critical to healing, and movement-based therapies therefore are an important technique for achieving this. This may be done with fairly unstructured, guided movement, as Chodorow (1994) described, or by directed movement, as in a group directed by a dance therapist. In either case, the encouragement to move outside of rigid and stunted body movements may begin to elicit emotionally charged patterns of movement that may emerge in a graded manner and in a safe environment. The fear and arousal associated with that movement pattern may then gradually be diminished through the process of extinction. Eventually this may allow the therapist to approach deeper levels of arousal that previously would have been intolerable and ultimately to complete the extinction. In addition, movement brings on line those regions of the brain that have been shut down by dissociation, again allowing the therapist to bypass the somatic dissociative block. In this process, as the patient begins to move more and more into the dissociated body region, the threat will diminish. The process will be cumulatively self-fulfilling, just as the process of constriction was self-perpetuating and progressive.

Equestrian therapy is another unique means of gradually regaining access to embodiment that has been lost to dissociation. I have used therapeutic riding in a number of patients, including several with complex trauma related to physical and sexual abuse as children. The technique involves simple riding instruction progressing to the patient's directing the horse around obstacles in the arena, always at a walking pace. Several features of equestrian therapy may have unique benefit. Gaining a source of empowerment and control is obvious. More importantly, the proprioceptive input provided by the reciprocal movements associated with the walking gait of the horse tap into the instinctual movement patterns of the human rider and reestablish patterns of the most basic procedural, instinctual memory for movement that the disembodied, dissociative patient has lost. It also is extremely common for trauma victims to form close bonds with animals, especially dogs, perhaps because they are the only beings that are perceived as safe. The bond of the horse and rider reflect not only empowerment but also meaningful engagement.

The use of *artistic media* plays a similar role in the release of dissociative blocks between emotion, somatic procedural memory, and consciousness. Such media include painting, drawing, sculpture, and manipulation of tangible symbols such as shapes and designs. This is especially true in children, where the words for feeling states are generally relatively undeveloped. Lacking a verbal context for the traumatic experience, the abused child will act out terror in disruptive or regressive behavior, some of which is meaningful and symbolic of the trauma. Based on the premises that I have presented, the presence of mental illness in a child virtually guarantees that the child was exposed to traumatic stress. The use of drawing, sculpting, and objects as symbols bypasses the verbal block and presents a perceptual, proprioceptive, and somatic approach to accessing trauma and to completing the dissociated motor action. The success of this type of approach in young children has been well established.

For basically the same reasons, the use of artistic media in adults who have experienced complex trauma, especially in early childhood, has met with considerable success. Victims of early childhood trauma carry the somatic experiences of those events in procedural memory, essentially creating unconscious symbols of continuing threat. Using artistic media such as drawing and sculpting to replicate the traumatic event, the traumatized child will often depict the somatic elements of the experience in realistic or symbolic form.

By releasing these experiences through symbolic repetition in this fashion, the truncated acts of escape and defense may be completed in much the same fashion as the stereotyped movements associated with SE. Drawing or sculpting the trauma realistically or symbolically presumably changes its meaning to the survival brain.

Elements of empowerment and extinction have been incorporated in a number of *self-defense training programs* for women. Most of these programs, such as "model mugging," are not specifically meant to be forms of trauma therapy. They are usually directed by lay personnel who may not have the skills to modulate arousal, dissociation, and emotional release in members of the class who may actually be victims of physical trauma. Predictably, it is not uncommon for members of such classes to be survivors of assault and rape. Along with teaching well-defined skills in physical self-defense, these classes do attempt to instill a sense of control and empowerment, both of which are appropriate goals in all forms of trauma therapy. The intense social bonding that often accompanies such classes also makes for an environment that fosters healing from trauma. Completion of the classes is often associated with intense emotional release, again occurring in an environment of social support. On the other hand, because these classes do not address the risks of pathological dissociation as part of traumatic reenactment, they do not monitor the potential adverse emotional reactions that may occur as a result of the intense traumatic exposure. They therefore pose a risk of flooding the vulnerable client with a past history of multiple, complex trauma, and causing an abreaction with worsening of the traumatic response.

That said, intentional physical reenactment of a defined traumatic event in a controlled and guided setting should provide a potential way to actually complete the act of survival defense. Indeed, many practitioners of somatically based trauma therapy employ this technique, actually guiding the patient through the defensive action to its completion based on the story of the event. Usually this is done after many sessions of therapy that have gradually diminished the intensity of arousal associated with the somatosensory messages of the trauma. At the completion of trauma therapy using these techniques, it also would make sense for the patient to expand her repertoire of survival skills by engaging in physical training.

Regaining Consciousness: Restitution of the Triune Brain

As noted in Chapter 2, imaging studies of the brain reveal that in the face of threat, there is an increase in blood flow to the areas of the brain on the right side that deal with arousal and the organization of brain and body function to deal with that threat. One doesn't need the higher cognitive functions, such as speech or logic, to initiate the immediate behavior in response to danger. What is needed is activation of learned motor responses that are instinctual or have been acquired and stored in our unconscious survival brain in conditioned, procedural memory. These learned responses are stored in the parts of the brain, including the cerebellum, basal ganglia, and motor cortex, that control instinctual motor reflexes and learned skilled motor functions, all of which are largely unconscious. This is where the trauma-related somatosensory cues that perpetuate the process of traumatization are also stored. The victim of trauma is essentially ruled by this unconscious area of the brain.

The concept of the triune brain, consisting of the brainstem, the limbic system, and the cerebrum, was proposed in the 1970s by Paul MacLean (1973). I briefly referred to this concept in Chapter 2. The brainstem, consisting of the primitive and reflexive lower centers of the brain (medulla, pons, cerebellum, and midbrain) is basically reptilian, in that reptiles survive on the functions that this part of the simple brain provides. Reptiles are spared but also deprived of the burdens of emotions and thoughts. As mammals evolved, however, the demands of life on land, with their implications for high-energy expenditure, required a more complex means of organizing behavior. The evolution of the ventral vagal complex of nerve cells provided a brake on the fight/flight response in order to conserve energy. Thus, mammals have evolved the limbic system (layered over the reptilian brain), which endows them with the ability to experience shades of arousal and emotion and to process conscious or declarative memory often linked to visual images, all designed to promote survival of the species. The limbic system incorporates the amygdala and hippocampus, as well as other brain centers that foster socialization, mating, nurturing of the infant, and other behaviors, some of which are unique to mammals. However, much of this subprimate mammalian behavior continues to be determined by instincts.

The third and most recently evolved region of the brain, unique to primates, is the cerebral hemispheres, especially the frontal regions of the cerebral cortex. These areas endow primates with the capacity to organize and interpret information in a way that enables them to exhibit novel and unique behavior that goes beyond conditioned learning. Such uniquely human functions as logic, problem solving, and novel creativity arise from the frontal areas of the cerebral cortex. Each region of the triune brain certainly is capable of independently creating "awareness" and therefore a level of consciousness. Each step up the triune ladder, however, increases the capacity to alter and vary behavior based on conscious intent, not just on instinct and conditioned learning through procedural memory.

Brain function in the victim of trauma has been altered. The hierarchy of function of the triune brain has been reversed, at least in part. When the traumatic experience periodically reemerges, whether from external or internal cues, the "thinking brain" shuts down, if only briefly. The cognitive perception that the person may experience in this instance may be a transient, negative, intrusive thought, a brief period of blankness of thought, a fleeting subjective impression of numbing or confusion, or any of a number of experiences that represent momentarily altered perception. Even more commonly, the person may not have any cognitive awareness of the occurrence of such episodes. They may simply complain of impairment of attention or concentration, stumbling over words, saying the wrong word, or inability to find words. When writing text, they may miss or write the wrong letters, make simple grammatical errors, or lose the context of their topic. Forgetfulness due to impairment of working and other types of declarative memory are prominent. Many such patients, if the person has been traumatized in an experience that involved violent movement, are labeled as experiencing symptoms of a cerebral concussion, with associated cognitive impairment. What differentiates them from the victim of a minor traumatic brain injury is the fact that, in a calm, cue- and stress-free environment, *their cognitive function will dramatically improve!* Nevertheless, the trauma victim indeed is at the mercy of the whims of the limbic system and reptilian brain that periodically interrupt the functions of the thinking brain.

When our minds are clear and free from the invasive interruption of threat-based limbic messages, we are able to interpret messages from our internal and external environments using our powers of logic and deduction. The aches and pains of daily life can be attributed to the basketball game that we played the previous day, the roiling in our stomach to the overdose of spicy pizza and beer at supper, the morning headache to the unaccustomed red wine the night before. Although these are crude examples, in the absence of the ability to apply cognitive interpretation to internal signals of discomfort, they may join with and assume the role of cues linked to threat. The arousal linked to them may also amplify their severity. This process may underlie the syndrome of somatization. In fact, somatization represents the tyranny of the limbic system in the victim of trauma. In essence, the limbic system and cortex perform a rhythmic dance in trauma, except that neither one seems to know who should be leading at any given time.

One of my patients, a ceramic sculptor whom I mentioned earlier, suffered a severe trauma when the platform of a cherry picker that she was standing on to decorate a school gym collapsed. In the fall, she fractured her nose and was concussed. She subsequently developed a postconcussion syndrome, as well as symptoms of PTSD, dissociation, and depression. She intuitively turned to her art as a means of healing, and in the process produced a series of sculptures that uncannily reflect the workings of the triune brain in trauma. Figure 10.1 illustrates the ambivalence of the relationship between the limbic system and cortex during early trauma. I see the "wolf," the newly acquired dancing partner of the trauma victim, as a metaphor for her limbic system, which was brought on line by another trauma that occurred after the fall in the gymnasium. Her cortex, the naked woman, is performing the dance of consciousness with the limbic system, with neither partner clearly leading the dance.

Figure 10.1
"Cautionary tale," images of dissociation, dances with the limbic system. (Caroline Douglas).

I have found that guided cognitive interpretation of all of the symptoms and perceptions that the trauma victim experiences often has a remarkable therapeutic effect. In fact, the more detailed and fact-based the explanation that I am able to provide, the more benefit the patient derives from the process. The exception, of course, are severely dissociated patients who most of the time have very little access to their cognitive brain. For these people, cognitive overload may actually be detrimental or even traumatizing. Nevertheless, enlightenment, which implies bringing the unconscious into consciousness, may be profoundly therapeutic. In fact, these concepts are in keeping with the observations of Breuer and Freud at the turn of the 19th century. I have had discussions about this with other practitioners of somatically based trauma therapy, and most agree that quenching and extinction of somatic cues and procedural memories alone is probably not adequate. These cues and the patterns of somatosensory response have been hardwired, so to speak, in the brain. Although they may have been extinguished from experience by effective therapy, the subtle conditioned link never totally disappears. Survival skills were meant to be permanent even if not used for years. The reemergence of regional myofascial pain under stress years after its disappearance through therapy is not unusual. Having acquired a cognitive meaning for that pain, however, the healed trauma victim now has a rational explanation for the symptom. He or she can now interpret it as a special message that he or she is under stress. This cognitive clarity dissipates the ability of the pain to become a source for further arousal and therefore for perpetuation of the somatic symptom itself. This cognitive awareness of one's own body may ultimately inhibit physical sensations from once again becoming incorporated into a kindled cycle linked to fear.

This ability to apply the power of one's thinking brain to the interpretation of life messages that previously contained implications for danger may be the ultimate expression of trauma healing and transformation. Figure 10.2

Figure 10.2
"Surrender," images of dissociation, emerging from the reptilian brain (Caroline Douglas).

dramatically illustrates the emergence of the "person" or the "self" from control by the reptilian brain. Shedding the snake-skin of the reptilian brain represents the initial release from the freeze/dissociation that had created the sculptor's previously disabling states of altered perception. She formed these images from her own unique perceptions of her inner self in relationship to her world during her descent into PTSD and dissociation and through her ultimate emergence via therapy and healing. Without any knowledge of the triune structure of the brain, she recreated an artistic metaphor for the model that MacLean (1973) has described and that I have applied to the process of traumatization. In Figure 10.3, the sculptor blended the concept of metamorphosis with that of traumatic transformation with the unfurling of the wings of an insect after emergence from the chrysalis, reflecting the awakening of the human mind. In Figure 10.4, she illustrated her healing transcendence through trauma therapy, with restoration of the hierarchy of the cerebral cortex/human atop the brainstem/reptilian brain, as represented by the tortoise. One is tempted to speculate that instinct led her to these startling artistic expressions of the process of her healing that uncannily reflect the underlying neurophysiology of trauma. I have taken considerable liberties in my interpretation of this woman's work. Her perceptions of the meaning of her art differ from those that I have presented, but the concepts of emergence and transformation are commonly held.

Figure 10.3
"Longing," images of dissociation, emerging from the chrysalis (Caroline Douglas).

Drug Treatment: Correcting the Chemicals or Tightening the Lid?

Drug therapy for psychiatric conditions has expanded greatly in recent years. This trend is based on an expanding knowledge of the chemicals in the brain that control the transmission of messages between brain regions. Modern psychiatry has progressively moved toward concepts of mental illness that emphasize genetic tendencies that predispose individuals to abnormalities in these so-called neurotransmitters. Major psychiatric illnesses, such as depression and schizophrenia, are now believed to be associated with abnormal levels of activity of brain neurotransmitters such as serotonin, norepinephrine, and dopamine. Many of

Figure 10.4
"Patience," images of dissociation, the restoration of the triume brain (Caroline Douglas).

the drugs currently used in psychiatric conditions act primarily as agents to enhance or inhibit the actions of neurotransmitters based on their theoretical relationship to the illness.

The unfortunate introduction of the advertisement of prescription pharmaceuticals on television has made the names of some of these neurotransmitters familiar to the general public. But it certainly has not provided an accurate understanding of the realities of scientific knowledge in this area. In fact, we really don't know if depression is a disease of "serotonin deficiency" or, for that matter, how drugs that produce higher amounts of serotonin within brain synapses actually work to improve symptoms of depression. Altering brain serotonin levels has a cascade of effects down the line in the brain, and they may produce therapeutic effects that have nothing to do with the role of serotonin per se. Many drugs are discovered by chance because they produce a useful effect quite different than the one for which they were being studied. Others are chemically related to a naturally occurring body chemical and are tested to see if they can replicate the effect of that chemical with fewer side effects than other drugs. Some have already been found useful for a disease and are then applied to other diseases with features similar to the original illness. Chance, conjecture, and solid deductive reasoning all play a role in the development of effective drugs.

The useful model of kindling, a condition that I have referred to repeatedly in this book, has also been applied to a number of other psychiatric conditions that are characterized by spontaneous and progressive worsening over time. Bipolar disorder, or manic/depressive illness, is perhaps the most salient psychiatric disorder that is believed to represent an example of kindling, or as some describe it, neurosensitization. Syndromes involving anxiety, panic, obsessive-compulsive disorder, and, of course, PTSD also are believed to present features of kindling. Based on the theoretical relationship between kindling and epilepsy, the use of a growing class of drugs with primarily anticonvulsant properties has been proposed and studied for these conditions, including for PTSD. Early drugs were Tegretol (carbamazapine) and Depakote (divalproex sodium). A variety of new, atypical anticonvulsants have now been developed, primarily for the treatment of major depression and bipolar disorder, including Neurontin (gabapentin), Topomax (topirimate), and Lamictal (lamotragine). All of these drugs are associated with a significant spectrum of side effects, both unpleasant and at times dangerous.

The use of anticonvulsants in trauma syndromes has been subjected to only limited scientific study. The only anticonvulsant that has been shown to improve symptoms of PTSD has been Lamictal, although the other drugs listed are in fairly wide use for PTSD (Hagerman et al., 2001). Their use in this manner is definitely "off label," or not included in the drug package insert describing the uses that have been approved by the FDA. In fact, despite the logic behind their use in posttraumatic syndromes, none of the anticonvulsant medications has been studied enough to be approved by the FDA for treatment of PTSD.

The antidepressant medications have been used widely in PTSD, and a number have been shown to be effective. A number of the serotonin reuptake inhibitors (SRIs) have been used the most in PTSD, have been tested in well-run scientific studies, and have been approved by the FDA for treatment of PTSD. These include Paxil (paroxitine) and Zoloft (sertraline). The primary use of SRIs has been in the treatment of depression and obsessive-compulsive disorders, but they also have demonstrated significant effectiveness in PTSD, including in the symptoms of numbing and avoidance that are often resistant to treatment. Interestingly, many other primary antidepressant drugs have also been tested in PTSD. Elavil (amitriptyline) and the MAO inhibitors have been shown to be helpful, but they also have unpleasant and even dangerous side effects (Hagerman et al., 2001).

Arousal and anxiety as part of the arousal/dissociation cycle are probably the most unpleasant posttraumatic symptoms. Unfortunately, antidepressant drugs may actually accentuate anxiety in some patients. Drugs belonging to the SRI class are not purely serotonergic (promoting serotonin activity). Depending on the drug, they also may promote the neurotransmitters dopamine and norepinephrine, both of which may enhance arousal. As a result, they also have the capacity actually to stimulate and aggravate arousal and trigger anxiety when treating PTSD. One of the problems with SRIs in the treatment of depression is the triggering of the manic phase of the manic/depression cycle in bipolar disorder. When treating a cyclical or bipolar psychiatric condition, which of course includes PTSD, one always faces the dilemma of striking a delicate balance between treating symptoms at one end of the extreme and producing symptoms the opposite end. The problem is also uniquely unpredictable in that the arousal/dissociation cycle in each trauma victim has its own traits of vulnerability and resistance to the effects of the various neurotransmitters. Judicious trial-and-error treatment with the SRIs is probably the only way to approach medication management in this group of patients.

At the opposite end of the spectrum, tranquilizers such as the benzodiazepine class (Valium, Xanax) may precipitate severe depression in bipolar disease and PTSD; consequently, they generally should not be used in trauma victims. This is especially true in patients with complex trauma, who are likely to present the most difficult challenges to drug treatment. In these patients, one must often treat both ends of the arousal/dissociation spectrum, leading to multiple drugs and the risk of multiple side effects.

One must also be aware that side effects are extremely common with trauma patients. In the general patient population, drug side effects can usually be managed fairly easily. Trauma victims, on the other hand, are prone to kindling, incorporating not only the somatic sensations of everyday life but also those of the side effects of the psychotropic drugs. This process rapidly makes the drugs intolerable and renders them useless. In using psychotropic drugs in this group of patients, one must start with subtherapeutic doses and increase by tiny increments. Trauma patients, of course, are also susceptible to the gastrointestinal symptoms of GERDS and IBS, which also are cyclical and unpredictable. In some cases the patient may misinterpret symptoms arising from these conditions as medication side effects, rendering the drug intolerable. It is important to realize that the patient's experience of these side effects is indeed real and represents an actual change in brain and body physiology.

Another dilemma in the drug treatment of trauma is the extremely common association of chronic pain in its victims. As I have noted, chronic pain in the absence of an acute cause probably is at least in part a manifestation of procedural memory. Even when there is a "legitimate" physical cause for the pain, that pain may be incorporated into the kindled cycle of arousal and therefore specifically linked to emotion and stress. This makes the pain resistant to most standard forms of treatment, including the use of narcotic analgesics, anti-inflammatory drugs, and physical measures such as cortisone injections or physical therapy.

There is a growing movement in the field of chronic pain treatment to use maintenance narcotic medications, often in high doses. Unfortunately, the patient's emotional state, specifically with regard to life trauma and its role in the pain cycle, has been largely ignored in this process. Regardless of the source of the pain, its linkage to arousal basically makes the pain indistinguishable from the associated emotional state. In essence, when treating chronic pain in this context, one actually may be primarily treating the emotion linked to it. Numbing through the use of narcotics in this context mimics the role of endorphins in dissociation that inhibits arousal. If the message of pain is linked to the arousal of a failed fight/flight experience, the pain will continue to be unconsciously perceived by the survival brain as a vital and necessary warning to promote survival. As a result, it can never be completely abolished with narcotics, resulting in the need for higher and higher doses to obtain any measure of relief. In my treatment of hundreds of patients with chronic pain, I was always impressed by their desperate need for narcotic medication even though effective pain relief was never achieved. In our clinic, graded and supported narcotic withdrawal was usually complicated more by the increased pain linked to emotional distress than by the autonomic and gastrointestinal symptoms of narcotic withdrawal. In short, narcotics are basically not a useful form of medication for fear-based emotions, and therefore they are not appropriate for the treatment of chronic pain that is linked to a history of trauma.

The always-changing face of the enemy makes drug treatment of the symptoms of trauma a tricky proposition. What works for one symptom often makes symptoms at the other end of the spectrum worse. Side effects assume a life of their own and create new symptoms to treat. Physical symptoms related to trauma-induced changes in the brain may be misperceived as being side effects to the drug. The end result, in my experience, often is a laundry list of half a dozen medications in constantly changing dosages treating kindling, anxiety, depression, and pain and covering the gamut of the spectrum of neurotransmitters. This drug-treatment balancing act tests the patience not only of the prescribing physician but also of the patient. More importantly, such psychotropic cocktails leave the patient in a state of mental dullness and physical collapse quite similar to sustained dissociation. The drugs may clamp a lid on the cauldron of the emotional cycle, but they do so at the expense of the patient's cognition and emotions. In this arrested state, the patient is ill-equipped to reap benefits from forms of restorative trauma therapy.

We cannot blame this dilemma on the physician managing this drug scenario. The progressive introduction of new medications is driven by the physical and emotional pain of the victims of complex trauma and the cycling of their varied symptoms. In fact, some victims of complex trauma are not amenable to standard means of psychotherapy, which may lead to flooding and disabling dissociation. The use of multiple medications may be the only means of enabling the patient to live in an environment other than an institution. However, although these multiple drug regimens allow patients to exist in an environment relatively free from external stimulation, they also prohibit any means of extinguishing internal or external traumatic cues. Without a sense of body, the trauma victim cannot regain a sense of self.

So how can one even begin a therapeutic process that helps the patient to break free from the bondage of the need for multiple drugs? One must start with the most basic of needs in these patients, the most important of which are engagement and empowerment. The value of engagement in groups with people who share traumatic experiences was dramatically demonstrated in veterans of World War II and especially of Vietnam. The most important resource to the combatant in war is his fellow soldier, and this resource remains after his return to civilian life. The high incidence of PTSD in Vietnam veterans is probably partially based on the social rejection they experienced after their return, and one of the most effective resources in recovering their lives was found within groups of their peers. The importance of peer-group support in healing trauma has also been dramatically documented with rape and cancer survivors. Humans and other mammals are social creatures, and social isolation is linked to many diseases and a shortened life span. Reengagement of the isolated and constricted trauma victim is one of the basic essentials for the process of expanding safe boundaries and extinguishing trauma-linked cues. Interpretation of distorted perceptions by one's peers, verbal encouragement to expand one's sense of safe boundaries, and reassurance that the resulting discomfort is not a danger may help victims to take the first steps toward finding the tiniest safe place.

Shame and self-blame are usually part of the shared heritage of trauma victims. Sharing stories and emotions with people who have experienced and survived similar intense and negative feeling states rekindles hope. Becoming aware that trauma is a universal syndrome, that we all experience pieces of it throughout our lives, and that their symptoms of terror are not unique to them provides the cognitive context to their own lives that begins the healing process. Engagement may begin the process of desensitization that ultimately allows the trauma victim to tolerate existence without multiple drugs.

Because helplessness is the core state that defines traumatization, healing must be associated with empowerment and the perception of control. The trauma victim may be empowered by the group process itself. Listening to stories of healing and redemption from those with similar life experiences expands victims' perceived options for healing. However, healing also inevitably requires recapturing the sense of embodiment that is lost in dissociation. It is impossible for victims to feel powerful if all they perceive is an overwhelming sense of physical weakness and collapse. If victims are to tolerate weaning from a multiple drug regimen (or, for that matter, any cognitive or somatic psychotherapeutic techniques) they must first recapture some sense of safety within their own mind, memory, and body. How this is achieved may depend on the ingenuity of the therapist and perhaps of the patient as well. The more "tangential" therapies that approach the trauma through perceptual sensory messages, such as the movement and art-related activities I discussed earlier, may be one way of beginning the process of embodiment. By dampening the kindling of traumatic sensorimotor cues, the trauma victim may begin to regain a modicum of boundary sense and therefore of safety. A recovered sense of self is a prerequisite for empowerment, and the restoration of a sense of body is a requirement for the perception of self.

In essence, I feel that the drug treatment of the varied states of trauma, including arousal, dissociation, numbing, avoidance, depression, pain, and somatic syndromes, is an often necessary but inevitably self-limiting therapeutic approach. All experiences, including the manipulation of levels of brain transmitters, change the chemical and physical environment of the brain itself. Studies may eventually show that drug treatment produces permanent and desirable alteration in brain pathways. On the flip side, they may also eventually show that prolonged drug treatment produces permanent changes that render the brain *more* vulnerable. If trauma, when broken down to its basic elements, is indeed a model for the effects of classical conditioning, behavioral therapy remains the best option for extinguishing the process. Medications in this model must be considered an adjunct and not a therapeutic end.

The Risks of Transformation

The paths we choose to follow in our lives are shaped by the myriad patterns of our positive and negative life experiences beginning in earliest childhood. We would be presumptuous to assume that our choices are based solely on the power of free will. It's not so much that we march in an unconscious lockstep toward goals that are determined by our parents, teachers, and mentors. Our choices, rather, are shaped from birth by our experiences related to reward and punishment. Our legacy of trivial to profound negative and positive life experiences largely determines those life choices. In the case of negative life experiences, this behavior unfortunately is based on many of the principles of traumatic reenactment and recapitulation.

We unconsciously seek to undo the negative experiences through the process of repetition, perhaps to achieve completion or to eventually get it right. Harville Hendrix (2001) noted that we often pick our mates based on their reflecting some of the negative traits of our caregivers. Some of this repetition behavior may be based on our having become familiar, and therefore more comfortable, with how to relate to those negative traits in another person. On the other hand, we may feel that underneath all of the abuse, our alcoholic father was basically a good man. So we marry another alcoholic male, unconsciously believing that we can reform him and, in doing so, banish the pain of our childhood. The compulsion to pursue a specific profession or the competitive need to climb the corporate ladder is fueled by our unconscious need for control, self-gratification, and completion. Certainly instinctual drives contribute to this process, but the direction they take is usually determined by early life experiences—primarily negative ones, I would venture to say.

In this process, we often find that our ultimate achievement, however gratifying, also entails incredible self-sacrifice and stress. The willingness of individuals to accept these sacrifices is often remarkable and inexplicable. The medical and legal professions are probably extreme examples of this. Why would one sacrifice health, happiness, family, and leisure in the completely voluntary pursuit of a vocational goal? Why would a doctor work 80 hours a week to the detriment of his personal health and relationships? I would suggest that the most likely explanation is that this behavior reflects the childhood behaviors for which the individual received parental reward or avoided parental punishment. In these cases there was an absence of intrinsic and unqualified parental love and bonding to provide the child with a sense of self-worth outside of personal achievements. As you know by now, I believe that the absence of adequate nurturing during infanthood is child abuse. However, the concept of nurturing goes well beyond early maternal bonding; it extends into the childhood and teenage years, when parents may make unreasonable demands for excellence or perfection and withhold intrinsic love and valuation of the child as a person. These traumatized children are rewarded only for doing what they do—not for simply being who they are. Lacking an intrinsic sense of self, the traumatized child is destined to endlessly recapitulate personal achievement as the only means of recapitulating his or her sense of self. Unfortunately, as Alice Miller (1997) noted, this life lesson usually becomes a generational and eventually a universal cultural pattern of acceptable behavior. In our culture, it has become the desired norm and fuels our widely admired capitalist economy

Although we pay a price for the burden of our life trauma, the negative effects of our choices and our patterns of behavior also contain rewards.

Conclusion

Financial security, material possessions, expanded freedom of choice, and the acknowledgement of achievement are a heady brew of positive reinforcement for an otherwise stressful life. Why would our marriages founder and our children be disturbed in the climate of such plenty? In fact, regardless of its rewards, the life based solely on achievement represents with remarkable accuracy the approach/avoidance conflict that creates an environment of helplessness in which trauma can occur.

I have seen a remarkable number of adult patients who have been traumatized by an apparently trivial negative life event, usually a minor fender-bender MVA. In many of these patients, significant childhood abuse had predisposed them to the complex physical response they had to MVA. A small but significant number, however, did not have childhood trauma. Instead, they were experiencing daily trauma due to marked ambivalence regarding their life pursuit of a profession. The higher they climbed up the academic, corporate, legal, or medical ladder of achievement, the more they were subjected to the administrative demands of superiors, and the more duress was imposed on them. In many cases, the patients were women subjected to unmistakable gender bias. One of my patients, a professor at a university, developed debilitating whiplash symptoms and depression after a minor MVA. Her core trauma was insidious gender discrimination at work, and her symptoms resolved when she relinquished her tenure. In other cases, the core trauma was an ongoing psychologically abusive marriage. In all of these cases, the victims unconsciously accepted the abusive situation as the norm because it allowed them to define their sense of self-worth in ways that were established in their childhoods—as the "successful professional" or the "dutiful wife and mother."

Many of these patients entered trauma therapy because they believed my assertions that their physical and emotional responses to the MVA were based solely on the traumatic nature of the accident, superimposed on their old burden of "little life traumas." A number of them successfully traveled the transformative road to full consciousness and awareness of themselves. In some cases, this acquired wisdom helped them recognize the core trauma of their life: their career path or their dysfunctional and abusive marriage. They now faced another approach/avoidance dilemma, one that required tremendous courage to resolve. Several took the path that seemed to contain the greatest threat to their safety, giving up their tenured professorships, their corporate vice-presidencies, and even businesses they owned or giving up the financial safety net of their dysfunctional marriages. But their newly acquired wisdom enabled them to look beyond the immediate message of that threat and have the courage to start over, seeking training in entirely new vocations, not surprisingly often in the healing arts. Some, empowered by their newly found self-awareness and more grounded sense of self, filed appeals, complaints, or suits against their employers, usually for gender discrimination.

Life changes of this sort carry with them their own burden of stress and pain. Facing them without personal resources is potentially traumatic. But true transformation from trauma changes the most critical aspect of trauma: its *meaning*. When one's sense of self is wrapped up in the endless demands of achievement, one basically can never find the professional Holy Grail or reach the end of the road. The ante is raised with each new step. But the alternative to the endless search may also be intolerable. If one's perception of self is totally bonded to achievement, giving up that life pattern may amount to a shattering of the self. That loss may be far more terrifying than the pain of the quest for professional success. This may be the reason that many patients during the course of their therapy reach a point where a new fear arises—not a fear of facing the terror associated with the core trauma, but rather a fear of what may be necessary to replace it. The traumatized mind may view that alternative as an undefined void far more frightening than the constricting but familiar defenses they have used throughout their lives. Under these circumstances, patients may inexplicably terminate therapy at the point of a real breakthrough.

Those who have retained a fragment of an intrinsic self-sense may find the courage to jump into that void and accept the unknown. As healing takes place and self-confidence emerges, the former victim may find deeply buried resources, goals, and desires that have been suppressed because they did not meet the goals of their childhood caregivers. Not surprisingly, their travel along the road to healing has given them remarkable insights, not only into their own newly found self, but also into the ways of the mind and the implications of having lost both the mind and the body through trauma. Transformation therefore implies that the person not only has recovered a degree of homeostasis but also has achieved a new level of adaptation and perception that can only be described as wisdom.

The concept of wisdom suggests the acquiring of practical life knowledge through the accumulation of a broad spectrum of life experiences—experiences both good and bad. It implies an awareness of both possibilities and limitations, opportunities and barriers, and perhaps especially an awareness of the finitude of life itself. Linley (2003) provided a learned review of the literature on the concept of wisdom as a positive adaptation to life trauma. In exploring the nature of wisdom, Linley defined its three fundamental dimensions. The first is the *recognition and management of uncertainties*. The uncertainties of life inevitably involve a possible loss of control. Acquiring wisdom entails an awareness of uncertainties but the development of the ability to manage them with adaptive changes in behavior rather than with fear, rage, or freeze.

The second dimension in wisdom is the *integration of affect and cognition*. With regard to trauma, the acquisition of wisdom implies that the person no longer experiences fear and its somatic sensations as intrinsic threats. The *meaning* associated with emotions and body states linked to fear becomes integrated with conscious awareness. These states then become detached from the old trauma, and consist of declarative memories of a past event that are used to expand one's practical life knowledge. Emotions previously experienced as threats now are incorporated in one's storehouse of conscious survival skills.

The third dimension is the *recognition and acceptance of human limitation*. Linley (2003) noted that this concept has been explored through the ages as the ultimate prerequisite for wisdom. More than any other person, the trauma survivor has witnessed the fragility of life and the certainty of its ultimate end. Healing from trauma therefore allows one to fully appreciate the value of one's existence. It allows one to move beyond the concerns in one's life that relate only to one's self and to empathize with others. Altruism as part of this world sense may be one of the most valuable of the traits acquired through the wisdom of healing, not only for society but also for the individual.

Transformation and the development of wisdom through healing from trauma provide dramatic evidence for the resiliency and power of the human spirit. Much has been written about the concept of the wounded healer, and about the unique insights and strengths of those who have overcome past life trauma. I have been told that in indigenous tribes, the shaman often arises from those members who have experienced significant hardship and traumatic loss. In my ongoing and numerous contacts with therapists in the field of traumatic stress, I have found something that everyone in this field already knew: The passion and unique insight of these dedicated people are often based on their own life traumas and the process of their healing. Knowing oneself allows one to know others and to refrain from judging them on the basis of one's own unconscious fears and prejudices that stem from retained internal traumatic messages. Having experienced and overcome trauma, one has gained wisdom, and with it has found empathy for the often-distressing behavior of trauma patients who continue to struggle with their own frightening emotions and body messages. Using the wisdom of the body to heal the brain restores embodiment, which in turn allows for a perception of self that is able to withstand the residual assaults of the past and to fully comprehend the experience of those who are still on the path of healing from trauma. Obviously not all people who have experienced the gift of traumatic healing enter the healing professions. There are members of society, however, who intrinsically seem to possess unique gifts of insight and social caring for their peers and for disadvantaged members of their society in general. Many of these unique people are able to give such altruistic gifts by virtue of their own experience with traumatic healing.

EPILOGUE

Understanding Your Life

The definition of trauma covers a vast continuum of negative life experiences, their relative importance based on their intrinsic meaning for survival to the particular person—or animal. In my model, trauma can occur from the time the parts of the brain in the fetus that process procedural memory come on line through death, unless one believes in past lives. The trauma may be as dramatic as torture or as subtle as shades of maternal/infant bonding. Even subtle negative experiences may approach the level of trauma if a state of helplessness accompanies the negative event.

Watching animal behavior is a useful means of understanding ourselves. The human forebrain puts such a complex structure on top of behavior that it's often hard to see the instinctual patterns that underlie it. Animals are much more honest, direct, and predictable. I think that Peter Levine had it right when he equated the freeze response and its discharge in animals with its counterpart in humans as the source of traumatization. The problem with making this ethological comparison is that the freeze response may be extremely subtle and hard to identify in our perplexing species. I have equated the psychological process of dissociation with the perceptual event that occurs with the freeze, acknowledging that dissociation per se is not always pathological. Nevertheless, the experience of dissociation implies that the person has experienced a life threat.

This threat, or course, may occur as a novel life experience or as an internal threat-based message arising from procedural memory for an old trauma. The real dilemma is why humans don't do what animals do when they have survived: shake, sweat, and breathe it all out.

On Christmas Day one year I experienced a family event that demonstrated why this usually doesn't occur. I had given my almost-3-year-old grandson a little car that could be run with a simple remote control. He had the remarkable idea to see whether it would run on the top of his head. In the course of this experiment, the wheels became entangled in his curly hair. It was obviously extremely painful, but he is a proud little boy, and although he was obviously terrified, he did not cry while I extracted his hair as gently as possible from the wheel. After I was finished, he ran to his mother and proceeded to scream in fear, pain, and rage for several minutes, striking out at no one in particular. His mother simply held him and allowed him to fully vent his fear, rage, and, I suspect, shame and embarrassment. In our culture, the "normal" adult behavior would be to reassure or suppress this "over-the-top" behavior, which in fact was a healthy completion of all the terror and rage that preceded his obvious freeze. This young mother, bonded and attuned to her child, instinctively knew just what he needed to do and averted one of life's "minor" traumas. Many patients have told me that, after a car accident, they began to shake all over and cry. Invariably, in an attempt to be reassuring, family members, police, and ambulance personnel urged these patients not to shake or cry, leading them to suppress this physiologically necessary but socially intolerable response.

Wailing, crying, and throwing oneself on the casket of a departed loved one at a funeral is considered inappropriate behavior in many cultures. Tantrums in children are treated with "time-out" isolation, not with touch and holding. We have lost the ability to tolerate the expression of vehement emotions in others. Perhaps this expression is impractical in a culture so tightly compacted both physically and emotionally. As I have noted, the only animals that seem to have lost the ability to spontaneously experience the behavior of the freeze discharge are domesticated or confined in a laboratory, circus, or zoo. Like these animals, perhaps we have found our own metaphorical cages through the behavioral entrapments of our culture.

The spectra of life events that are considered capable of causing traumatization by the DSM-IV are defined as "extreme traumatic stressors" (American Psychiatric Association, 1994). Although the DSM-IV list of horrific life events is qualified by the phrase "but not limited to," there is no mention of subtle life events that may be traumatizing because of their meaning in relation to past trauma. No consideration is given to preverbal trauma. Although "being diagnosed with a life-threatening illness" is listed as an example, there is no consideration given to the traumatic nature of the medical and surgical experience itself, especially in children. Psychological abuse in the dysfunctional family, marital relationship, or workplace, discrimination, and grinding poverty in the culture based on race, gender, religion, or nationality are not considered. And yet few people who have experienced fear in the context of such experiences would deny that they were traumatic. Limiting the definition of trauma to extreme stress is like defining the iceberg by its tip. Trauma rather must be defined by the specific physiological changes that occur in the body and brain related to any negative life experience and to the perpetuation of those changes over time.

Obviously such a definition is useless for studying the epidemiology of trauma. Behavioral science must place limits on its definitions, and it generally does so based on the negotiations of a panel of experts. Fortunately I am not constrained by such limitations and am free to speculate and postulate my ideas, with the only risk being the rejection of such experts. But in one respect, I think we would all agree: We all are victims of trauma, and we all are traumatized at some point in our lives. Another thing that we will agree on is that most people exposed to trauma do not appear to be traumatized. Whether in an indigenous tribe or a modern urban culture, life threats occur, and may do so many times throughout one's life. We are equipped to handle these threats through the instinctual autonomic systems in our brains and bodies. However, we also have a finite "allostatic load," the cumulative amount of stress that we tolerate before we begin to deteriorate from the stress-related diseases. It is the nature and degree of this traumatic life experience that defines us in almost every way imaginable.

I have discussed at length the role of maternal/infant bonding in developing resilience to threat and stress throughout the lifespan. Disorders of personality—obsessive/compulsive, borderline, narcissistic—are essentially a product of early childhood abandonment and trauma, usually within the first few years. Phobic, anxiety, and panic disorders also reflect a reduction in tolerance to threat based on negative early experience. These examples, as well as the spectrum of depressive disorders, almost certainly reflect the switching on of a gene through early life trauma. Even schizophrenia, a decidedly genetic trait, often is precipitated by a life stress or illness. Trauma essentially plays a role in causing or triggering most if not all mental illness.

Our choices throughout the lifespan are a reflection of what we have been taught as a child, but often the "teacher" was one or a series of traumas. It is the more subtle traumas that we disregard that perhaps make the most difference. I have had many patients relate a happy childhood but then acknowledge that one parent was alcoholic and either was unavailable as a parental resource or was to be avoided when he or she was intoxicated because of erratic behavior. The core trauma of other patients occurred in an abusive and punitive parochial school setting, with regular physical punishment, scorn, and belittlement. Alice Miller (1983) suggested that the culturally determined, abusive style of parental upbringing of children in pre–World War II Germany determined the pathological behavior of that nation during the Nazi regime.

The developing child is in no position to assess or judge the normality of his or her particular early life experience. It's basically the only world the child knows, and he or she assumes that's how the rest of the world operates, too. Thus, the child in the dysfunctional family unconsciously adopts those dysfunctional patterns. Life experiences that are physically painful, such as injuries, accidents, or surgical procedures, imprint the postures, tics, aches and pains of those events on procedural memory throughout the lifespan. They form the substrate for our physical behaviors, skills, appearance, and health. The DSM-IV notes that traumatized children may express their trauma only through repetitive play that is reflective of the trauma, or in physical complaints such as headache and stomachache. Any parent recognizes these symptoms in children as being related to stress. In fact, these somatic symptoms reflect fear related to an impending visit to an environment that contains a serious threat. For some reason, when these physical symptoms occur in adulthood, we no longer relate them to the same meaning that they had when we were children.

We all have categories of events in our lives that "set us off" or that we call our "pet peeves." These often relate to specific and peculiar behaviors of others that are intolerably irritating to us. Like every other life trait, these pet peeves represent childhood events or behavior-specific triggers for fear and secondarily for rage. They inevitably represent a conditioned association and response to a life event that represented a threat that was never successfully resolved. If the peeve is a behavioral trait, it will be similar to a trait in a caregiver, teacher, religious figure, or other authority figure over whom we had no control and who behaved in a way that induced fear.

Our tastes in food often reflect the association of that food with negative experiences in childhood that may have been linked to meals, such as arguments between our parents at the dinner table. Sensitivity to certain smells may be linked to odors, such as perfume, cologne, tobacco, or body odors, associated with an abuser. Choices in styles of dress, types of music, or forms of recreation often reflect identification with positive experiences, but also avoidance of negative childhood experience. Finally, our choices in mates and profession are especially influenced by our negative life experiences, as I noted earlier. Interestingly, our choices in these two most important areas often reflect, at least in part, traumatic repetition, the most maladaptive response to traumatic stress.

Personality features, life choices, behavioral traits, physical habits, habitual moods, smiles and facial expressions, habitual body postures, tics and nervous movement patterns, levels of personal hygiene and neatness, and a host of other idiosyncrasies all reflect our personal and quite individual responses to the conditioning influence of our multiple life traumas. Some are adaptive, many are merely curious, and others place us at risk for vulnerability to the inevitable exposure to small traumas that we all face, literally until we die. Some may be endearing, others a source of irritation to others. We often observe ourselves with whimsy and curiosity, wondering how we ever developed those weird little habits. Usually, however, we are basically oblivious to our own peculiar personal nuances. After all, this is the only body and mind that we have lived in.

Perhaps the most interesting thing we may gain in the process of transformation from trauma is insight not only the into the meaning of previously distressing and even disabling symptoms, but also into these other personal features we have always assumed we inherited from our parents. Recognizing these traits for what they are allows us to view ourselves not only with empathy and understanding but also with a little humor. Perhaps the ability to laugh at ourselves with wisdom and without regret is the ultimate gift of healing from trauma.

References

American Psychiatric Association. *Diagnostic and Statistical Manual of Mental Disorders, Fourth Edition (DSM-IV)* (1994). Washington, DC: American Psychiatric Association.

Anderson, G., Behnke, M., Chung, H., Conlon, M., & Wyler, F. (1995). Effect on and correlation between infant crying and salivery cortisol. *Pediatric Research, 33*(21), 12A–57.

Antelman, S., Austin, M., Caggiula, A., Edwards, D., Gershon, S., Kiss, S., & Kocan, D. (1997). Stressor-induced oscillation: A possible model of the bi-directional symptoms of PTSD. *New York Academy of Sciences, 21,* 296–305.

Ardrey, R. (1966). *The Territorial Imperative.* New York: Dell.

Beebe, G. (1975). Follow-up studies of World War II and Korean War POWs: II. Morbidity, disability and maladjustments. *American Journal of Epidemiology, 197*(101), 400–422.

Bok, S. (1998). *Mayhem.* Reading, MA: Addison-Wesley.

Borenstein, D., Boden, S., Jacobson, A., Lauerman, W., O'Mara, J., Platenberg, C., Schellinger, D., & Wiesel, S. (2001). The value of magnetic resonance imaging of the lumbar spine to predict low back pain in asymptomatic subjects: A seven-year follow-up study. *Bone and Joint Surgery, A*(9), 1306–1311.

Bowlby, J. (1976). *Attachment, Second Edition.* New York: Basic.

Bremner, D. (2002). *Does Stress Damage the Brain? Understanding Trauma-Related Disorders From a Mind-Body Perspective.* New York: W. W. Norton & Company.

Breslau, J., & Seidenwurm, D. (2000). Socioeconomic aspects of spinal imaging: Impact of radiological diagnosis on lumbar spine-related disability. *Topics in Magnetic Resonance Imaging, 11*(4), 218–223.

Breuer, J., & Freud, S. (1957). *Studies in Hysteria.* New York: Basic.

Brown, T. (1989). Cartesian dualism and psychosomatics. *Psychosomatics, 30*(3), 322–331.

Cannon, W. B. (1957). "Voodoo" death. *Psychosomatic Medicine, 19,* 182–190.

Catalano, R., & Hartig, T. (2001). Communal bereavement and the incidence of very low birthweight in Sweden. *Journal of Health and Social Behavior, 42*(4), 333–341.

Chagnon, N. (1992). *Yanomamo: The Last Days of Eden.* New York: Harcourt Brace.

Chamberlain, D. (1998a). Babies Don't Feel Pain: A Century of Denial in Medicine. In Dumit, J. & Davis-Floyd, R., (Eds.), *Cyborg Babies: From Techno-Sex to Techno-Tots.* New York: Routledge.

——— (1998b). *The Mind of Your Newborn Baby.* Berkeley, CA: North Atlantic Books.

Charpak, N., Charpoak, Y., de Figueroa, C., & Ruiz-Pelaez, N., (2001). A randomized, controlled trial of Kangaroo Mother Care: Results of follow-up at 1 year of corrected age. *Pediatrics, 108*(5), 1072–1079.

Chodorow, J. (1994). *Dance Therapy & Depth Psychology: The Moving Imagination.* New York: Routledge.

Cuny, H. (1965). *Ivan Pavlov: The Man and His Theories.* New York: Paul S. Erickson.

Damasio, A. (1994). *Descartes' Error: Emotion, Reason, and the Human Brain.* New York: Avon.

——— (1999). *The Feeling of What Happens: Body and Emotion in the Making of Cnsciousness.* New York: Harcourt.

Davis-Floyd, R., & St. John, G. (1998). *From Doctor to Healer: The Transformative Journey.* New Brunswick, NJ: Rutgers University Press.

de Casper, A., Busnel, M-C., Granier-Deferre, C., Lecanuet, J-P., & Mangeais, R. (1994). Fetal reactions to recurrent maternal speech. *Infant Behavior and Development, 17*(20), 159–164.

Didi-Huberman, G. (2003). *Invention of Hysteria: Charcot and the Photographic Iconography of the Salpêtrière.* Cambridge, MA: MIT.

Engel, G. I. (1971). Sudden and rapid death during psychological stress: Folklore or folk wisdom? *Annals of Internal Medicine, 74,* 771–782.

References

Felitti, V., Anda, R., Nordenberg, D., Williamson, D., Spitz, A., Edwards, B., Koss, M., Marks, J. (1998). Relationship of childhood abuse and household dysfunction to many of the leading causes of death in adults: The adverse chidhood experience (ACE) study. *American Journal of Prevetentative Medicine*, 14(4), 245–58.

Ferenczi, S. (1921). Psychoanalytic observations on tics. In *Further Contributions in Psychoanalysis*. (Quoted in van der Hart, 2000)

Flexner, A. (1910). *The Flexner Report on Medical Education in the United States and Canada, 1910*. Washington, DC: Science and Health Publications, Inc.

Flor, H. (2002). The modification of cortical reorganization and chronic pain by sensory feedback. *Applied Psycophysiology and Biofeedback*, 27(3), 215–227.

———— (2003). Cortical reorganization and chronic pain: Implications for rehabilitation. *Journal of Rehabilitation Medicine*, (41 Suppl), 66–72.

Freud, S. (1938). *The Basic Writings of Sigmund Freud*. New York: Random House.

———— (1954). Beyond the pleasure principle (1920). In J. Strachey (Ed. and Trans.), *Complete Psychological Works, Standard Edition*, Vol. 3. London: Hogarth Press.

———— (1962). The Aetiology of Hysteria. In J. Strachey, J. (Ed and Trans.), *The Standard Edition of the Complete Psychological Works of Sigmund Freud*, 15, 1–240, 16, 241–496, London: Hogarth Press.

Freze, M. (1989). *They Bore the Wounds of Christ: The Mystery of the Sacred Stigmata*. Huntington, IN: Our Sunday Visitor Books.

Friedman, M. (1994). Neurobiological sensitization models of posttraumatic stress disorder: Their possible relevance to multiple chemical sensitivity syndrome. *Toxicology and Industrial Health*, 10(4–5), 49–462.

Friedman, M., & Schnurr, P. (1995). The relationship between trauma, posttraumatic stress disorder and physical health. In Charney, D., Deutsch, A., & Friedman, M., (Eds.), *Neurobiological and Clinical Consequences of Stress: From Normal Adaptation To PTSD* (pp. 518–524). Philadelphia: Lippincott-Raven.

Gawande, A. (2002). *Complications: A Surgeon's Notes on an Imperfect Science*. New York: Metropolitan Books.

Giannakoulopoulos, X., Fisk, N., Glover, V., Kourtis, P., & Sepulveda, W., (1994). Fetal plasma cortisol and B-endorphins response to intrauterine needling. *Lancet*, 344, 77–81.

Ginsberg, H. (1974). Controlled vs. non-controlled termination of immobility in domestic fowl (Gallus gallus): Parallel with the learned helplessness phenomenon. Unpublished manuscript, as quoted in Seligman, M. (1975). *Helplessness*. New York: W. H. Freeman and Company.

Goddard, G., Leetch, C., & McIntyre, D., (1969). A permanent change in brain functioning resulting from daily electrical stimulation. *Experimental Neurology, 25*, 295–330.

Goldstein, J., Ed. (1998). *Why We Watch: The Attractions of Violent Entertainment*. New York: Oxford University Press.

Goodall, J. (1990). *Through a Window*. Boston: Houghton Mifflin.

Grigsby, J., & Stevens, D. (2000). *Neurodynamics of Personality*. New York: Guilford.

Grossman, D. (1995). *On Killing: The Psychological Cost of Learning to Kill in War and Society*. New York, NY: Little Brown & Company.

Hagerman, I., Anderson, H., & Jorgenson, M. (2001). Posttraumatic stress disorder: A review of psychobiology and pharmacotherapy. *Acta Psychiatrica Scandinavia, 104*(6), 411–422.

Harlow, H. (1958). The nature of love. *American Psychologist, 13*, 673–685.

Hendrix, H. (2001). *Getting the Love You Want: A Guide for Couples*. New York: Henry Holt.

Herman, J. (1997). *Trauma and Recovery: The Aftermath of Violence, from Domestic Abuse to Political Terror*. New York: Basic.

Janet, P. (1920). *The Major Symptoms of Hysteria*. New York: MacMillan.

Johnson, E., Moutsopoulos, H., & Skopouli, F., (2000). Neuroendocrine manifestations in Sjogren's syndrome. *Rheumatologic Disease Clinics of North America, 6*(4), 927–949.

Jung, C. (1916). The transcendent function. *Collected Works, 8*, 67–91, Princeton, NJ: Princeton University Press, 1975.

Jung, C. (1965). *Memories, Dreams, Reflections*. New York: Vintage.

Kaplan, M., Ed. (1966). *Essential Works of Pavlov*. New York: Bantam.

Klaus, M., & Kennel, J. (1976). *Maternal-Infant Bonding: The Impact of Early Separation or Loss on Family Development*. St. Louis, MO: Mosby.

Krakow, B., Clark, J., Hollifield, M., Johnston, L., Koss, M., Melendrez, D., Pacheco, M., Pedersen, B., Schrader, R., & Warner, T., (2002). Sleep-disordered breathing, psychiatric distress, and quality of life impairment in sexual assault survivors. *Journal of Nervous and Mental Diseases, 190*(7), 442–52.

Krappel, F., & Harland, U. (2001). MRI diagnosis of intervertebral disc disease. *Der Orthopade*, (8), 502–513.

Kroll, J. (2002). Posttraumatic symptoms and the complexity of responses to trauma. *JAMA*, 290(5), 667–670

Leakey, R. (1994). *The Origins of Humankind*. New York: Basic.

Levine, P. (1997). *Waking the Tiger*. Berkeley, CA: North Atlantic Press.

Linley, P. (2003). Positive adaptation to trauma: Wisdom as both process and outcome. *Journal of Traumatic Stress*, 16(6), 601–610.

MacLean, P. (1973). *A Triune Concept of the Brain and Behavior*. Toronto: University of Toronto Press.

Maeda, M., Hayashi, A., Shoji, S., & Tamaoka, A., (1995). A case of HLA-DR2, DQw1 negative posttraumatic narcolepsy. *Rinsho Shinkeigaku*, 3(5), 811–813.

Mailis-Gagnon, A., Giannovlis, I., Downar, J., Kwan, C., Mikulis, D., Crawley, A., Nicholson, K., & Davis, K., (2003). Altered central somatosensory processing in chronic pain patients with "hysterical" anesthesia. *Neurology*, 60(9), 1501–7.

Mason, W., & Berkson, G. (1975). Effects of maternal mobility on the development of rocking and other behaviors in rhesus monkeys: A study with artificial mothers. *Developmental Psychobiology*, 8, 197–221.

Mead, V. (2003). *Somatic Psychology Theory and the Origins of Chronic Illness: A Case Study of Type I Diabetes*. Thesis, Naropa University, Boulder, CO.

Melzack, R., Coderre, T., Katz, J., & Vaccarino, A. (2001). Central neuroplasticity and pathological pain. *Annals of the New York Academy of Science*, 933, 157–174.

Miller, A. (1983). *For Your Own Good: The Roots of Violence in Child-rearing*. New York: Farrar, Straus and Giroux.

———— (1997). *The Trauma of the Gifted Child: The Search for the True Child*. New York: Basic.

Mitchell, S., Keen, W., & Morehouse, G., (1864). *Gunshot Wounds and Other Injuries*. Philadelphia: J. B. Lippincott Co.

Montagu, A. (1986). *Touching: The Human Significance of the Skin*. New York: Harper & Row.

Nathanielsz, P. (1999). *Life in the Womb*. Ithaca, NY: Promethean.

Odent, M. (2000). Between circular and cul-de-sac epidemiology. *Lancet*, 355, 1371.

Overpeck, M., Berendes, H., Brenner, R., Trifletti, L., & Trumble, A., (1998). Risk factors for infant homicide in the United States. *The New England Journal of Medicine*, 339(17), 1211–1216.

Panksepp, J. (1998). *Affective Neuroscience: The Foundation of Human and Animal Emotions*. New York: Oxford University Press.

Perry, B. (1995). Childhood trauma, the neurobiology of adaptation, and "use-dependent" development of the brain: How "states" become "traits." *Infant Mental Health Journal*, 16(4), 271–291.

Porges, P. (1998). Love: An emergent property of the mammalian autonomic nervous system. *Psychoneuroendicrinology*, 23(8), 837–861.

Porges, S. (1995). Orienting in a defensive world: Mammalian modification of our evolutionary heritage. A polyvagal theory. *Psychophysiology*, 32, 301–318.

Prescott, J. (2002). *America's Lost Dream: 'Life, Liberty and the Pursuit of Happiness.'* The Association for Prenatal and Perinatal Psychology and Health, Tenth International Congress, December 6–9, 2001.

Rauch, S., Alpert, N., Fischman, A., Fisler, R., Jenike, M., Orr, S., Pitman, R., Savage, C., & van der Kolk, B., (1996). A symptom provocation study of posttraumatic stress disorder using positron emission tomography and script-driven imagery. *Archives of General Psychiatry*, 53, 380–387.

Reynolds, W., Lue, F., Moldofsky, H., & Saskin, P, (1991). The effects of cyclobenzaprine on sleep physiology and symptoms in patients with fibromyalgia. *Journal of Rheumatology*, 18, 454–454.

Ridley, M. (2003). *Nature via Nurture*. New York: Harper Collins.

Sa, D., Mailis-Gagnon, A., Nicholson, K., & Lang, A., (2003). Posttraumatic painful torticollis. *Movement Disorders*, 18(12), 1482–91.

Salapatek, P., & Cohen, L. (1987). *Handbook of Infant Perception*, Vol I. New York: Academic Press.

Saul, L. (1966). Sudden death at impasse. *Psychological Forum*, 1, 88–89.

Schore, A. (1994). *Affect Development and the Origin of the Self: The Neurobiology of Emotional Development*. Hillsdale, NJ: Lawrence Erlbaum.

——— (2002). Dysregulation of the right brain: A fundamental mechanism of traumatic attachment and the psychopathogenesis of posttraumatic stress disorder. *Australian and New Zealand Journal of Psychiatry*, 36, 9–30.

Schreiber, S., & Galai-Gat, T. (1993). Uncontrolled pain following physical injury as the core-trauma in posttraumatic stress disorder. *Pain*, 54, 107–110.

References

Scordo, K. (1996). *Taking Control: Living with Mitral Valve Prolapse.* Cincinnatti, OH: Kardinal Publishing.

Seligman, M. (1975). *Helplessness.* New York: W. H. Freeman and Company.

Selye, H. (1956). *The Stress of Life.* New York: McGraw-Hill.

Starlanyl, D., & Copeland, M. (1998). *Fibromyalgia & Chronic Myofascial Pain: A Survival Manual.* Oakland, CA: New Harbinger Publications.

Starr, P. (1982). *The Social Transformation of American Medicine.* New York: Basic.

Taddio, A., Doren, G., Goldblach, M., Ipp, M., & Stevens, B., (1995). Effect of neonatal circumsion on pain responses during vaccination of boys. *Lancet, 345,* 291–292.

Taylor, G., Bagby, R., & Parker, J. (1997). *Disorders of affect regulation: Alexithymia in medical and psychiatric illness.* Cambridge, UK: Cambridge University Press.

Textor, R. (1967). *A Cross Cultural Study.* New Haven: HRAF Press.

Tinker, R., & Wilson, S., (1999). *Through the Eyes of a Child: EMDR With Children.* New York: W. W. Norton & Company.

van der Hart, O., van Dijke, A., & van Son, M. (2000). Somatoform dissociation in traumatized World War I combat soldiers: A neglected clinical heritage. *Journal of Trauma and Dissociation, 1*(4), 33–66.

Van der Kolk, B. (1989). The compulsion to repeat the trauma. *Psychiatric Clinics of North America, 12,* 2: 389–411.

Van der Kolk, B., van der Hart, O., & Weisath, L., (1996). The History of Trauma in Psychiatry. In B. Van der Kolk, A. MacFarlane, & L. Weisath, (Eds.), *Traumatic Stress.* New York: Guilford.

Verny, T. (1986). The Psychotechnology of Pregnancy and Labor. *The Journal of Pre- and Perinatal Psychology and Health, 1*(1), 31–51.

——— (2002). *Tomorrow's Baby: The Art and Science of Parenting from Conception through Infancy.* New York: Simon & Schuster.

Vohr, B., Bauer, C., Broyles, S., Delaney-Black, V., Dusick, A., Fleisher, B., Kaplan, R., Mele, L., Papile, L., Simon, N., Steichen, J., Verter, J., Wilson, D., Wright, L., & Yolton, K., (2000). Neurodevelopmental and functional outcomes of extremely low birth weight infants in the National Institute of Child Health and Human Development Neonatal Research Network, 1993–1994. *Pediatrics, 10596,* 1216–26.

Wadwha, P. (1998). Prenatal stress and life-span development. In *An Encyclopedia of Mental Health*. Howard S. Friedman, (Ed.). San Diego, CA: Academic Press.

Weight, D., & Bigler, E. (Eds.), (1998). Neuroimaging in Psychiatry. *The Psychiatric Clinics of North America, 21*, 4: 725–759.

Whitfield, C. (2003). *The Truth about Depression: Choices for Healing*. Deerfield Beach, FL: Health Communications, Inc.

Wilson, S., Burbridge, J., Fisler, R., Kradin, T, & Van der Kolk, B., (1999). Phenotype of blood lymphocytes in PTSD suggests chronic immune activation. *Psycho-Somatics, 40, 222–25*.

Yehuda, R., Binder-Brynes, K., Giller, E., Schmeidler, J., & Siever, L., (1998). Relationship between posttraumatic stress disorder characteristics of Holocaust survivors and their adult offspring. *American Journal of Psychiatry, 155*(6), 841–843.

Zuckerman, B., Bauchner, H., Parker, S., Cabral, H. (1990). Maternal depressive symptoms during pregnancy and newborn irritability. *Journal of Developmental and Behavioral Pediatrics, 11*(4), 190–4.

Index

abreaction, 189
abulia, 179, 192
acupuncture, 260, 262
addiction, 89, 90–91
adrenal glands, 206, 207, 244
adrenaline, 206–207
adrenocorticotropic hormone, 52, 207
advertising, 93
afferent nerves, 22
AIDS, 208
alcoholism, 80, 130
alexithymia, 180
allopathy, 158
alternative and complementary medicine, 157–158, 167
Alzheimer's disease, 39
ambivalence, 34–35
amniocentesis, 112–113
amygdala, 52, 63, 73, 74, 105, 269
anesthesia, 236
anhedonia, 179
animals in captivity, 49, 54–55
Antelman, S., 214
anticonvulsant drugs, 274–275
antidepressant drugs, 275
anxiety disorders, 72, 287
aphasia, 82
approach/avoidance conflict, 33, 34
    life stress and, 211–212, 281
Ardrey, R., 6
art therapy, 267–268
assessment
    biopsychosocial approach, 153
    brain imaging technology, 71–73
    diagnostic criteria, 78–79
    sensory cues, 64
    sociocultural considerations, 129
    whiplash syndrome, 231
atropine, 56

attachment theory, 117, 119
attention deficit hyperactivity disorder, 72, 122–123, 248–249
autonomic nervous system, 9, 22, 50, 102–103
    biofeedback, 24
    in freeze response, 45, 213, 215–217
    in infant–caretaker interaction, 120
    stress response, 24, 25
    trauma-associated diseases of, 214–227
    vasomotor instability in conversion hysteria, 195

benzodiazepines, 275–276
biofeedback, 24, 262
bipolar disorder, 80–81, 274, 275–276
blinking, 236
blood flow, 16–17
    cognitive demands, 73
    imaging technology, 72
    in somatic dissociation, 230, 243
    threat response, 206, 207
    traumatization effects, 73–74
    vasomotor instability in conversion hysteria, 195–196
body memory, 63
body piercing, 90
body scanning, 256
Bok, S., 134, 144–145, 147
bowel problems, 4, 221
Bowlby, J., 115, 119
brain injury, 4
    memory disorders related to, 39
    trauma effects, 8
    see also neurophysiology
brain/mind/body continuum, 26–27, 203–204
    body systems in, 20–26
    brain structure and function, 16–19
    function of mind in, 19–20
    holistic medical practice, 169

interrelationship of elements, 14, 16
motor skill acquisition and, 16, 21–22
in perception of reality, 14–16
brainstorm, 51, 269
breast-feeding, 92, 118, 119, 120, 137, 138
Bremen, D., 73, 74, 75
Brendan, T., 161
Brier, J., 187, 188, 189, 195, 259
Brown, T. M., 13
bruxing, 50

Cannon, W., 48
cardiovascular function
in freeze response, 45, 46–47
mitral valve prolapse/dysautonomia syndrome,
222–223
in sudden unexplained death, 47–48
threat response, 45–46, 206
carpal tunnel syndrome, 234
Catalano, R., 107
cataplexy, 250
causes of traumatic stress, 7–8, 97–98
birth experience, 114–115
childcare effects, 121–122, 124
chronic pain, 182
cortisol effects, 75
Freudian model, 187–190
genetic factors, 8, 87
as inappropriate survival response, 29, 42, 58
inhibited freeze response, 48–49, 75
killing in war, 147
learned helplessness model, 56–57
life-threatening experience, 12, 13
in medical care, 114–115, 151–152, 170–171
memory-based sensory cues in, 18, 58, 59–62,
63, 192–193
neurosensitization, 62–64
resiliency factors, 54–55
scope of, 97–98, 285–289
sociocultural sources, 6–7, 97, 98, 127,
129–133, 149–150
traumatizing potential of types of trauma, 259
cerebral cortex, 19, 51, 269–270
Chamberlain, D., 101, 104
Charcot, J-M., 185–187
Charpak, N., 143
chemical sensitivity, 217, 223–225
child abuse and neglect
art therapy for victims of, 267–268
associated diseases, 209–210
attention deficit hyperactivity disorder and, 248
conversion hysteria and, 175
epidemiology, 134–135
postpartum depression in victims of, 241–242
social relationship problems in adulthood for
victims of, 70
in whiplash syndrome etiology, 228
childbirth, 8, 106
C-sections, 113, 114

electronic fetal monitoring, 113
historical development, 110–112
legal environment, 112
maternal anesthesia, 111
medical practice, 110–111, 112–114, 118
postpartum depression, 241–242
risk of traumatization of neonate in, 114–115
childhood experience
compulsive reenactment of trauma, 89–90,
279–280
daycare, 125, 130
exposure to violence, 144
of extreme sports participants, 91–92
in families with alcoholic parent, 80, 130
in formation of personality and behavior, 18,
78, 88, 287–289
infantile amnesia, 39, 101
infant sentience, 99–105
manifestations in trauma, 2
mother's, and subsequent caretaking style, 117
neonatal intensive care, 107–110
popular conceptualization of, 99
preverbal trauma, 8, 97
psychopathology risk, 80–81, 287
risk of dissociative response to subsequent
trauma, 262–263
sociocultural determinants, 130, 143
subsequent social behavior and, 142–143
see also child abuse and neglect; childbirth;
fetal experience; infant–mother relations;
preverbal trauma
Chodorow, J., 266
chronic fatigue syndrome, 217–220
chronic pain, 3–4, 238–241
pelvic, 243
trauma pharmacotherapy and, 276–277
cognitive functioning
brain blood flow related to, 73
brain structure for, 269–270
concept of mind, 19–20
creative thought, 37
in dissociation, 177, 179–181, 216
in freeze response, 48
in healing process, 255
hemispheric division of brain, 51
infant capacity, 99–100, 103–104
intrusive thoughts, 64–65
trauma effects, 247–248, 252, 270–271
in whiplash syndrome, 231
in wisdom, 282–283
complex trauma, 215, 262
computed tomography, 72
conditioning
brain changes in, 25, 83–84
classical, 29, 30–32
concentration of excitation, 32
creative thought and, 37
definition, 17
experimental neurosis, 33–35

Index

fight/flight/freeze response, 28–29
  influence of, 31, 37
  irradiation of effects, 32
  memory in, 38
  neurophysiology of, 102–103
  reinforcement, 31
  sensitivity, 31
  survival function, 32–33
  trauma model, 5, 7–8, 42
  traumatic reenactment and, 94–95
  in utero, 105
conversion hysteria, 1, 9
  characteristics, 183, 193–194
  clinical conceptualization, 175, 185–192
  neurological alteration in, 194–196
  rationale, 175–176
  somatic dissociation and, 193
cortisol, 210, 215
  endocrine regulation, 52, 244
  fetal exposure, 97, 107
  fetal expression, 106
  immune regulation, 246
  infant expression in stress, 109, 115–116, 118, 122
  prolonged exposure effects, 74, 75
  side effects, 207–208
  in stress physiology, 206–208
  in threat response, 207
coughing, 236
creative thought, 37
critical incident debriefing, 261
culture, see society and culture
cumulative trauma disorder, 233–235
cyclical patterns in homeostasis, 53
cystitis, interstitial, 217, 243–244

Damasio, A., 24–25, 71, 82, 104
dance therapies, 266–267
Davis-Floyd, R., 154, 157, 162–163, 169
death, 19–20
  sudden unexplained, 47–48
de Caspar, A., 105
declarative memory, 38–39, 103–104
decorticate rigidity, 258–259
definition of trauma, 6, 58, 205, 285, 286–287
  concept of stress and, 205–206
  conceptual evolution, 1–2, 97
  continuum conceptualization, 8, 97, 205
Depakote, 274
depression, 287
  pharmacotherapy, 273–274
  postpartum, 241–242
Descarte, R., 13–14
desensitization
  in medical school training, 156, 171
  to violence, 147
diabetes, 207–208, 245
Diagnostic and Statistical Manual of Mental Disorders, Fourth Edition, 2, 97, 261, 286–287

dissociation, 45
  autonomic nervous system in, 45, 213, 215–217
  characteristics, 177, 179–181
  clinical conceptualization, 185
  cognitive functioning in, 216
  in complex trauma, 215
  in conversion hysteria, 175, 183
  early studies in hysteria, 185–192, 193, 195
  freeze response and, 36–37, 74–75, 266, 285
  implications for treatment, 255, 262–264
  in infants, 121, 122
  involuntary motor responses in therapy and, 257
  motor impairment in, 184–185
  neurophysiology, 179–180, 183
  non-pathological, 178, 257, 285
  perceptual distortion in, 75, 179
  predisposing factors, 262
  as reward stimulus, 263–264
  in shellshock, 183–185
  stigmata and, 198
  therapeutic interventions to address, 264–268
  see also somatic dissociation
dissociative identity disorder, 179
dizziness, 59
dopamine, 138, 142
  pharmacotherapy rationale, 273–274
dreams, 25, 66–67, 218–219
dystonia, 237

eating disorders, 90, 91
ecstatics, 196, 197, 198
effects of traumatization, 252–253
  brain changes, 74–76, 270
  cognitive functioning, 252, 270–271
  compulsive reenactment, 88–95, 279–280
  dissociation, 177–178
  inappropriate defensive behaviors, 69
  memory defects, 74–75
  sense of time, 58, 67, 70, 75, 252, 253
  social relationship problems, 69–70
  susceptibility to subsequent traumatization, 67–68
  traumatizing potential of types of trauma, 259
  see also symptoms of traumatization
efferent nerve, 22
Elavil, 275
Emotional Freedom Therapy, 260
emotional functioning
  brain structure and function in, 52, 82
  dissociation manifestations, 179, 182
  emotional memory, 40–41
  facial expression, 50
  medical conceptualizations, 13, 14
  medical school training and, 156–157
  societal control through emotional manipulation, 127–129
  survival behavior and, 49
  visceral system and, 24–25

in wisdom, 283
endocrine function
  health risks in stress adaptation, 53–54
  neurophysiology, 52
  threat response, 207
  trauma-associated diseases, 244–245
endorphins, 91, 92, 149, 217, 263
  in dissociation, 180, 181, 182–183
  fetal expression, 106
  in freeze response, 44
  in traumatic re-enactment, 89–90, 94
Engel, G., 47, 153
entertainment, violence in, 127, 144
epicondylitis, 234
epilepsy, 274
epinephrine, 44, 210
episodic memory, 38
equestrian therapy, 267
evolutionary theory, 11, 26, 28
  brain development, 19, 269–270
  gender differences in violent behavior, 134,
    136–137
  sociocultural evolution, 126–127
explicit memory, 38–39
exposure therapy, 255, 262
extinction of conditioning, 31, 61
  treatment goals, 254–255
Eye Movement Desensitization and Reprocessing,
  197–198, 260, 261, 262

facial expression, 50, 104
  infant-mother bonding, 119–120
fatigue, 4
  in fibromyalgia, 217, 218, 219
fear, 146
  societal control through, 128–129
  of therapeutic change, 282
Felitti, V., 209, 245
felt sense, 255–256
Ferenczi, S., 183–184, 236
fetal experience, 8, 84
  capacity for sentience, 104–105
  maternal stress and, 106–107
  sensory stimulation, 108–109
  sources of trauma in, 97
  trauma exposure, 106–107
fibromyalgia, 217–220
fight/flight/freeze response, 7
  determinants of, 43
  energy metabolism in, 45–46
  function, 28
  human response, 43
  induction, 43
  learning, 28–29
  neurophysiology, 44, 210
  see also freeze response
Flexner, A., 158–159
food and feeding, 93
freedom instinct, 49

freeze response, 5
  autonomic nervous system in, 45, 213, 215–217
  cognitive functioning in, 216
  dangers of, 46–47
  dissociation and, 36–37, 45, 266, 285
  freeze discharge, 29, 44–45, 48–49, 54, 211, 212
  function, 29, 44
  hypnosis and, 36
  neurophysiology, 44, 45, 46–47, 211, 213
  trauma and, 29–30, 48–49, 149–150, 192–193,
    212–213, 285
  visceral responses in, 215–216
  see also fight/flight/freeze response
Freud, S., 7, 66, 89, 187–190, 192, 193, 195, 259
Freze, M., 196
Friedman, M., 224
frontal lobe syndrome, 82–83
functional magnetic resonance imaging, 71–72

Gage, Phinneas, 82–83
gastroesophageal reflux disease, 217, 221–222
Gawande, A., 161, 166
gender differences, 6
  in preference for violent entertainment, 146
  trauma vulnerability, 132
  violent behavior, 133–134, 136, 139–140
gender discrimination and sexual harassment, 132
general adaptation syndrome, 53, 207
genetics, 8
  developmental significance, 12
  effects of experience in determining influence
    of, 17–18, 81, 84–87, 88
  influence of, 77–78
  influence on personality and behavior, 83,
    84–87, 88
  predisposition to violent behavior and,
    133–134, 136–137, 140–141, 148
  psychopathology risk and, 78–81
  trauma risk and, 8, 87
  twin studies, 87
Giannakoulopoulos, X., 106
glucose metabolism, 16–17, 44, 73, 206–207
  normal, 215
Goldstein, J., 146, 147, 148
Goodall, J., 139–140
Grave's disease, 245–246
Grigsby, J., 84, 85
guided imagery, 260
Gulf War syndrome, 224

hallucinations, 250
Harlow, H., 141, 143
Harlow, J., 82
Hashimoto thyroiditis, 245–246
headache, see migraine
health haintenance organizations, 160–161
helplessness, 47–48
  in experimental neurosis, 35
  forms of, 211

Index

freeze response and, 49, 55, 56, 211
learned, 56–57
in shellshock etiology, 184
social control and, 127, 132, 149–150
in trauma experience, 5, 12, 56–57, 59, 132, 189, 211, 212
treatment considerations, 278–279
whiplash syndrome etiology, 229–230
Hendrix, H., 279–280
Herman, J., 70
hippocampus, 17, 73, 74, 269
infant development, 101, 102
memory function, 39, 52, 103
regenerative capacity, 76
trauma effects, 74, 75
Hippocrates, 13
holistic medicine, 13
Holocaust survivors, 79
homeostasis, 195
body systems in maintenance of, 53
cyclical patterns in, 53
definition, 52–53
disruption, 53–54
neurophysiology, 52
hopelessness, 47–48
hormonal system
infant-mother bonding and, 118
in stress-related disease, 206
5-hydroxyindoleacetic acid, 142
hyperthyroidism, 244–245
hypnagogic hallucinations, 250
hypnosis, 36–37, 44, 189
hypochondriasis, 64
hypothalamic/pituitary/adrenal axis, 52, 75, 244
infant–caretaker interaction and, 119, 120
hypothalamus, 52
hysteria. see conversion hysteria

immune function
cortisol effects, 208
trauma-associated diseases, 245–247
implicit memory, 40–42
imprinting, 86
infant–caretaker relations, 3, 8, 83
attention deficit hyperactivity disorder and, 122–123
bonding, 117–125
conservation-withdrawal behaviors, 121, 122
developmental significance, 115–117, 118–124
feeding experience, 92–93
gaze interaction, 119, 120
hormonal system and, 118
infant neurophysiology and, 119–123, 138, 141–142, 143
infant personality development and, 84–85
maternal deprivation effects, 141–142
negative interactions, 121–122
psychopathology risk and, 78, 79–80, 85, 287

separation effects, 86, 115–116, 118, 119, 129–130
social violence and, 137–139, 143–144
instinctive behavior, 6, 17–18
survival function, 33
threat response, 20, 28
insulin, 245
insurance system, 159, 235
intrusive thoughts, 64–65
irradiation of conditioned response, 32, 61–62, 94–95
irritable bowel syndrome, 217, 220–221

Janet, P., 89, 186–187, 190–192, 193, 195, 197
jaw muscles, 49–50, 230
Jung, C., 265

kindling, 62–64, 75
in psychopathology, 274
treatment goals, 262
Klaus, M., 115, 117
Kroll, J., 129

Lamictal, 274–275
language and communication, 19
brain structure and function in, 82
dissociation manifestations, 180
doctor–patient relationship, 168
facial expression, 50, 119–120
tic-related speech disorders, 236–237
see also preverbal trauma
Leakey, R., 134
learned helplessness, 56, 59, 89
legal system, 131
Levine, P., 4–5, 48, 256, 285
limbic system, 93, 156, 168, 240, 269
clinical significance, 270–271
Linley, P., 283
little traumas, 2–3, 97, 98, 127–128, 129–133, 149
livido reticularis, 217, 220
locus ceruleus, 51–52
Lorenz, K., 86
lupus erythematosis, 245–246

MacLean, P., 269
magnetic resonance imaging, 71–72
Mailis-Gagnon, A., 194
Mason, W., 141
Mead, V., 117
Meaney, M., 116
meaning, trauma and, 2, 64, 211, 253
clinical significance, 282, 283
mechanism of healing, 254
medial prefrontal cortex, 74
medical practice, 128, 129–130
biopsychosocial and holistic approaches, 153, 167, 169, 172–173
in childbirth, 110–111, 112–115

cost of care, 159–160, 161
doctor–patient relationship, 157, 167–171, 172
education and training for, 152–158, 165–167
evolution of U.S. system, 158–162
health insurance system, 131–132, 159, 235
intrauterine surgery, 106
malpractice litigation, 161–162
neonatal intensive care, 107–110
physician errors, 166
sociocultural values and, 162–163
as source of trauma, 8, 97, 114–115, 132,
    151–152, 170–171
strategies for improving, 171–174
technological orientation, 164–165, 170
medulla, 47
memory
in conditioning, 38
disorders of, 39
in dissociation, 177
dreams and, 66–67
emotional, 40–41
explicit/declarative, 38–39
fetal capacity, 105
implicit/nondeclarative, 40–42
infant capacity, 39, 101, 103–104
interference of intrusive thoughts, 64–65
kindling effects, 62–64, 75
learned helplessness model of trauma, 56–57
neurophysiology, 39, 52, 103
past/present boundaries, 253
in perception of reality, 15–16
in phantom limb pain, 239–240
stability of, 39
in threat response, 29, 41–42, 49, 55–56
trauma-associated defects, 74–75
in trauma experience, 7, 18, 42, 58, 94,
    177–178, 192–193
treatment goals, 254
see also procedural memory
menstrual irregularity, 245
migraine, 225–227
Miller, A., 280
mind/body relationship, 7
Cartesian model, 1, 11
continuum model, 11
historical conceptualizations, 13–14
holistic medicine rationale, 13
trauma response and, 12
see also brain/mind/body continuum
Mitchell, S., 200
mitral valve prolapse/dysautonomia syndrome,
    217, 222–223
monoamine oxidase inhibitors, 275
Montagu, A., 119–120
motor behaviors
conditioned defensive reactions, 68–69, 234–235
in conversion hysteria, 194
cumulative trauma disorder etiology, 234–235
in dissociation, 184–185

in hysteria, 191
irradiation of conditioned responses, 68–69
muscle bracing in sleep, 218–219
therapeutic movement, 265–267, 268
therapeutic response in somatic experiencing,
    256–257
tics, 235–238
vestibular-cerebellar self-stimulation, 141–142
motor skill acquisition
brain changes in, 21–22
brain/mind/body continuum in, 16
infant development, 120–121
memory function in, 41
survival skills, 41–42
motor vehicle accidents, 3–4, 60, 131, 228, 230
    see also whiplash syndrome
movement therapy, 266–267, 268
multiple chemical sensitivities, 217, 223–225
multiple sclerosis, 245–246
musculoskeletal system, 20–21
autonomic innervation, 49–50
cumulative trauma disorder, 233–235
fibromyalgia symptoms, 218
reflexive action, 22–23
survival behavior functions, 49–50
myofascial pain, 232–233, 238, 243, 265

narcolepsy, 250
narcotics, 276–277
Nature via Nurture (Ridley), 85–86
near-death experience, 15–16
Nemeroff, C., 115
Neurontin, 274
neurophysiology
brain imaging studies, 70–74
brain/mind/body continuum, 14, 15–19
brain structure and function, 16–19, 269–270
of compulsive reenactment of trauma, 89–90
concept of mind, 20
of conditioning, 102–103
of conversion hysteria, 194–196
development in neonatal intensive care, 109
of dissociation, 179–180, 181, 183
endocrine regulation, 244
experience-based changes in, 17, 83–84
fight/flight/freeze response, 44, 210–211
freeze response, 44, 45, 46–47
hemispheric division of brain, 51
infant development, 99, 100–101, 115–116
infant–mother relations and, 8, 119–123, 138,
    141–142, 143
of learning, 83–84
of memory, 39, 103
motor skill acquisition, brain changes in, 21–22
neurosensitization, 62–64
pharmacotherapy rationale, 273–274
psychopathology, brain changes in, 70, 72–73,
    81–82
regenerative capacity, 76

Index

of stress-related disease, 206–209
survival behavior functions, 49–50
of threat response, 51–52, 73, 206–208, 268–269
trauma experience, 7–8, 11, 12, 58, 74–76, 270
traumatic reenactment, 94
triune brain model, 269–270
unconscious body functions, 21–22
see also brain injury
neurosis
approach/avoidance conflict in, 33
experimental, 33–35, 49
genetic predisposition, 85–86
vulnerability, 35
nondeclarative memory, 40–42
nonsteroidal anti-inflammatory drugs, 238
norepinephrine, 52, 210

obesity, 92–93, 123, 207
obsessive-compulsive disorder, 72, 275
Odent, M., 124
olfactory sense, 224–225
orbitofrontal cortex, 52, 73, 120, 244
orienting response, 46, 50, 238
outcomes research, 261
oxytocin, 118

pain
chronic, 238–241, 276–277
chronic pelvic, 243
dissociation and, 178, 179–180, 182–183
experimental induction of neurosis, 33–35
of extreme sports, 90–92
fetal capacity to experience, 106
in fibromyalgia, 217–220
infant capacity to experience, 99–102, 108
myofascial, 232–233
phantom limb, 61, 182, 239–240
as source of trauma, 182
trauma experience and, 3–4, 181–182, 239–241
traumatic reenactment, 89–90
use of touch in therapy, 265
palpitations, 59
pancreas, 245
Pavlov, I., 17, 25, 30, 33, 35, 36, 49, 103–104
Paxil, 275
pelvic pain, 243
Perry, B., 134
personality
brain structure and function in, 82–83
childhood experience in formation of, 18,
287–289
determinants of, 83–85
genetic and environmental influences, 84–87,
88
infant–caretaker relations in development of,
84–86, 87
vulnerability to neurosis, 33, 35
phantom limb phenomena, 61, 182, 239–240

pharmacotherapy, 135
anticonvulsant drugs, 274–275
antidepressant, 275
arousal induced by, 275
chronic pain, 241, 276–277
rationale, 273–274
side effects, 275–276, 277
tranquilizers, 275–276
trauma treatment, 274–278
phobia, 35, 287
physical manifestations of trauma, 8–9, 60, 62,
151–152, 251
autonomic nervous system dysfunction, 214–217
bimodal presentation, 216
conceptual basis, 12, 175–176, 209–214
cumulative trauma disorder, 233–235
diseases of somatic dissociation, 242–244
dysfunctional postures and movement patterns,
23–24
endocrine disorders, 244–245
fetal experience, 107
fibromyalgia, 217–220
gastroesophageal reflux disease, 221–222
immune disorders, 245–247
infant bonding experience and, 122–123
irritable bowel syndrome, 220–221
migraine, 225–227
mitral valve prolapse/dysautonomia syndrome,
222–223
multiple chemical sensitivities, 223–225
myofascial pain, 232–233
neonatal intensive care outcomes, 109–110
reflex sympathetic dystrophy, 200–204, 243
scope of, 176, 209–210, 211, 213–214
syndromes of procedural memory, 227
tics, 235–238
vasomotor instability, 195–196
weight gain, 207
whiplash syndrome, 227–231
see also conversion hysteria; stigmata
pineal gland, 14
piriformis syndrome, 233, 243
pitocin, 114, 118
pituitary gland, 52, 207, 244
Planetree, 172–173
Plotsky, P., 115
Porges, S., 46–47
positron emission tomography, 71–72
postconcussion syndrome, 4
posttraumatic stress disorder
as autonomic regulation dysfunction, 214–215
brain imaging studies, 72
clinical conceptualization, 2
diagnostic categorization, 73, 261
diagnostic criteria, 78–79, 129
freeze response theory, 4–5, 48
genetic risk factors, 79
intrusive thoughts in, 65

life-threatening illness and, 151, 152
memory defects in, 74–75
neurosensitization in, 63
outcomes research, 261–262
somatic experiencing in treatment of, 5
somatic therapeutic modalities, 260–261
time perception in, 70
power relations, 6–7
social structures, 126–127
predator–prey relationship, 28, 43, 44, 126
premenstrual syndrome, 241
Prescott, J., 134, 137, 142
preverbal trauma, 8, 97
fetal experience, 106–107
infant capacity for, 99–105
in neonatal intensive care, 107–110
procedural memory
definition, 41
infant capacity, 103
in learning, 41
life-threatening experience, 41–42
survival function, 49, 55–56, 59
trauma-associated cues in, 42, 59–62
trauma-related syndromes of, 227
prolactin, 118
protective factors
genetic, 87
threat response, 54–56

race/ethnicity, 6
Raynaud's phenomena, 217, 220
reality, 14–15
reenactment of trauma, 67–68, 88–95, 144,
148–149, 279–280
reflexes, 22–23
reflexive behavior, 40
reflex sympathetic dystrophy, 9, 175–176,
200–204, 213, 243
reinforcement, 31
religion and spirituality, 19–20
concept of stigmata, 196–197
religious conflict, 6–7
rheumatoid arthritis, 245–246, 247
Ridley, M., 85–86, 87, 133
risk-taking behaviors, 91–92, 147
rituals, 127–129, 133
in doctor training, 154–155

Sa, D., 238
Saul, L., 47–48
schizophrenia, 72, 78, 287
Schore, A., 119, 121
Scordo, K., 223
self-abuse, 89–90. *see also* suicide
self-defense training, 268
self-perception, 70–71
in dissociation, 177
of doctors-in-training, 154–155, 156–157
therapeutic change, 272–273, 281–283

Seligman, M., 56
Selye, H., 13, 53, 74, 206, 207, 208–209, 221
semantic memory, 38
Semelweiss, E., 110
sensory processes
brain function in, 16–17
brain/mind/body continuum, 14, 21
in classical conditioning, 30, 102–103
in conversion hysteria, 175, 193–194
experience of neonates in intensive care,
108–109
fetal experience, 104–105, 108–109
infant capacity, 99–105
infant–caretaker interaction, 119, 142, 143
memory-based sensory cues in traumatization,
18, 59–62
multiple chemical sensitivities, 224–225
pain perception, 101–103
perception of reality, 14–15
post-traumatic cue-based sensitization, 63–64,
94–95
in somatic experiencing, 255–256
somatosensory deprivation, 142, 143
survival behavior functions, 49, 51–52
in whiplash syndrome, 230–231
sentinel experience, 1
serotonin, 138, 142
pharmacotherapy rationale, 273–274
serotonin reuptake inhibitors, 275
sexual behavior, 136
sexual trauma, 189–190
shame, 121, 128, 278
shellshock, 1, 183–185, 236
sicca, 217
single photon emission computed tomography,
71–72
Sjogren's syndrome, 245–246, 247
sleep patterns, 4
in fibromyalgia, 218–219
trauma-related disorders, 249–250
social relations
child abuse outcomes in adulthood, 70
dissociation manifestations, 179
effects of inappropriate defensive behaviors, 69
in healing process, 168–169, 172
influence of childhood experience, 78,
142–144, 279–280
process of social isolation, 69–70
therapeutic significance, 278–279
see also infant–caretaker relations
society and culture, 8
acceptance of traumatizing experiences, 3, 127
child caretaking practices, 123–125, 138–139,
143
conceptualization of trauma in context of, 1,
129
control mechanisms in, 127–128, 147–148, 149
expression of strong emotion, 286
family functioning, 130

healthcare system and, 162–163
human evolution, 126
implications for assessment, 129
neurosis formation and, 33
obstacles to scientific research, 7
patriarchies, 162–163
personality development and, 87
power relations in, 126–127
predisposition to violent behavior, 138–139,
140–141, 143–144
primate societies, 139–141
self-abuse behaviors and, 90
sources of trauma in, 6–7, 97, 98, 127, 129–133,
149–150
trauma of societal rituals, 127–129
violent entertainment and, 144–149
somatic dissociation, 230
associated diseases, 243–244
conversion hysteria and, 175–176, 193
definition, 178
dystrophic change in, 199
implications for therapy, 264
manifestations, 178, 242–243, 264
somatic experiencing, 4–5
dissociated patient, 255, 262–268
involuntary movement patterns and postures in,
256–258
mechanism of change, 255–256, 271–272
safety of therapeutic setting, 255, 258
therapeutic relationship in, 256
touching in, 256, 264–265
for trauma without sensorimotor experience,
258–259
somatic nervous system, 21
somatoform dissociation, 183, 185
somnolence, daytime, 250
soul, 13–14, 19–20
spasmodic torticollis, 237–238
spastic dysphonia, 237
sports, 41
pain of extreme sports participation, 90–92
as violent entertainment, 145–146
SRY gene, 133–134, 137
St. Francis of Assisi, 196
Starlanyl, D., 220
stigmata, 9, 175–176, 192
definition, 196
dissociation and, 198
physiology, 197, 198–200
religious significance, 196–197, 198
stress-related disease
clinical conceptualization, 205–206
physiology, 206–209
stuttering, 236–237
substance abuse, 210
sudden unexplained death, 47–48
suicide, 135
survival of the fittest, 126–127

sympathetic nervous system, 102–103
in fight/flight/freeze response, 44
in reflex sympathetic dystrophy, 201
vasomotor instability in conversion hysteria,
195
symptoms of traumatization, 8
childhood experience and, 2
as conditioned behavioral responses, 5, 42,
60–61
health risks in stress adaptation, 53–54
intrusive thoughts, 65
nightmares, 66–67
psychological manifestations, 4
scope of, 42
self-perception, 70–71
sociocultural context, 129
time perception, 70
worsening over time, 63–64
see also effects of traumatization; physical
manifestations of trauma

tattoos, 90
technology, 164–165
Tegretol, 274
tendonitis, 234
Territorial Imperative, The (Ardrey), 6
Textor, R., 137
thalamus, 73
therapeutic relationship, 157, 167–171, 172
in somatic experiencing, 256
therapist qualities, 283–284
Thieriot, A., 171–172
Thought Field Therapy, 260
threat response
cue associations in, 59, 94–95
energy metabolism for, 45–46, 206
fear as, 128
gender differences, 134
health risks in stress adaptation, 53–54
as instinctual behavior, 20, 28
memory function in, 41–42, 59
musculoskeletal anatomy for, 49–50
neurophysiology of, 49–50, 51–52, 73, 206–208,
268–269
orienting response, 46
in somatoform dissociation, 183
survival behavior, 28
in traumatization, 12, 23, 42, 58, 94–95
unconscious learned behaviors for, 21, 32–33,
40
vulnerability vs. resiliency in, 54–56
see also fight/flight/freeze response
thyroid, 244–245
tics, 61, 183, 184, 191, 235–238
therapeutic response, 256–257, 258
time, perception of, 58, 67, 70, 75, 252, 253
Tinker, R., 197
Topomax, 274

torticollis, 237–238
tranquilizers, 275–276
Traumatic Incident Reduction, 260
treatment, 9
    brain plasticity and, 76
    conceptual and technical evolution, 1
    with dissociated patient, 255, 262–268
    effectiveness, 261
    as extinction of conditioning, 254–255
    fibromyalgia, 220
    freeze discharge techniques, 48
    irritable bowel syndrome, 221
    mechanism of healing, 254, 255, 261–262, 266
    patient self-perception, 281–283
    patient understanding of symptoms, 271–272
    psychoanalytic approach, 188–190
    rationale for somatic therapies, 255
    resistance to change, 282
    social support in, 278–279
    somatic therapeutic modalities, 260–261
    therapist qualities, 283–284
    titration of elicited arousal in, 255
    see also pharmacotherapy; somatic experiencing
tryptophan, 138
twin studies, 86–87
tyramine, 226

unconscious learned behavior, 17
    memory function in, 40, 41
    survival function, 32–33, 40, 42
    see also conditioning

vagal complex, 46–48, 215, 269
van der Hart, O., 178, 183, 184
van der Kolk, B., 89, 134, 263
vasomotor control, 195–196, 197–198, 200, 202
    in somatic dissociation, 242–243
vengeance, 146

Verny, T., 113
vertigo, 230–231
vestibular system, 141–142
violent behavior
    desensitization to, 147
    epidemiology, 134–136
    exposure effects, 3, 144–149
    human nature and, 133–134, 136–137
    infant–caretaker relations and, 137–139,
        143–144
    primate behavior, 139–141
    vengeance, 146
visceral system, 22, 24–25, 50, 215–216
    fibromyalgia complications, 219–220
    freeze response, 216
Visual Kinetic Dissociation, 260
voodoo death, 48

war, 127, 133
    causes of, 6–7
    conceptual development of trauma, 1, 97
    shellshock victims, 183–185
    soldier training for, 147
Weight, D., 72
Weir, P., 92
whiplash syndrome, 60, 192
    clinical conceptualization, 5, 228, 229, 230–231
    cognitive problems in, 231
    symptoms, 4, 227–229, 231
    vision problems in, 231
wisdom, 282–284
workplace stress, 131, 132, 281–282
Wright, T., 13

Yehuda, R., 79, 115

Zoloft, 275
Zuckerman, B., 106–107